Cognitive Strategy Research

Christine B. McCormick
Gloria Miller
Michael Pressley
Editors

Cognitive Strategy Research:

From Basic Research
to Educational Applications

With 23 Figures

Springer-Verlag
New York Berlin Heidelberg
London Paris Tokyo

Christine B. McCormick
College of Education
Department of Educational Psychology
University of South Carolina
Columbia, SC 29208
USA

Gloria E. Miller
Department of Psychology
University of South Carolina
Columbia, SC 29208
USA

Michael Pressley
Department of Psychology
The University of Western Ontario
London, Ontario
Canada N6A 5C2

Library of Congress Cataloging-in-Publication Data
Cognitive strategy research: from basic research to educational
  applications / edited by Christine B. McCormick, Gloria Miller,
  Michael Pressley.
     p. cm.
   Includes indexes.
   ISBN 0-387-96869-5 (U.S.)
   1. Cognitive learning. 2. Cognition—Research. 3. Cognition in
children. 4. Learning, Psychology of. I. McCormick, Christine.
II. Miller, Gloria E. III. Pressley, Michael.
LB1062.C645 1989
370.15′2—dc19   89-5971
                                                      CIP

Printed on acid-free paper.

Typeset by Publishers Service, Bozeman, Montana.
Printed and bound by Edwards Brothers, Ann Arbor, Michigan.
Printed in the United States of America.

9 8 7 6 5 4 3 2 1

ISBN 0-387-96869-5 Springer-Verlag New York Berlin Heidelberg
ISBN 3-540-96869-5 Springer-Verlag Berlin Heidelberg New York

Preface

A substantial body of literature has been directed at theoretical explanations of cognitive strategies and their influence upon competent academic performance. Initially, much of this research was conducted in laboratory settings. Recently, more emphasis has been placed upon studying strategic behavior in contexts approximating real life academic situations. The content of this volume reflects this transition from laboratory to educational settings. In the final analysis, this body of literature suggests that we should be quite optimistic about the utility of strategy instruction research.

In particular, at least two major advances have been made in the field of strategy instruction. First, the development of more complex models of competent thinking has allowed for greater precision in identifying critical strategies. Moreover, this work has led to a greater understanding of factors that lead to individual differences in academic performance. Second, researchers have begun to focus on the development of instructional designs to promote competent performance with an emphasis upon assessing the value and effectiveness of strategy instruction in naturalistic settings. This work has allowed for a greater understanding of current strategy practices and also of possible impediments to successful strategy instruction in educational settings.

Consistent with these areas of major advancement, we have divided this volume into two sections. The first section provides coverage of recent advances in basic research on models of competent learning and related instructional issues. The second section addresses more specific educational applications within the academic domains of reading, writing, mathematics, and science. The distinctions between the two sections are useful for organizational purposes but sometimes blur under close scrutiny.

The goal of the volume is to depict accurately the state of the art in cognitive stragegy research. We have not attempted to complete an exhaustive review of this burgeoning research area. Instead, we feel this volume reflects the Zeitgeist of important issues for theoreticians, researchers, and members of the educational community at large. This volume can provide valuable insights for novices, experts, and all others on the continuum of competence in the field of education.

Our editing of this book benefited greatly from the encouragement and assistance provided by the Springer-Verlag staff. Christine B. McCormick's participation in this project was partially supported by a grant from the National Science Foundation. The contribution by Gloria Miller was partially supported by a Biomedical Research Grant from the University of South Carolina. Michael Pressley's editorial work was made possible through a grant by the Natural Sciences and Engineering Research Council of Canada.

Christine B. McCormick
Gloria Miller
Michael Pressley

Contents

Part II: Educational Applications

Contributors

LINDA BAKER, Department of Psychology, University of Maryland-Baltimore Co., Catonsville, MD 21228, USA

CAROLE R. BEAL, Department of Psychology, Dartmouth College, Hanover, NH 03755, USA

TERESA CARIGLIA-BULL, Department of Psychology, University of Western Ontario, London, Ontario, Canada N6A 5C2

LUIS A. CORDON, Department of Psychology, University of Notre Dame, Notre Dame, IN 46556, USA

JEANNE D. DAY, Department of Psychology, University of Notre Dame, Notre Dame, IN 46556, USA

SHARON J. DERRY, Department of Psychology, Florida State University, Tallahassee, FL 32306-1051, USA

GERALD G. DUFFY, Department of Teacher Education, College of Education, Michigan State University, East Lansing, MI 48824-1034, USA

ANNETTE DUFRESNE, Department of Psychology, University of Windsor, Windsor, Ontario, Canada N9B 3P4

JOAN K. GALLINI, Department of Educational Psychology, College of Education, University of South Carolina, Columbia, SC 29208, USA

MARY LOUISE KERWIN, Department of Psychology, University of Notre Dame, Notre Dame, IN 46556 USA

AKIRA KOBASIGAWA, Department of Psychology, University of Windsor, Windsor, Ontario, Canada N9B 3P4

RICHARD LAPAN, Department of Educational Studies, College of Education, University of Delaware, Newark, DE 19716, USA

RICHARD LEHRER, Department of Educational Psychology, University of Wisconsin, Madison, WI 53706, USA

MICHAEL PRESSLEY, Department of Psychology, University of Western Ontario, London, Ontario, Canada N6A 5C2

RALPH E. REYNOLDS, Department of Educational Studies, University of Utah, Salt Lake City, UT 84112, USA

LAURA R. ROEHLER, Department of Teacher Education, College of Education, Michigan State University, East Lansing, MI 48824-1034, USA

WILLIAM D. ROHWER, JR., Department of Educational Psychology, University of California, Berkeley, CA 94720, USA

ELIZABETH J. SHORT, Department of Psychology, Case Western Reserve University, Cleveland, OH 44106, USA

BARBARA L. SNYDER, Department of Psychology, University of Western Ontario, London, Ontario, Canada N6A 5C2

SONYA SYMONS, Department of Psychology, University of Western Ontario, London, Ontario, Canada N6A 5C2

JOHN W. THOMAS, Far West Laboratory, 1855 Folsom St., San Francisco, CA 94103, USA

WOODROW TRATHEN, Department of Educational Studies, University of Utah, Salt Lake City, UT 84112, USA

JAMES P. VAN HANEGHAN, Department of Psychology and Human Resources, George Peabody College, Vanderbilt University, Nashville, TN 37203, USA

SUZANNE E. WADE, Department of Educational Studies, University of Utah, Salt Lake City, UT 84112, USA

JILL A. WEISSBERG-BENCHELL, Department of Psychology, Case Western Reserve University, Cleveland, OH 44106, USA

Part I
Basic Research

The first three chapters in this section address recent attempts to broaden theoretical approaches to strategy instruction. The final three chapters in this section pertain to advances in instructional design and to issues relevant to the success of strategy training in naturalistic settings.

An overview of past and present trends in strategy training is presented in the lead chapter by Symons, Snyder, Cariglia-Bull, and Pressley (Chapter 1). Three current information-processing models of competent thinking are presented and promising instructional approaches that have evolved in light of this process-oriented research are reviewed. These researchers leave us hopeful that important improvements in children's knowledge and use of strategies can be obtained through carefully designed comprehensive instruction. Short and Weissberg-Benchell (Chapter 2) further specify the need for a broad conceptualization of strategy training, especially with respect to learning-disabled children. These authors present a detailed analysis of critical variables that differentiate successful and unsuccessful learners and stress the need for a triple alliance between cognitive, metacognitive, and motivational strategy instruction in order to enhance the academic performance of learning-disabled children. In particular, these authors explicate the motivational aspects of LD children's school failures, especially in regards to the impact of attributional style and self-concept on motivation in the classroom. In addition, factors affecting the success of remediation techniques to foster cognitive processing, metacognitive knowledge, and motivation to learn in learning-disabled students are reviewed.

Dufresne and Kobasigawa (Chapter 3) also adhere to a broad conception of competent strategy use in their examination of factors contributing to individual differences in children's utilization of study time. Competent learners distribute study time differentially according to certain priorities (differential allocation) and make effective decisions regarding the amount of study time needed to reach a prescribed goal (sufficient allocation). Dufresne and Kobasigawa provide a detailed analysis of critical task and learner characteristics that affect the ease with which these allocation processes are employed and pose problems for future research in this area.

The latter three contributions in this section focus on issues critical in the design of effective strategy instruction. In Chapter 4, Day, Cordon, and Kerwin explore the role of social interaction in academic competence in young children. They evaluate Vygotsky's theory of cognitive development as a framework for thinking about instructional environments. According to this theoretical approach, "scaffolded" instruction, in which a more competent learner mediates the learning experiences of a young child, is the primary vehicle for promoting cognitive skills in young children. Observational studies of interactions between children and adults (or more competent peers) in "informal" educational settings are reviewed. There is little evidence either for consistent improvement in children's cognitive performance as a consequence of scaffolded instruction or for the superiority of scaffolding over other forms of instruction. Instead evidence pointed to the advantages of exposure to variability in teaching style. The implication of this work is that there may be no one ideal strategy training method beneficial for all children.

Both Rohwer and Thomas (Chapter 5) and Duffy and Roehler (Chapter 6) explore current educational practices that create impediments to successful strategy training. Rohwer and Thomas focus on problem solving, comprehension, and memory strategies in specific academic domains (e.g., mathematics, science, English, and history). They cite numerous inconsistencies between what research reveals about effective strategy instruction and what is occurring in classrooms in terms of cognitive demands and instructional support. According to Rohwer and Thomas, recent advances in theory and research can lead to instructional reform only if instructors demand and support students' acquisition and deployment of effective strategies without furnishing compensations that reduce or eliminate the need for strategic learning. Duffy and Roehler address this same basic issue by discussing difficulties inherent in teaching reading strategies. An instructional theory designed to remediate these problems is presented. While their work is based on a programmatic series of studies documenting the mental processing involved in teaching reading strategies to at-risk learners, their conception of "mental modeling" and other related ideas are applicable to all instruction in which the goal is student regulatory control. Duffy and Roehler agree with Rohwer and Thomas that the future success of strategy instruction rests with broad educational reforms in teacher training and changes in societal attitudes regarding the importance of self-regulated learning.

In summary, it is obvious from these chapters that future advances in strategy instruction will necessitate the delineation of more complex models of learning and instruction. Clearly, educators and researchers have begun to address this challenge by illuminating complex interactions between students, teachers, and instructional materials as a means of increasing our understanding of how to foster strategic learning in educational settings.

1
Why Be Optimistic About Cognitive Strategy Instruction?

SONYA SYMONS, BARBARA L. SNYDER, TERESA CARIGLIA-BULL, AND MICHAEL PRESSLEY

An enormous amount of attention has been devoted to cognitive strategy instruction in the last 20 years, with strategies considered controllable processes that can facilitate particular performances (e.g., Pressley, Forrest-Pressley, Elliott-Faust, & Miller, 1985). Most of this interest has been on the part of researchers, who have often focused on basic paradigms (e.g, paired-associate learning, list learning) that do not represent well or completely the complexity of educational tasks. See, for instance, Pressley, Heisel, McCormick, and Nakamura's (1982) review of strategy instruction with respect to basic memory research. There is now more reason for the educator community to be optimistic, however, for cognitive psychologists and educational researchers are currently studying more complex strategies that are more appropriate for the tasks children ordinarily encounter in school. For example, when school children try to learn spelling words by looking away from the words, writing them down, and comparing them with the correct spelling, they are engaging in strategic behavior—The children are consciously carrying out processes aimed at learning how to spell words. When a writer plans a paper by preparing an outline, followed by construction of a first draft and revision, that writer is being strategic. There have been many demonstrations that children can be taught to execute these types of procedures with subsequent improvements in performance. As a result, educators have embraced the strategy instructional approach (e.g., January, February, & March 1987 issues of *Journal of Learning Disabilities*; Jones, Palincsar, Ogle, & Carr, 1987).

Despite the availability of and apparent enthusiasm for strategy research and theory by the educator community, the evidence is overwhelming that strategy instruction has not been incorporated into the curriculum on a large scale (e.g., Applebee, 1984, 1986; Durkin, 1979; Thompson, 1985). The many reasons for this state of affairs and many challenges to the implementation of strategy instruction are reviewed elsewhere, with a strong case made that the obstacles to strategy instructional implementation can be overcome (Pressley, Goodchild, Fleet, Zajchowski, & Evans, 1989). The purpose of this chapter is to spell out the many reasons why continued optimism is justified with respect to the development of realistic educational interventions, despite the fact that strategy instruction is not fully developed at this point.

There are at least three reasons to be optimistic about strategy instruction and strategy instructional research. First, more realistic and complete information-processing models of competent performance have become available. Compared to previous theories that focused only on cognitive factors (e.g., Atkinson & Shiffrin, 1968), more recent models capture the cognitive, metacognitive, social-personality, and style factors that can affect classroom functioning. Second, there are more complete information-processing models of instruction that address the many factors involved in good thinking. Third, researchers are becoming extremely sophisticated at conducting both laboratory and classroom research that is informative about realistic educational goals.

Theoretical Models of Competent Thinking

In this section, we outline the nature of some current information-processing conceptions of competent thinking, models that capture the complexity of thinking as it occurs when pursuing educationally important goals. Three models are presented as representative of the general information-processing approach to cognition.

BARON'S PROBLEM-SOLVING MODEL OF THINKING

Baron defines thinking as a conscious, goal-directed episode consisting of a series of interdependent phases (Baron, 1985, chap. 3). Essentially, these phases are search processes in which the thinker seeks to define a goal or criterion for ending the thinking episode; tries to find various potential means for achieving that goal (possibilities); and then collects evidence for and against the alternative possibilities. Thus, thinking is a process in which evidence is used to choose among potential possibilities in order to satisfy a goal. The search processes are often executed internally (i.e., in long-term memory) with stored knowledge and schema brought to bear on a current problem. Information can be provided by the external environment as well. For instance, goals may be clarified by asking someone; possible solutions and relevant evidence may be obtained by watching others attempt to solve the same problem.

The aim of the search processes is to find the best solutions to problems. However, there are costs associated with these processes in terms of their expected success and the time and effort required for their execution. In order to maximize the utility of these processes, the thinker should continue to search as long as the expected gains outweigh the costs. Ideal thinking involves maximizing the utility of the search processes for any given task, as well as using the available evidence in such a way that all possibilities are fairly evaluated.

Individual thinkers, however, differ with respect to knowledge, capacities, and emotions. These factors produce differences in how individuals weigh the costs and benefits of their search processes. Thus, the amount of searching considered satisfactory may not be optimal in terms of actually maximizing performance. Baron defines a systematic deviation from optimal search on a particular task as a bias, while a consistent bias across tasks is defined as a cognitive style. For instance, a bias toward impulsivity on some task would produce insufficient allocation of effort to search processes and too little self-criticism in the search for and use of evidence.

The execution of search processes and weighing of available evidence are managed by heuristics that the thinker possesses. Within this model, a heuristic is defined as a rule or strategy for directing search processes or for using evidence in a particular class of situations. One problem-solving heuristic is forward search. This heuristic entails searching for possibilities using evidence as a cue (Baron, 1985). Forward search is most beneficial when there are many possible ways to satisfy a goal, although the evidence concerning many of them can be used to eliminate most possibilities (Baron, 1985).

For example, consider an adolescent girl who is reading social studies text with the goal of preparing for an examination. She can simply read the text over and over, she could sleep with the book under her pillow; or she could construct summaries of the to-be-learned content (e.g., Taylor & Beach, 1984). Assuming the adolescent knows the strategies and their relative effectiveness, sleeping on the text might be eliminated since it would not produce learning of the content. Rereading is also an inefficient way to learn the material compared to summarization. Thus, the adolescent might select summarization.

Baron's model of thinking (1985) then suggests that when confronted with a problem-solving task, a good thinker executes a series of processes aimed at identifying a goal and choosing the means to achieve that goal from a number of possibilities based on an unbiased analysis of evidence. The search processes by which goals, possibilities, and evidence are obtained, as well as the evaluation of evidence, are monitored and regulated by heuristics that have an executive role in the thinking process (Derry, this volume, chap. 11; Derry & Murphy, 1986). Baron emphasizes that many of the difficulties thinkers experience are due to biased search processes, which may in turn lead to biased heuristics (inadequate monitoring and self-regulation) (Baron, 1981). Biased thinking (e.g., impulsive thinking) is considered modifiable however, particularly by training general heuristics for guiding search processes (Baron, 1985). See, for instance, Meichenbaum (1977) for many examples of how impulsivity can be modified by training children to search systematically.

STERNBERG'S COMPONENTIAL MODEL

Sternberg (1979, 1982) presents both "a logic and a methodology for isolating component thinking processes that underlie certain task domains" (Derry & Murphy, 1986, p. 5). Based on his analyses of complex problem-solving tasks such as analogical reasoning, classification, series completion, and syllogistic logic, Sternberg (1979, 1982) has developed a process-oriented model of intelligence that focuses on two levels of information processing. The components (or steps) involved in a thinking task constitute the first level. The second level consists of higher-order processes known as metacomponents that perform planning and decision-making functions during thinking.

At the first level, there are four different types of components. A component is defined as an elementary information process that operates on the thinker's internal representations of objects or symbols (Sternberg, 1979, 1982). The four lower-level components differ in terms of the functions they perform. For instance, performance components include processes such as encoding and responding that occur during problem solving. Acquisition components store information in long-term memory. The processes used to access previously stored knowledge are called retention (retrieval) components. Finally, transfer components permit application of knowledge across a variety of related tasks.

The lower-level components can be combined into strategies, which are sets of components that are always performed in combination for certain classes of thinking tasks. For instance, in order to execute a text-summarization strategy, performance components enabling discrimination between main ideas and details would be grouped with acquisition and retention components governing storage and recall of the main ideas from long-term memory.

At the second level, Sternberg (1982) defines six types of metacomponents. The metacomponents perform an executive or metacognitive role in thinking. They are responsible for determining what to do and how to do it (Sternberg, 1982). The functions of the metacomponents include: (a) recognizing the problem or goal of thinking; (b) selecting lower-order components or strategies to be employed; (c) deciding how to sequence the components (and/or strategies); (d) selecting the form of representation or organization that information will take in memory; (e) deciding how much effort to allocate to the component processes in order to balance the trade-off between speed and accuracy in executing these processes; and (f) monitoring the progress of thinking. The sixth metacomponent is responsible for keeping track of what has been done, what is currently being done, and what remains to be done toward meeting the goal of the thinking task (Sternberg, 1982). Monitoring may lead to a change in goals or strategies. This metacomponent regulates the other metacomponents as well as the lower-level components.

According to Sternberg (1979, 1982, 1983), competent thinking is mainly a function of the speed and facility with which a given thinker performs the basic operations defined by the components and metacomponents (Derry & Murphy, 1986). While the knowledge that the thinker possesses is not emphasized as a determinant of competency, it is not completely disregarded. The acquisition, retrieval, and transfer components can be regarded as processes that would have a strong influence on the scope and depth of the knowledge base (Borkowski, 1985).

In terms of attempting to improve thinking skills, Sternberg's (1979, 1982) model suggests that components, strategies, and metacomponents can all be trained. Indeed, Sternberg has argued that instruction aimed at augmenting thinking skills "should provide explicit training in both executive and nonexecutive information processing, as well as interactions between the two kinds of information processing" (Sternberg, 1983, p. 9).

The Good Strategy User Model

According to the good strategy user model developed by Pressley and his colleagues (Pressley, 1986; Pressley, Borkowski, & Schneider, 1987; Pressley, Goodchild, et al., 1989), the elements of good thinking include an array of techniques (strategies) for accomplishing goals; knowledge about when and how these techniques should be used (metacognition); and an extensive nonstrategic knowledge base that is used in conjunction with the strategic and metacognitive processes. Strategic processing is goal-directed and with practice may become automatized (Pressley, Borkowski, & O'Sullivan, 1985; Pressley, Goodchild, et al., 1989).

Thinkers possess different types of strategies. For instance, task-limited strategies are used for very specific goals in particular domains. These are tricks for aiding performance on particular tasks. For instance, one may use the phrase "Man very early made jars stand up nearly perpendicular" to remember the order of the planets in the solar system (i.e., Mercury, Venus, Earth, Mars, Jupiter, Saturn, Uranus, Neptune, and Pluto). Often, task-limited strategies are specific instantiations of more broadly applicable strategies. The example just given employs a first-letter mnemonic strategy (Morris, 1979). However, task-limited strategies may be applied with certain tasks even if the learner has not extracted the rules for using a similar strategy across domains. Goal-limited strategies, on the other hand, are used to accomplish particular goals that occur in many content areas such as remembering, comprehending, and problem solving. For example, if a first-letter mnemonic strategy was used across domains to remember information it would be considered a goal-limited strategy. Finally, general strategies regulate the task-limited and goal-limited strategies. General strategies include monitoring performance, altering processing when current strategies are not succeeding, allocating attention to the task, and searching for relationships between the present task and previous tasks accomplished via strategic mediation.

Good strategy users also posses metacognitive knowledge about specific strategies. Each strategy in a thinker's repertoire is qualified by detailed information specifying the utility of the procedure, including when and where the procedure should be implemented. This knowledge is considered crucial for autonomous strategy use and transfer of strategies to novel situations (O'Sullivan & Pressley, 1984; Pressley, Borkowski, & O'Sullivan, 1984; Pressley, Goodchild, et al., 1989).

The knowledge base also plays an important role in this model. On the one hand, knowledge of certain facts may render strategic processing unnecessary. For instance, the child who has memorized basic math facts does not need to employ a strategy to solve the problem $5 + X = 9$ (Carpenter, 1985). On the other hand, some strategies may be impossible without relevant non-strategic knowledge (Pressley, Goodchild, et al., 1989). The child who has not mastered basic math facts will not be capable of using more complex mathematical problem-solving strategies such as those taught in the TAPS program (Derry, Hawkes, & Tsai, 1987) described in the next section.

In addition to strategies, metacognition, and an extensive knowledge base, the good strategy user model also emphasizes motivational beliefs and cognitive styles. Beliefs about competency for particular tasks in specific domains (e.g., "I am good at math"), or about ability in general (e.g., "I am a capable learner"), will affect the thinker's motivation to perform strategically and to acquire new procedures. These motivational beliefs are tied to self-esteem (McCombs, 1986) in that those who see themselves as able to control their own cognition will be more likely to allocate effort and attention to strategic processing. In the long run, motivational beliefs are also related to the thinker's cognitive style, where cognitive style is defined as the habitual way that a thinker responds to cognitive tasks (similar to Baron, 1985). Motivational beliefs or attributions may create a general tendency to respond to thinking tasks in a certain way.

In summary, good strategy use involves the coordination of strategies, metacognition, styles, motivational beliefs, and the knowledge base (Pressley, Goodchild, et al., 1989). A competent thinker analyzes task situations to determine the strategies that would be appropriate. A plan is then formed for executing the strategies, and progress during strategy execution is monitored. In the face of difficulty, ineffective strategies are abandoned in favor of more appropriate ones. These processes are supported by appropriate motivational beliefs and a general tendency to think strategically.

SUMMARY

Information-processing models of competent thinking differ in terms of the specific elements of thinking that are emphasized. For example, while Baron (1985) stresses the importance of stylistic tendencies that produce biased search processes, Sternberg (1979, 1982) and Pressley (1986; Pressley, Borkowski, & Schneider, 1987; Pressley, Goodchild, et al., 1989) stress strategic and metacognitive processes. Sternberg pays more attention to the components that make up strategies than do Baron or Pressley and his associates.

On the other hand, beliefs are considered more explicitly as determinants of performance by Baron and Pressley than by Sternberg.

Despite differences in emphasis, there are striking similarities between the contemporary information-processing models. All explain thinking more in terms of processing than "architectural" variables (i.e., neurological deficiencies) (e.g., Campione & Brown, 1978). Thus, these models imply that intervention is possible, since processing can be altered with appropriate instruction, which in turn can affect performance. Most, like the three reviewed here, contain modifiable metacognitive elements [i.e., heuristics (Baron, 1985); metacomponents (Sternberg, 1979, 1982); and general strategies and metacognition (Pressley, Goodchild, et al., 1989)] and hypothesize that competent thinking follows from a variety of factors in interaction. Such complex models present a challenge in that the interactions between factors are not clearly understood. Nevertheless, these models permit clear predictions about interventions that should be effective in producing competent thinking. Specifically, improved performance should follow from long-term explicit instruction that addresses strategic processes (Baron, 1985; Pressley, Goodchild, et al, 1989; Sternberg, 1983). Instructional efforts should also be made to improve metacognitive knowledge of strategies, nonstrategic knowledge, and motivational beliefs (Pressley, Goodchild, et al., 1989; Short & Weissberg-Benchell, this volume, chap. 2). These instructional perspectives have been elaborated in detail in models of strategy teaching that were informed by information-processing analyses of thinking like the ones reviewed in this section. Three such models of teaching are taken up in the next section.

Instructional Theories

The increase in knowledge about the nature of competent thinking has been coupled with interest in relating principles of cognitive psychology to instruction (Glaser, 1985). The result has been much more complete models of instruction than have been available in the past. These new models of instruction address many of the skills and much of the knowledge that constitute good strategy use. We briefly review three especially complete models of instruction that have evolved in light of these new models of thinking. The first two are general instructional prescriptions and the third was developed for strategy instruction in the domain of mathematical problem solving.

INSTRUCTION ACCORDING TO THE GOOD STRATEGY USER MODEL

Pressley (1986; Pressley, Goodchild, et al., 1989) argues that strategy instructors should directly teach all the components of good strategy use (i.e., strategies, metacognition, motivation, and knowledge). In order to encourage students to think strategically, instructors need to emphasize the link between strategy use and competent performance. The knowledge that good performance depends on appropriate strategies rather than luck or ability while poor performance is often due to inappropriate procedures motivates children to use strategies (Borkowski, Carr, Rellinger, & Pressley, in press; Clifford, 1984).

Students also need to be encouraged to adopt intellectual styles that are consistent with good strategy use (e.g., reflective & low anxious styles). The instructional setting should promote a comfortable, reflective pace and calm academic activity rather than anxiety. When given an academic task, students need to know that it is appropriate to reflect upon what is required in the particular situation. They need to be impressed that some thought should be given to strategy selection.

Pressley, Snyder, and Cariglia-Bull (1987) analyzed the various methods that can be used to teach strategies, from very indirect approaches like discovery learning to more explicit, single-component approaches (behavioral modeling, textbook presentations) to multicomponent, extremely direct approaches (e.g, direct explanation of strategies by teachers as they behaviorally model strategies, followed by student practice with corrective feedback; Duffy, Roehler, Meloth, et al., 1986). The available evidence suggested that the direct approach was more likely than other instructional methods to produce accurate knowledge of strategies. Thus, Pressley's instructional perspective is that strategic procedures should be explained and modeled by teachers, and that guided practice and corrective feedback should be provided as children attempt to use strategies.

Pressley and his associates argue that when students are taught a new strategy, they also need to be taught where and when to use it. There is a unique set of information for each strategy specifying the range of appropriate application, metacognitive knowledge about specific strategies (which is often abbreviated to "specific strategy knowledge"). The good strategy user instructional perspective is that this information should be provided explicitly. Children are not efficient at discovering such information on their own (Pressley, Borkowski, & O'Sullivan, 1984, 1985; Pressley, Levin, & Ghatala, 1984), nor do they automatically apply such information even if they do discover it independently (e.g., Pressley, Ross, Levin, & Ghatala, 1984). On the other hand, direct instruction of specific strategy knowledge increases the likelihood that elementary-school students will appropriately and effectively apply strategies (Duffy, Roehler, Sivan et al., 1987; O'Sullivan & Pressley, 1984). For example, when teaching a prediction strategy aimed at enhancing reading comprehension (e.g., Palincsar & Brown, 1984), students should be informed that the strategy is most appropriate when text is covering content where a person's prior knowledge is almost certainly correct (e.g., Alvermann, Smith, & Readence, 1985; Hasselhorn & Körkel, 1986).

Pressley and his colleagues also recognize the importance of nonstrategic knowledge. Because there are many strategies that simply cannot be executed without a well-developed knowledge base, strategy instruction should also address the development of nonstrategic knowledge. For instance, it would do no good to instruct a child to use a categorizing-organizational strategy to mediate learning of lists of categorizable items if the child was not familiar enough with the items in the list to divide them into appropriate categories (cf. Rabinowitz, 1984). It is generally beneficial to activate prior knowledge about the content of to-be-read material, although this strategy is futile if the reader knows nothing about the topic beforehand (Hasselhorn & Körkel, 1986) and may be counterproductive if the child possesses errant prior knowledge (e.g., Alvermann et al., 1985). Similarly, brainstorming to retrieve all that is known about a topic before beginning to write is only useful when writers possess prior knowledge about the topic. Otherwise, a better strategy is to seek information from external sources.

Strategy instruction from the good strategy user perspective is seen as long term. While it is true that some particular strategies can be taught relatively quickly, the teaching of many strategies so that they are used generally and effectively in a coordinated manner requires a lot of instruction and practice. Students need to learn the strategic procedures and associated specific strategy knowledge well enough so that the strategies are executed efficiently in appropriate situations. It is very easy to understand the need for extended instruction by considering the large number of strategies that can be taught to learners (e.g., Devine, 1987; Gagné, 1985).

THE UNIVERSITY OF KANSAS STRATEGY INTERVENTION MODEL (SIM)

Donald Deshler and his associates at the University of Kansas have developed a model of strategy instruction intended for special education settings, although many of its components are probably more generally applicable. The Kansas group advocates instruction of a core group of strategies that advance the academic and social skills that are important in school. For instance, the memory and comprehension strategies include paraphrasing, self-questioning, visual imagery, first-letter mnemonics, and error monitoring, among others.

Each strategy is first described to the students, with this description including some important metacognitive information about it. The rationale for the strategy is explained, as are the types of results that can be expected and the situations to which the strategy can be applied. A teacher models use of the strategy, using "think aloud" procedures. Students begin to use the strategy with teacher-led demonstrations giving way to guided practice. Students verbally rehearse the steps in the strategy until they have mastered them. During practice and feedback phases, students practice with fairly simple materials first and then with grade-appropriate content. Both speed and accuracy are encouraged as students learn the strategies to mastery. Reinforcement and corrective feedback are provided throughout the procedure.

A main strength of the SIM model is its concern with instruction for generalized strategy use (Deshler, Schumaker, & Lenz, 1984; Ellis, Lenz, & Sabournie, 1987a, 1987b). There are explicit efforts to make students aware of the contexts in which a strategy can be applied. Multiple exemplars are used at every phase of instruction; reminders are provided to students about where strategies can be used; and consistent practice is given in applying the strategy to class assignments. Students are taught to prompt themselves to use strategies with self-talk and are given many reminders to be alert to cues that would suggest use of a particular strategy. Sometimes they are provided with cue cards that contain summaries of the strategies that they have learned as aids to generalization. Students are also given practice integrating strategies to accomplish all of the demands posed by multiple-component academic tasks.

Motivation is maintained in this program by having students decide what strategies they are going to acquire and what educational goals they will target. They are also taught to keep track of their daily performance through charting, to monitor and evaluate their progress, and to reinforce themselves for doing well. Students are made aware of the generally important role of strategy use by the creation of a "strategic environment" in the classroom. This is accomplished by teachers consistently modeling strategy use during class activities. The students are repeatedly exposed to social role-taking strategies, communication strategies, and academic learning strategies through this mechanism.

It is very clear that Deshler's model requires explicit and extensive teaching that is very different from the instruction that often goes on in school. As Deshler and Schumaker (1986) put it:

> The following teacher behaviors appear to be critical to optimizing instructional gains through learning strategy instruction: providing appropriate positive and corrective feedback using organizers throughout the instructional session, ensuring high levels of active academic responding, programming youth involvement in discussions, providing regular reviews of key instructional points and checks of comprehension, monitoring student performance, requiring mastery learning, communicating high expectations to students, communicating rationales for instructional activities, and facilitating independence. (pp. 586–587)

Training Arithmetic Problem-Solving Skills (TAPS)

Sharon Derry and her associates at Florida State University (Derry, this volume, chap. 11; Derry et al., 1987) have developed an instructional technology for teaching elementary-school children to solve complex arithmetic word problems that require the application of several strategies. In this program students are taught to plan their problem solving, to include specific mathematical procedures in their plans, to check, and to self-monitor their problem-solving behavior. There are four strategic plans that children are taught to use. One is the "change" plan that should be applied when a problem specifies an initial set of items that is changed in quantity either by addition or subtraction. A second is the "combine plan" that involves adding two subsets to create a superset (e.g., 6 red squirrels + 8 gray squirrels = 14 squirrels). The "compare" strategic plan is applied to problems requiring the determination of a difference between a larger set and a smaller set. Finally, the "vary" plan involves setting up a problem with a missing value that is equal to the number of units in the whole set multiplied by the value per unit (e.g., the price of 10 gallons of gas = \$1.50/gallon × 10 gallons).

The training includes providing information about how to recognize which strategic plan is appropriate. The goal is for students to be able to quickly and accurately recognize the situations that call for the change, combine, compare, and vary plans. During this phase students are presented with diagrams and explanations of the four plans. They practice matching simple problems to the appropriate solution plan. They also receive practice mapping problems to diagrams that specify the steps in the solution plans. Practice at plan identification is continued to the point where students can quickly and accurately identify which plan to use without the benefit of diagrams. Students then practice generating problems that require each of the four strategic plans.

The next phase of training includes practice carrying out calculations involving the four different plans, solving for different pieces of missing information (e.g., in a difference problem, the larger and smaller sets are sometimes given with solution of the difference required, while the larger set and the difference are given at other times with solution for the smaller set required). Again, diagrams are used at first, but these are faded as training proceeds.

The students are also given practice chaining the plans, so that solutions determined by using one plan can be used to solve problems involving another plan. They are also taught specific ways to change the strategies. For example, they are taught that a method known as *forward chaining* is fast and efficient when it can be applied. Forward chaining involves solving for the first unknown encountered in a problem and then holding the answer in memory and continuing to read the problem to find the next unknown that must be determined. If that method fails, there is the alternative of *backward chaining*. This involves finding the ultimate answer that the child is supposed to generate, and then seeking values that can be used to generate the ultimate answer, including the identification of unknowns that must be determined in order to calculate the final answer. Students practice solving problems using forward and backward chaining, and receive corrective prompts along the way. Following this, students learn to solve problems that require three of the solution plans.

Metacognitive information is provided at a number of points. The value of the plans is emphasized, as is the relative value of forward to backward chaining. Students are taught the features of problems that call for particular plans. Confusing and ambiguous problems are used to train monitoring and checking—These problems normally lead to wild goose chases. The students are taught to monitor whether they are goose chasing or engaging in productive problem solving, and to consider the possibility that additional information may be needed to solve the problem if they are not making progress.

A strength of the instructional model devised by Derry et al. (1987) is that a great deal of diagnoses are made to determine the problem-solving behaviors that students do and do not possess. Instruction is then tailored to specific weaknesses, and thus, our summary of the program includes steps that may not be necessary for all students.

Derry et al. (1987) are also very much aware of the need for nonstrategic knowledge. They do not even begin instruction of the four strategic plans with children who do not know the basic arithmetic operations (add, subtract, multiply, and divide) and the related math facts required to carry out those operations.

Although Derry et al. (1987) do not deal extensively with motivational issues, they make clear to students throughout instruction that there are educational gains associated with use of the strategic plans that are instructed as part of TAPS. In addition, the TAPS framework is aimed at reducing behaviors that can have a devastating effect on student motivation, including wild goose chasing, trial-and-error learning, and failing to monitor patently unproductive behaviors.

In summary, Derry et al. (1987) have designed an instructional intervention that addresses a particular, but extremely difficult mathematical acquisition: the solution of word problems. The graduates of this treatment know strategic plans for solving word problems, know when to apply the mathematical plans that they know, can apply the plans quickly, check their performance regularly, and seem generally competent. These graduates should experience less frustration solving problems than students who received less extensive and systematic instruction, and hence mathematical motivation should be enhanced for TAPS students.

Discussion

The three instructional approaches reviewed here share at least eight similarities:

1. Strategies

All of these models prescribe teaching people procedures that efficiently accomplish important educational goals. Although there are innumerable strategies that can enhance specific aspects of performance, in all cases reviewed here, there is a bias toward teaching only a few strategies at a time and teaching them well, rather than teaching many strategies concurrently and superficially. This point deserves emphasis, because there is little evidence that teaching a number of strategies to children quickly produces important changes in processing (cf., Chipman, Segal, & Glaser, 1985; Segal, Chipman, & Glaser, 1985). The evaluations that are available suggest that teaching a few strategies at a time works better (Derry, this volume, chap. 11; Duffy & Roehler, this volume, chap. 6; Duffy, Roehler, Meloth, et al., 1986; Ellis et al., 1987a, 1987b; Mayer, 1986; Nickerson, Perkins, & Smith, 1985; Palincsar & Brown, 1984; Pressley, Cariglia-Bull, & Snyder, 1984).

2. Teach Monitoring

Checking strategies are emphasized in all of these models. As students execute strategies and perform educational tasks, they should monitor performance to determine their progress. Students are also instructed to try to remediate the problems they are experiencing once detected. The emphasis on on-line checking of cognitive progress has developed in light of research establishing that even good students sometimes fail to monitor performance adequately and/or fail to take corrective measures when problems are spotted (e.g., Garner, 1987; Markman, 1981; Schneider & Pressley, 1988, chap. 7; Van Haneghan & Baker, this volume, chap. 9). Again, surveys of strategy research conducted in the 1960s and 1970s turn up little or no emphasis on the teaching of monitoring (e.g., Pressley, Heisel et al., 1982).

3. Metacognition About Strategies

All of these models emphasize the importance of making certain that students know when and where to use strategies. This can be accomplished by telling such information to students; it can also be accomplished by providing students with extensive experience across settings where strategies can be employed. The latter tactic is especially likely to work if students are taught methods for noting when and whether the strategies they are using work (e.g., Pressley, Borkowski, & O'Sullivan, 1984). This type of metacognition is important because it is critical to generalization and maintenance of strategies. Effective deployment of strategies depends on students being armed with knowledge about when strategies should be used. The explicit attention to metacognition about strategies in these models contrasts with the great bulk of work on strategy instruction, in which there has been little or no attention to information about when and where to use the strategies that are being taught (for commentary, see Belmont, Butterfield, & Ferretti, 1982; Brown, Bransford, Ferrara, & Campione, 1983; Pressley, Heisel, et al., 1982).

4. Maintain Student Motivation

Students are most likely to be motivated to use strategies if they are aware that the strategies do in fact enhance performance (e.g., Brown et al., 1983). Thus, all of these instructional programs include explicit provisions to highlight the utility of strategies, such as explaining how strategies aid performance, providing feedback about strategy-mediated performance, and charting students' progress while using strategies. Motivation can also be dealt with more globally. For instance, Borkowski et al. (in press) and Pressley, Goodchild et al. (1989) argue that children need to be made aware that competent functioning is often a result of using the right strategies. Further, they should be taught that they can become competent thinkers by employing the strategies used by successful learners. Although the role of motivation has been understudied to date, theorists and researchers are beginning to offer detailed models of how motivation can affect strategy use (Borkowski et al., in press; McCombs, 1986).

5. Teach in Context

Strategies are not to be taught as a separate curriculum entry (an approach often advocated in the past; Chipman et al., 1985; Segal et al., 1985). They are to be taught as part of the actual academic tasks that students face. Important strategies for reading, math, and memory are best learned when they are practiced with kinds of materials that students are expected to master using the strategies.

6. Interactions Between Strategies and the Knowledge Base

There is a clear realization that teaching of strategies alone is not sufficient. There are many pieces of knowledge that the good student possesses, with strategy use largely dependent on having this knowledge. Success cannot be attributed to either strategies or knowledge alone (e.g., Glaser, 1984) but to strategies and other knowledge operating in combination.

7. Interactive and Direct Teaching

A gradual releasing of control from the teacher to the student, with teachers resuming greater control as needed, is emphasized in these models. Although teachers describe and model strategies initially, a great deal of supervised student practice is required for students to learn strategies so that they can be executed efficiently. Teachers are most effective when they monitor this practice, offering individually tailored corrective feedback and encouragement. Teachers also encourage generalization of strategies, in that they provide guidance and reminders to students about when and how strategies can be extended to new situations. This information is provided directly and explicitly. This contrasts with alternative models that view the teacher as someone who should explain procedures briefly and then assign unsupervised practice, or as someone who should supervise discovery-learning procedures (e.g., Brainerd, 1978; Pressley, Snyder, & Cariglia-Bull, 1987).

8. Long-Term Teaching

Because competent information processing involves many strategies and teaching of each of these strategies should be thorough according to these models, strategy instruction is not viewed as a quick fix by these instructional theorists. Rather, instruction is long-term and detailed, with extensive presentation of information about strategies and extended practice in applying strategies.

Strategy Research

Recent strategy instructional research has been extremely informative about interventions that have real-world utility. One reason is that contemporary strategy researchers and theorists recognize how various research questions about strategy instruction are related to one another. A second reason is that researchers are gaining savvy in designing studies that answer these questions.

RESEARCH QUESTIONS

Perhaps the most fundamental question is whether a proposed strategy can affect performance as intended. Strategy researchers have spent more time on this question than any other (e.g., Pressley, Heisel, et al., 1982), investigating the effectiveness of many strategies for many domains. The method of evaluation is straightforward. One group of subjects is taught to process in a fashion consistent with the strategy; the control group is provided with no strategy instruction.

Once it is known that a population benefits from instruction to use a strategy, there remains the question of whether students can be trained to use the strategy consistently and appropriately. That is, can the population in question be trained to maintain and generalize a strategy? Although failures to generalize instructed strategies are widely known and frequently bemoaned, our perspective is that strategy generalization is not a form of "litmus test" for strategy instruction. Strategy generalization experiments reveal whether generalization is possible given current instructional technology and how it can be promoted. They can also specify when generalization is unlikely, difficult, or very costly. On these latter occasions, it is often not appropriate to abandon a strategy that is otherwise effective. Even if autonomous strategy use cannot be achieved, it is often the case that prompting can elicit the strategy in order to accomplish the same educational goals. In addition, materials can often be modified to tap the advantages identified in strategy research (e.g., Education Development Center, 1988; 1985; Gagné & Bell, 1981; Mayer, 1987, chap 6; Pressley, 1983). For example, even if children cannot be taught to self-question and self-test as they read text, it is sometimes possible to place adjunct questions in text that prompt self-testing and provide the cognitive and metacognitive benefits that follow from self-questioning (Anderson & Biddle, 1975; Pressley, Snyder, Levin, Murray, & Ghatala, 1987).

In short, researchers today recognize the need for programmatic research. Such a program includes identification of processing that can affect performance, study of instruction that might promote widespread use of procedures that are learned, and engineering efforts aimed at providing the gains of strategy use when self-regulated processing cannot be produced. In addition to the research questions and issues addressed explicitly in this subsection, the contemporary theories of strategic functioning reviewed earlier suggest many individual differences dimensions that might affect whether students execute and use strategies (e.g., style factors, functional short-term memory constraints, preferences). Thus, there are potential instruction by individual differences interactions that should be studied in exhaustive research programs (Cronbach & Snow, 1977). Often it is also profitable to compare two different strategies that are designed to accomplish a particular goal in order to assess their relative strengths and weaknesses. Given such diverse questions about use and instruction of strategies, it is not surprising that strategy research is often a long-term, multiexperiment endeavor.

RESEARCH METHODS

Marx, Winne, and Walsh (1985) considered the obstacles facing the researcher who wishes to study cognitive and strategic processes, particularly in classrooms (also see Levin, 1985). For instance, in the classroom there are complex reciprocal interactions between teachers and students that are not always easily characterized or easily controlled for research purposes (e.g., disciplinary encounters, friendly exchanges mediated by a long history of good student-teacher relations). There are also many theoretically uninteresting variables that can affect cognitive performance in the classroom (e.g., what the student ate for lunch, whether there was a high-spirited assembly).

Peterson and Swing (1983) outlined additional obstacles. For example, processing in the classroom must be done in "real time"; children may not be able to slow down their cognitive processing in class in order to carry out strategies. Another way of thinking about this problem is to recognize that strategy execution requires use of short-term memory capacity, as does processing of other input that occurs in class. To the extent that strategies must be executed while processing other classroom input, there is potential for a short-term memory bottleneck. The child simply may not have enough capacity to process input from the class while executing a strategy. Peterson and Swing (1983) also argued that the problem of strategy generalization may be more pronounced in classrooms than in the laboratory given the greater diversity of materials and cognitive processes that are experienced in class.

Despite Peterson and Swing's (1983) concerns about potential difficulties in the implementation of cognitive strategies, they close their chapter by citing what is certainly the most important motivation for doing classroom research on strategies:

. . . Many students are passing through our educational system without learning the basic skills in reading and mathematics. Other students are not achieving at high levels in these areas. Strategies to enhance vocabulary learning, reading comprehension, and mathematical problem solving have potential for directly improving students' achievement in reading and mathematics. Thus, from an educational standpoint, research on classroom implementation of cognitive strategy instruction should be given a high priority. (p. 283)

Many agree with Peterson and Swing's (1983) assessment that classroom strategy instruction is challenging, but worth it. Most notably, in this context, Marx et al. (1985) closed their chapter by pointing out that, " . . . Not only is the study of students' cognitions in classrooms a scientific challenge, it is also fundamental to bettering education" (p. 200). Fortunately, the challenge is being met in part. We review two exemplary research efforts here. These were selected because the authors evaluated potentially important educational strategy instruction in well-designed experiments.

Direct Explanation of Reading Strategies

There has been an increased emphasis in recent years on the importance of direct explanation of strategies to students. Duffy and Roehler and their associates at Michigan State University have taken the lead in arguing for such instruction with respect to reading (Duffy & Roehler, 1986, 1987, this volume, chap. 6; Duffy, Roehler, & Putnam, 1987). In particular, they argue that teachers who work with poor readers should explain explicitly the mental processing associated with strategies used by good readers. Duffy and Roehler also argue that young readers should be taught "to develop thoughtful and conscious reasoning about problems encountered in real text (such as trade books and magazines), where each situation demands a slightly different response" (p. 415). Teachers should explain when particular strategies can be used and how they can be applied proficiently. This perspective strongly emphasizes direct, explicit instruction about the reasoning that is involved in the use of reading strategies.

Recently, Duffy and Roehler and their colleagues offered an ambitious and important experiment to support their position (Duffy, Roehler, Sivan, et al., 1987). One strength of the experiment is that treated reading groups were assigned to experimental and control conditions randomly. Ten teachers and their low-achieving third-grade reading groups were assigned to participate in a "direct explanation" condition. Teachers in this condition were taught to explain reading skills as strategies and to include metacognitive information about those strategies as part of teaching. Ten other third-grade teachers and their low-achieving students were assigned to a treated control condition. Teachers in this condition were taught to apply behavioral management principles with their classes. That both groups believed they were "treated" groups reduced the possibility that any gains in the direct explanation condition would be the result of a "Hawthorne effect" (Campbell & Stanley, 1966).

Another strength of the study was the inclusion of a variety of dependent measures that captured the many concerns of the study. The quality of teachers' explanations of strategies was assessed by analyses of transcripts of actual lessons. Student awareness was measured with "lesson interviews" that tapped awareness of lesson content. These interviews were conducted immediately following some piece of instruction. During a "concept interview" at the end of the year, students' awareness of the need to be strategic when reading was determined. Several measures of reading achievement were also included. Perhaps the most challenging of these was the reading portion of the Michigan Educational Assessment Program (MEAP) that was administered approximately five months after the experiment ended. Classroom measures were also taken, including assessments of the management of the classroom, attendance in school, and content coverage.

Teachers in the direct explanation condition were more explicit than control teachers in explaining reading strategies. In addition, after a year of instruction, the direct explanation children were more aware of the content covered in class and the reading strategies that had been taught. Direct explanation subjects were more likely than control subjects to believe that reading is a self-directed activity, that reading involves problem solving, that skills and rules aid comprehension, that the purpose of reading is to get meaning, that reading involves conscious processing, and that reading involves selection of strategies. Post-treatment achievement test differences favored the direct explanation subjects, with the most impressive result being a significant difference favoring treated classrooms on the five-month-delayed MEAP.

One notable aspect of these analyses is that the units of treatment and the units of analysis were the same (i.e., the reading group), consistent with methods of statistical analyses that are widely recommended (e.g., Levin, 1985). The alternative approach, which involves using the individual subject as the unit of analysis, inflates the Type I error rate well beyond the nominal rate since there is a violation of the independence of errors assumption (e.g., Kirk, 1982).

In summary, Duffy, Roehler, Meloth, et al. (1986) performed a true experiment evaluating direct explanation. They accomplished this goal with actual teachers in a classroom setting using the textbooks traditionally employed in reading instruction. There were striking increases in awareness of reading processes and reading achievement as a function of direct explanation, making clear that teachers can be taught to engage in direct explanation of reading strategies so that their students profit. We note in closing that one reason this experiment is so strong is that it is the culmination of several years of work, including preliminary studies (e.g., Duffy, Roehler, Meloth, et al., 1986). The development and evaluation of an important educational intervention takes time (Duffy & Roehler, this volume, chap. 6).

Reciprocal Teaching of Comprehension Strategies

Annemarie Palincsar, Ann Brown, and their associates have studied an approach to increasing children's reading comprehension. The heart of the intervention is a particular form of interaction between students and teachers. In their best known experiments (Palincsar & Brown, 1984), seventh-grade students who could decode print but had difficulty comprehending were trained to use four reading strategies: predicting what information would be presented in text; generating questions about text; summarizing text; and clarifying text. Early in instruction teachers provided much support. They modeled expert use of the four strategies and coached students to use the techniques. Gradually, use of the strategies was transferred to the students such that during the later stages of instruction the teacher provided prompting and assistance only as needed. An important aspect of this approach is that part of the transfer of responsibility to students involved having them serve as teachers of the strategies to others in their reading group. Reading comprehension was improved substantially by this treatment.

Palincsar (1987) studied whether this interactive approach involving transfer of responsibility from teachers to students could be used to teach similar listening comprehension strategies to younger children (first grade). First, extensive pretesting was conducted in order to identify students who were at risk for school difficulties, especially those related to comprehension. Once identified, at-risk students were randomly assigned to the reciprocal instruction condition or to the control condition, with the experimental and control students in the same classrooms (i.e., there were three classrooms, each containing treated and control subjects).

The training took place over a series of 25 sessions and was administered to small groups by the classroom teachers. During the first five sessions, the teacher introduced the four comprehension strategies explicitly. This was followed by 20 sessions of dialogue in which students were led to use the four strategies with expository text that was read to them. Throughout training, comprehension was assessed by having students respond to factual questions as well as some gist and analogy questions. Control subjects also received these practice tests.

Palincsar (1987) produced a great deal of evidence that the intervention affected children's performance as intended. The teachers' role changed over the course of instruction as expected, with the teacher providing explicit information early in instruction and serving more as a coach later in instruction. As instruction continued, students were more likely to seek clarification immediately when they heard information that was unfamiliar or hard to understand. The most striking data, however, were on performance measures taken at and near the conclusion of the study. In general, students in the experimental condition outperformed students in the control condition on these measures. Even when the effect was not significant (i.e., on gist questions), there was a strong trend favoring the experimentals over the controls.

Particularly impressive was Palincsar's attention to the performance of the individual subjects. In this experiment, all but two of the trained subjects showed gains over the course of treatment. We note that this attention to individual performance has characterized all of the Palincsar studies and is a great strength of the work on reciprocal instruction. Another strength is the collection of comparable performance measures throughout the study, permitting determination of when the intervention began to have an effect. In general, the experimental and control means did not diverge until the second half of the intervention period.

DISCUSSION

Classroom Research

What are good classroom studies like? They are motivated by clearly articulated theories and important instructional issues. Actual teachers carry out the instruction, with teaching occurring over an extended period of time. The studies are true experiments (i.e., there is random assignment of participants to instructed and control conditions). A variety of dependent measures are collected in order to assess the multidimensional impacts of the interventions. Palincsar's consistent analysis of individual subjects' progress (e.g., Palincsar & Brown, 1984; Palincsar, Brown, & Martin, 1987) is praiseworthy—It is important to know not only whether group means are changed for the better by an intervention, but also what percentage of children benefit from the treatment as individuals. Duffy, Roehler, Meloth, et al.'s (1986) use of a treated control condition is a method that other researchers should note, since potential Hawthorne effects are reduced or eliminated if all participants believe that they are in treated conditions.

Although neither of the experiments considered in detail in this section provided information about their active components, we do not view this as a particularly important flaw. While component analysis certainly has its place in a program of classroom research (Pressley, Forrest-Pressley, & Elliott-Faust, in press), establishing that a package is effective is a logical prerequisite to conducting research that decomposes the treatment into more and less active ingredients. Frank Kline of the Institute for Research on Learning Disabilities at the University of Kansas provided an analogy that seems appropriate:

If one conceives of strategy instruction as a cook conceives of devising a new soup recipe, the importance of component analysis and its position in relation to other research becomes apparent. Just as the experienced cook doesn't throw just anything into the pot, so the researcher/educator carefully selects only the elements of instruction that he feels from past experience and research are important.

The cook's first priority is to get a good taste. The particular taste that the cook looks for is dependent on many things, but ultimately lies with the audience that will consume his soup. In a similar fashion, the curriculum chosen by the researcher/educator will include the particular components proven to be effective with the particular clients he serves.

Once the overall good taste of the soup has been established (often by limited tastings as well as experience), the cook can then begin to refine the recipe into its final version. This refinement can take the form of adding or subtracting different ingredients to find out what effect they have on the soup.

The researcher/educator will also be interested in forming his product through piloting selected parts of it (tasting) as well as bringing his full range of experience to bear. Eventually though, a full-scale test with the intended audience is necessary to establish the efficacy of the general program. Component analysis is appropriate, but only after the initial efficacy (taste) of the package is established. Once the general usefulness is established, component analysis becomes a useful tool to provide the most potent and cost-effective program possible. It also contributes heavily to the creation of the next program by informing the researcher/educator which components are most effective. (Kline, personal communication, 1987)

It seems to us that Duffy, Roehler, Palincsar, and their associates are pretty good cooks, and it is a good bet that the recipes they have prepared will be tried and experimented with by others. Their recipes will be adapted to specific situations not considered in the original reports. Some adaptations will improve the flavor of the soup; others will destroy it. Identification of both types of components will permit the development of more potent and cost-effective interventions.

Laboratory Research

Recent laboratory research provides insight into real-world strategy use that complements research generated in the classroom. As an example, consider contemporary research on imagery and elaboration:

1. Laboratory researchers are investigating more educationally valid tasks. At the beginning of the 1970s, most basic research on imagery and elaboration processes was conducted in paired-associate and other basic paradigms (e.g., Paivio, 1971). In recent years, however, lab studies of elaboration have focused on more educationally relevant tasks such as vocabulary learning (e.g., Pressley, Levin, & Delaney, 1982), prose retention (e.g., McCormick & Levin, 1984, 1987), and acquisition of science and social studies facts (e.g., Levin et al., 1983; Pressley, Symons, McDaniel, & Snyder, 1988).
2. There are increasingly analytical studies of individual differences. Thus, there are studies that are sensitive to individual differences in the knowledge base (e.g., Rohwer, Rabinowitz, & Dronkers, 1982) and functional short-term memory capacity (Pressley, Cariglia-Bull, Deane, & Schneider, 1987) necessary to construct elaborations.

3. There are head-on comparisons of one strategy with another. Particularly important are comparisons of strategies that have traditionally been uncritically accepted as educationally important and potent (e.g., McDaniel, Pressley, & Dunay, 1987; Pressley, Levin, & McDaniel, 1987).
4. A large data base has been generated regarding children's monitoring of performance as they use elaboration strategies. It is clear that young children do not monitor proficiently (e.g., Ghatala, 1986; Lodico, Ghatala, Levin, Pressley, & Bell, 1983; Markman, 1981), and that it is not especially easy to teach them to monitor (e.g, Ghatala, Levin, Pressley, & Goodwin, 1986; Ghatala, Levin, Pressley, & Lodico, 1985). More positively, it is possible to teach monitoring so that children are able to spot problems and continue to do so for some time following the termination of instruction (e.g., Elliott-Faust & Pressley, 1986; Ghatala et al., 1986; Miller, 1985).
5. There have been studies of how to add metacognitive information to instruction to increase maintenance and generalization of elaboration strategies (e.g., Borkowski, Carr, & Pressley, 1987; Kurtz & Borkowski, 1987; O'Sullivan & Pressley, 1984). It appears that information about when and where to use trained strategies can be added to instruction directly, although there are individual differences in susceptibility to such instruction (e.g., impulsive children with low prior metacognition seemed not to benefit much from metacognitive information about trained strategies in Kurtz & Borkowski, 1987).
6. Laboratory researchers have demonstrated that strategy effects are very specific. This suggests that there are many diverse strategies, rather than a few general ones, that will need to be integrated into the curriculum and taught over an extended period of time. For instance, elaborative strategies affect learning of associative relations without affecting other aspects of learning (e.g., Pressley, Levin, Kuiper, Bryant, & Michener, 1982), and some methods of elaboration have positive effects on incidental learning without benefiting intentional learning (e.g., provision of precise elaborations of mutually confusing sentences; Pressley, McDaniel, Turnure, Wood, & Ahmad, 1987).
7. Laboratory researchers have also determined that it is not possible to generalize conclusions about a given strategy from research on another strategy. Thus, the developmental functions that describe children's use of interactive imagery are very different from those describing the use of rehearsal strategies (see Schneider & Pressley, 1988). There are different developmental levels when it is profitable to educate rehearsal versus imagery strategies.

In summary, recent laboratory research is more informative about strategy instruction and strategy use than studies conducted a decade ago, many of which boiled down to an instructional test of a single strategy applied to a laboratory task (Pressley, Heisel, et al., 1982). The rich matrix of laboratory data being generated in the late 1980s provides many hints about what might work in the classroom and complements classroom research efforts.

Closing Comments

Those who are interested in strategy instructional theories and research efforts are thinking beyond the theories and the extant research studies. A new vision of education is emerging. It is one in which children are provided procedural instruction throughout their academic careers, one in which strategy instruction is at the heart of education. This reflects the belief that a major goal of schooling is to teach people *how* to read, write, and solve problems (e.g., Jones et al.,1987).

Entire volumes are appearing that carry this message, along with guidelines for how this goal might be reached. An impressive example is *Effective Instruction for Special Education* by Margo A. Mastropieri and Thomas E. Scruggs (1987). This book is tailored for special educators, but includes information about strategies that are appropriate for elementary education in general. Mastropieri and Scruggs review strategic instruction that can be used for reading, language arts, mathematics, social studies, and science. In addition, they cover general strategies of classroom management, the strategic development of social skills, and strategies that can be taught to special students to ease the transition to the world of employment. The discussion of strategies is embedded in a discussion of mainstream topics surrounding these curriculum problems, so that the information about strategies is tied to information more traditionally taught in special education courses. Books like this are invaluable in that they provide a bridge to the teacher corps that has not been made before (see also Gagné, 1985; Mayer, 1987). Teachers and prospective teachers are provided with high-quality information about scientifically validated strategies that are applicable in a school environment. A main message in these volumes is that strategy instruction is at the heart of professional-level teaching.

For the most part, the examples cited in this chapter have been about teacher-directed instruction. However, environments that are completely supportive of strategy development would involve more than this. Texts would encourage development and use of strategies with explicit commentary about strategies for remembering and understanding material. In addition, other support materials would be available, possibly including bulletin board displays prompting acquisition and deployment of new strategic skills; study skills kits that can be used on an individualized basis by students; and videotaped programming about use of various strategies. The school library would stock a good supply of books that detail strategies for various domains (see Pressley, Goodchild et al., 1989, for candidate volumes). These books would be prominently displayed and their circulation and use widely encouraged. The presence of these elements in school would go far to make clear to the student that use of appropriate strategies is central to good thinking. It would become obvious that there are better and poorer ways of accomplishing virtually every educational task and that there is great motivation to learn the more effective procedures.

In addition to being surrounded by materials that encourage use of strategies, the student would be exposed to people who use strategies and would be willing to pass on their procedural knowledge to others. Teachers would routinely and overtly select and use strategies. They would "think aloud" to reveal how they were monitoring strategy use and making decisions to continue or switch strategies. For instance, Deshler and Schumaker (in press) argue that teachers should model strategic thinking during execution of even the most mundane tasks (e.g., taking role, reviewing assignments) so that students become aware of the universal applicability (e.g., Miller, Galanter, & Pribram, 1960) of strategic planning. Peers often can serve as models and teachers. The Kansas group has also completed work on peer instruction of strategies, producing evidence that learning-disabled children who have learned a strategy can teach it to learning-disabled peers (Ellis, Lenz, & Sabornie, 1987a). Parents can be involved too. In fact, a variety of theoretical perspectives support the position that parents value opportunities to pass important skills from their generation to the next (e.g., Erikson, 1968; Vygotsky, 1978). Vygotsky, in particular, argues that the acquisition of intellectual skills by the child often involves adult-child interaction in which the parent provides sensitive guidance that is gradually faded as the child assumes greater and greater control of skills that are mastered (Day, Cordon, & Kerwin, this volume, chap. 4). A variety of data support the conclusion that parents can directly guide their children's acquisition of important skills, ones that take many sessions and many months to develop (Ellis & Rogoff, 1982; Laboratory of Comparative Human Cognition, 1983; Ninio, 1980, 1983; Rogoff & Gardner, 1984; Saxe, Gearhardt, & Guberman, 1984; Wood, Bruner, & Ross, 1976).

There is plenty of reason to believe that children's knowledge about strategic processes can be developed through instruction. The research we have touched upon suggests that there is abundant motivation to increase knowledge and use of strategies since these procedures mediate important real-world tasks. Our perspective is that current models of thinking, instructional theories, and approaches to research combine to fuel enthusiasm for additional research on and development of strategy instruction, research, and development that is critical if really effective strategy instruction is to be created and disseminated.

Acknowledgments.

Writing of this chapter was supported by a grant from the Natural Sciences and Engineering Research Council to Michael Pressley. Authors Symons and Snyder were supported by graduate scholarships from the same agency.

REFERENCES

Alvermann, D.E., Smith, L.C., & Readence, J.E. (1985). Prior knowledge activation and the comprehension of compatible and incompatible text. *Reading Research Quarterly 20*, 420–436.

Anderson, R., & Biddle, W. (1975). On ask people questions about what they are reading. In G.H. Bower (Ed.), *The psychology of learning and motivation*, Vol. 9 (pp. 90–132). New York: Academic Press.

Applebee, A.N. (1984). *Contexts for learning to write*. Norwood, NJ: Ablex.

Applebee, A.N. (1986). Problems in process approaches: Toward a reconceptualization of process instruction. In A.R. Petrosky, D. Bartholomae, & K.J. Rehage (Eds.), *The teaching of writing: Eighty-fifth yearbook of the National Society for the Study of Education* (pp. 95–113). Chicago: University of Chicago Press.

Atkinson, R.C., & Shiffrin, R.M. (1968). Human memory: A proposed system and its control processes. In K.W. Spence & J.T. Spence (Eds.), *The psychology of learning and motivation*, Vol. 2. New York: Academic Press.

Baron, J. (1981). Reflective thinking as a goal of education. *Intelligence, 5*, 291–309.

Baron, J. (1985). *Rationality and intelligence*. Cambridge, England: Cambridge University Press.

Belmont, J.M., Butterfield, E.C., & Ferretti, R.P. (1982). To secure transfer of training instruct self-management skills. In D.K. Determan & J.R. Sternberg (Eds.), *How and how much can intelligence be increased?* (pp. 147–154). Norwood, NJ: Ablex.

Borkowski, J.G. (1985). Signs of intelligence: Strategy generalization and metacognition. In S.R. Yussen (Ed.), *The growth of reflection in children* (pp. 105–144). Orlando, FL: Academic Press.

Borkowski, J.G., Carr, M., & Pressley, M. (1987). "Spontaneous" strategy use: Perspectives from metacognitive theory. *Intelligence, 11*, 61–75. *11*, 61–75.

Borkowski, J.G., Carr, M., Rellinger, E., & Pressley, M. (in press). Self-regulated cognition: Interdependence of metacognition, attributions, and self-esteem. In B.F. Jones & L. Idol (Eds.), *Dimensions of thinking and cognitive instruction*. Hillsdale, NJ: Erlbaum & Associates.

Brainerd, C.J. (1978). Learning research and Piagetian theory. In L.S. Siegel & C.J. Brainerd (Eds.), *Alternatives to Piaget: Critical essays on the theory* (pp. 69–109). New York: Academic Press.

Brown, A.L., Bransford, J.D., Ferrara, R.A., & Campione, J.C. (1983). Learning, remembering, and understanding. In J.H. Flavell & E.M. Markman (Eds.), *Handbook of child psychology*, Vol. III, *Cognitive development* (pp. 177–266). New York: John Wiley & Sons.

Campbell, D.T., & Stanley, J.C. (1966). *Experimental and quasi-experimental designs for research*. Chicago: Rand McNally.

Campione, J.C., & Brown, A.L. (1978). Toward a theory of intelligence: Contributions from research with retarded children. *Intelligence, 2*, 279–304.

Carpenter, T.P. (1985). Learning to add and subtract: An exercise in problem solving. In E.A. Silver (Ed.), *Teaching and learning mathematical problem solving: Multiple research perspectives* (pp. 17–40). Hillsdale, NJ: Erlbaum & Associates.

Chipman, S.F., Segal, J.W., & Glaser, R. (Eds.). (1985). *Thinking and learning skills*, Vol. 2, *Research and open questions*. Hillsdale, NJ: Erlbaum & Associates.

Clifford, M.M. (1984). Thoughts on a theory of constructive failure. *Educational Psychologist, 19*, 108–120.

Cronbach, L.J., & Snow, R.E. (Eds.). (1977). *Aptitudes and instructional methods.* New York: Irvington/Naiburg.

Derry, S.J., Hawkes, L.W., & Tsai, C-J. (1987). A theory for remediating problem-solving skills of older children and adults. *Educational Psychologist, 22,* 55–87.

Derry, S.J., & Murphy, D.A. (1986). Designing systems that train learning ability: From theory to practice. *Review of Educational Research, 56,* 1–39.

Deshler, D.D., & Schumaker, J.B. (1986). Learning strategies: An instructional alternative for low-achieving adolescents. *Exceptional Children, 52,* 583–590.

Deshler, D.D., & Schumaker, J.B. (in press). An instructional model for teaching students how to learn. In J.L. Graden, J.E. Zins, & M.J. Curtis (Eds.), *Alternative educational delivery systems: Enhancing instructional options for all students.*

Deshler, D.D., Schumaker, J.B., & Lenz, B.K. (1984). Academic and cognitive interventions for LD adolescents (Part i). *Journal of Learning Disabilities, 17,* 108–117.

Devine, T.G. (1987). *Teaching study skills: A guide for teachers.* New York: Allyn & Bacon.

Duffy, G.G., & Roehler, L.R. (1986). *Improving classroom reading instruction: A decision-making approach.* New York: Random House.

Duffy, G.G., & Roehler, L.R. (1987). Improving reading instruction through the use of responsive elaboration. *The Reading Teacher, 40,* 514–520.

Duffy, G.G., Roehler, L.R., Meloth, M., Vavrus, L., Book, C., Putnam, J., & Wesselman, R. (1986). The relationship between explicit verbal explanation during reading skill instruction and student awareness and achievement: A study of reading teacher effects. *Reading Research Quarterly, 21,* 237–252.

Duffy, G.G., Roehler, L.R., & Putnam, J. (1987). Putting the teacher in control: Basal textbooks and teacher decision making. *Elementary School Journal, 87,* 357–366.

Duffy, G.G., Roehler, L.R., Sivan, E., Rakliffe, G., Book, C., Meloth, M., Vavrus, L., Wesselman, R., Putman, J., & Bassiri, D. (1987). The effects of explaining the reasoning associated with using reading strategies. *Reading Research Quarterly, 22,* 347–368.

Durkin, D. (1979). What classroom observations reveal about reading comprehension instruction. *Reading Research Quarterly, 14,* 481–538.

Education Development Center. (1988). *Improving textbook usability.* Newton, MA: Education Development Center.

Elliott-Faust, D.J., & Pressley, M. (1986). How to teach comparison processing to increase children's short- and long-term listening comprehension monitoring. *Journal of Educational Psychology, 78,* 27–33.

Ellis, E.S., Lenz, B.K., & Sabornie, E.J. (1987a). Generalization and adaptation of learning strategies to natural environments: Part 1, Critical agents. *Remedial and special education, 8,* 6–20.

Ellis, E.S., Lenz, B.K., & Sabornie, E.J. (1987b). Generalization and adaptation of learning strategies to natural environments: Part 2, Research into practice. *Remedial and special education, 8,* 6–23.

Ellis, S., & Rogoff, B. (1982). The strategies and efficacy of child versus adult teachers. *Child Development, 53,* 730–735.

Erikson, E.H. (1968). *Identity: Youth and crisis.* New York: Norton.

Gagné, E.D. (1985). *The cognitive psychology of school learning.* Boston: Little, Brown & Co.

Gagné, E.D., & Bell, M.S. (1981). The use of cognitive psychology in the development and evaluation of textbooks. *Educational Psychologist, 16,* 1128–1138.

Garner, R. (1987). *Metacognition and reading comprehension*. Norwood, NJ: Ablex.

Ghatala, E.S. (1986). Strategy-monitoring training enables young learners to select effective strategies. *Educational Psychologist, 21,* 43–54.

Ghatala, E.S., Levin, J.R., Pressley, M., & Goodwin, D. (1986). A componential analysis of the effects of derived and supplied strategy-utility information on children's strategy selection. *Journal of Experimental Child Psychology, 41,* 76–92.

Ghatala, E.S., Levin, J.R., Pressley, M., & Lodico, M.G. (1985). Training cognitive strategy monitoring in children. *American Educational Research Journal, 22,* 199–216.

Glaser, R. (1984). Education and thinking: The role of knowledge. *American Psychologist, 39,* 93–104.

Glaser, R. (1985). Learning and instruction: A letter for a time capsule. In S.F. Chipman, J.W. Segal, & R. Glaser (Eds.), *Thinking and learning skills,* Vol. 2, *Research and open questions* (pp. 609–618). Hillsdale, NJ: Erlbaum & Associates.

Hasselhorn, M., & Körkel, J. (1986). Metacognitive versus traditional reading instructions: The mediating role of domain-specific knowledge on children's text processing. *Human Learning, 5,* 75–90.

Jones, B.F., Palincsar, A.S., Ogle, D.S., & Carr, E.G. (Eds.). (1987). *Strategic teaching and learning: Cognitive instruction in the content areas*. Alexandria, VA: Association for Supervision and Curriculum Development.

Kirk, R.E. (1982). *Experimental design: Procedures for the behavioral sciences*. Monterey, CA: Brooks/Cole.

Kurtz, B.E., & Borkowski, J.G. (1987). Development of strategic skills in impulsive and reflective children: A longitudinal study of metacognition. *Journal of Experimental Child Psychology, 43,* 129–148.

Laboratory of Comparative Human Cognition (1983). Culture and cognitive development. In P. Mussen (General Ed.) & W. Kesson (Volume Ed.), *Handbook of child psychology,* Vol. 1 (pp. 295–356). New York: John Wiley & Sons.

Levin, J.R. (1985). Some methodological and statistical "bugs" in research on children's learning. In M. Pressley & C.J. Brainerd (Eds.), *Cognitive learning and memory in children* (pp. 205–233). New York: Springer-Verlag.

Levin, J.R., Dretzke, B.J., McCormick, C.B., Scruggs, T.E., McGivern, J.E., & Mastropieri, M.A. (1983). Learning via mnemonic pictures: Analysis of the presidential process. *Educational Communication and Technology Journal, 3,* 161–173.

Lodico, M.G., Ghatala, E.S., Levin, J.R., Pressley, M., & Bell, J.A. (1983). The effects of strategy-monitoring on children's selection of effective memory strategies. *Journal of Experimental Child Psychology, 35,* 263–277.

Markman, E.M. (1981). Comprehension monitoring. In W.P. Dickson (Ed.), *Children's oral communication skills* (pp. 61–84). New York: Academic Press.

Marx, R.W., Winne, P.H., & Walsh, J. (1985). Studying student cognition during classroom learning. In M. Pressley & C.J. Brainerd (Eds.), *Cognitive learning and memory in children* (pp. 181–203). New York: Springer-Verlag.

Mastropieri, M.A., & Scruggs, T.E. (1987). *Effective instruction for special education*. Boston: Little, Brown, & Co.

Mayer, R.E. (1986). Teaching students how to think and learn: A look at some instructional programs and the research: A review of J.W. Segal, S.F. Chipman, & R. Glaser's (1985), *Thinking and learning skills,* Vol. 1, *Relating instruction to research* and S.F. Chipman, J.W. Segal, & R. Glaser's (1985), *Thinking and learning skills,* Vol. 2, *Research and open questions*. *Contemporary Psychology, 31,* 753–756.

Mayer, R.E. (1987). *Educational psychology: A cognitive approach.* Boston: Little, Brown & Co.

McCombs, B.L. (1986, April). *The role of the self-system in self-regulated learning.* Paper presented at the annual meeting of the American Educational Research Association, San Francisco.

McCormick, C.B., & Levin, J.R. (1984). A comparison of different prose-learning variations of the mnemonic key word method. *American Educational Research Journal, 21,* 379–398.

McCormick, C.B., & Levin, J.R. (1987). Mnemonic prose-learning strategies. In M.A. McDaniel & M. Pressley (Eds.), *Imagery and related mnemonic strategies: Theories, individual differences, and applications* (pp. 392–406). New York: Springer-Verlag.

McDaniel, M.A., Pressley, M., & Dunay, P.K. (1987). Long-term retention of vocabulary after keyword and context learning. *Journal of Educational Psychology, 79,* 87–89.

Meichenbaum, D.M. (1977). *Cognitive behavior modification.* New York: Plenum.

Miller, G.E. (1985). The effects of general and specific self-instructional training on children's comprehension monitoring performance during reading. *Reading Research Quarterly, 20,* 616–628.

Miller, G., Galanter, E., & Pribram, K. (1960). *Plans and the structure of behavior.* New York: Holt, Rinehart, & Winston.

Morris, P.E. (1979). Strategies for learning and recall. In M.M. Gruneberg & P.E. Morris (Eds.), *Applied problems in memory* (pp. 25–57). London, England: Academic Press.

Nickerson, R.S., Perkins, D.N., & Smith, E.E. (Eds.). (1985). *The teaching of thinking.* Hillsdale, NJ: Erlbaum & Associates.

Ninio, A. (1980). Picture-book reading in mother-infant dyads belonging to two subgroups in Israel. *Child Development, 51,* 587–590.

Ninio, A. (1983). Joint book reading as a multiple vocabulary acquisition device. *Developmental Psychology, 19,* 445–451.

O'Sullivan, J.T., & Pressley, M. (1984). Completeness of instruction and strategy transfer. *Journal of Experimental Child Psychology, 38,* 275–288.

Paivio, A.U. (1971). *Imagery and verbal processes.* New York: Holt, Rinehart, & Co.

Palincsar, A.S. (April 1987). *An apprenticeship approach to the instruction of comprehension skill.* Paper presented at the annual meeting of the American Educational Research Association, Washington DC.

Palincsar, A.S., & Brown, A.L. (1984). Reciprocal teaching of comprehension-fostering and monitoring activities. *Cognition and Instruction, 1,* 117–175.

Palincsar, A.S., Brown, A.L., & Martin, S.M. (1987). Peer interaction in reading comprehension instruction. *Educational Psychologist, 22,* 231–254.

Peterson, P.L., & Swing, S.R. (1983). Problems in classroom implementation of cognitive strategy instruction. In M. Pressley & J.R. Levin (Eds.), *Cognitive strategy research: Educational applications* (pp. 267–287). New York: Springer-Verlag.

Pressley, M. (1983). Making meaningful materials easier to learn: Lessons from cognitive strategy research. In M. Pressley & J.R. Levin (Eds.), *Cognitive strategy research: Educational applications* (pp. 239–266). New York: Springer-Verlag.

Pressley, M. (1986). The relevance of the good strategy user model to the teaching of mathematics. *Educational Psychologist, 21,* 139–161.

Pressley, M., Borkowski, J.G., & O'Sullivan, J.T. (1984). Memory strategy instruction is made of this: Metamemory and durable strategy use. *Educational Psychologist, 19,* 94–107.

Pressley, M., Borkowski, J.G., & O'Sullivan, J.T. (1985). Children's metamemory and the teaching of memory strategies. In D.L. Forrest-Pressley, G.E. MacKinnon, & T.G. Waller (Eds.), *Metacognition, cognition, and human performance* (pp. 111–153). Orlando, FL: Academic Press.

Pressley, M., Borkowski, J.G., & Schneider, W. (1987). Cognitive strategies: Good strategy users coordinate metacognition and knowledge. In R. Vasta & G. Whitehurst (Eds.), *Annals of Child Development*, Vol. 5 (pp. 89–129). New York: JAI Press.

Pressley, M., Cariglia-Bull, T., Deane, S., & Schneider, W. (1987). Short-term memory, verbal competence, and age as predictors of imagery instructional effectiveness. *Journal of Experimental Child Psychology, 43*, 194–211.

Pressley, M., Cariglia-Bull, T., & Snyder, B.L. (1984). Are there programs that can really teach thinking and learning skills?: A review of Segal, Chipman, & Glaser's *Thinking and learning skills*, Vol. 1, *Relating instruction to research*. *Contemporary Education Research, 3*, 435–444.

Pressley, M., Forrest-Pressley, D.L., & Elliott-Faust, D.J. (in press). How to study strategy instructional enrichment: Illustrations from research on children's prose memory and comprehension. In F. Weinert & M. Perlmutter (Eds.), *Memory development: The Ringberg conference*. Hillsdale, NJ: Erlbaum & Associates.

Pressley, M., Forrest-Pressley, D., Elliott-Faust, D.L., & Miller, G.E. (1985). Children's use of cognitive strategies, how to teach strategies, and what to do if they can't be taught. In M. Pressley & C.J. Brainerd (Eds.), *Cognitive learning and memory in children* (pp. 1–47). New York: Springer-Verlag.

Pressley, M., Goodchild, F., Fleet, J., Zajchowski, R., & Evans, E.D. (1989). The challenges of classroom strategy instruction. *Elementary School Journal, 89*, 301–342.

Pressley, M., Heisel, B.E., McCormick, C.B., & Nakamura, G.V. (1982). Memory strategy instruction with children. In C.J. Brainerd & M. Pressley (Eds.), *Verbal processes in children* (pp. 125–159). New York: Springer-Verlag.

Pressley, M., Levin, J.R., & Delaney, H.D. (1982). The mnemonic keyword method. *Review of Educational Research, 52*, 61–92.

Pressley, M., Levin, J.R., & Ghatala, E.S. (1984). Memory strategy monitoring in adults and children. *Journal of Verbal Learning and Verbal Behavior, 23*, 270–288.

Pressley, M., Levin, J.R., Kuiper, N.A., Bryant, S.L., & Michener, S. (1982). Mnemonic versus nonmnemonic vocabulary-learning strategies: Additional comparisons. *Journal of Educational Psychology, 74*, 693–707.

Pressley, M., Levin, J.R., & McDaniel, M.A. (1987). Remembering versus inferring what a word means: Mnemonic and contextual approaches. In M. McGeown & M.E. Curtis (Eds.), *The nature of vocabulary acquisition* (pp. 107–127). Hillsdale, NJ: Erlbaum & Associates.

Pressley, M., McDaniel, M.A., Turnure, J.E., Wood, E., & Ahmad, M. (1987). Generation and precision of elaboration: Effects on intentional and incidental learning. *Journal of Experimental Psychology: Learning memory, and cognition, 13*, 291–300.

Pressley, M., Ross, K.A., Levin, J.R., & Ghatala, E.S. (1984). The role of strategy utility knowledge in children's strategy decision making. *Journal of Experimental Child Psychology, 38*, 491–504.

Pressley, M., Snyder, B.L., & Cariglia-Bull, T. (1987). How can good strategy use be taught to children?: Evaluation of six alternative approaches. In S. Cormier & J. Hagman (Eds.), *Transfer of learning: Contemporary research and applications* (pp. 81–121). Orlando, FL: Academic Press.

Pressley, M., Snyder, B.L., Levin, J.R., Murray, H.G., & Ghatala, E.S. (1987). Perceived readiness for examination performance (PREP) produced by initial reading of text and text containing adjunct questions. *Reading Research Quarterly, 22,* 219–236.

Pressley, M., Symons, S., McDaniel, M.A., & Snyder, B.L. (1988). *Elaborative interrogation facilitates acquisition of confusing facts. Journal of Educational Psychology, 80,* 268–278.

Rabinowitz, M. (1984). The use of categorical organization: Not an all-or-none situation. *Journal of Experimental Child Psychology, 38,* 338–351.

Rogoff, B., & Gardner, W. (1984). Adult guidance of cognitive development. In B. Rogoff & J. Lave (Eds.), *Everyday cognition: Its development in social context* (pp. 95–116). Cambridge, MA: Harvard University Press.

Rohwer, W.D., Jr., Rabinowitz, M., & Dronkers, N.F. (1982). Event knowledge, elaborative propensity, and the development of learning proficiency. *Journal of Experimental Child Psychology, 33,* 492–503.

Saxe, G.B., Gearhart, M., & Guberman, S.R. (1984). The social organization of number development. In B. Rogoff & J.V. Wertsch (Eds.), *Children's learning in the zone of proximal development.* In W. Damon (Editor-in-chief), *New directions for child development,* No. 23. San Francisco: Jossey-Bass.

Schneider, W., & Pressley, M. (1988). *Memory development between 2 and 20.* New York & Berlin, FRG: Springer-Verlag.

Segal, J.W., Chipman, S.F., & Glaser, R. (Eds.). (1985). *Thinking and learning skills,* Vol 1., *Relating research to instruction.* Hillsdale, NJ: Erlbaum & Associates.

Sternberg, R.J. (1979). The nature of mental abilities. *American Psychologist, 34,* 214–230.

Sternberg, R.J. (1982). A componential approach to intellectual development. In R.J. Sternberg (Ed.), *Advances in the psychology of human intelligence,* Vol. 1. Hillsdale, NJ: Erlbaum & Associates.

Sternberg, R.J. (1983). Components of human intelligence. *Cognition, 15,* 1–48.

Taylor, B.M., & Beach, R.W. (1984). The effects of text structure instruction on middle-grade students' comprehension and production of expository prose. *Reading Research Quarterly, 19,* 134–146.

Thompson, A.G. (1985). Teachers' conceptions of mathematics and the teaching of problem solving. In E.A. Silver (Ed.), *Teaching and learning mathematical problem solving* (pp. 281–294). Hillsdale, NJ: Erlbaum & Associates.

Vygotsky, L.S. (1978). *Mind in society: The development of higher psychological processes.* Cambridge, MA: Harvard University Press.

Wood, D.J., Bruner, J.S., & Ross, G. (1976). The role of tutoring in problem solving. *Journal of Child Psychology and Psychiatry, 17,* 89–100.

2
The Triple Alliance for Learning: Cognition, Metacognition, and Motivation

ELIZABETH J. SHORT AND JILL A. WEISSBERG-BENCHELL

Effective learning in schools today requires children to coordinate numerous skills in a variety of content domains. In an attempt to maximize educational output, skilled learners are presumed to balance their cognitive skills, metacognitive skills, and motivational styles. This delicate balance can be seen in skilled learners' sensitivity to the tetrahedral nature of learning (Jenkins, 1979). According to Jenkins' tetrahedral model, skilled learners remain constantly aware of four critical factors: (a) the characteristics of the learner, (b) the demands of the task, (c) the nature of the materials, and (d) the learning activities possessed by the student and those required by the task. Skilled learners are aware of their cognitive strengths and weaknesses in a particular content domain and are usually motivated to utilize their strategic skills to master any academic challenge.

Learning-disabled (LD) children can be distinguished from their skilled counterparts in numerous ways. The most salient distinguishing feature of LD students is that psychometric intelligence does not predict their achievement, whereas intelligence does predict the achievement of their more skilled peers (Keller & Hallahan, 1987; Short, Feagans, McKinney, & Applebaum, 1984; Taylor, Fletcher, & Satz, 1984). We believe that this gap between actual and expected achievement in LD children can be explained by an analysis of cognitive, metacognitive, and motivational variables. Thus, this chapter will present current information regarding the influences of critical cognitive, metacognitive, and motivational factors on young students' academic learning. After describing how LD and skilled learners differ in terms of cognition, metacognition, and motivation, effective instruction with LD students will be described.

Cognitive Skills

In an attempt to understand the cognitive deficits of the LD learner, researchers have explored a wide variety of cognitive processes, including attention, memory, and language (Ceci, 1986; McKinney & Feagans, 1983;

Torgesen & Wong, 1986). Not surprisingly, skilled learners are more efficient than LD learners with respect to most cognitive skills and contents. These differences between skilled and LD learners in basic cognitive abilities increase linearly as a function of years in school (McKinney & Feagans, 1984). This should not come as a great surprise if we accept Nickerson's (1984) analogy that cognitive processes are like the "muscles of the mind." The assumption is that the LD students' cognitive skills/muscles are not as well developed as skilled learners' cognitive skills/muscles because LD students do not exercise their skills as often. With each new year, skilled students further refine and strengthen their muscles through extensive use, whereas LD students' muscles begin to atrophy as a result of their failure to use these cognitive muscles. Thus, the gap in skills enlarges with time.

Although a useful analogy, it is critical to recognize that LD learners are not uniformly deficient (McKinney, 1988). Because of our inability to precisely define what is meant by learning disabilities, the LD population is quite diverse. The great variability or heterogeneity that exists within the LD population has made it quite difficult to unravel which skills or combination of skills are critical factors in school failure (McKinney, Short, & Feagans, 1985). Despite the uncertainty regarding sample definition, there appears to be some consensus regarding the primary importance of at least three cognitive skills for successful academic achievement. These include attention (Short, Friebert, & Andrist, 1988), memory (Swanson, 1988a), and language (Feagans & Applebaum, 1986). A review of the literature may help shed insight into how and why attention, memory, and language skills affect achievement in schools.

ATTENTION

The importance of attentional processes in successful academic performance has been well documented (Krupski, 1986). Classroom environments are filled with an abundance of stimuli, with many appealing and potentially distracting stimuli lacking in educational relevance (e.g., fun-loving peers, hallway commotions, toys and animals in the corner of the room, outdoor panorama). Successful students need to learn to filter out appealing distractions (Keogh & Margolis, 1976), concentrating instead on educationally relevant information. Three specific attentional skills appear most critical to success in school. These include students' ability to: (a) attend selectively to relevant task information, (b) sustain attention on tasks, and (c) deploy attention flexibly across tasks (Krupski, 1986; Reynolds, Wade, Trathen, & Lapan, this volume, chap. 7).

Not only are attentional skills and processes obviously critical to academic success, but so too are they important to the development of intelligence (Zeamon & House, 1963). Sternberg (1977) has prominently placed attentional resources in his triarchic theory of intelligence. As limited information processors, LD students need to learn to allocate their cognitive resources efficiently, recognizing that some situations call for swift processing, whereas others require more reflective processing. The flexible allocation of resources (i.e., knowing when to be fast and when to be slow) is critical for achieving automaticity and is one of the hallmarks of successful school performance. Skilled learners strive for automaticity in processing to avoid taxing their attentional resources to the point of exhaustion (Schneider, Dumais, & Shiffrin, 1984). Therefore, low academic functioning may be a secondary consequence of a more fundamental attentional deficit, with attentional rigidity seen as the critical factor (Krupski, 1986).

Where Are the Attentional Deficits?

The attentional difficulties experienced by LD children are quite diverse and appear to affect achievement in numerous ways (Keogh & Margolis, 1976). According to Keogh and Margolis (1976), LD children experience attentional difficulties in three areas: (a) "coming to attention" or focusing attention on the task, (b) "making decisions" or carefully considering all the alternatives to a problem, and (c) "maintaining attention" or sustaining attention on a task for a period of time. For example, if children have difficulty focusing their attention on an analogy task, they will not encode successfully the relevant stimulus attributes of the (A:B) pair (Sternberg, 1977). As a result, when they decide how to map the relationship observed between the A:B pair to the C:D pair, they will not consider all the possible alternatives to the problem. In addition, they will have difficulty maintaining their attention on the task and will be more inclined to make a haphazard guess. Consequently because of poor attentional skills, the LD learner will be more prone to error than the skilled learner.

Multifaceted Nature of Attentional Deficits

Little if any subtyping research has been done on the attention skills of the LD student. Yet few researchers would disagree that there exists a diverse array of attentional profiles in LD populations. Recently, Short, Friebert, et al. (1988) explored the variety of potential attentional problems experienced by LD learners. This developmental study of second, fourth, and sixth graders enabled an examination of two competing hypotheses: developmental delay and developmental difference. To determine whether LD learners were deficient in their ability to stay on task (sustained attention), the continuous performance task (CPT) was employed. The CPT performance involved students' prolonged attention to a computer screen for approximately 15 minutes. During this time interval, students were to signal on the joy stick the presence of a target letter "x" in a continuous stream of letters. The task employed was deliberately constructed to avoid taxing children's cognitive resources in order to determine why attentional difficulties develop. On the CPT, the LD learners were comparable to their skilled learner counterparts in sustaining their attention. Therefore, when cognitive resources are not taxed heavily, it appears that young and LD learners are as able as their older and more skilled counterparts to sustain their attention on the task.

In order to determine whether differences in sustained attention were a function of the cognitive complexity of the task, a paper and pencil analog of the CPT (the 2 & 7 task; Ruff, Evans, & Marshall, 1984) was employed in this study. The 2 & 7 task involves students coordination of attentional and visual scanning skills. Students were presented with 20 15-second trial blocks, each comprised of two rows of stimuli. Students were instructed to scan the arrays from the right to left, crossing out the target numbers as quickly as possible. Results for the 2 & 7 test indicated that LD students' performance was inferior to their skilled counterparts. In fact, LD sixth graders were less proficient than their second-grade skilled counterparts. Thus, while no differences emerged between skilled and LD learners' sustained attention on the simple CPT task, LD learners were deficient in sustaining their attention on a higher-level task that involved a visual search component.

Not only do students need to stay on task for successful school performance, but learners also need to flexibly deploy their attention in the face of changing task demands. Therefore Short, Friebert, et al. (1988) employed two tasks designed to tap flexible deployment of attention: (a) verbal fluency (Das, 1984) and (b) nonverbal fluency (Ruff et al., 1984). The verbal fluency task involved subjects' speeded generation of words satisfying a letter condition (i.e., words beginning with the letter "B" or "L"). The nonverbal fluency task involved subjects' speeded generation of straight line designs based on five dot configurations. Five 60-second trial blocks were employed. Scores from both fluency tests included number of unique words/designs and number of perseverative errors. Both tasks were assumed to require flexible deployment of attention in that subjects had to spontaneously generate unique words/designs without rigidly generating multiple instances of the same class of words or designs. On both the verbal and nonverbal fluency tasks, LD students were deficient compared to their skilled counterparts. Like the complex sustained attention task, LD learners did not improve with age in their flexible deployment of attention in either the verbal or nonverbal domain, whereas skilled learners improved consistently with age. In addition, LD learners were comparable to the second graders in flexible deployment of attention.

Finally, selective attention or the subjects' ability to attend to relevant information while ignoring irrelevant information was examined by Short and her colleagues via two tasks. The first, the Stroop test (Golden, 1978), was assumed to minimally tax cognitive resources while requiring speeded selective attention. Scores included the number of stimuli verbalized in a 60-second trial block and the number of errors. The second, the Wisconsin Card Sorting Test (Heaton, 1981) was more cognitively taxing, yet no speeded component was imposed. This task involved four standard stimuli and a test deck of 64 cards. The stimuli differed on three dimensions: color (red, green, blue, yellow), number (1, 2, 3, 4 elements), and form (stars, crosses, circles, & triangles). Subjects were asked to generate sorting rules using experimenter feedback regarding the accuracy of their rules. Scores included the number of rules generated and the number of perseverative errors. On both tasks, LD learners were inferior to their skilled counterparts. Again developmental differences emerged within the skilled learner group, whereas the profile for the LD group was flat. Thus, it appears that selective attention skills improve between second and sixth grade for the skilled group, with no similar gain in proficiency experienced by the LD group. These attentional gains experienced by normally achieving children parallel their achievement gains, with no significant improvement in either arena experienced by LD students.

Taken together, these data suggest LD learners' attentional skills affect achievement performance in diverse ways. When tasks are too challenging for the LD learner, deficits appear in both sustaining attention and selective attention. LD students are capable of sustaining attention on simple tasks, but apparently are overwhelmed as task complexity increases.

Memory

School learning depends on children's ability to remember new information presented during the course of the day, as well as the ability to retrieve information previously learned. Skilled learners are able to learn new information quickly, creating permanent records of this information in long-term memory. In addition, they make use of previously learned facts to clarify the significance of new information and to facilitate knowledge acquisition. Without memory skills, learning could not take place. Each experience would be a "novel" one, with no benefit afforded by previous experience.

Where Are the Memory Deficits?

Researchers have long recognized the importance of memory skills for academic achievement and have extensively documented differences between skilled and LD learners (Ceci, 1984; Torgesen, 1985; Worden, 1986). Deficits in memory performance may be global or tied specifically to one of several subskills (i.e., encoding, storage, and retrieval skills). Deficits in the memory performance of LD students have been attributed to both structural and strategic deficits, with heated debates among those favoring one position or the other as the primary cause for academic retardation (Swanson, 1982).

For some LD learners, structural deficits may in fact exist (Pascul-Leone, 1970). These LD children may not have the capacity to attend actively to as many units of information as their skilled counterparts. This capacity limitation imposed on the learner due to a structural deficit decreases the probability that LD learners will successfully remember as much information as their skilled peers. Nevertheless, the extant data in memory does not support the conclusion that structural deficiencies characterize the majority of low achievers (Dempster, 1979).

Instead, the data suggest that nearly all LD learners fail to process information strategically and therefore do not maximize their structural capacity (Chi, 1977). According to the strategy deficit hypothesis, many LD learners would perform more effectively if they used the strategies employed by more capable learners (Pressley, 1986; Pressley, Johnson, & Symons, 1987; Ryan, Short, & Weed, 1986). Considerable support for this strategy deficit hypothesis has been obtained in research examining memory for words (Bauer, 1977), digits (Torgesen & Houck, 1980), simple sentences (Kee, Worden, & Throckmorton, 1984), and simple and complex narratives (Wong & Jones, 1982). These studies suggest that training LD learners to use appropriate strategies dramatically improves their performance on the target task.

Although task-specific strategies play an important role in improving LD students' working memory processes, the strategic use of background knowledge can and often does affect memory performance as well. Students can be encouraged to "activate their background knowledge" about the "to be learned material" (Bartlett, 1932; Hasselhorn & Körkel, 1986) and thereby improve the memorability of new information. The facilitative effects of topical scripts (i.e., restaurant/grocery store) have been documented extensively for skilled learners (Feagans & Short, 1984; Spiro & Tirre, 1979), as well as for reading disabled learners (Ryan, Sheridan, & Short, 1981). Increasing knowledge about and use of the inherent organizational structure of texts (i.e., story grammars/summarization rules) has also been shown to facilitate the reading comprehension and writing performance of less skilled and young learners (Buss, Yussen, Mathews, Miller, & Rembold, 1983; Day, 1981; Short & Ryan, 1984).

In an attempt to tease out structural differences from strategic differences in long-term memory, Chi (1977) explored differences between child chess experts and adult novices. Her research with these children and adults strongly suggested that structural differences in memory span do not exist. Instead, the memory differences observed were a function of a complex interaction between a person's knowledge base and strategy selection. Further support for the facilitative effects of background knowledge on memory has been obtained by Schneider, Körkel, and Weinert (1987). Comparisons were made among four groups of students on their recall of texts about soccer. Students were classified as either academically successful or unsuccessful, with these groups further differentiated by their expertise in soccer. Thus, the four groups of children in this study were academically successful soccer experts, academically successful soccer novices, academically less successful soccer experts, and academically less successful soccer novices. All soccer experts outperformed novices, with no advantage in memory afforded by virtue of the skilled learner status. These data suggest that extensive background knowledge can override potentially powerful learner differences. Given findings like these, it is not surprising that educators are quite concerned about differential development of and use of background knowledge by skilled learners. In sum, not only do LD learners differ from their skilled peers in their development of the knowledge base, but they also do not activate background knowledge relevant to the task at hand.

Multifaceted Nature of Memory Deficits

Although many LD researchers have looked to either short-term memory capabilities or long-term memory skills as the reason why these children fail in school, it has more recently been recognized that the single deficit approach is probably incorrect, particularly with LD populations. Two recent studies highlight the difficulty of searching for simple solutions to LD learners' memory difficulties (Speece, 1987; Swanson, 1988a). The assumption made by these researchers is that LD learners experience a variety of memory problems, with no two students experiencing exactly the same difficulties. Both studies examined individual differences in memory performance within LD samples using cluster analyses to isolate distinct profiles of learners that were predictive of school achievement. For some LD students, memory problems may not solely be a function of capacity limitations but rather strategic deficits may prevent the students from utilizing their existing capacity. For other LD students, memory problems may not solely be a function of strategy deficits but rather capacity limitations may hinder the learner's use of strategies.

Swanson (1988a) observed one common memory deficit in all LD students: they were inferior to skilled students in "accessing structural resources on demanding tasks." By "structural resources," Swanson meant that LD students were less able to activate and effectively utilize their background knowledge on demanding tasks compared to their skilled counterparts. Only 20% of the LD learners were more specifically classified as passive learners according to Swanson. These passive learners failed to activate their relevant background knowledge during the encoding phase. The largest subtype of LD children observed (50% of the total sample) had difficulty "forming multiple connections between task material and information in memory (i.e., they do not elaborate material)." While Swanson did not interpret this deficiency as a strategy deficit, many others have concluded that failure to elaborate reflects a lack of strategic processing (Pressley, Johnson, & Symons, 1987). Interpretations aside, these data strongly suggest that memory deficiencies plague the LD learner. It is noteworthy that Swanson observed that LD students with less pronounced memory problems were more capable in both reading and math than LD students with severe memory deficiencies. Clearly, memory contributes greatly to the academic difficulties experienced by LD students.

Further support for the importance of memory skills to academic performance has been offered by Speece's (1987) study of information-processing subtypes. Examination of the memory deficiencies of a reading-disabled group revealed that four of the six subtypes of reading-disabled children (63% of the sample) experienced significant memory problems. More specifically, half of these LD children had speed of processing and encoding deficits, with the other half demonstrating storage deficits (e.g., strategy or organization). These processing deficits are consistent with Daneman and Carpenter's (1980) contention that LD readers have little processing space available for the long-term storage of new information because they must allocate most of their resources to overall phonetic processing. Therefore working memory is overtaxed and reduced academic efficiency is the net result.

Taken together, these data suggest LD learners' memory skills affect their academic performance in diverse ways. Many children have strategic processing and background knowledge deficits, with perhaps some children experiencing structural deficits. These strategy, knowledge, and structural deficits not only individually affect the quantity of learning, but all three factors may interact in powerful ways to produce important memory deficiencies that contribute significantly to LD students' achievement difficulties.

LANGUAGE

Language processing has been cited quite consistently as a factor that is both critical to school success and that differentiates skilled from LD learners. This should not come as any great surprise, since school learning is largely dependent on the oral communication of information by both teachers and students. Teachers rely heavily on language skills to disseminate information in the classroom. Teachers expect students to express their understanding of material using language. Limited language skills may force less skilled learners to be passive in their learning environment. Skilled students monitor the messages communicated by speakers more effectively than do their LD counterparts (Speece, 1982). The logical conclusion derived from this research is that LD students are less effective than their skilled counterparts in monitoring the effectiveness of classroom communications (i.e., lessons), and therefore are less likely to ask questions when communication failures occur. Classroom observational data clearly suggest that skilled learners do in fact ask and answer more questions than their less skilled counterparts (Brophy & Good, 1985). Perhaps skilled students' active learning style is largely due to superior language skills. While this relationship is somewhat speculative to date, mounting evidence supports this contention (Bialystok & Ryan, 1985).

Where Are the Language Differences?

Differences between skilled and LD learners have been observed in four general language areas: grammatical knowledge, syntactic knowledge, phonological knowledge, and discourse or narrative knowledge (Bialystok & Ryan, 1985; Feagans & Short, 1984). Difficulties in any of these four general language areas would affect not only the oral communication process, but also the students' written communication and reading processes (Ryan,

1981; Short & Ryan, 1984). In addition, LD learners have been characterized as deficient in both expressive and receptive language skills (Feagans &
Short, 1986).

Given these language differences, it is not surprising that LD learners are
less automatic in their language skills than their more skilled peers, and that
their academic performance in school is depressed. LD learners' passive style
may largely be a function of their inferior language skills. Given LD learners'
expressive language deficits, the passivity witnessed during classroom interactions may simply be a function of their inability to construct or answer a
question. Some evidence in support of this contention has been obtained in
a recent longitudinal study of referential communication in skilled and LD
students (Feagans & Short, 1986). Comparisons were made between skilled
and LD students' ability to serve as both speakers and listeners in a communication task, as well as their ability to rephrase the message upon request. LD
students were less effective in both the speaker and listener role than their
skilled counterparts. Even when they had demonstrated nonverbal comprehension of the message, LD students were less able to communicate the message or rephrase the message in a unique way for a confused listener. Feagans
and Short (1986) further demonstrated that LD students' communication
skills are a good predictor of reading comprehension both concurrently and
longitudinally, whereas IQ is not (see Beal, this volume, chap. 8, for a discussion of the relationship between communication skills and writing skills in
normal children). Elementary school children during their first three years of
school were asked to communicate a message about six steps needed to open
a puzzlebox to a puppet. Comprehension of the six-step sequence was
demonstrated nonverbally by all children by opening the box independently.
Even after all children demonstrated perfect comprehension of the sequence,
LD students had more trouble initially communicating this sequence to the
puppet and demonstrated less flexibility rephrasing their message upon
request. Although LD students were as proficient as their skilled counterparts on the nonverbal comprehension of this task, their ineffective verbal
skills masked their performance. Thus, perhaps LD students' poor linguistic
skills are in part responsible for the gap between IQ and achievement.

Multifaceted Nature of Language Deficits

Although language differences have been observed consistently between
skilled and less skilled learners (Ryan, 1981), not all LD children demonstrate the same deficiencies in language. In a recent study by Feagans and
Applebaum (1986), individual differences in language skills within an LD
sample were examined via hierarchical cluster analysis. Language skills were
examined at three levels: syntactic, semantic, and discourse. Based on findings suggesting the importance of discourse skills in the classroom (Feagans
& Short, 1984), Feagans and Applebaum (1986) hypothesized that subtypes
deficient in discourse skills would have the bleakest academic prognosis. To

summarize the results of this study, 42% of the school-identified LD sample had deficient discourse skills, while 44% of the LD children demonstrated strengths in discourse skills as compared to syntactic skills. Students deficient in discourse skills demonstrated lower achievement in reading recognition, reading comprehension, and math across a three-year period than did LD students proficient in narrative skills.

Summary

Not surprisingly, there are consistent attention, memory, and language differences between skilled and LD learners of all ages. Not only do between-group differences consistently emerge, but within-group differences are readily identified as well. One obvious conclusion from this research is that as task difficulty increases, processing capacity must be applied quickly and flexibly or task demands will overwhelm the learner's cognitive capacity. While cognitive skills are most certainly important for academic success, considerable evidence is mounting that cognitive skills are a necessary but not sufficient condition for academic success. In the next two sections, the importance of metacognitive strategies and motivational style for effective school performance will be emphasized. Particular attention will be paid to instances where metacognitive performance and motivational style appeared to compensate for the cognitive deficiencies of LD learners.

Metacognition

Metacognition has been defined as students' awareness of their own cognitive activity and of the methods employed to regulate their own cognitive processes (Brown, 1978). The first portion of the definition addresses whether or not the learner is aware of how knowledge about the "self," the "task," and the "strategies" influences performance. Flavell and Wellman (1977) hypothesized that with each educational experience, learners gain additional knowledge about how person, strategy, and task variables affect both the quality and quantity of learning.

Successful students have the opportunity to learn about themselves with each new academic experience. For example, they learn about their differential effectiveness on tasks (e.g, I am quite skilled in math, but less skilled in reading). Also, successful task performance provides information regarding the utility of selected strategies, whereas failure provides information regarding the ineffectiveness of selected strategies on the task (Pressley, Levin, & Ghatala, 1984). Because skilled learners predominantly experience success in academic endeavors, coping with failure appears to be less difficult for the skilled learner than the LD learner. Skilled learners recognize the importance of "personal effort channeled into strategic activity" (Pressley, Borkowski, & Schneider, 1987). In contrast, LD learners appear to profit less from their academic experiences. Failure experiences reinforce LD learners' feelings of inadequacy in academic contexts (Pearl, 1982). Although the failure experiences can be instructive of strategy/task mismatches for skilled learners, the overabundance of these failure experiences for LD learners appears to be far from instructive. Consistent failure does not provide information about what the LD learner should do strategically to insure success. Rather, consistent failure convinces LD learners that nothing they do will change their academic fate.

• The second portion of the definition of metacognition addresses how students direct, plan, and monitor their cognitive activity (Brown, 1978). Students should regulate their cognitive activities throughout the school day by engaging in active checking, planning, monitoring, testing, revising, evaluating, and thinking about their cognitive performance (Baker & Brown, 1984; Van Haneghan & Baker, this volume, chap. 9). Only when students consciously monitor their cognitive activity do they benefit from failure, abandoning strategies that proved ineffective.

Zimmerman and Pons (1986) have explored extensively the differences in this self-regulation component of metacognition in high- and low-achieving high-school students. Based on structured interviews designed to explore self-regulated learning strategies of students in both academic and social contexts, Zimmerman and Pons concluded that skilled learners used more strategies consistently across contexts than do less skilled learners, with consistent and flexible use of strategies characterizing skilled learners. Self-regulation depends not only on knowledge of strategies, but on the consistent use of strategies as well.

WHERE ARE THE METACOGNITIVE DEFICITS?

The profile of the LD learner's metacognitive skills is comparable to that of his or her cognitive skills. LD and hyperactive learners demonstrate deficiencies in metamemorial knowledge (Borkowski, Peck, Reid, & Kurtz, 1983), in meta-attention (Loper, Hallahan, & Ianna, 1982), and in metalinguistic knowledge (Bialystok & Ryan, 1985). That is, they lack sophisticated knowledge about the person, task, and strategy variables of metacognition as they pertain to memory, attention, and linguistic skills. Not only is their metacognitive knowledge deficient as compared to their skilled counterparts, but they are also less able to regulate academic activity spontaneously, which is presumably controlled by metacognitive variables and processing (Forrest-Pressley & Waller, 1980; Short & Ryan, 1984).

Children exhibiting these strategy deficits have been commonly referred to as "passive or inactive learners" (Ryan, Short, & Weed, 1986; Torgesen, 1977). This style of passive learning predisposes students to failure, even when their cognitive skills are intact. The research in metacognition has shed considerable light on the strategic skills employed by active learners to promote successful performance in school (Pressley, 1986). According to Pressley's (1986) "good strategy user" model, successful learners must (a) process information in a goal-directed fashion, (b) monitor strategic progress made toward achieving the goal, (c) be motivated and not anxious, and (d) be knowledgeable about the world and strategies. The idea is that "good strategy users" must employ strategies to set both their "mind" and their "environment" so that optimization of academic competence is the net result. Thus, they must actively pursue and explore information sources in their environment.

MULTIFACETED NATURE OF METACOGNITIVE DEFICITS

Little research has been done on the multifaceted nature of metacognitive deficits with LD learners. One interesting study done by Swanson (1988b) attempted to explore the role metacognition plays in the problem-solving performance of both high- and low-aptitude students. Swanson assessed metacognition via a 17-item open-ended questionnaire designed to tap the person, strategy, and task variables of metacognition, as well as the importance of knowledge base. All questions were rated on a five-point scale, with high scores indicating sophisticated metacognitive knowledge. In addition, cognitive aptitude was assessed via the Cognitive Abilities Test (CAT). Students were classified as high in metacognitive knowledge provided their total score on the 17 questions exceeded 42, with students scoring less than 39 on the battery classified as low in metacognitive knowledge. High-aptitude students achieved above 120 on the CAT, with low-aptitude students scoring below 106 on the CAT. In this two-by-two design, Swanson demonstrated that high metacognitive knowledge proved to be a better predictor of problem-solving performance than did cognitive aptitude. It should be noted that within the high- and low-metacognitive groups, aptitude was a useful predictor. However, the high-metacognitive/low-aptitude group was superior to the high-aptitude/low-metacognitive group in problem-solving performance. These findings suggest that metacognitive knowledge can compensate for low aptitude in the fourth and fifth grades. Although group classification was based on all 17 metacognitive questions, the questions tapping the person variable and the importance of prior knowledge proved to differentiate low- and high-aptitude students most effectively.

SUMMARY

Taken together, these findings suggest that skilled learners are more aware than their LD peers of their learning styles, the demands of the task, the strategies appropriate for the task, and the relevance of using their background knowledge to facilitate learning. Sophisticated metacognitive knowledge and strategies enable skilled learners to better use their cognitive resources to solve problems, both in and out of the classroom. Preliminary evidence suggests that metacognitive knowledge can enable the less skilled learner to compensate for lower cognitive ability, although future research is needed on this issue with LD populations. •

Motivational Style

The fact that motivation plays a critical role in classroom learning is well established. Motivational factors have often been implicated in LD learners' failure in school. Several motivational explanations have been offered for the gap between LD students' IQ and their achievement. Although too numerous to list in their entirety, possible factors include lack of effort, lack of persistence, low self-concept, and task avoidance. Despite the consensus on the importance of motivation to LD children's achievement, the exact role motivation plays in achievement is still an area of active investigation, challenging researchers from a variety of theoretical perspectives. Two common lines of research related to motivation are causal attributions and self-concept. These two perspectives will be examined as they relate to potential reasons why LD students fail to perform optimally in school.

WHERE ARE THE ATTRIBUTIONAL DIFFERENCES?

The impact of students' attributional style on their motivation in the classroom has received considerable attention to date. Students' perceptions about the causes of their academic success and failure are quite diverse, with the impact of ability, effort, task difficulty, and luck most often studied (Wiener, 1979). LD learners seem to adopt a maladaptive attributional profile and are often characterized as "learned helpless." LD students often believe their failures are due to low ability, while attributing their successes to the ease of the task. Thus, they accept responsibility for their failures, but do not accept credit for their successes (Butkowsky & Willows, 1980; Jacobsen, Lowery, & DuCette, 1986; Pearl, Bryan, & Donahue, 1980). This maladaptive attributional style not only leads to a decline in motivation, but this profile also discourages task analysis, task persistence, and optimal task selection. All three areas deserve separate mention because of the critical role they play in determining the probability that LD students will experience future success.

Students' attributional profiles affect performance by influencing the task-analysis process. Since LD children attribute failure to factors beyond their control and assume they cannot change task outcomes, no attempt to engage in task-analysis is made. Skilled children, however, will develop hypotheses regarding poor performance because task outcome is believed to be within their control (Pearl, Bryan, & Herzog, 1983). Moreover, as task difficulty increases, LD children tend to attribute their successes to luck and their failures to poor ability, while skilled children will attribute successes to high effort and failure to task difficulty (Aponick & Dembo, 1983).

Causal attributions also impact performance by affecting students' task selection. In a study by Fyans and Maehr (1979), elementary-school children were asked to choose one of three angle-matching tasks. Although none of the tasks differed in reality, the children were told that success could be achieved for one task via ability, another via effort, and the third via luck. Children chose tasks in accordance with their beliefs regarding the causes of their own successes. That is, those who believed that success is mostly due to ability tended to choose ability tasks, and so forth.

Causal attributions also impact performance by affecting students' task persistence (Butkowsky & Willows, 1980). If children perceive a task to be extremely difficult, they will become discouraged and discontinue their effort. By not trying, skills will not improve and success will not be achieved. On the other hand, tasks that are perceived to be exceptionally easy will not encourage effort either. Tasks need to be sufficiently challenging so that students can achieve success with some effort. Once students see that persistence at a task leads to success, their motivation on future tasks will increase, as will their skills. Unfortunately, neither researchers, educators, nor students perform effective task analyses to determine which tasks will foster intrinsic motivation. As a result of either faulty or nonexistent task analysis, we may unwittingly be discouraging students' motivation.

Although many LD students have maladaptive attributional profiles, the pervasiveness of the adverse effects are harder to determine. A recent study by Jacobsen et al. (1986) assessed the pervasiveness of LD students' maladaptive attributional profile on academic, social, and random events. The attributional possibilities were: ability, effort, task difficulty, luck, emotions (good vs. bad mood), and someone else (help vs. no help). Compared to skilled children, LD students offered a wider array of attributional possibilities (i.e., mood and other people) for their successes on all three events. By ascribing success to factors other than ability and effort, the opportunity to build self-esteem was greatly diminished.

In contrast, others have found LD learners' maladaptive profiles to be tied to specific domains. For example, Pearl (1982) found that although LD children attributed lack of effort to be the cause of reading failure, lack of effort was not believed to be the cause of social failure. Instead, bad luck was seen as the cause of social failures. According to this study, then, LD children do not seem to accept responsibility for their social failures, although they do accept responsibility for their failures in other tasks. Perhaps the conflicting findings may be a function of the types of LD children studied. Whereas reading-disabled children probably do generalize their maladaptive attributional styles across tasks, math-disabled children may not evidence maladaptive profiles across all situations. This finding is consistent with Licht's (1983) data that reading-disabled children have difficulty in many content areas due to their reading problem and therefore generalize their low perceptions of competence across these domains. In contrast, since math-disabled children may only experience difficulty in the math content area, they tend not to generalize their low perceptions of competence across domains.

MULTIFACETED NATURE OF ATTRIBUTIONS

Subtyping studies have been conducted to unravel the great heterogeneity in attributional profiles obtained in both skilled and LD populations (Covington & Omelich, 1979a, 1979b; Short, Weissberg-Benchell, & Evans, 1988). Covington (1987) and his colleagues differentiated subtypes based on performance outcome and effort attributions. Two successful subtypes were identified. In the first subtype, success was accomplished with little to no effort leading to beliefs of high ability and feelings of pride. Thus, this ability subtype appears to be self-motivated and eager to face challenging tasks since success in future endeavors is expected. The second subtype is composed of students whose success is accomplished with a great deal of effort. These "effortful" success experiences do not lead to beliefs of high ability and feelings of pride, but often lead to self-doubt about academic competence instead. Because of high fear of failure, high effort/success students will probably choose tasks that minimally challenge their skill level, and therefore limit their opportunities to learn new things.

Besides success subtypes, two failure subtypes exist: those students who fail despite effort and those students who fail due to a lack of effort. Students who fail despite a great deal of effort believe themselves to have low ability. These low-ability ascriptions may be inappropriate, since often the learner's effort was misdirected through poorly selected strategies (Clifford, 1984). The failure causes them to feel shame and distress, expect failure, and appear less task-persistent in the future. These students are probably motivated to avoid all academic tasks in order to avoid the ascription of low ability and the accompanying feelings of low self-worth. Students who fail when exerting little or no effort avoid the ascription of low ability because they did not try. They are able, therefore, to avoid feeling shame and distress, since their self-worth is not challenged. Such students are most likely to choose tasks that are either too easy or too difficult for them, insuring either success or an excuse for failure. This "self-defensive motivation" (Covington & Omelich, 1979a) practically insures students of learning little during their academic careers. Because teachers tend to reward effort and punish the lack of it, these students are likely to be chastised by their teachers.

The overwhelming desire of students to "avoid appearing dumb" results in effort becoming a "double-edge sword" (Covington & Omelich, 1979b). When failure results from low effort, low-ability ascriptions are avoided but teacher punishment is likely. When failure occurs despite high effort, punishment is avoided but ascriptions of low ability are inevitable. This dilemma may be avoided by providing students with reasons, other than low ability, for a high-effort/failure scenario. Covington and his colleagues suggest offering students poor task-analysis and goal-setting as appropriate reasons for failure. Strategic behavior and task analysis are skills that can be learned and improved, and can offer the student hope for future success.

WHERE ARE THE SELF-CONCEPT DIFFERENCES?

Children who are lacking in self-confidence are likely to adopt a passive style of relating to both adults and peers. Recently, educators have expressed concerns about the pervasiveness of passivity and low self-esteem among LD learners. One critical question is: Do LD children perceive themselves to be uniformly incompetent or do they recognize their strengths and weaknesses? If in fact LD students were identified based on a specific deficit, we should expect students' self-concept to be notably deficient in that specific academic subject. The data on this point are equivocal. Some studies have reported that LD children generalize their feelings of low competence across a variety of academic and nonacademic domains (Butkowsky & Willows, 1980), whereas others suggest that LD children demonstrate low self-concepts in specific arenas (i.e., athletic, social, academic: Renick, & Harter, 1986). The mixed findings in the literature may be a function of the type of disability evidenced by the LD children in these studies. As Licht (1983) has pointed out, reading-disabled students probably do generalize their perception of low competence across domains, as reading ability is necessary for success in most academic and nonacademic tasks. In contrast, math-disabled students may not generalize their perceptions of low competence across domains, as math ability is necessary for only a few academic tasks expected of children. Obviously, this is an important area for future research. Future studies need to determine how different subtypes of learning-disabled children differ in their perceptions of competence in a variety of domains.

SUMMARY

Taken together, the attributional and self-concept findings suggest the importance of raising the self-esteem of all students in the classroom. In order to accomplish this, teachers should explicitly teach students to recognize the multitude of causes responsible for failure situations, including such factors as mood, fatigue, lack of background knowledge, unproductive effort, and poor task analysis. Students should not be afraid to face failure: rather, they should analyze each failure outcome and thereby profit from the experience. Preliminary data on attribution retraining suggests strongly that only when students recognize that their personal effectiveness depends on the use of appropriate strategies will improvement gains be generalized (Schunk & Gunn, 1986). By encouraging students to monitor their learning performance, teachers will foster more effective learning styles in their students.

Remediation

THE ROLE OF TEACHERS IN FOSTERING AN EFFECTIVE TRIPLE ALLIANCE

Specific suggestions can be offered to educators regarding how to foster cognitive processing, metacognitive knowledge and processing, and the motivation to learn (Bondy, 1984). First, teachers should actively promote a general awareness of cognitive, metacognitive, and motivational processes. Bondy offers two suggestions for enhancing awareness: (a) encourage students to keep a "daily learning log" and (b) model and discuss appropriate strategies. Research by D'Arcy (1981) clearly supports the utility of learning logs for some learners. Students were asked to think about their academic activities daily and write about points of confusion, generate questions for further clarification and self-study, and summarize insights gained from the activity. The shift from product to process learning should encourage an active learning style in students. Although these learning logs appear to be an effective means for teaching both cognitive and metacognitive skills (e.g., strategic effectiveness, self-monitoring, self-evaluation) and motivating the skilled learners, research is still needed on the utility of this method with LD learners.

Support for the importance of modeling appropriate cognitive, metacognitive, and motivational strategies can be drawn from a variety of sources (Bandura, 1977; Pressley, Borkowski, & Schneider, 1987; Whimbey & Lochhead, 1986; see also Duffy & Roehler, this volume, chap. 6). Often students cannot appreciate the significance of strategic behavior unless they witness the facilitative effects of strategies on another's behavior (see also Duffy and Roehler, this volume, chap. 6). One such technique is the "think aloud" technique (TA). Much of the groundwork for think aloud techniques has been laid by Vygotsky (1978), Meichenbaum (1977), and Kendall (1984). The clinical utility of overt verbalizations has long been recognized with LD populations (Harris, 1986), mentally retarded children (Kendall, Borkowski, & Cavanaugh, 1980), attention deficit disorder (ADD) children (Torgensen, 1977), and impulsive children (Kendall & Braswell, 1982).

Think aloud techniques require teachers to verbalize the thought processes and strategies they are using to tackle a specific problem-solving situation (Whimbey & Lochhead, 1986). By thinking aloud, teachers will demonstrate their own effective strategies for tackling novel and/or difficult problems, with opportunities available for modeling coping and repair strategies. For example, when solving an analogy the teacher would say:

... apple is to tree as grape is to _____ . Let's see, in the first place the problem is a semantic analogy. The way I recognize this is that the first word apple forms some semantic relationship to the second word tree. Now I know that an apple is a red piece of fruit that grows on a tree. That is it — the apple grows on the tree. Now I need to apply this same semantic relationship to the third and fourth elements. In the third box I see the word grape so I first think about where the grapes grow and then I look through all the possible answers for the word that indicates where the grapes grow—here it is, vine. So I put an x in the box which contains the word vine.

The teacher's modeling of the steps in strategic processing should enable students to then imitate these strategies during their own problem-solving attempts. Recent evidence for the facilitative effects of the TA manipulation has been obtained in diverse areas of academic performance, including reading comprehension and problem solving (Davey & Porter, 1982; Short, Evans, Dellick, & Cuddy, 1988). More research is needed on differential responsivity to the TA manipulation as a function of skill level, developmental level, and strategic knowledge.

In addition to promoting general awareness of initial encoding activity, teachers should facilitate conscious monitoring on the part of learners. Often the educational system actively discourages independent monitoring by young learners. Instead of encouraging children to check their own work, children are reinforced for speed of processing (i.e., when your worksheet is done you can go out to recess). Despite skilled performance, children seldom think they can determine their own accuracy and instead learn to rely on the teacher for feedback (Miller, 1985).

How to Promote Active Learning

Several ways of encouraging active monitoring by skilled and LD students can be offered. First, teachers should provide a variety of feedback opportunities for their students (Bondy, 1984). Although it is often important for the teacher to provide explicit feedback regarding accuracy/inaccuracy of solution, the type of feedback dictates the results obtained. Feedback aimed at the product (i.e., how many problems are solved correctly) is not as instructive as feedback aimed at the processes used to solve the problems (i.e., strategies). If feedback is geared towards the processes used to produce the outcome, both success and failure experiences will be instructive. Success experiences would provide information regarding task-appropriate strategies, whereas failure would provide feedback regarding task-inappropriate strategies. Process-oriented feedback should encourage students to engage actively in assessment of the match between the strategy they chose and the task at hand.

Not only might diverse feedback opportunities encourage active learning, but active learning can also be encouraged through comprehension-monitoring training. Research on the teaching of monitoring skills has strongly suggested that by making students reflect on the relationship between task performance and strategic behavior, learners are apt to select more powerful strategies on future tasks (Ghatala, Levin, Pressley, & Goodwin, 1986). Similarly, Day (1981) argues that by encouraging students to write summaries of new material, monitoring of comprehension is also encouraged since concrete evidence is self-generated about their depth of understanding.

Finally, teachers should encourage a deliberate and systematic approach to learning. Students must be taught to approach problems systematically prior to, during, and after problem-solving exercises. Cognitive behavior therapists have long advocated this approach (Meichenbaum, 1977). Although true for all learners, it is especially critical to foster "thinking skills" in the LD learners. Students should have a clear sense of the purpose of and reason for completing a particular task. Often students' task definition is quite different from that of their teachers' task definition (Canney & Winograd, 1978). Given these differences, it is not surprising that students often fail to meet the expectations of their teachers. Even when teachers and students have similar purposes for performing a task, goals are often not met because the processes employed during the task are not executed accurately or completely. Finally, even when students and teachers are in synchrony in the problem-definition stage and the strategic-processing phase, errors may arise after the task is completed. Students may not accurately engage in the monitoring or checking process and therefore make careless errors. If students are taught to actively check their own work, rather than passively relying on the teacher for feedback, accuracy should be greatly enhanced.

EFFECTIVE APPROACHES FOR REMEDIATING "INACTIVE LEARNING"

One obvious way of encouraging active participation in learning by LD students is through the use of self-directing verbalizations (Meichenbaum, 1977). For example, Short and Ryan (1984) demonstrated that reading comprehension skills could be improved for disabled readers by asking themselves five "wh" questions about story grammar components of narratives (main character, setting, actions, ending, and feeling). This story grammar strategy has been adapted to the domain of writing successfully by Harris and Graham (1985). Like most self-instructional strategies, the story grammar strategy was initially employed in an other-regulated manner, with the experimenter prompting for strategy implementation. However, the self-instructional nature of training encourages self-regulation and therefore experimenter prompting is eventually faded out of the program.

The benefits of self-instructional training have been stressed repeatedly by advocates of metacognitive theory and cognitive behavior therapy (Ryan, Weed, & Short, 1986). Self-instruction seems to be most potent when learners are enlightened about the purpose of strategies (Brown, Bransford, Ferrara, & Campione, 1983; Kennedy & Miller, 1976). Complete instruction to use self-instructions should include information about where, when, and why students should use the strategies that are trained and how strategies can be modified for novel tasks. Brown et al. (1983) refer to such instruction as self-control training. Two experimental techniques, reciprocal teaching and self-questioning, have been quite successful for delivering process feedback, increasing monitoring skills, and promoting strategic learning for diverse populations. Both techniques nicely adhere to the suggestions put forth by the "self-control" training.

First, the reciprocal teaching technique (Palincsar & Brown, 1984) alters the nature of the teaching relationship. The technique capitalizes on the method of socratic dialogue in disseminating information about strategies. The 20-day training program teaches four strategies designed to promote self-regulated learning, including summarization, prediction, question generation, and clarification. Initially, the teaching technique is modeled by the teacher and is therefore other-regulated. Eventually students begin to assume both the role of the learner and the role of the teacher during the teaching process. By allowing students to teach segments of the text to the class, clear feedback is provided regarding the depth of their understanding. When students encounter difficulty teaching the lesson, it becomes readily apparent where comprehension difficulties exist to both the teacher and the learner. Although monitoring skills were not formally evaluated by Palincsar and Brown (1984), these skills are critical to teaching effectiveness. Unless the student evaluates the quality of the message, no corrective action can be taken. Future studies should evaluate whether reciprocal teaching techniques improve monitoring skills.

A second method designed to place the locus of control for feedback and learning in the hands of the student is the self-questioning technique (Wong, 1985). This approach was designed to promote active strategic learning through the use of self-verbalizations (Meichenbaum, 1977). Students can be taught to employ self- or experimenter-generated questions as a means of monitoring their own comprehension (Miller, 1985, 1987; Miller, Giovenco, & Rentiers, 1987; Short & Ryan, 1984; Weissberg-Benchell, 1986; Wong & Jones, 1982). By employing the self-questioning techniques, students are able to assess first hand the quality of their understanding of new material. Students profit from the self-generated feedback obtained from testing their comprehension with questions in that they recognize their test readiness or need for further study.

To date, self-control training has proven effective in improving skilled and LD learners' memory, attention, and language skills, but often these newly acquired skills have limited generalizability. Efforts must be made to teach students how to generalize their newly acquired skills to a variety of contexts and tasks (Borkowski & Cavanaugh, 1979; Brown et al., 1983). Not only is it important to train flexible application of newly acquired strategies; students also need to be taught to analyze tasks and the environment for information about where and when to apply which strategies. In order to foster optimal strategy selection by LD learners, educators should build in relational metacognitive knowledge (Borkowski, Weyhing, & Turner, 1986). Learners need to recognize that some strategies are more effective at improving specific performances than are others (Clifford, 1984; Pressley, Borkowski, et al., 1987). Through extensive practice and the provision of explicit performance feedback, children will learn to recognize which strategies are more effective and to objectively employ the better ones (Pressley, Borkowski, & O'Sullivan, 1984).

HAS METACOGNITIVE AND MOTIVATIONAL TRAINING ENHANCED COGNITION?

Recent metacognitive and motivational training studies have attempted to simulate the balancing act performed by skilled learners between cognitive, metacognitive, and motivational skills. A series of studies by Dale Schunk and his colleagues illustrates the metacognitive and motivational benefits of training students to approach tasks strategically. In one recent study, Schunk (1983) taught subtraction skills and self-regulation strategies to elementary-school children with poor math abilities. They were trained to monitor their on- and off-task behavior, evaluate their performance, and determine their reinforcement for the outcome. Not only did the children's sense of self-efficacy improve, but so too did their task persistence and subtraction skills. In a second study, Schunk (1984) trained math-disabled students to set small, easily attainable goals on subtraction tasks and to administer self-rewards for attaining their goals. Again, learning to approach tasks strategically improved students' expectations for future success, their perceived self-efficacy, and their math skills. Similar findings were obtained in a study designed to train LD adolescents to set realistic task goals. Learning to set realistic goals in the learning environment not only improved task performance, but also affected LD adolescents' attributions, with shifts toward a more adaptive attributional profile (Tollefson, Tracey, Johnson, Farmer, & Buenning, 1984).

Training students to set realistic goals, administer self-rewards, and monitor their behaviors are all effective ways to improve skills and increase motivation. Research on training students to use task-specific strategies has also shown important motivational benefits. Schunk and Gunn (1986) taught math-disabled students to use task-specific strategies on division problems. During training, the importance of consistent strategy use for improved performance was stressed. The results included: (a) children attributed their successful performance to enhanced ability; (b) subsequent tasks were perceived to be easier; (c) self-efficacy was enhanced; and (d) math skills improved.

Despite these promising effects for math-disabled students, less consistent results have been obtained for reading-disabled students, (e.g., Reid & Borkowski, 1985; Short & Ryan, 1984; Weyhing, 1986). Attribution retraining studies have not met with consistent success for several reasons. First, telling students to "try hard" will not result in increased effort unless they are taught to use an effective strategy. Too often as educators we suggest that students must "try again" to solve a problem yet we fail to provide the students with insight into the strategy most appropriate for the task. Perhaps equally as important, we rarely explain concretely what it was about the unsuccessful strategy that led to the student's failure. Without this information, task persistence is not likely to occur.

Attribution retraining programs need to be flexible so that they can include specific strategies tailored both to the student's need and to the task demands (Borkowski, Weyhing, & Turner, 1986). First, as was noted by Clifford (1984), effort is often not a sufficient condition for success; rather, effort in conjunction with the correct strategy will yield success. Second, attribution retraining programs often fail because of the limited nature of training (i.e., session length, context domain). Attributional profiles were not acquired overnight, and therefore it is absurd to assume that we can alter maladaptive profiles after brief training in limited contexts. Third, the type of subject employed in the study may largely determine whether or not the training is effective. It is possible that the maladaptive attributional profile is less pervasive for some children than others. The more pervasive the dysfunctional attributions, the less likely that short-term training is liable to make a difference.

Summary

Taken together, the training research presented in this section suggests that programs are only effective when they adopt a comprehensive view of learning. Simply teaching cognitive skills appears not to be enough to alter the academic profile of the LD student. In addition, simply teaching metacognitive strategies and altering attributional profiles may produce task-specific gains, but the long-standing educational significance of these gains has yet to be seen. Programs designed to improve all three domains simultaneously in the LD student have shown the most promise (Arbitman-Smith & Haywood, 1980; Deshler, Warner, Schumacher, & Alley, 1983). Future research should examine the modifiability of attributional profiles by employing both parents and teachers as consistent trainers. Interventions should not only include coping statements, but also training in a specific learning activity (i.e., goal-setting, mnemonic rehearsal).

Factors Missing from this Triple Alliance Model

Several factors would alter any straightforward relationship among cognitive, metacognitive, and motivational skills (Short, 1987). Such factors include developmental level, time available for processing, and contextual constraints. The triple alliance between cognitive, metacognitive, and motivational skills is not developmentally invariant, but rather varies with developmental level. A realistic profile of a young, skilled learner would be a high score on both the cognitive and motivational axes, with a low or moderate-to-low score on the metacognitive axis. Despite adequate cognitive and motivational skills, young skilled learners appear to be somewhat deficient in their planfulness, comprehension monitoring, and deliberate strategic performance as compared to older skilled learners (Baker & Brown, 1984). As a result, young skilled learners are less able to demonstrate their academic talents consistently than are older skilled learners. Nonetheless, a metacognitive deficiency in the preschooler would not have the same educational significance as a metacognitive deficiency in the college student. Environmental support structures are more readily available for the young child (e.g., parents, teachers) than for the adolescent or young adult. During early and middle childhood, society does not expect self-regulation, but rather other-regulation is the norm. With increasing age, more and more responsibility for regulation is shifted to the adolescent and therefore the need to self-regulate becomes stronger. This shift from other- to self-regulation can be seen in the academic arena, the medical arena, and the social arena. As Lerner (1986) points out in his "Goodness of Fit Model," the adaptive significance of behavior changes as a function of both developmental age and context.

Not only do developmental factors influence the adaptive significance of these profiles, but the modifiability of the strength of individual components of the triple alliance model may vary with age as well. Strategies can be easily taught to young learners; however, the net result is often rigid application. In contrast, strategies are sometimes difficult to teach to skilled learners, since they may prefer an alternative strategy to that which was instructed (Brown et al., 1983). Therefore training programs would need to be sensitive to these developmental issues.

A second factor that affects the triple alliance is time available for processing (see Dufresne & Kobasigawa, this volume, chap. 3, for a discussion of study time allocation). Given ample time to complete a simple task, it may not be maladaptive to be deficient in strategic planning skills. However, as task demands begin to exceed the student's cognitive capabilities, poor planning will certainly hinder effective learning. Students must learn to be flexible and adaptable in the learning environment. Moreover, the triple alliance becomes even more complicated with age, since more is expected of the learner. As skilled learners' metacognitive knowledge becomes more sophisticated, they are increasingly able to make use of their academic strengths and weaknesses to strike better balances between cognition, metacognition, and motivation regardless of temporal considerations.

In addition to learner characteristics, a third factor, contextual constraints, would affect the triple alliance model. Two important contexts that would affect this model are the school and the home environment. Classroom goal structures affect student learning and motivation in a powerful way (Schunk, 1985). According to Nicholls (1984), the three basic types of classrooms are: (a) competitive or norm-referenced learning (i.e., ego-involved learning), (b) mastery or criterion-referenced learning (i.e., task-involved learning), and (c) cooperative learning (i.e., group approach). Allowing students to set realistic goals reaps great motivational benefits, particularly for LD students (Schunk, 1984, 1985; Tollefson et al., 1984). Research by Covington and Omelich (1981) indicated that learning in a mastery-referenced setting offers increased knowledge and understanding as the primary goal, whereas learning in a competitive-referenced setting encourages students to concentrate on avoiding failure rather than pursuing knowledge. Moreover, within the mastery-learning setting, retesting is allowed. Setting realistic goals and retesting oneself to monitor progress increases students' grade aspirations and confidence, as well as increasing beliefs in the value of effort for success (Covington & Omelich, 1981; Nicholls, 1984). Further, LD students placed in resource rooms or self-contained classrooms (where learning goals are individualized) perceive themselves to be more academically competent than those LD children placed in a regular classroom (Renick, 1985). Less conclusive data are available on the effects of cooperative learning environments on the triple alliance, although what is available suggests cooperative learning can have powerful effects. Cooperative learning settings seem to be most beneficial for children with low academic self-concepts; when their group succeeds, group success raises all group members' feelings of pride and satisfaction (Ames & Felker, 1979). One foreseeable problem with this type of learning setting could be that LD students may assume responsibility when the group fails, however. This failure would further diminish the self-concept of LD children. Important considerations for group placement might include probability of group success and group involvement. Given these data, it should not be surprising to note that most training studies adopt a mastery orientation. Similar suggestions can be offered regarding the home environment. Research has largely ignored the early learning environment of the LD student and instead focused on the school context. The reason for this stems largely from the fact that LD is a condition brought about at school age. Future research should explore the learning environment of the LD student outside the confines of the school.

Conclusions

Learning to balance cognitive, metacognitive and motivational skills is quite an accomplishment for most students, but especially LD students. Teachers and parents of LD students need to provide practice in the use and significance of a strategy. Also, parents and teachers need to instruct children about the significance of planning, monitoring, and evaluating their strategic behavior. Providing LD children with the opportunity both to produce and regulate the strategic activity should enhance the likelihood of systematic strategic performance in everyday contexts (Brown et al., 1983; Meichenbaum, 1977; Paris, Newman, & McVey, 1982; Short & Ryan, 1984). In the home, opportunities present themselves for observable strategic behavior. Parents need to be explicit about their use of lists (e.g., grocery, jobs around the house), their check-out system for monitoring whether tasks have been completed, and their method of coping with failure (e.g., next time allow more time for the job, next time make a more comprehensive list). In the school, numerous opportunities present themselves for observable strategic behavior. Teachers use lists consistently in the classroom (e.g., children who didn't complete assignments, classroom jobs) and could easily develop a lesson around the function of lists (e.g., discuss the fallibility of memory and the assistance gained from lists). Teachers can model strategic use of self-questioning both to direct cognitive behavior and to monitor progress toward goals (e.g., reading story to answer five questions and comprehension check achieved through these questions). Finally, teachers can teach their students to cope with failure by making attributions about lack of effort with the correct strategy. This effort-attribution link up should promote learning in the classroom.

Explicit, concrete, and extensive instruction has been effective with skilled learners, although more research is needed with LD populations. Particular attention should be paid to the faulty alliances that may develop between cognition, metacognition, and motivation in LD students as a result of a long history of academic failure. To date, the faulty alliance between cognition and motivation that results in learned helplessness is the most heavily researched. Future research might explore the faulty alliances that are developed by LD students and how they affect achievement.

REFERENCES

Ames, C., & Felker, D. (1979). An examination of children's attributions and achievement-related evaluations in competitive, cooperative, and individualistic reward structures. *Journal of Educational Psychology, 71,* 413–420.

Aponick, D., & Dembo, M. (1983). LD and normal adolescents' causal attributions of success and failure at different levels of task difficulty. *Learning Disability Quarterly, 6,* 31–39.

Arbitman-Smith, R., & Haywood, C.H. (1980). Cognitive education for learning disabled adolescents. *Journal of Abnormal Child Psychology, 8,* 51–64.

Baker, L., & Brown, A.L. (1984). Metacognitive skills and reading. In D. Pearson, R. Barr, M. Kamil, & P. Mosenthal (Eds.), *Handbook of reading research* (pp. 353–394). New York: Longman.

Bandura, A. (1977). *Social learning theory.* Englewood Cliffs, NJ: Prentice-Hall, Inc.

Bartlett, F.C. (1932). *Remembering.* London: Cambridge University Press.

Bauer, R. (1977). Memory processes in children with learning disabilities: Evidence for deficient rehearsal. *Journal of Experimental Child Psychology, 24,* 415–430.

Bialystok, E., & Ryan, E.B. (1985). A metacognitive framework for the development of first and second language skills. In D.L. Forrest-Pressley, G.E. MacKinnon, & T.G. Waller (Eds.), *Metacognition, cognition, and human performance,* Vol. 1 (pp. 207–252). New York: Academic Press.

Bondy, E. (1984). Thinking about thinking: Encouraging children's use of metacognitive processes. *Childhood Education, 60,* (4), 234–238.

Borkowski, J.G., & Cavanaugh, J. (1979). Maintenance and generalization of skills and strategies by the retarded. In N.R. Ellis (Ed.), *Handbook of mental deficiency: Psychological theory and research* (pp. 120–220). Hillsdale, NJ: Erlbaum & Associates.

Borkowski, J.G., Peck, V.A., Reid, M.K., & Kurtz, B. (1983). Impulsivity and strategy transfer: Metamemory as a mediator. *Child Development, 54,* 459–473.

Borkowski, J.G., Weyhing, R.S., & Turner, L.A. (1986). Attribution retraining and the teaching of strategies. *Exceptional Children, 53,* 130–137.

Brophy, J., Good, T. (1985). Teacher behavior and student achievement. In M.C. Wittrock (Ed.), *Handbook of research on teaching* (3rd ed.). New York: MacMillan Press.

Brown, A.L. (1978). Knowing when, where, and how to remember. In R.Glaser (Ed.), *Advances in instructional psychology,* Vol. 1 (pp. 77–167). Hillsdale, NJ: Erlbaum & Associates.

Brown, A.L., Bransford, J.D., Ferrara, R.A., & Campione, J.C. (1983). Learning, remembering, and understanding. In P. H. Mussen (Ed.), *Handbook of child psychology: Cognitive development,* Vol. III (pp. 77–166). New York: John Wiley & Sons.

Buss, R.R., Yussen, S.R., Mathews, S.R., III, Miller, G.E., & Rembold, K.L. (1983). Development of a story schema to retrieve information. *Developmental Psychology, 19,* 22–28.

Butkowksy, I.S., & Willows, D.M. (1980). Cognitive-motivational characteristics of children varying in reading ability: Evidence for learned helplessness in poor readers. *Journal of Educational Psychology, 72,* 402–422.

Canney, G., & Winograd, P. (1978). *Schemata for reading and reading comprehension performance* (Tech. Rep. No. 120). Urbana, IL: University of Illinois Center for the Study of Reading.

Ceci, S.R. (1984). A developmental study of learning disabilities and memory. *Journal of Experimental Child Psychology, 38,* 352–371.

Ceci, S.R. (1986). *Handbook of cognitive, social, and neuropsychological aspects of learning disabilities.* Hillsdale, NJ: Erlbaum & Associates.

Chi, M.T. (1977). Age differences in memory span. *Journal of Experimental Child Psychology, 23,* 266–271.

Clifford, M.M. (1984). Thoughts on a theory of constructive failure. *Educational Psychologist, 19,* 108–120.

Covington, M.V. (April, 1987). *The role of motivational and cognitive variables in autonomous learning.* Paper presented at the annual meeting of the American Educational Research Association, Washington, DC.

Covington, M.V., & Omelich, C.L. (1979a). Are causal attributions causal? A path analysis of the cognitive model of achievement motivation. *Journal of Personality and Social Psychology, 37,* 1487–1504.

Covington, M.V., & Omelich, C.L. (1979b). Effort: The double-edged sword in school achievement. *Journal of Educational Psychology, 71,* 169–182.

Covington, M.V., & Omelich, C.L. (1981). As failures mount: Affective and cognitive consequences of ability demotion in the classroom. *Journal of Educational Psychology, 73,* 796–808.

Daneman, M., & Carpenter, P.A. (1980). Individual differences in working memory and reading. *Journal of Verbal Learning and Verbal Behavior, 19,* 450–466.

D'Arcy, P. (1981). Putting your own mind to it. *Forum for the discussion of new trends in education, 23,* 38–40.

Das, J.P. (1984). Aspects of planning. In J.R. Kirby (Ed.), *Cognitive strategies and educational performance* (pp. 35–50). New York: Academic Press.

Davey, B., & Porter, S. (1982). Comprehension-rating: A procedure to assist poor comprehenders. *Journal of Reading, 26,* 197–202.

Day, J.D. (April, 1981). *Training summarization skills: A comparison of training methods.* Paper presented at the biennial meeting of the Society for Research in Child Development, Boston.

Dempster, F.N. (1979). Memory span and short term memory capacity: A developmental study. *Journal of Experimental Child Psychology, 26,* 419–431.

Deshler, D.D., Warner, M.M., Schumacher, J.B., & Alley, G.R. (1983). Learning strategies intervention model: Key components and current status. In J. D. McKinney & L. Feagans (Eds.), *Current topics in learning disabilities* (pp. 245–283). Norwood, NJ: Ablex.

Feagans, L., & Applebaum, M.I. (1986). Validation of language subtypes in learning disabled children. *Journal of Educational Psychology, 78,* 365–372.

Feagans, L., & Short, E.J. (1984). Developmental differences in the comprehension and production of narratives by reading disabled and normally achieving children. *Child Development, 55,* 1727–1736.

Feagans, L., & Short, E.J. (1986). Referential communication and reading performance in learning disabled children over a 3-year period. *Developmental Psychology, 22,* 177–183.

Flavell, J.H., & Wellman, H.M. (1977). Metamemory. In R.V. Kail & J.W. Hagen (Eds.), *Perspectives on the development of memory and cognition* (pp. 3–33). Hillsdale, NJ: Erlbaum & Associates.

Forrest-Pressley, D.L., & Waller, T. (April 1980). *What do children know about their reading and study skills?* Paper presented at the annual meeting of the American Educational Research Association, Boston.

Fyans, L., & Maehr, M. (1979). Attributional style, task selection, and achievement. *Journal of Educational Psychology, 71,* 499–507.

Ghatala, E.S. Levin, J.R., Pressley, M., & Goodwin, D. (1986). A componential analysis of the effects of derived and supplied strategy information on children's strategy selection. *Journal of Experimental Child Psychology, 41,* 76–92.

Golden, C.J. (1978). *Stroop Color and Word Test.* Chicago: Stoelting Co.

Harris, K.R. (1986). The effects of cognitive-behavior modification on private speech and task performance during problem solving among learning-disabled and normally achieving children. *Journal of Abnormal Child Psychology, 14,* 63–67.

Harris, K.R., & Graham, S. (1985). Improving learning disabled students' composition skills: Self-control strategy training. *Learning Disability Quarterly, 8,* 27–36.

Hasselhorn, M., & Körkel, J. (1986). Metacognitive versus traditional reading instructions: The mediating role of domain-specific knowledge on children's text processing. *Human Learning, 5,* 75–90.

Heaton, R.K. (1981). *Wisconsin card sorting test manual.* Odessa, FL: Psychological Assessment Resources.

Jacobsen, B., Lowery, B., & DuCette, J. (1986). Attributions of learning disabled children. *Journal of Educational Psychology, 78,* 59–64.

Jenkins, J.J. (1979). Four points to remember: A tetrahedral model and memory experiment. In L.S. Cermak & F.I.M. Craik (Eds.), *Levels of processing in human memory* (pp. 429–446). Hillsdale, NJ: Erlbaum & Associates.

Kee, D., Worden, P.E., & Throckmorton, B. (1984). Sentence demonstration ability in reading disabled vs. normal college students. *Bulletin of the Psychomonic Society,* 22, 183–185.

Keller, C.E., & Hallahan, D.P. (1987). *Learning disabilities: Issues and instructional interventions.* Washington, DC: National Educational Association Professional Library.

Kendall, C.R., Borkowski, J.G., & Cavanaugh, J.C. (1980). Maintenance and generalization of an interrogative strategy by EMR children. *Intelligence, 4,* 255–270.

Kendall, P.C. (1984). Cognitive processes and procedures in behavior therapy. *Annual Review of Behavior Therapy Theory and Practice, 9,* 132–179.

Kendall, P.C., & Braswell, L. (1982). Cognitive-behavioral self-control therapy for children: A components analysis. *Journal of Consulting and Clinical Psychology, 50,* 672–689.

Kennedy, B.A., & Miller, D.J. (1976). Persistent use of verbal rehearsal as a function of information about its value. *Child Development, 47,* 566–569.

Keogh, B.K., & Margolis, J. (1976). Learn to labor and wait: Attentional problems with children with learning disorders. *Journal of Learning Disabilities, 9,* 276–286.

Krupski, A. (1986). Attention problems in youngsters with learning handicaps. In J.K. Torgesen & B.Y.L. Wong (Eds.), *Psychological and educational perspectives on learning disabilities* (pp. 161–192). New York: Academic Press.

Lerner, R.M. (1986). *Concepts and theories of human development* (2nd ed.). New York: Random House.

Licht, B. (1983). Cognitive-motivational factors that contribute to the achievement of learning-disabled children. *Journal of Learning Disabilities, 16,* 483–490.

Loper, A.B., Hallahan, D.P. & Ianna, S.O. (1982). Meta-attention in learning disabled and normal students. *Learning Disability Quarterly, 5,* 29–36.

McKinney, J.D. (1988). Research on conceptually and empirically derived subtypes of specific learning disabilities. In M.C. Wang, M.C. Reynolds, & H.J. Walberg (Eds.), *The handbook of special education: Research and practice,* Vol. 2 (pp. 253–281). Oxford, England: Pergamon Press.

McKinney, J.D., & Feagans, L. (1983). *Current topics in learning disabilities,* Vol. 1. Norwood, NJ: Ablex.

McKinney, J.D., & Feagans, L. (1984). Academic and behavioral characteristics: Longitudinal studies of learning disabled children and average achievers. *Learning Disability Quarterly, 7,* 251–265.

McKinney, J.D., Short, E.J., & Feagans, L. (1985). Academic consequences of perceptual-linguistic subtypes of learning disabled children. *Learning Disabilities Research, 1,* 6–17.

Meichenbaum, D.M. (1977). *Cognitive behavior modification: An integrative approach.* New York: Plenum Press.

Miller, G.E. (1985). The effects of general and specific self-instruction training on children's comprehension monitoring performances during reading. *Reading Research Quarterly, 20* (5), 616–628.

Miller, G.E. (1987). Influence of self-instructions on the comprehension monitoring performance of average and above average readers. *Journal of Reading Behavior, 19,* 303–316.

Miller, G.E., Giovenco, A., & Rentiers, K.A. (1987). Fostering comprehension monitoring in below average readers through self-instructional training. *Journal of Reading Behavior, 19,* 379–393.

Nicholls, J. (1984). Conceptions of ability and achievement motivation: A theory and its implications for education. In S. Paris, D. Olson, & H. Stevenson (Eds.),

Learning and motivation in the classroom (pp. 211–237). Norwood, NJ: Erlbaum & Associates.

Nickerson, R.S. (1984). Kinds of thinking taught in current programs. *Educational Leadership, 42,* 26–36.

Palincsar, A.S., & Brown, A.L. (1984). Reciprocal teaching of comprehension-fostering and comprehension-monitoring activities. *Cognition and Instruction, 1,* 117–175.

Paris, S.G., Newman, R.S., & McVey, K.A. (1982). Learning the functional significance of mnemonic actions: A microgenetic study of strategy acquisition. *Journal of Experimental Child Psychology, 34,* 490–509.

Pascul-Leone, J. (1970). A mathematical model for the transition rule in Piaget's developmental stages. *ACTA Psychologia, 32,* 301–345.

Pearl, R. (1982). Learning disabled children's attributions for success and failure: A replication with a labeled learning disability sample. *Learning Disability Quarterly, 5,* 173–176.

Pearl, R., Bryan, T., & Donahue, M. (1980). Learning disabled children's attributions for success and failure. *Learning Disability Quarterly, 3,* 3–9.

Pearl, R., Bryan, T., & Herzog, A. (1983). Learning disabled and nondisabled children's strategy analyses under high and low success conditions. *Learning Disability Quarterly, 6,* 67–74.

Pressley, M. (1986). The relevance of the good strategy user model to the teaching of mathematics. *Educational Psychologist, 21,* 139–161.

Pressley, M., Borkowski, J.G., & O'Sullivan, J.T. (1984). Memory strategy instruction is made of this: Metamemory and durable strategy use. *Educational Psychologist, 19,* 94–107.

Pressley, M., Borkowski, J.G., & Schneider, W. (1987). Cognitive strategies: Good strategy users coordinate metacognition and knowledge. In R. Vasta & G. Whitehurst (Eds.), *Annals of child development,* Vol. 4 (pp. 89–129). Greenwich, CT: JAI Press.

Pressley, M., Johnson, C., & Symons, S. (1987). Elaborating to learn and learning to elaborate. *Journal of Learning Disabilities, 20,* 76–91.

Pressley, M., Levin, J.R., & Ghatala, E.S. (1984). Memory strategy monitoring in adults and children. *Journal of Verbal Learning and Verbal Behavior, 23,* 270–288.

Reid, M.K., & Borkowski, J.G. (April, 1985). *A cognitive-motivational program for hyperactive children.* Paper presented at the biennial meeting of the Society for Research in Child Development, Toronto.

Renick, M.J. (April, 1985). *The development of learning disabled children's self perceptions.* Paper presented at the biennial meeting of the Society for Research in Child Development, Toronto.

Renick, M.J., & Harter, S. (1986). *The development of learning disabled students' self-perceptions and the impact of the social comparison process.* Unpublished manuscript, University of Denver, Denver, CO.

Ruff, R.M., Evans, R.W., & Marshall, L. (1984). *Verbal and figural fluency in head injured adults.* Unpublished manuscript, University of California at San Diego, San Diego, CA.

Ryan, E.B. (1981). Identifying and remediating failures in reading comprehension: Toward an instructional approach for poor comprehenders. In G.E. MacKinnon & T.G. Waller (Eds.), *Advances in reading research,* Vol. 3 (pp. 224–262). New York: Academic Press.

Ryan, E.B., Sheridan, E.M., & Short, E.J. (April, 1981). *Individual differences in schema utilization by skilled and less skilled readers.* Paper presented at the annual meeting of the American Educational Research Association, Los Angeles.

Ryan, E.B., Short, E.J., & Weed, K.A. (1986). The role of cognitive strategy training in improving the academic performance of learning disabled children. *Journal of Learning Disabilities, 19*, 521–529.

Ryan, E.B., Weed, K.A., & Short, E.J. (1986). Cognitive behavior modification: Promoting active, self-regulatory learning styles. In J.K. Torgesen & B.Y.L. Wong (Eds), *Psychological and educational perspectives on learning disabilities* (pp. 367–397). New York: Academic Press.

Schneider, W., Dumais, S., & Shiffrin, M. (1984). Automatic and control processing and attention. In R. Parasuraman & D. Daviez (Eds.), *Varieties of attention* (pp. 1–28). Orlando, FL: Academic Press.

Schneider, W., Körkel, J., & Weinert, F. (April 1987). *The knowledge base and memory performance: A comparison of academically successful and unsuccessful learners.* Paper presented at the annual meeting of the American Educational Research Association, Washington, DC.

Schunk, D. (1983). Progress self-monitoring: Effects on children's self-efficacy and achievement. *Journal of Experimental Education, 51*, 89–93.

Schunk, D. (1984). Sequential attribution feedback and children's achievement behaviors. *Journal of Educational Psychology, 76*, 1159–1169.

Schunk, D. (1985). Self-efficacy and classroom learning. *Psychology in the Schools, 22*, 208–223.

Schunk, D., & Gunn, T. (1986). Self-efficacy and skill development: Influence of task strategies and attributions. *Journal of Educational Research, 79*, 238–244.

Short, E.J. (April, 1987). *The educational implications of cognitive, metacognitive, and motivational subtypes.* Paper presented at the annual meeting of the American Educational Research Association, Washington, DC.

Short, E.J. Evans, S., Dellick, D.M., & Cuddy, C. (1988). *Thinking aloud during problem solving: Facilitation effects.* Manuscript submitted for publication.

Short, E.J., Feagans, L., McKinney, J.D., & Applebaum, M.I. (1984). Longitudinal stability of LD subtypes based on age- and IQ-achievement discrepancies. *Learning Disability Quarterly, 9*, 214–225.

Short, E.J., Friebert, S.E., & Andrist, C.G. (1988). *Individual differences in attentional processes as a function of age and skill level.* Manuscript submitted for publication.

Short, E.J., & Ryan, E.B. (1984). Metacognitive differences between skilled and less skilled readers: Remediating deficits through story grammar and attribution training. *Journal of Educational Psychology, 76*, 225–235.

Short, E.J., Weissberg-Benchell, J.A., & Evans, S. (1988). *Attributional differences between skilled and less skilled learners: Group versus subtype approaches.* Manuscript submitted for publication.

Speece, D.L. (October, 1982). *Comprehension monitoring in normally achieving and learning disabled children.* Paper presented at the 4th International Conference of Learning Disabilities. Kansas City, MO.

Speece, D.L. (1987). Information processing subtypes of learning disabled readers. *Learning Disability Research, 2*, 91–102.

Spiro, R.J., & Tirre, W.C. (1979). *Individual differences in schema utilization during discourse processing.* (Tech. Rep. No. 111). Urbana, IL: University of Illinois Center for the Study of Reading.

Sternberg, R.J. (1977). *Intelligence, information processing, and analogical reasoning: The componential analysis of human abilities.* Hillsdale, NJ: Erlbaum & Associates.

Swanson, H.L. (1982). A multidirectional model for assessing learning disabled students' intelligence: An information processing framework. *Learning Disability Quarterly, 5,* 312–326.

Swanson, H.L. (1988a). *Memory subtypes in learning disabled readers.* Manuscript submitted for publication.

Swanson, H.L. (1988b). *The influence of metacognitive knowledge and aptitude on problem solving.* Manuscript submitted for publication.

Taylor, H.G., Fletcher, J.M., & Satz, P. (1984). Neuropsychological assessment of children. In G. Golstein & M. Hersen (Eds.), *Handbook of psychological assessment* (pp. 211–234). New York: Pergamon.

Tollefson, N., Tracy, D., Johnson, E., Farmer, A., & Buenning, M. (1984). Goal setting and personal responsibility training for learning disabled adolescents. *Psychology in the Schools, 21,* 224–233.

Torgesen, J. (1977). Memorization processes in reading disabled children. *Journal of Educational Psychology, 69,* 571–578.

Torgesen, J. (1985). Memory processes in reading disabled children. *Journal of Learning Disabilities, 18,* 350–357.

Torgesen, J., & Houck, D. (1980). Processing deficiencies of learning-disabled children who perform poorly on digit span test. *Journal of Educational Psychology, 72,* 141–160.

Torgesen, J.K., & Wong, B.Y.L. (1986). *Psychological and educational perspectives on learning disabilities.* New York: Academic Press.

Vygotsky, L.S. (1978). *Mind in society: The development of higher psychological processes* (M. Cole, V. John-Steiner, S. Scribner, & E. Souberman, Eds. and trans.). Cambridge, MA: Harvard University Press.

Weiner, B. (1979). A theory of motivation and attribution for some classroom experiences. *Journal of Educational Psychology, 75,* 530–543.

Weissberg-Benchell, J.A. (1986). *Preschoolers' story knowledge.* Unpublished master's thesis, Case Western Reserve University, Cleveland, OH.

Weyhing, R.S. (1986). *Effects of attributional retraining on beliefs about self efficacy and reading comprehension in learning disabled adolescents.* Unpublished master's thesis, University of Notre Dame, Notre Dame, IN.

Whimbey, A., & Lochhead, J. (1986). *Problem solving and comprehension: A short course in analytic reasoning.* San Francisco, CA: Freeman.

Wong, B.Y.L. (1985). Metacognition and learning disabilities. In D.L. Forrest-Pressley, G.E. MacKinnon, & T.G. Waller (Eds.), *Metacognition, cognition, and human performance,* Vol. 2 (pp. 137–180). New York: Academic Press.

Wong, B.Y.L., & Jones, W. (1982). Increasing metacomprehension in learning disabled and normally achieving students through self-questioning training. *Learning Disability Quarterly, 5,* 228–240.

Worden, P. (1986). Prose comprehension and recall in disabled learners. In S. Ceci (Ed.), *Handbook of cognitive, social, and neuropsychological aspects of learning disabilities,* Vol. 1 (pp. 240–261). Hillsdale, NJ: Erlbaum & Associates.

Zeamon, D., & House, B.J. (1963). The role of attention in retardate discrimination learning. In N.R. Ellis (Ed.), *Handbook of mental deficiency* (pp. 159–223). New York: McGraw-Hill Book Co.

Zimmerman, B.J., & Pons, M.M. (1986). Development of a structured interview for assessing student use of self-regulated learning strategies. *American Educational Research Journal, 23,* 614–628.

3
Children's Utilization of Study Time: Differential and Sufficient Aspects

ANNETTE DUFRESNE AND AKIRA KOBASIGAWA

A quote from Bloom (1974) seems a fitting way to begin this chapter: "All learning, whether done in school or elsewhere, requires time." Thus, from the learner's perspective, in addition to the need to process information to be learned in some manner, some expenditure of time is also required for learning. We can refer to time, then, as a necessary, but not sufficient, condition for learning to occur. In many situations, a learner has considerable freedom in terms of spending time for learning activities; for example, whether to spend time studying for a test, how long to study, what material to spend the most time on. It is our goal in this chapter to examine some of the key processes involved in children's utilization of time for studying and to suggest some promising directions for future research.

In the first section, we present a broad perspective for studying children's utilization of study time. To this end, two key aspects of study-time utilization are delineated, along with a discussion of the major factors that are likely to affect how study time is allocated. Next, we present some illustrative experimental studies relevant to developmental issues surrounding allocation of study time and discuss the current state of knowledge in this area. In the final section, we outline important future research directions in the context of the framework presented in the first section.

Aspects of Allocation of Study Time

FOCUS OF CHAPTER

According to Bandura (1986), people constantly have to decide what activities to pursue and how long to continue ones they have initiated. These two decision processes suggest that children's effective use of study time can be examined in two ways: (a) differential allocation—whether a learner allocates more time to certain tasks or units of tasks (e.g., more important or difficult units) and (b) sufficient allocation—whether a learner allocates enough time so that the study goal can be met (Dufresne & Kobasigawa, in press).

What should be emphasized for studying and how much time should be spent for studying represent two frequent decisions that students must make while studying. Consequently, skills related to the two aspects of study-time usage (differential and sufficient allocation) are useful across numerous study situations. Generally, the effective way to use study time would be to spend more time on task-relevant or less well-learned material. This ability to distribute study time *differentially* according to certain priorities becomes especially important as children face constraints on the time they have available for studying and on the amount of material they can absorb. Differential allocation of study time, however, does not always lead to successful test performance. To do well on the criterion task, as Carroll's (1963) model for school learning suggests, children must also learn to spend a *sufficient* amount of study time to reach the study goal. While there are additional aspects of utilization of study time (e.g., timing—determining when to begin studying for a test), we will focus in this chapter on children's differential and sufficient allocation of study time.

Several researchers on cognitive development (e.g., Brown, Bransford, Ferrara, & Campione, 1983; Flavell, 1977; Rohwer, 1984), have suggested that a person's use of study strategies (e.g., rehearsal, elaboration; see Rohwer & Thomas, this volume, chap. 5) is determined by complex interactions of characteristics of tasks and the learner. We have also found it useful to look at these two classes of variables in examining children's allocation of study time. Decisions as to how to distribute time across different units of material, and decisions as to when a sufficient time has been spent must be made by considering various characteristics of the task and the learner. For instance, which materials should be studied longer than others depends on what materials a particular learner is having more difficulty in understanding (learner characteristics) as well as what materials will be emphasized on the test (task characteristics). Furthermore, the ease with which a learner can make decisions on "what to study" and "how long to study" is affected by, for example, the availability of external help (task) and the learner's skills to assess time requirements (learner). To elaborate on these points, we identify in the next section some crucial variables under each of these two categories (task and learner).

Task Characteristics Affecting Utilization of Study Time

Similar to allocation of other resources, how to allocate study time must be decided in terms of a goal or objective. We can use an analogy of allocation of resources by business or government, where the first step is an identification of goals (e.g., Bender, 1983). One must also consider the environment or the context in which one is operating, both for devising plans and strategies to allocate resources and for evaluating and perhaps revising goals.

Study Goals

Two properties of goals that have been studied by researchers (e.g., Bandura, 1986; Morgan, 1985) are likely to affect the ease of allocating time differentially and sufficiently. First, study goals can differ in terms of the *explicitness* or specificity with which they describe what skills or concepts are expected to be learned and how the acquired knowledge will be assessed subsequently. Explicitly stated goals are important for learners to identify task-relevant information and decide what should be emphasized for studying (differential allocation) or to select task-appropriate self-testing strategies for determining whether study goals have been achieved (sufficient allocation).

Second, study goals can differ with respect to their *time frame* or proximity, which also affects the ease with which students can use study time effectively. For instance, students may study a list of pictorial items for an immediate recall test under a self-terminated procedure or study five chapters for an exam three months from now. In the first case, children are simply required to spend sufficient time by monitoring recall readiness. In the second case, however, students additionally need to estimate the time that will be required for the task and decide when to begin studying so that there will be enough time available to meet the study goal. Furthermore, students need to set subgoals and distribute study time over the three-month period considering other activities that they have to complete in the meantime.

Context

The context in which a study task is carried out can differ with regard to the availability of various resources (e.g., teacher, study questions) or support that can facilitate or constrain the use of strategies of time allocation (see Duffy & Roehler, this volume, chap. 6, for a discussion of other related teacher-focused resources). For instance, students may use a sufficient amount of time for studying for a test when a teacher estimates how long the material should be studied and set aside this amount of class time so that students can study in class. Students may not allocate study time effectively, however, when they are at home and must independently ensure that enough time is spent studying. Even in the second situation, of course, support may be provided by parents, for example, "You have problems with your multiplications, so you should spend some more time learning them" (differential allocation).

The context of a study situation may also differ with respect to the availability of time itself. The manner in which time should be distributed may vary depending on how much time is available. When ample time is available, the best strategy may be to spend more time on those topics one is having difficulty in learning. When study time is highly limited, however, the best strategy may be to focus on those topics where better learning results can be expected in a short time period.

The learner's criterion for deciding whether they have studied sufficiently can also vary depending on the amount of time available. If the allotted time is more than needed, a learner may study until he or she can answer all the questions he or she thinks could possibly be on the test. When the study time is highly limited, however, the same learner may decide that sufficient time has been spent when he or she knows the answers to the questions that are most likely to be on the test.

Under ordinary study situations, the issue of time constraints can emerge because children typically engage in study activities with other goals in mind—they want to or must participate in extracurricular activities, watch a special TV program, have peer interactions, and complete routine chores. To use time effectively under these conditions, children need to set up priorities by considering time constraints and the attractiveness of various activities as well as their importance. To allocate a sufficient amount of time to a particular task, children may also consider the availability of external support, for example, a "delegate" who can complete some of their tasks in their place (Oerter, 1981).

LEARNER CHARACTERISTICS AFFECTING UTILIZATION OF STUDY TIME

While characteristics of the task can affect the ease with which study time can be used appropriately, to determine how an individual is likely to allocate study time, we must also examine characteristics of the learner. As we will discuss in detail shortly, two important characteristics the learner brings to study situations are (a) metacognition and (b) motivation. The importance of these two variables in the context of the development of study strategies is discussed in detail by Pressley, Goodchild, Fleet, Zajchowski, and Evans (1989).

Metacognition.

The term metacognition can be used to refer to (a) metacognitive knowledge and (b) monitoring and regulatory skills of current cognitive activities (e.g., Brown et al., 1983; Flavell, 1979). Metacognitive knowledge represents a person's knowledge stored in long-term memory concerning how his or her abilities, the nature of study materials, the study goal, and study strategies will affect the course and outcome of learning. One can see the significance of a learner's metacognitive knowledge in that, although task characteristics (e.g., study goal) may affect how time should be utilized, the learner is unlikely to allocate study time appropriately if he or she is unaware of the effect of task variables on learning. To illustrate, the amount of study time that is required varies depending on whether one must learn the gist of the story or learn the story word for word. A young child who does not know that word for word recall is more difficult than gist recall (Kreutzer, Leonard, & Flavell, 1975) is unlikely to vary the amount of time spent for these two tasks.

As indicated previously, metacognition also includes the learner's skills to regulate the course of current study activities, for example, by planning the approximate amount of time to be allocated to the task and then monitoring the progress of study activities (e.g., Brown, 1978). To use study time effectively, according to this framework, a learner must know (a) the nature of the material, for example, which units are more important; (b) the goal of studying, for example, verbatim recall; (c) the current state of learning, for example, how well a particular topic is learned relative to the study goal; and (d) how to use these pieces of information for allocating time for studying (Brown et al., 1983). Information a is useful for allocating study time differentially, information b is important for deciding an appropriate strategy to assess the current state of learning (component c), and information c is relevant to allocating study time differentially (spend more time on less well-learned topics) as well as sufficiently.

Motivation

Task-appropriate metacognitive knowledge and regulatory skills may not ensure that study time is allocated appropriately if children are not sufficiently motivated (e.g., Bandura, 1986). One can easily think of instances where students are aware that they do not know the material very well, and yet do not study the material a longer time.

While we cannot provide an extensive discussion on the concept of motivation here, we can refer to two important sources of motivation that are included in most motivational theories (see, for example, Dweck & Elliott, 1983; Maehr, 1983, for more complete discussions; see also Short & Weissberg-Benchell, this volume, chap. 2 for a discussion of motivational issues with a special population). One important source of motivation is a person's perceived value of the outcomes of his or her actions. Thus, even though reviewing study notes a little longer may result in a high grade, if this outcome does not have a high value for the individual, he or she may not study the material sufficiently. Another important source of motivation for the selection and persistence of goal-directed behavior is a person's belief that his or her actions will produce specified results and that one has the ability to perform these activities. As a result, children may not spend a greater portion of study time for a harder task (lack of differential allocation) or may terminate studying prematurely (lack of sufficient allocation) if they believe that they are not capable of achieving the goal even if they try. In fact, researchers (e.g., Dweck, Davidson, Nelson, & Enna, 1978) have shown that children are likely to discontinue working on challenging tasks if they attribute their previous failure on the task to lack of ability. In contrast, children showed high persistence on tasks when their self-judgments of efficacy were enhanced (e.g., Schunk, 1984).

In closing this section, it should be pointed out that a person's strong will to work hard is insufficient for using study time effectively. To this end, high motivation needs to be supplemented by knowledge about, for example, which materials are and are not essential for achieving study goals.

SUMMARY

We have conceptualized utilization of study time as consisting of two inter-related aspects: (a) allocating more time to a certain task than to others (differential allocation) and (b) allocating a sufficient amount of time to reach a study goal (sufficient allocation). Our attempt has been to show that an "effective" manner of allocation of study time is determined by complex inter-actions of characteristics of tasks (e.g., what is emphasized by a study goal) and the learner (e.g., how well the learner is knowledgeable of the task). We have also indicated that, depending on certain properties of study goals (e.g., explicitness) and contexts under which such goals are pursued (e.g., availability of external help), decision processes can be simple or complex regarding how time should be spent for studying. Two important characteristics of a learner are metacognition and motivation. A learner's metacognitive knowledge about task demands and the current state of learning is necessary for effective regulation of study time. The learner's metacognitive knowledge, however, may not guarantee that study time is allocated appropriately if the outcomes of studying are not valued or if the learner does not believe that he or she has the ability to produce the outcomes.

Empirical Studies

In this section we will review major research procedures and findings relevant to children's tendency and ability to (a) distribute study time unevenly across different units of material and (b) spend a sufficient amount of study time in order to achieve a study goal. Most of the studies in this area were conducted to assess children's skills to monitor characteristics of tasks and the current state of knowledge and use such information to regulate utilization of study time (see Van Haneghan & Baker, this volume, chap. 9, for a discussion of monitoring issues in the math domain). Most of the information available, therefore, concerns the effect of age-related improvements in metacognition (i.e., learner characteristics) on children's allocation of study time. At the same time, it will be shown that children's effective use of study time emerges at different age levels depending on different characteristics of tasks.

DIFFERENTIAL ALLOCATION OF STUDY TIME

In different situations learners may decide how to distribute their study time on the basis of the progress of learning (e.g., "I am not learning this section of material well so I should spend more time on it"), or on the basis of charac-teristics of the material (e.g., spending more time on difficult as opposed to easy units of material), or on some combination of these. The focus of this sec-tion is: Do children monitor the relevant aspects of the task, materials, or their own learning (e.g., Do I know this unit well?) and use that information to regulate the use of study time?

One of the most basic instances of differential allocation is allocating study time to relevant, as opposed to irrelevant, items in simple memory tasks. According to Miller and her associates (Miller, Haynes, DeMarie-Dreblow, & Woody-Ramsey, 1986; Miller & Weiss, 1981), children around third grade begin to show such time-allocation strategies. In their studies, children were specifically asked to memorize one set of pictorial items (household objects or animal). The items were concealed under doors that had a drawing of either a cage (for animal pictures) or a house (for household items). During a study period (25 sec), children were allowed to look under whatever doors they wanted, as many times as they wanted. Grade-3 or older students spent a greater portion of study time examining the task-relevant items. Grade-2 or younger children, on the other hand, spent about the same amounts of study time for studying the relevant and irrelevant material. Results complementary to those reported by Miller et al. have been observed in classroom situations. Kobasigawa, Chouinard, and Dufresne (1988) asked grade-4 and -8 students to read prose passages and prepare study notes for a subsequent test in which they would be asked to recall four different attributes of different kinds of bears. Both grade-4 and -8 students copied significantly more relevant than irrelevant facts; about 75% of students' study notes contained information relevant to the performance objectives.

In the preceding studies, the experimenter essentially identified for children which items should be emphasized for studying. In other situations, however, children must identify for themselves which units of materials should be emphasized for studying on the basis of, for example, which items they are learning well. The question of how well children utilize this type of information to distribute their study time was assessed by Masur, McIntyre, and Flavell (1973). These researchers asked grade-1, -3, and college students to memorize a series of pictorial items over three study trials. For the second and third trials, participants were asked explicitly to select out half of the items for further study (45 sec). Grade-3 and college students were found to select those items that they failed to recall on the preceding trial while grade-1 children were found to select an approximately equal amount of recalled and unrecalled items.

What was the problem for grade-1 children in the Masur et al. study? Apparently, their problem was not in identifying which items they had and had not recalled previously; these young children were capable of discriminating recalled from missed items. Perhaps, this knowledge of item difficulty might not have occurred to them spontaneously during study trials. If young children are reminded of the differences in task difficulty during study, do they allocate study time differentially by using this information? Recall that Masur et al. forced children to be selective by asking them to choose only one half of the study items for additional study. Do children show similar selectivity on a spontaneous basis? These issues were examined by Dufresne and Kobasigawa (in press).

The materials for the Dufresne and Kobasigawa study consisted of two types of booklets of picture paired-associate items: "easy" booklets, which contained highly related items (dog-cat) that children of all age levels could learn perfectly following a brief study period, and "hard" booklets, which contained unrelated items (book-frog) that chidren of all age levels could also learn perfectly with some reasonable effort. Grade-1, -3, -5, and -7 children initially received two self-terminated study trials ("Study until you are sure you can recall all the pairs perfectly"), each trial with a different set of two booklets, under one of two conditions: (a) a prompt condition in which they were asked to identify an "easy" booklet after naming the paired items but before studying them, or (b) a no-prompt condition in which they were not required to do so. Following the second recall trial, children were asked questions to assess their knowledge of how to allocate study time differentially (e.g., which booklet will be easier to learn, how they should study so they can remember the hard and the easy booklet equally well) and sufficiently (e.g., knowledge of self-testing strategies). A third self-terminated trial was then administered to provide preliminary information regarding the limits of children's ability to allocate study time strategically.

Whether or not they were reminded of the difference in difficulty, grade-1 and -3 children spent about the same amount of study time on hard pairs as they did on easy pairs during the first two study trials (see also, Bisanz, Vesonder, & Voss, 1978; Dufresne & Kobasigawa, 1988). The metamemory data indicated that, as was observed in the Masur et al. study, many of these younger children did know the distinction in the materials. The problem for grade-1 children appeared to lie in their lack of knowledge of regulatory skills that permit them to use knowledge of the difference in item difficulty to allocate more time to hard pairs. One interesting observation was that grade-3 but not grade-1 children spent significantly longer on the hard items on trial 3 (after metamemory questions). This finding suggests that eliciting various aspects of knowledge related to allocating study time through metamemory questions may lead to differential allocation in grade-3 children. (A follow-up study by the same researchers clearly confirmed this observation.) Grade-5 and -7 students were especially prone to spend more time on the hard items (see Bisanz et al., 1978, for a similar conclusion). These older students appeared to use several sources of information for regulating study time: (a) their readily evocable knowledge that the unrelated pairs should be studied longer (metamemory data), (b) information about the current state of learning through some form of self-testing (approximately 50% of the older students were observed to use self-testing strategies), and (c) feedback on their performance on trial 1 that indicated how poorly they had performed on the hard task (mainly grade-7 students increased the amount of study time for hard pairs on trial 2).

In the Dufresne and Kobasigawa study (in press), grade-5 children's knowledge related to differential allocation of study time was more elaborate and usable than younger children's. In other conditions, though, grade-5 students may not be particularly sensitive to the task difficulty, and consequently, may not distribute study time differentially across different tasks. In a study by Owings, Petersen, Bransford, Morris, and Stein (1980), two groups of grade-5 students, academically successful and unsuccessful (based on teacher ratings and an achievement test), were asked to study two stories under a self-terminated procedure for a subsequent test. One of the stories contained information that was readily understandable in terms of what the children already knew (e.g., the hungry boy ate a hamburger), and thus would be easy to learn. In the other story, the predicates were arbitrarily re-paired with sentence subjects (e.g., the hungry boy took a nap), and thus would be difficult to learn. The successful students were aware that they had more difficulty learning the less sensible stories, and spent more time studying the difficult stories than the easy stories. In contrast, the unsuccessful students were much less aware of the difference in difficulty between the two stories, and tended to distribute their study time equally between the easy and difficult stories. (For a similar study with college students, see Hunter-Blanks, Ghatala, Pressley, & Levin, 1988.)

In the studies reviewed so far, children were asked to recall information in the same form in which it was originally presented. How do children use extra study time when they are required to recall the gist of a story? To this end, students must be able to discriminate between main ideas and trivial points, and then organize those important units for retelling the story. When these are required, only grade-7 or older students allocate study time differentially according to the importance of units of text, at least when processing long and complex stories. In a study by Brown and Smiley (1978), grade-5, -7, -12, and college students were asked to read a story for gist recall. Prior to the outset of this investigation, the story was divided into linguistic subunits, and independent groups of college students rated the structural importance of these subunits for the main theme of the story using a four-point scale (Brown & Smiley, 1977). These researchers found that, with additional study time, grade-7 or older students showed improved recall for important units of material but not for less important units. Grade-5 students, on the other hand, did not benefit from the additional study time. An examination of study behaviors during the additional time indicated that grade-7 (41%) and -12 (76%) students were more likely than grade-5 students (28%) to underline or write down the most important passages. Even when they were prompted to underline sentences during study, about 70% of grade-5 students who used this technique selected important and trivial units with equal frequency. When asked to recall such complex materials as stories, then, the majority of grade-5 students does not distribute study time in accordance with the importance of units of text even though, as demonstrated in previous research (Brown & Smiley, 1977), they can discriminate units of the highest level of importance from the remaining units.

Summary

We began this section with the question: Do children (a) monitor the relevant aspects of the task, materials, or their own learning and (b) use that information for regulating the use of study time? In typical list-learning situations,

grade-2 or younger children may not allocate more study time to more important or more difficult units of material even when the task-relevant items are
identified by the experimenter or when the knowledge of the difference in
item difficulty is evoked through prompt questions. Grade-3 children are only
beginning to use study time differentially. Children around this grade level
are likely to use this strategy when the importance of items are explicitly
identified for them, when they are asked to be selective, or when various
aspects of relevant metamemory are evoked through prompt questions. With
age, children distribute study time differentially across different units of
material on the basis of information from several sources (knowledge of item
difficulty and the current state of learning). When high cognitive demands
are imposed on students (e.g., gist recall), however, even older elementary-
school children (grade-5) fall back to an indiscriminative study strategy
without using the apparently available task-relevant knowledge (just as younger children frequently do in simple list-learning situations).

Sufficient Allocation of Study Time

In virtually any learning situation, students should be able to assess the
progress of studying towards their study goals. If the assessment is that
material is well learned, then the learner decides to terminate studying. If, on
the other hand, the assessment is that material is not well learned, then study
continues (e.g., Brown, Campione, & Barclay, 1979). Children, of course, may
bring rules other than those just described for determining whether or not
they have allocated the time needed to reach the goal, for example, "Read the
hard unit first, then read the easy unit, and then read the hard unit once again.
Then I should do well on a test," (Dufresne & Kobasigawa, in press). In the
present section, we will focus on children's ability to use self-testing strategies
as well as externally available test items as a means for determining recall
readiness. In all of the reviewed studies items to be recalled and criterion testing procedures were explicitly explained to children.

A classic study by Flavell, Friedrichs, and Hoyt (1970) examined children's
ability to assess their readiness to recall a set of pictorial items. Children in
nursery school, kindergarten, grade-2, and grade-4 were asked to memorize
pictorial items until they thought they could remember all the items perfectly. The list length was set at each child's previously assessed memory span.
To expose a picture for study, the child was required to press a button beneath
that particular picture. These researchers used recall scores as a measure of
children's ability to monitor recall readiness. More than 80% of the grade-2
and -4 children showed perfect recall on all three trials, while only 7% of nursery school and 14% of kindergarten children performed in this manner. Interesting findings with regard to the use of self-testing were that nearly all of the
grade-2 and -4 children employed an anticipation strategy (before exposing
the picture of the object, the child first says that object's name and then
presses the button to see if he or she was correct). In contrast, the use of this
strategy was low in nursery school and kindergarten children (38%). In a

related study by Leal, Crays, and Moely (1985), though, it was observed that when the list length was set equal to the child's memory span plus one item, grade-3 children terminated study activities quite prematurely and many of them did not use any form of self-testing unless they were explicitly instructed to do so. Apparently, a slight modification of task difficulty seems to affect young children's spontaneous use of self-testing strategies. This point is further illustrated by the Dufresne and Kobasigawa (in press) study that we described previously.

The materials used in the Dufresne and Kobasigawa study were two booklets of paired-associate items (one booklet contained highly related pairs and one contained unrelated pairs), which children were requested to study until they felt they could recall all the pairs perfectly. The list length was varied across grade levels to make the task approximately equally difficult for all ages. Recall scores indicated that older students were better able than younger students to monitor when they had studied the material sufficiently. First, older students' (grade-5 and -7) recall scores were consistently higher than younger students' (grade-1 and -3) across three trials. Second, significantly more older than younger students achieved perfect recall on trial 2 (24% vs. 3%) and trial 3 (41% vs. 4%), but not on trial 1. Yet, many students even in the oldest grade (70% on trial 2 and 50% on trial 3) were not completely successful at assessing their recall readiness.

Children's knowledge and use of self-testing strategies were also examined in the Dufresne and Kobasigawa study. Although a small proportion of grade-1 and -3 children did go over *both* easy and hard booklets two or three times, the majority of the younger children studied by simply looking at each item once, with no attempt to self-test how well they had learned the material (see also Neimark, Slotnick, & Ulrich, 1971). As evidenced by their responses to the metamemory questions, one difficulty for these children, especially grade-1 children, might be their lack of knowledge about how to monitor the current state of learning or the utility of self-testing strategies. Grade-3 children seem somewhat more ready to adopt the use of self-testing strategies. Following the metamemory questions concerning self-testing strategies, a small proportion of grade-3 children (20%) began using a self-testing strategy appropriate for the paired-associate task (covering the response picture and trying to guess what the covered picture would be). While grade-3 children who used a self-testing strategy had difficulty in consistently remembering to cover the response picture before looking at it, these younger self-testing users' recall scores (82% correct) were much closer to the study goal than nonusers' (51%), and were as high as older self-testing users' (83%).

In contrast to younger students, grade-5 and -7 students were more sensitive to the need for assessing the progress of learning by using some type of self-testing strategy. Although the number of students spontaneously using a self-testing strategy appropriate for the paired-associate task was rather small (20%), about one-half of the older students spontaneously used some form of self-testing on trials 1 and 2 (observational data and verbal reports combined). Following the metamemory questions, the proportion of older students using a paired-associate self-testing strategy increased to 40% (trial 3). However, even older self-testing users showed several difficulties, for example, using or suggesting a self-testing strategy more appropriate for a serial- or free-recall task (e.g., checking how many items could be recalled without looking at the booklet), or terminating study activities when they did not remember all the items during self-testing. With a somewhat more complex task (studying two booklets of paired-associate items, one of which requires three trials to learn), then, it appears that even many of the older elementary-school students have difficulty monitoring recall readiness accurately. Our speculation is that when children first begin to allocate study time strategically considering the study goal, they mainly use information concerning the level of difficulty of materials (e.g., study the easy task once but study the hard task two or three times, and terminate study). Only later do these children begin to use information from previous learning trials and information about their current state of learning assessed by task-appropriate self-tests for allocating study time sufficiently.

This observation regarding older children's difficulty in the use of sufficient study time may not be particularly surprising when we consider the accuracy of college students in monitoring recall readiness. D'Ydewalle, Swerts, and De Corte (1983) asked college students to study 30 pieces of factual information (names of people, historical dates) under a self-terminated procedure. The amount of time allocated by these college students was appropriate for recalling only 43% of the items. See Hunter-Blanks et al. (1988) and Pressley, Snyder, Levin, Murray, and Ghatala (1987) for further evidence of college students' difficulty in allocating sufficient study time. In addition, in a survey conducted by Anderson (1980) of the types of study strategies used by college students, very few students mentioned the use of self-testing strategies.

In the studies reviewed so far, children had to think about using some form of self-testing to determine how well material had been learned. If children are provided with test items of a criterion task, how effectively do they use such test items for regulating study time for achieving the study goal (100% accuracy)? This question was examined by Gettinger (1985).

Gettinger devised a paradigm to assess the amount of time children needed for learning a reading task to 100% mastery (i.e., sufficient allocation) as well as the amount of time children allocate for learning the same reading task under a self-terminated procedure. In the first phase of the experiment, grade-4 and -5 students studied factual information contained in a passage while listening to a taped presentation and then took a test consisting of 10 multiple-choice items. Children did not receive any feedback as to how well they had performed on the test. The number of trials needed for each child to reach 100% accuracy on the test defined that child's time-needed-to-learn score. In the second phase of the experiment, children studied a new but equivalent form of the reading task using the same study-test procedure. They were told that they were working for 100% accuracy on the test but were free to terminate their study when they were sure they had learned the material sufficiently. Gettinger's findings (see also Gettinger, 1984) suggest that spontaneous allocation of sufficient time for studying is not a simple matter for school children, even under a seemingly optimal condition — the availability of test-taking opportunities. When students were allowed to self-determine the number of trials, they spent about 68% of the time they actually needed to master the reading task.

Why did children not monitor their recall readiness effectively even when test-taking opportunities were provided to them? Ghatala, Foorman, Levin, and Pressley (in press) reasoned that taking a multiple-choice test, as was done in the Gettinger study, may not enable children to monitor the progress of learning accurately. Multiple-choice tests typically include distractors that are plausible in nature. By responding to such highly plausible distractors, children may erroneously inflate their confidence in their incorrect choices and terminate study activities prematurely. These researchers hypothesized that children's assessment of recall readiness can be improved by requiring them to respond to short-answer-recall questions. In addition to determining this hypothesis, the Ghatala et al. study examined the following question as well: Do children allocate study time more sufficiently when they have test items during study than when they do not?

In general, Ghatala et al. asked grade-4 children to learn a reading task similar to that used by Gettinger (1985), until they were sure they could perfectly recall eight pieces of factual information and then to take a recall test. In a control condition (study condition), children simply studied the reading passage for as many trials as they felt were needed before indicating that they were ready for the test. In another condition (study-test condition), children studied the passage once and took the recall test without receiving any performance feedback. These children were allowed to repeat this study-test procedure as many times as they wished until they were sure they reached the study goal. If children's test performance did not meet the study goal (100% recall) following the self-terminated trials, they received additional trials until they reached the criterion performance (a measure of time needed to learn).

Ghatala et al.'s outcomes suggest that a short-answer recall test provides children with a better opportunity to assess their current state of memory more accurately than does a multiple-choice test. Recall that children in the Gettinger study spent only 68% of the study time that they actually needed. In contrast, the amount of study time spontaneously allocated by children in the study-test condition (i.e., in the Ghatala et al. study) closely matched the amount of time needed to master the reading material; they spent 86% of the time needed to reach the study goal. Furthermore, their findings also indicated the importance of test-monitoring opportunities by using externally provided test items. Thus, those children who simply repeated study trials (i.e., study condition) spent only 47% of the time needed to achieve perfect recall. It should be pointed out, however, that Pressley, Levin, Ghatala, and Ahmad (1987) have reported that grade-2 or younger children's test monitoring tends to be less accurate compared to grade-4 or older children's, even when both younger and older children have performed equally well on a test. Consequently, younger children (e.g., grade 2) may not use experimenter-provided test items as effectively as grade-4 children did in the Ghatala et al. study for regulating study time.

As an alternative to experimenter-provided practice questions, several investigators instructed children on how to use self-testing strategies to improve their assessment of recall readiness. Leal et al. (1985) trained grade-3 children to use a self-testing strategy useful for serial- and free-recall tasks and obtained promising results. These children not only maintained the trained strategy but also generalized it to other study situations, outperforming nontrained children on various memory tasks. Dufresne and Kobasigawa (1987) found that many grade-3 children readily responded to instructions on how to use a self-testing strategy that was appropriate for paired-associate tasks, and that the use of self-testing greatly improved children's recall performance. Given that many children at this grade level do not use self-testing strategies as a means for allocating a sufficient amount of study time, additional training studies that include school-like materials would be informative.

Finally, we briefly consider the role that children's motivation may play in the use of study time. Although the reviewed studies were not designed to examine motivational factors, could the findings that many children do not study sufficiently be explained in terms of motivational variables? Perhaps, in a few cases, the observed results could be a consequence of children's beliefs that they would not achieve the study goal even if they worked hard on the task. In typical experimental situation, most children are sufficiently motivated by the ample individual attention they receive from the experimenter. Researchers (Dufresne & Kobasigawa, in press; Ghatala et al., in press) reported that, when they terminated studying, most children, especially younger ones, predicted that their recall would be perfect or close to perfect. In addition, observations of children's behavior indicated that many children were surprised when they could not recall items on the recall test. We believe, therefore, that a lack of motivation may not be a major factor for children's failure to allocate a sufficient amount of study time in most of these cases.

Summary

Children's tendency to allocate sufficient study time so that a study goal is met increases with age. Despite such age-related improvements in the use of study time, we have also seen that many older students are not always proficient at assessing whether they have studied sufficiently.

One factor that accounts in part for the observed developmental differences in allocating sufficient study time is the use of self-testing strategies that permit assessment of the current stage of learning, for example, trying to remember items without looking at them before terminating study. Like many other study strategies, children's skills to use self-testing skills are initially limited to simple tasks (e.g., learning lists equal to one's memory span). With age, such skills become more differentiated and usable in a task-appropriate manner. While the data are limited, it appears that self-testing strategies appropriate for serial or free-recall tasks seem to appear before self-tests that are appropriate for paired-associate tasks (e.g., Dufresne & Kobasigawa, in press). Thus, in addition to the knowledge that self-testing is a useful thing to do, a mature use of self-testing involves (a) knowing what is required by a criterion task, (b) selecting a self-testing strategy that is appropriate to the learning goal, and (c) deciding whether to study longer by comparing the current state to the study goal. Since different criterion tasks require different self-testing strategies, component b should be included in instructions of future training studies.

Concluding Remarks

The studies reviewed in this chapter highlight the fact that students have a great many choices and decisions in terms of how they utilize their time for studying. Researchers have, for many years, focused on the issue of how teachers can more effectively manage time for teaching and learning (e.g., Fisher & Berliner, 1985; Stallings, 1980). A shift to include the role students play in managing their own time for learning would seem fruitful.

This chapter was centered around two key decisions students must make to utilize time for studying: (a) how to distribute study time among different materials or units of materials and (b) how to allocate a sufficient amount of study time to reach the goal. Similar to many other areas of cognition, developmental increases in strategic allocation of study time were demonstrated. Thus, older students were more likely than younger students to distribute their study time unevenly among different materials to be studied and use self-testing strategies to assess the progress of learning. Not only were older students able to utilize strategies to help allocate study time, they were also able to take different characteristics of tasks into account (e.g., free recall vs. paired-associate tasks) and generalize the use of such strategies across a variety of study situations.

What factors seem to account for such developmental increases? One explanatory factor that has guided much of the research in this area is the concept of metacognition. The studies reviewed support the view that one of the things that develops is children's knowledge about the effective use of study time. Older children are also more likely than younger children to use the available task-appropriate metacognitive knowledge. It seems reasonable that as children go through school, they are exposed more frequently to different study situations that require strategic allocation of time, and practice different components of such strategies (e.g., Leal et al., 1985). With increased familiarity with different academic tasks, then, the coordination of various forms of knowledge (e.g., nature of material, demands of criterion test, components of self-testing strategies) for allocating study time should become increasingly less effortful and demanding for older students.

The studies reviewed in this chapter, then, have provided preliminary information concerning developmental differences in children's use of study time and some possible underlying psychological mechanisms (metacognitive knowledge and skills). However, because the focus of research thus far has been placed on a narrow range of study situations, more information is needed before we can arrive at a comprehensive picture of the component skills involved in allocation of time for studying. In the studies reviewed: (a) students were to carry out study activities immediately without having freedom to participate in alternative activities (e.g., studying a different subject, playing with peers) at that time; (b) students' use of study time was observed in a single study session in the absence of time constraints; and (c) students typically received explicit instructions as to the questions that would be asked on the criterion test (almost always verbatim recall). In contrast to these situations, students usually face more complex situations in school settings. As described in the beginning of this chapter, strategic use of time for studying under such situations can be more complex than illustrated by the studies reviewed (see Symons, Snyder, Cariglia-Bull, & Pressley, this volume, chap.1).

Following from the observations described herein regarding existing studies in this area, one promising avenue for future research would be to examine differential and sufficient allocation of study time under a broader range of task conditions. We can refer again to the framework presented at the beginning of this chapter in looking at how task conditions might be varied. First, it would be useful to investigate children's use of study time under conditions where students are less certain as to what will be on a subsequent test (specificity of study goal) or where students have an opportunity to study for a test that will be given at a set time in the future (proximity of study goal). By using these situations, researchers can observe further components of allocation of study time, for example, how children plan how much time will be needed to achieve a study goal and ensure that studying is begun at a time so that sufficient time will remain. Second, research should be conducted in the context where studying must be done when there is some choice of activities to be performed (studying for a test, playing with peers). Such research would permit an examination of children's ability to set up priorities and sequence activities considering both the availability of resources (e.g., help from parents) and time constraints.

In looking at utilization of study time under a wider range of task conditions, we would suggest that both metacognitive and motivational factors would be important in accounting for individual differences in allocation of time for studying. We have indicated previously that the effect of motivational variables on children's use of study time may not be easily observed in usual experimental situations where studying is done immediately following the experimenter's instructions in a room where distractions are minimized. Motivational concepts have been used to explain the choices that people make in the presence of alternative activities and people's persistence in the selected activities over a period of time (e.g., Bandura, 1986). Therefore, in those situations described in the preceding paragraph where, for example, children can make a choice between studying and other activities, in addition to metacognitive knowledge of how study time should be allocated, motivational factors such as a belief that one's actions will produce valued outcomes would also be important.

Throughout this chapter, we have been discussing how children utilize their time for studying. We recognize that the study activities performed by children during the time they spend studying are important determinants of learning. It has been our aim in this chapter, however, to discuss some aspects of what children must be capable of in order to allocate time for studying in an effective manner. Underlying our manner of approaching this topic is our view that effective allocation of time for studying does not mean simply that more time should be spent studying, but rather that the amount of time spent studying should vary in accordance with such factors as the goals for the task, the ability and knowledge state of the learner, and study strategies. Skills to manage effectively an important resource such as time would surely be useful throughout life.

ACKNOWLEDGMENTS

Preparation of this chapter was facilitated by a Doctoral Fellowship awarded to the first author by the Social Sciences and Humanities Research Council of Canada (SSHRC) and by a SSHRC grant (No. 410-87-0328) to the second author.

REFERENCES

Anderson, T.H. (1980). Study strategies and adjunct aids. In R.J. Spiro, B.C. Bruce, & W.F. Brewer (Eds.), *Theoretical issues in reading comprehension* (pp. 483–502). Hillsdale, NJ: Erlbaum & Associates.

Bandura, A. (1986). *Social foundations of thought and action: A social cognitive theory.* Englewood Cliffs, NJ: Prentice-Hall.

Bender, P.S. (1983). *Resource management: An alternative view of the management process.* New York: John Wiley & Sons.

Bisanz, G.L., Vesonder, G.T., & Voss, J.F. (1978). Knowledge of one's own responding and the relation of such knowledge to learning: A developmental study. *Journal of Experimental Child Psychology, 25,* 116–128.

Bloom, B.S. (1974). Time and learning. *American Psychologist, 29,* 682–688.

Brown, A.L. (1978). Knowing when, where, and how to remember: A problem of metacognition. In R. Glaser (Ed.), *Advances in instructional psychology,* Vol. I (pp. 77–165) Hillsdale, NJ: Erlbaum & Associates.

Brown, A.L., Bransford, J.D., Ferrara, R.A., & Campione, J.C. (1983). Learning, remembering and understanding. In J.H. Flavell & E.M. Markman (Eds.), P.H.

Mussen (Series Ed.), *Handbook of child psychology* 4th ed. *Cognitive development*, Vol. 3 (pp. 77–166). New York: John Wiley & Sons.

Brown, A.L., Campione, J.C., & Barclay, C.R. (1979). Training self-checking routines for estimating test readiness: Generalizing from list learning to prose recall. *Child Development, 50*, 501–512.

Brown, A.L., & Smiley, S.S. (1977). Rating the importance of structural units of prose passages: A problem of metacognitive development. *Child Development, 48*, 1–8.

Brown, A.L., & Smiley, S.S. (1978). The development of strategies for studying texts. *Child Development, 49*, 1076–1088.

Carroll, J.B. (1963). A model of school learning. *Teachers College Record, 64*, 723–733.

Dufresne, A., & Kobasigawa, A. (in press). Children's spontaneous allocation of study time: differential and sufficient aspects. *Journal of Experimental Child Psychology.*

Dufresne, A., & Kobasigawa, A. (1987). [Allocating study time: How to distribute study time and how to terminate studying]. Unpublished raw data.

Dufresne, A., & Kobasigawa, A. (1988). Developmental differences in children's spontaneous allocation of study time. *Journal of Genetic Psychology, 149*, 87–92.

Dweck, C.S., Davidson, W., Nelson, S., & Enna, B. (1978). Sex differences in learned helplessness: II. The contingencies of evaluative feedback in the classroom. III. An experimental analysis. *Developmental Psychology, 14*, 268–276.

Dweck, C.S., & Elliott, E.S. (1983). Achievement motivation. In E.M. Hetherington (Ed.), *Handbook of child psychology: Socialization, personality, and social development*, Vol. 4 (pp. 643–691. New York: John Wiley & Sons.

D'Ydewalle, G., Swerts, A., & De Corte, E. (1983). Study time and test performance as a function of test expectations. *Contemporary Educational Psychology, 8*, 55–67.

Fisher, C.W., & Berliner, D.C. (Eds.). (1985). *Perspectives on instructional time.* New York: Longman.

Flavell, J.H. (1977). *Cognitive Development.* Englewood Cliffs, NJ: Prentice-Hall.

Flavell, J.H. (1979). Metacognition and cognitive monitoring: A new area of cognitive-developmental inquiry. *American Psychologist, 34*, 906–911.

Flavell, J.H., Friedrichs, A.G., & Hoyt, J.D. (1970). Developmental changes in memorization processes. *Cognitive Psychology, 1*, 324–340.

Gettinger, M. (1984). Achievement as a function of time spent in learning and time needed to learn. *American Educational Research Journal, 21*, 617–628.

Gettinger, M. (1985). Time allocated and time spent relative to time needed for learning as determinants of achievement. *Journal of Educational Psychology, 77*, 3–11.

Ghatala, E.S., Foorman, B.R., Levin, J.R., & Pressley, M. (in press). Improving children's regulation of their reading PREP time. *Contemporary Educational Psychology.*

Hunter-Blanks, P., Ghatala, E.S., Pressley, M., & Levin, J.R. (1988) A comparison of monitoring during study and during testing on a sentence-learning task. *Journal of Educational Psychology, 80*, 279–283.

Kobasigawa, A., Chouinard, M.A., & Dufresne, A. (1988). Characteristics of study-notes prepared by elementary school children: Relevancy and efficiency. *Alberta Journal of Educational Research, 34*, 18–29.

Kreutzer, M.A., Leonard, C., & Flavell, J.H. (1975). An interview study of children's knowledge about memory. *Monographs of the Society for Research in Child Development, 40* (1, Serial No. 150).

Leal, L., Crays, N., & Moely, B.E. (1985). Training children to use a self-monitoring study strategy in preparation for recall: Maintenance and generalization effects. *Child Development, 56*, 643–653.

Maehr, M. (1983). On doing well in science: Why Johnny no longer excels; why Sarah never did. In S. Paris, G. Olson, & H.W. Stevenson (Eds.), *Learning and motivation in the classroom* (pp. 179–210). Hillsdale, NJ: Erlbaum & Associates.

Masur, E.F., McIntyre, C.W., & Flavell, J.H. (1973). Developmental changes in apportionment of study time among items in a multitrial free recall task. *Journal of Experimental Child Psychology, 15,* 237–246.

Miller, P.H., Haynes, V.F., DeMarie-Dreblow, D., & Woody-Ramsey, J. (1986). Children's strategies for gathering information in three tasks. *Child Development, 57,* 1429–1439.

Miller, P.H., & Weiss, M.G. (1981). Children's attention allocation, understanding of attention, and performance on the incidental learning task. *Child Development, 52,* 1183–1190.

Morgan, M. (1985). Self-monitoring of attained subgoals in private study. *Journal of Educational Psychology, 77,* 623–630.

Neimark, E., Slotnick, N.S., & Ulrich, T. (1971). Development of memorization strategies. *Developmental Psychology, 5,* 472–432.

Oerter, R. (1981). Cognitive socialization during adolescence. *International Journal of Behavioral Development, 4,* 61–76.

Owings, P.A., Petersen, G.A., Bransford, J.D., Morris, C.D., & Stein, B.S. (1980). Spontaneous monitoring and regulation of learning: A comparison of successful and less successful fifth graders. *Journal of Educational Psychology, 72,* 250–256.

Pressley, M., Goodchild, F., Fleet, J., Zajchowski, R., & Evans, E.D. (1989). The challenges of classroom strategy instruction. *Elementary School Journal, 89,* 301–342.

Pressley, M., Levin, J.R., Ghatala, E.S., & Ahmad, M. (1987). Test monitoring in young grade school children. *Journal of Experimental Child Psychology, 43,* 96–111.

Pressley, M., Snyder, B.L., Levin, J.R., Murray, H.G., & Ghatala, E.S. (1987). Perceived readiness for examination performance (PREP) produced by initial reading of text and text containing adjunct questions. *Reading Research Quarterly, 22,* 219–236.

Rohwer, W.M. (1984). An invitation to an educational psychology of studying. *Educational Psychologist, 19,* 1–14.

Schunk, D.H. (1984). Self-efficacy perspective on achievement behavior. *Educational Psychologist, 19,* 848–857.

Stallings, J. (1980). Allocated academic learning time revisited, or beyond time on task. *Educational Researcher, 9,* 11–16.

4
Informal Instruction and Development of Cognitive Skills: A Review and Critique of Research

JEANNE D. DAY, LUIS A. CORDON,
AND MARY LOUISE KERWIN

Children grow up surrounded by other people. These people tell children things, sharing thoughts, feelings, knowledge, and attitudes; they help children accomplish tasks, completing parts children cannot; and they tend to offer less assistance as children become able to do more on their own. Children are also exposed, however, to people who do not share their knowledge and skills (or do so poorly), do not help children attempt new tasks, and/or do not encourage independent performance. Somehow, amid these myriad interactions, children learn and develop new skills. Two tempting hypotheses are that: (a) children develop because of the formal and informal instruction they receive and (b) those who receive better, more supportive instruction, have superior developmental outcomes. In this chapter we examine both hypotheses, and are forced to conclude that the causal links between informal instruction and cognitive development have not been established empirically. Rather than entertain the rival hypothesis that social interactions and cognitive development are parallel processes without cause-effect relations, we suggest conceptual and methodological refinements that may enable researchers to document how informal instructional interactions and cognitive development are related.

Our concern in this chapter is not with the methods used in formal education, but rather with the strategies employed by adults and more capable peers in informal instructional interactions with children. Often, however, formal cognitive intervention programs are based on the type of teaching thought to occur informally (e.g., Gelzheiser, 1984; Palincsar & Brown, 1984; Schumaker, Deshler, & Ellis, 1986). To the extent that the effectiveness of informal instruction is unexamined, the foundations of some formal interventions can be questioned. Thus, some of our discussion is relevant to both formal and informal instructional interactions.

Vygotsky's (1978) theory of cognitive development provides a framework for thinking about the role of social interaction in cognitive development and is often cited as the rationale behind research on informal instructional interactions. We therefore begin with an overview of this theory and its relationship to the processes of informal instruction, especially those described by

Wood, Bruner, & Ross (1976). After a brief review of some empirical literature on the tutorial process, we argue that to search for an ideal teaching method may be overly simplistic and we present evidence that suggests that learners may benefit from a variety of teaching styles. Finally, in light of the extant research literature, methodological considerations are suggested that might improve the quality and applicability of future research.

Informal Instruction: Vygotsky's Theory and Scaffolding

Vygotsky (1978) argued that all higher psychological functions (e.g., perception, voluntary attention, intentional memory) have social origins. Specifically, he claimed that adults and more capable peers mediate the child's experiences. They organize the environment (e.g., by making some objects available and others not), interpret and give meaning to events, and direct attention to relevant dimensions of experience. They also provide ways to cope with information, showing children, for example, how to categorize, memorize, retrieve, integrate, and talk about their experiences. In these ways, adults not only tell children about their world, they also show children ways to think about that information. Thus, knowledge *and* cognitive processes are socially transmitted.

Individuals in a mediating role provide an indirect link between stimuli and children's responses, and they supply the tools for problem solving that children eventually internalize. These socially provided tools, once internalized, continue to serve mediating function and form the basis of children's independent thought. Thus, the knowledge and cognitive processes to which the child is exposed become, through internalization, his or her own. One implication of a theory such as Vygotsky's is that the child's eventual cognitive status is determined by the power and breadth of the knowledge and strategies to which he or she has been exposed.

An important aspect of Vygotskian theory is that children can often complete tasks when working with other people that they could not accomplish working independently. Vygotsky suggested that those abilities children demonstrate when given assistance are in the process of becoming internalized. These abilities are not yet mature; they are maturing. The distance between what the child can do working alone and what he or she can accomplish with aid was labeled "the zone of proximal development." Vygotsky hypothesized that measurement of the "zone" might provide excellent predictive information about the child's performance in the near future (Brown & French, 1979; Day, 1983; Luria, 1928, 1961; Vygotsky, 1929, 1978; Wozniak, 1975).

If, as Vygotsky suggested, higher psychological functions have social origins, adults (e.g., parents, teachers) and more capable peers (e.g., older siblings, friends) should engage in certain behaviors as they work with children to solve problems. First, adults and more capable peers should express the knowledge and cognitive strategies involved in problem solution. This externalization of skills could take several forms: for instance, telling the child what needs to be done, stepping the child through the problem, modeling appropriate strategies, and/or modeling while simultaneously explaining (see Duffy & Roehler, this volume, chap. 6). Thus, we should be able to identify how the "expert" thinks a problem should be solved. Second, the expert should help the child by reducing the cognitive "workload," taking responsibility for some parts of the task while allowing the child to concentrate on other components. The adult should do those parts of the task that the child cannot while allowing the child to participate as fully as possible. Adults thereby structure the task and the child's participation to permit the child to employ his or her fragile skills successfully. This exercise of skills within the zone of proximal development facilitates their internalization. In addition, such teaching/learning interactions may provide opportunities for the more expert to demonstrate skills that lie outside the learner's current zone of proximal development, but which will, in time, become skills the learner can practice. Third, because the eventual goal of instruction is for the child to be able to act independently, adults and more capable peers should take on less of the workload as children demonstrate increasing competence. They should, over time, transfer control of the task to the child. This ceding of control encourages the child to complete more of the task on his or her own.

Wood et al. (1976) also have described the tutoring process as involving modeling of correct solution strategies, simplifying task demands to allow the child to use his or her nascent skills, and intervening less as the child develops expertise. They have suggested that tutors provide a scaffold that

enables a child or novice to solve a problem, carry out a task or achieve a goal which would be beyond his unassisted efforts. This scaffolding consists essentially of the adult "controlling" those elements of the task that are initially beyond the learner's capacity, thus permitting him to concentrate upon and complete only those elements that are within his range of competence. (p. 90)

Wood et al. (1976) identified six functions of the tutor: (a) to recruit the child into working on the task; (b) to reduce the number of constituent acts required to solve the task so that the learner can complete the components that he or she can manage; (c) to maintain the learner's interest and motivation; (d) to mark relevant features of the task, interpreting discrepancies between the child's productions and correct solutions; (e) to control the level of frustration experienced by the learner; and (f) to demonstrate or model solutions to the task. Some of these ideas (particularly functions b and f) obviously correspond with Vygotsky's (1978). In addition, Wood et al. (1976) warn of a potential danger of creating too much dependence on the tutor and they observe that the tutorial function "withers away" as the child develops competence. Finally, they argue that scaffolding "can potentially achieve much more for the learner than an assisted completion of the task. It may result, eventually, in development of task competence by the learner at a pace that would far outstrip his unassisted efforts" (p. 90). Scaffolded instruction, therefore, is one means of enhancing a child's skills.

Empirical Studies of the Tutoring Process

Researchers have attempted to verify that people do, indeed, teach children as Vygotsky and Wood et al. (1976) suggested. Typically, an observational methodology is used; behaviors are recorded as an adult tries to help a child solve some problem (e.g., prepare for a memory test, complete a puzzle). Mothers and their preschool children are usually the subjects (e.g., McGillicuddy-DeLisi, 1982, 1985; McGillicuddy-DeLisi, DeLisi, Flaugher, & Sigel, 1987; McGillicuddy-DeLisi, Sigel, & Johnson, 1979; Sigel, 1982) although occasionally fathers (e.g., Barton & Ericksen, 1981; Frankel & Rollins, 1983), older siblings (Cicirelli, 1967, 1972, 1973, 1976), or other adults (e.g., Childs & Greenfield, 1980; Wood et al., 1976) are asked to teach and sometimes school-age children are taught (e.g., Rogoff, Ellis, & Gardner, 1984). These observational studies tend to take two general forms. One is to provide an ethnographic interpretation of an ongoing instructional interaction (e.g., Cazden, 1981; Cazden, Cox, Dickinson, Steinberg, & Stone, 1979; Gardner & Rogoff, 1982; McNamee, 1979; Mehan, 1979). The other is to examine how the frequencies of general classes of instructional behavior (e.g., number of directives or questions) change with children's age or experience. Most of this work has been cross-sectional (e.g., Childs & Greenfield, 1980; Greenfield, 1984; Wertsch, 1979; Wertsch, McNamee, Budwig, & McLane, 1980), although a few longitudinal studies have been published recently (e.g., Adams, 1987; Adams, Sartore, & Bullock, 1988; Heckhausen, 1987; Hodapp, Goldfield, & Boyatzis, 1984; Rogoff, Malkin, & Gilbride, 1984).

The data obtained from studies of instructional interactions are, as with most observations of human interaction, rich, complex, complicated, and difficult to summarize and/or quantify. Determination of what behaviors to code is problematic, especially since the meaning of a particular behavior can vary with the context. In addition, it is difficult to develop a coding scheme that is both sufficiently fine-grained to capture the nuances of human interaction and can be used reliably, and that produces large enough frequencies in each category to allow meaningful statistical analyses. These problems are exacerbated when the looked-for behaviors are subtle ones such as "providing a scaffold for children to practice nascent skills," and "reducing support as children develop competence." How are we to determine, for instance, that an adult provided just enough and not too much assistance? How are we to know that the child is practicing nascent skills and not ones that have already been internalized? How can we show that the adult ceded control quickly enough? Nevertheless, researchers have sought evidence for the tutorial processes described by Vygotsky (1978) and Wood et al. (1976). We review evidence for three of these processes, the externalization of cognitive skills, reductions in cognitive workload, and ceding of control to the learner, now.

EXTERNALIZATION OF SKILLS

The claim that adults and peers can externalize cognitive skills is perhaps the least controversial as it is the most easily observed. As a matter of course, children are shown and told how to do certain things. Adults teach children to wave bye-bye, to count, to say the alphabet, to tie their shoes, etc. Even young children (e.g., four-year-olds) externalize certain problem-solving skills when asked to tutor younger children, employing various techniques (e.g., physical demonstration, provision of assistance, and verbal explanation) to do so (e.g., Koester & Bueche, 1980). Adults can express some rather sophisticated strategies. For example, Gardner and Rogoff (1982) described how a mother assisted her eight-year-old son to prepare for a memory test. The child's task was to remember the organization of 18 household items so that he could arrange them in a predetermined order on six shelves in a simulated kitchen. The mother assisted the child by classifying the items, talking aloud about her thoughts, modeling a rehearsal strategy, and providing metamemorial information relevant to the task. Thus, the mother externalized strategies that made success more likely for her child.

REDUCTIONS IN WORKLOAD

That adults reduce the cognitive workload for children to allow them to practice their nascent skills has also been documented. DeLoache (1984), observed mothers and their 12-, 15-, and 18-month-old children read a picture book together. She found that if a mother believed that her child knew the name of an object, she would ask the child to give its label. If the mother thought the word was one the child did not know she was more likely to provide the label herself or to skip the picture altogether. Adults and more competent peers are more likely to provide support for especially young and/or inexperienced learners or for tasks which they consider difficult. Ludeke and Hartup (1983) noted that 9- and 11-year-olds used more repetitions and provided more direct assistance to younger (7-year-old) than older (9- or 11-year-old) tutees. Similarly, Greenfield (1984) described girls learning to weave in Zinacantan and reported that intervention was scaled to the needs of the learner; expert weavers were less likely to intervene on easy parts of weaving and with more experienced learners. Greenfield (1984; Childs & Greenfield, 1980) also found that expert weavers took over the weaving at technically difficult parts of the process, allowing the learner to complete a piece of woven cloth and permitting her to observe the more experienced weaver modeling the requisite skills.

Some of the clearest support for reductions in cognitive workload, however, comes from the numerous examples of adults becoming increasingly directive and/or explicit when children fail to respond correctly. For instance, Greenfield (1984; Reilly, Zukow, & Greenfield, 1978; Zukow, Reilly, & Greenfield, 1982) reported that mothers create additional scaffolding if their children fail to acknowledge an offer. If her child did not respond to a verbal offer of a banana, for example, the mother might tap on the table to direct the child's attention toward the banana or she might pick it up and extend it toward the child. Similarly, McNamee (1979) described a kindergarten teacher's efforts to get a five-year-old child, Karen, to retell a story. The teacher began by making a general request (e.g., "Tell me the story . . ."), which failed to elicit much of a response from Karen. The teacher then asked more specific questions (e.g., "What could the first Chinese brother do?" "Remember he went fishing?") which enabled Karen to start recounting the story. When Karen was unable to continue retelling the story, the teacher first prompted by asking a general question; *if* that was unsuccessful she followed it with a more specific question that demanded less "work" on Karen's part. The teacher thereby reduced the cognitive workload for Karen sufficiently to allow her to continue. Thus, across a variety of tasks (e.g., picture book reading, language learning, story retelling, and weaving, among others) adults have been found to arrange tasks so that children can employ their fragile skills successfully.

CEDING CONTROL TO THE LEARNER

Finally, evidence has also accumulated for the claim that adults take on less of the workload as children demonstrate increasing competence. Wertsch et al. (1980) observed mothers helping their 2-1/2-, 3-1/2-, or 4-1/2-year-old children complete a jigsaw puzzle. Mothers of the youngest children were more likely to direct the child's attention to the model and to intervene between the child's gaze at the model and the correct insertion of a puzzle piece. The proportions of other-regulated gazes at the model and of intervention between other-regulated gazes and correct placement of a puzzle piece declined across age. As children got older, therefore, mothers less frequently directed appropriate puzzle-solving behavior (looking at the model) and were less likely to intervene to make certain that information from the model was used appropriately. Like the mothers in Wertsch's studies (1979; Wertsch et al., 1980), the expert weavers observed by Childs and Greenfield (1980) were found to decrease their level of intervention as the learners' competence increased. Beginners received many commands, a very direct form of verbal aid, whereas learners who had woven two or more articles were more likely to be guided by statements. Similarly, the frequency of multimodal instruction (verbal and nonverbal combined) declined and the percentage of purely verbal messages increased as learners acquired more experience.

Wertsch's (1979; Wertsch et al., 1980) and Childs and Greenfield's (1980) data indicate that older or more advanced learners receive less assistance than younger or less experienced learners. However, because these studies are cross-sectional they only indirectly support the claim that tutors cede control of a task to a learner as his or her competence increases. Kerwin, Day, and Maxwell (in preparation), therefore, studied how mothers' involvement in problem solving changed over the course of a single (1-1/2-hour) instructional session. Thirty-three mothers were observed as they taught their 8- to 13-year-old children how to solve balance scale problems. (Mothers were given a written description of balance scales and an explanation of how to compute moments to solve balance scale problems before they began teaching.) The entire instructional interaction was videotaped and divided into episodes which were identified by any change in the arrangement of weights on the balance scale. Two measures of maternal involvement were then scored for each episode (i.e., problem): (a) the proportion of words spoken by the mother and (b) the completeness of her explanation as evaluated by how many of a possible 12 points about the balance scale and associated strategy she mentioned. If all mothers had presented the same number of problems (episodes) to their children, we could have compared directly how mothers' involvement changed from the first to the last problem. However, because the number of episodes varied across mothers, we needed to create a summary statistic that could describe any linear trends in the two dependent measures across time and which would be independent of number of episodes. For each mother, therefore, we regressed each of the two dependent measures (proportion of words and completeness of explanation) onto the number of episodes that mother employed. The unstandardized regression coefficients (one for proportion of words and one for the completeness of explanation) for each mother were then used in subsequent analyses to determine whether there was a linear change in mothers' involvement. The linear trends for both proportion of words and completeness of explanation were described by a negative slope and both mean trends (averaged over subjects) were significantly different from zero. Thus, mothers talked less and their explanations became less complete as the instructional interaction progressed. Concomitantly, their children talked more, and gave more complete explanations for the operation of the balance scale (on the same 12-point scale used to rate mothers) as the interaction progressed.

Is There an "Ideal" Tutoring Process?

Although considerable evidence has accumulated to indicate that tutors model cognitive processes, assist children as they practice fragile skills, and cede responsibility for more aspects of the task to children as their competence increases, several issues remain unresolved. The two issues that we see as most critical are that studies have demonstrated neither an improvement in children's skills as a consequence of scaffolding nor the superiority of scaffolding over other methods of instruction. Vygotsky (1978) and Wood et al. (1976) suggest that "good" instruction will enable the child to complete tasks on his or her own that were not possible before instruction. However, most investigations do not indicate whether children's competencies actually do improve as a function of tutoring. Reliance on cross-sectional data obscures the problem. Older, more experienced children perform better on many tasks, but whether that improvement is due to scaffolding or some other factor (e.g., rote learning, practice, or maturation) is an open question. What is needed are studies that include pre- and posttest comparisons of learners' abilities. At the very least, these studies could document that children's skills improved after they received scaffolded instruction. In addition to demonstrating that scaffolding "works" (that is, it leads to improvements in cognitive skill), we need evidence that the "ideal" pattern is somehow superior to other forms of instruction. To properly investigate this hypothesis, studies must include different styles of tutoring and compare and contrast their consequences. To our knowledge only one such study has been conducted (Wood, Wood, & Middleton, 1978). We will return to their results later.

Our data lead us to wonder whether the types of teaching/learning interactions described by Vygotsky (1978) and Wood et al. (1976) are predictive of the learner's acquisitions and whether they are better than other techniques. The Kerwin et al. study (in preparation) described earlier included pretest, posttest, and transfer assessments. Mothers and children took pretests on a 4-peg balance scale and posttests on the 4-peg scale, a 10-peg scale, a 10-peg scale with pans, and a teeter-totter. We were, therefore, able to determine whether mothers' instruction resulted in improvements in their children's understanding of balance scale tasks. Indeed, we found that most mothers were effective teachers. Not only did their children's performance improve from pretest to posttest, but most children also showed some spontaneous transfer. Specifically, although mothers scored reliably higher than their children on both pretest and posttest, both mothers and children showed significant improvement from pretest to posttest. Although no mothers were at Siegler's (1976) Rule IV on the pretest, 85% were on the posttest. Similarly, no children were at Siegler's Rule IV on the pretest whereas 50% were on the posttest. Only six children failed to improve at all; one of the six actually regressed to lower levels of rule use. Most mothers and children also generalized the strategy. Again, mothers scored significantly higher than their children on both pretest and transfer tests. However, both mothers and children performed reliably better on the generalization tasks than they had on the pretest, although their performance began to decline as the generalization task became less like the training task.

Clearly, then, most mothers managed to improve their children's understanding of balance scales. However, the question remains whether children's gains were related to the mothers' teaching styles. That is, were mothers who taught in an "ideal" pattern (i.e., intense involvement early during the interaction followed by a linear decrease in involvement), more successful teachers? Did their children score highest on the posttest and transfer tests? Multiple regression models were employed to answer these questions. The linear trends of both maternal teaching variables (proportion of words per episode and completeness of explanation per episode) and the child's standard scores on the Vocabulary and Block Design subtests of the WISC-R were the predictor variables. Children's postinstructional performance, summarized as the sum of their z-scores on posttest and the three transfer tasks, was the dependent variable. The multiple regression equation was not significant ($R^2 = 0.19$, adjusted $R^2 = 0.08$); none of the predictor variables was significantly related to the children's posttest performance. Apparently, mothers' teaching style, whether or not it followed an ideal pattern, was not significantly related to children's postinstructional performance—at least not for these mothers on this task.

Results from a small pilot study increase our suspicion that the cognitive consequences of various teaching styles are less clear cut than some would have us believe. We asked fathers to teach their 9- to 12-year-old children how to solve balance scale tasks. As in the Kerwin et al. (in preparation) study, fathers received written instructions about the operation of the balance scale and how to compute moments before they taught their children. In addition, children's understanding of the scale was assessed before and after instruction and their ability to transfer the trained strategy was evaluated. Like mothers, fathers were very effective teachers; all of the children learned and transferred the strategy. However, we could detect no consistencies across fathers that might account for their success. Fathers' teaching was extremely varied, even controlling for children's initial competence (e.g., by looking only at those children who were at Siegler's (1976) Rule II at pretest and at Rule IV at posttest). The amount of time spent teaching varied across fathers from 4 to 43 minutes; the number of problems presented ranged from 6 to 41; the proportion of words spoken by fathers in the first episode varied from 0.89 to 0.99 and from 0.50 to 0.85 in the last episode; the completeness of explanations provided by the fathers (rated on a 12-point scale) in the first and last episodes were also highly variable, ranging from 0 to 6 and 0 to 5, respectively. And, although one father seemed to decrease his involvement in a linear fashion, the rest did not. Our informal observations of the interactions were that even fathers who appeared insensitive to their children's understanding of the scale succeeded in teaching the strategy. Thus, we are left with the distinct impression that there exists more than one way to enhance children's skills and that claims from the superiority of one method of teaching over another are premature.

Although our data lead us to doubt that one instructional style is necessarily better than all others we recognize that we have not proved our case. The major problem is our reliance on observational data. We might be poor observers of human behavior, overlooking critical dimensions of teaching that determine cognitive outcomes. Alternatively, mothers and fathers might be highly variable in their teaching because they are responding to their children's idiosyncrasies. The variability we observe across parents might actually be indicative of an underlying consistency (e.g., instruction contingent on their children's needs) or it might be symptomatic of some more general and not identified underlying factor. The relative effectiveness of different styles of instruction is, therefore, best evaluated through experimental rather than observational research. Clearly defined instructional manipulations allow dimensions of teaching to be studied systematically and random assignment of children to these different instructional conditions helps to disentangle questions about the direction of causality.

The experimental manipulation of teaching strategies thought to be characteristic of different parents was attempted by Wood et al. (1978). An instructor (i.e., not the child's parent) was trained in four teaching styles: contingent, verbal, swing, and demonstration. Contingent instruction was closest to the "ideal" pattern described by Vygotsky (1978) and Wood et al. (1976). Contingent instruction involved presenting the child with problems, setting goals, and making requests that lay beyond the child's current ability level but not so far beyond that he or she was unable to comprehend. If the child succeeded in following an instruction, the instructor offered less assistance on the next attempt; if the child failed, the instructor provided more assistance. Verbal instruction, as its name implies, involved extensive use of verbal prompts. Because these verbalizations were not augmented by demonstration, they often failed to make the task requirements sufficiently concrete to enable the child to understand the underlying structure or logic of the task. The swing strategy is a strategy of extremes. If the child failed to respond to a general verbal prompt from the instructor, the child was immediately shown what to do, after which he or she received another general verbal prompt. Finally, demonstration involved the instructor showing the child what to do without explaining verbally her actions. These four teaching styles were employed with three- to five-year-old children as they tried to solve a difficult block-construction task. Children's postinstructional skill at putting the blocks together (both with and without assistance) provided measures of the effectiveness of each intervention.

Not surprisingly, children taught with the contingent strategy were better able to correctly assemble more pieces of the model than children taught with other strategies. They were also more efficient in their constructions; that is, they required fewer attempts to be successful. Thus, the superiority of contingent instruction seems clear. However, as Wood et al. (1978) reported, children in the contingent group were not more autonomous than children in other groups. They were as likely as other children to require assistance (as defined by asking for help, attempting to leave the situation, or displaying obvious frustration). In addition, although the three noncontingent groups performed less well on the average than the contingent one, Wood et al. (1978) reported that within each group, one child performed as well as or even better than some children in the contingent group. As Wood et al. (1978) cautioned, the data did not support overgeneralizations about ideal teaching strategies. "Ideal" teaching might be good for most children, but some children may do well with other strategies. Thus, the meager experimental data are also ambiguous with respect to whether scaffolding is necessary or a superior method of enhancing children's skills.

Is Variability the Ideal?

Tutorial processes such as those described by Vygotsky (1978) and Wood et al. (1976) have considerable face validity and yet the benefits associated with them are not always evident. Perhaps our conceptualization of the tutoring process and the search for an "ideal" method has been overly simplistic. Humans are diverse; inter- and intraindividual differences are substantial. The teaching style that works for one child on one task might not work for that same child on a different task or for a second child on any task. Similarly, a teacher who can express cognitive skills on one task, guide the child's use of those skills, and sensitively relinquish control to the child may not be able (or may not care) to engage in those processes on another task or with a different child. Good teaching may vary not only with students and teachers but also across tasks. Rote memorization or blind imitation may be the best methods for learning some tasks. Attempts to teach those tasks through scaffolded interactions might be inefficient, actually retarding the acquisition of skill.

Even if an ideal instructional style does exist (which we doubt) the question arises whether children do, or should, receive such instruction consistently. That all adults and more capable peers would be able to teach in an ideal fashion seems unlikely. Furthermore, given the constraints on time and energy faced by parents and teachers, children may often have to make do with incomplete or even no instruction. Exposure to a variety of instructional styles may enable the child to learn more independently or at least to make the most of poor instruction when it is encountered.

If variability in instructional styles is the norm, as we believe, questions about how much variability is good and how much is detrimental arise as do questions about whether children require some minimum exposure to given styles to profit from them. Prolonged observations of adult-child interactions in everyday settings may be one way to address these questions. Tizard (Tizard, 1985; Tizard & Hughes, 1984; Tizard, Hughes, Carmichael, & Pinkerton, 1983a, 1983b; Tizard, Hughes, Pinkerton, & Carmichael, 1982), for example, audiotaped mothers and children as they engaged in their typical afternoon routines at home. These extended observations could provide data about baseline rates of different types of teaching as well as information about what skills parents normally teach. In laboratory settings or when observed for brief periods of time, adults and/or peers may elect to teach in ways congruent with what they believe investigators expect (e.g., Renshaw & Gardner, 1987). In addition, the variety of tasks which can be taught in brief periods of time in the laboratory is limited and the child's initiation of instructional interactions nonexistent. Therefore, observations over extended time periods in natural settings provide better data for determining if different teaching behaviors vary in frequency.

Methodological Suggestions for Future Research

The relationships between instruction and cognitive growth are complex, bidirectional, and nonstatic, making unambiguous findings in this area difficult to establish. Several methodological refinements, however, may strengthen and disambiguate some claims. First, the consequences, both cognitive and noncognitive, expected from various instructional methods have to be specified and evaluated accordingly. Second, the processes by which social interaction produces the observed changes must be stated clearly. Third, more attention should be directed to how characteristics of students affect both the outcomes and the instruction they receive. And fourth, although observational and correlational research in this area is important, it should be augmented with experimental methods as frequently as possible.

CONSEQUENCES OF INSTRUCTION

Social interaction may be essential for the development of some cognitive skills and irrelevant to others. Furthermore, some of the skills that develop only in social interaction might be more important and/or general than others. Based on the tasks researchers have employed and their discussions, one might conclude that categorization (Adams, 1987; Hess & McDevitt, 1984; Hess & Shipman, 1965, 1967; Rogoff et al., 1984), puzzle construction (Wood et al., 1976), computation of balance scale moments (Kerwin et al., in preparation), long-division (Petitto, 1983), peekaboo and roll the ball (Hodapp et al., 1984), weaving (Childs & Greenfield, 1980), tortilla-making (Rogoff, 1986), recall (DeLoache, 1984; McNamee, 1979), communicative competence (Bruner, 1981; Greenfield, 1984; Ninio & Bruner, 1978; Snow, 1979), event knowledge (Nelson, 1980; Nelson & Gruendel, 1981), memory strategies (Gardner & Rogoff, 1982), representational thought (McGillicuddy-DeLisi, 1982; Sigel, 1982), self-regulation (Wertsch, 1979; Wertsch et al., 1980), metacognition (Day, French, & Hall, 1985; Gardner & Rogoff, 1982), and executive processes (Gardner & Rogoff, 1982; Hartup, 1985) are at least some of the cognitive skills that are thought to be enhanced through social interaction. One might ask what skills do *not* develop socially. Clearly, a theory that differentiates those abilities that are thought to originate in social interaction from those that originate in individual activity is needed (Hartup,

1985). Moreover, a theory that identifies those skills that are dependent on social input for their complete manifestation is needed.

One way in which skills acquired through social interaction may differ from those acquired through solitary activity is in their range of applicability. The explanations that people can give each other for various activities as they work together may result in knowledge that is more coherently organized and better integrated with existing cognitive structures. For example, in our studies with the balance scale task, many parents began instruction by pointing out that the balance scale was like a teeter-totter—that smaller children had to sit further away from and bigger children closer to the middle for the two to be equal. By anchoring instruction in existing knowledge, parents may have increased the accessibility and generalizability of the trained skill. This improved "packaging" of knowledge may enable greater generalization of trained skills. Thus, evaluations of this instructional approach may be best obtained on generalization measures.

An example of the necessity of focusing on generalization is our work on peer interaction and cognitive development (Kerwin & Day, 1987). On the basis of a pretest, college students were diagnosed as using Siegler's Rule III or Rule IV to solve balance scale problems. Four types of groups were then formed: (a) students using Rule III were paired together; (b) students using Rule III were paired with students using Rule IV; (c) students using Rule III worked alone; and (d) students using Rule IV worked alone. Students were asked to figure out how the balance scale operated, talking aloud as they did so. All students at Rule III paired with students at Rule IV learned how to solve problems on a 4-peg balance scale and virtually all generalized the skill to a 10-peg scale, a 10-peg scale with pans, and a teeter-totter with a moveable fulcrum and different weight barrels (although performance did decline on the teeter-totter). A few of the Rule III students who had been paired together and few who had worked alone figured out how to solve problems on the 4-peg scale. Of those who were able to figure out how the 4-peg scale worked, some were able to generalize the skills to the 10-peg scale. However, their performance declined substantially as the transfer tasks became even less like the training task. Thus, not only was the acquisition of a skill (computation of moments) more likely to be learned in interaction with more capable peers but the skill was also more easily generalized.

Social interaction may also have important noncognitive consequences. The style of instruction may have little effect on whether a skill is acquired, but tremendous impact on how the child feels about that skill and on whether that skill is voluntarily implemented in the future. In other words, different instructional methods may have different affective, motivational and attributional consequences (see Short & Weissberg-Benchell, this volume, chap. 2, for implications for special population). The child taught a skill through contingent instruction(Wood et al., 1978) may experience more success and less stress and anxiety than a child taught that same skill through the swing (Wood et al., 1978) strategy. The contingent approach might, therefore, promote feelings of self-worth, trust in one's tutor, and willingness to engage in the skill in the future. The swing strategy, on the other hand, might promote independence (because the child learns to rely on him or herself) and a dislike for one's tutor. Similarly, the use of open-ended questions (Sigel, 1982) might convey to the child that his or her thoughts are valued whereas closed questions might promote anxiety because a right or wrong answer is implied. Just as children who observe peers modeling problem-solving strategies have higher feelings of self-efficacy than children who watch adult models (Schunk & Hanson, 1985; Schunk, Hanson, & Cox, 1987), children receiving various instructional styles may experience different affective consequences.

Identification of the cognitive and noncognitive skills believed to develop in social settings is the first step toward showing how social factors influence growth. A final suggestion for further investigations on the importance of social interaction in instruction is the administration of both pre- and post-tests to document whether the expected developments have occurred. Assessments also should be made of the child's ability to generalize the skills (both cognitive and affective). Finally, abilities that should not be affected by dialogue about a particular task should be assessed in order to help establish the boundaries of social interaction. In any event, thoughtful and rigorous study is essential if a better understanding of social influences on cognitive development is to emerge.

IDENTIFICATION OF UNDERLYING PROCESSES

In addition to identifying what develops, researchers need to specify how social interaction produces observed changes, that is, what behaviors in the ongoing dialogue are related to cognitive outcomes and why they have the effects they do. Sigel (1982), for instance, has argued that open-ended inquiries demand reflective activity from the respondent and so promote the development of mental representation. Observational methods may not be the most powerful means of supporting his hypothesis, but he has isolated what needs to be coded in a complex stream of behavior, enabling experimental evaluation of his claims. Similar analyses could be conducted on other aspects of instruction. Instruction is multidimensional, involving explanation, demonstration, question-asking, practice, testing, etc., and hypotheses about how these various components affect the acquisition of skills could be developed. For example, tutors who repeatedly and explicitly test their students' progress may make the goal of independent performance highly salient. Their students may quickly become test-wise—able to anticipate what information will be quizzed and to respond appropriately. Alternatively, tutors who provide numerous examples and counter-examples may enhance students' ability to generalize the trained skill.

Several benefits are associated with delineating how particular behaviors relate to specific outcomes. The decision about what behaviors to code in observational research or to manipulate in experimental work becomes much clearer if one can identify in advance what behaviors are thought to be most important. Similarly, decisions about what tasks to use and what types of pre- and posttests to administer become relatively straightforward. More important, however, is that the complexity of instructional effects on cognitive functioning can be preserved and studied. Correlations between parental teaching and global indicators of the child's abilities (e.g., IQ or school performance) would be of less concern than: (a) how different styles of instruction (e.g., explanation vs. demonstration) in fluence particular skills (e.g., learning how to compute moments), and (b) whether different skills (e.g., learning how to compute moments vs. memory strategies) are best acquired through certain styles of teaching (e.g., guided practice). Thus, inter- and intravariability in instruction and cognition would become the objects of research.

CHILD CHARACTERISTICS

In addition to specifying expected cognitive outcomes and how they are achieved, researchers must be concerned with how characteristics of the child affect both instructional processes and outcomes. Studies of how social interaction affects cognitive growth tend to focus on one side of a bidirectional process—what teachers do to help children learn. But instructional style and cognitive outcome are as dependent on the child as on the teacher. Children bring different interests and talents to an instructional session; they may be more predisposed to learn some skills than others; and their style (e.g., their willingness to ask questions, to contradict, introject, even to attend) has enormous impact on how teachers act. Variations in children's behaviors make conclusions about the direction of effect from teacher to child questionable (Bell, 1968, 1979). Children may cause tutors to teach as they do. Children may learn because of the questions they ask, the objections they raise, and their manipulation of task materials. Both sides of the relationship, from teacher to student and from student to teacher, have to be considered. In other words, child characteristics such as starting competence, talkativeness, inquisitiveness, etc., must be included in investigations of teaching/learning interactions.

CLARIFYING CAUSAL RELATIONSHIPS

Unfortunately (for researchers), student and tutor behaviors are interdependent. Students' behaviors affect how tutors teach, which influences how students act. Less able students may elicit less competent teaching, which assures them little advancement. More able students may demand better teaching and so learn more. Because of this interdependence of behaviors, the direction of causality is unclear—who is causing whom to behave how to what end? Studies in which parents or siblings are observed teaching younger members of their family provide correlational data about the relationship between informal instruction and child outcome. However, claims about causal relationships based on these studies are inappropriate; the interdependence of behaviors is already established. Structural equation modeling might, depending on one's perspective (e.g., Cohen, 1981; Ling, 1982), make stronger claims about causal relationships possible.

Although causal linkages are difficult to establish through observational research, such work is essential to understanding how parents and older peers teach children. In addition, observations can provide clues as to how good instruction proceeds and supply hypotheses which can be tested experimentally. However, even studies that manipulate the components thought to be related to successful instruction are unlikely to document absolutely the causal linkages between informal instruction and cognitive development. Informal instruction occurs over an extended time period during which its content (what is taught) and form (how teaching proceeds) probably change. These adjustments in instruction across time are confounded with changes in the person receiving instruction and the reasons for teaching. In addition, instruction is multifaceted and various components may complement or offset one another. These subtleties of instruction and difficult to manipulate experimentally while maintaining adequate controls (see Duffy & Roehler, this volume, chap. 6; Symons, Snyder, Cariglia-Bull, & Pressley, this volume chap. 1). Nevertheless, experimental research could augment observational research by supplying evidence about how limited aspects of instruction are related to various outcomes. Studies that control for child characteristics could strengthen causal claims about the influence of teaching style on child outcomes by removing some of the variables that could provide alternative explanations. Such research could make contact with an extensive instructional literature (e.g., Borkowski & Cavanaugh, 1979; Brown, Campione, & Barclay, 1979; Campione, Brown, & Ferrara, 1982; Pressley, Borkowski, & O'Sullivan, 1985; Pressley & Dennis-Rounds, 1980) as a source of hypotheses about the relationships between learner characteristics, task demands, evaluation criteria and teaching effectiveness. A more complete picture of the causal factors involved in teaching and learning might, therefore, emerge.

Summary and Conclusions

In summary, theoretical expectations about how adults and more capable peers promote cognitive functioning have been illustrated empirically. More advanced individuals can, as Vygotsky (1978) and Wood et al. (1976) suggest: (a) externalize knowledge and cognitive skills, (b) lessen the cognitive workload for learners, and (c) cede control to students as their competence develops. However, that people can teach in this manner, does not imply that they do so routinely. In addition, research has yet to document convincingly that children's cognitive functioning improves as a consequence of informal instruction or that the form of instruction described as ideal is superior to any other type of instruction. We argue that an ideal method of instruction may not exist and further, that variability in teaching style may be both normal and advantageous. Finally, we suggest that in the future researchers: (a) specify the cognitive and noncognitive consequences of instruction, (b) state the particular processes by which social interaction produces the observed changes, (c) identify how student characteristics affect both the outcomes and processes of instruction, and (d) utilize experimental methods to augment observational data as frequently as possible.

Future research may well show that children not only receive and learn from a variety of instructional methods but also that exposure to a number of teaching styles is actually beneficial because it prepares children to deal with the diversity that they will inevitably encounter. Such results would not preclude studying whether certain styles are better suited to particular skills, teachers, or learners. Nor would studies of the relationships between how children are taught at home and how they perform in school become irrelevant, although the focus would probably shift to questions about how much variability in home instruction is necessary and how much detrimental. If variability in teaching style is both normal and advantageous, research issues do become more complicated; however, they may also better reflect the complexities inherent in human development.

References

Adams, A.K. (1987). *Classifier as apprentice: The novice-expert shift in categorization of animal types.* Unpublished manuscript, University of Hawaii, Department of Psychology, Honolulu.

Adams, A.K., Sartore, P., & Bullock, D. (1988). *Language-games and linguistic tools: Context and typicality effects on lexical specificity in maternal speech to toddlers.* Unpublished manuscript, University of Hawaii, Department of Psychology, Honolulu.

Barton, K., & Eriksen, L.K. (1981). Differences between mothers and fathers in teaching style and child-rearing practices. *Psychological Reports, 49,* 237–238.

Bell, R.Q. (1968). A reinterpretation of effects in studies of socialization. *Psychological Review, 75,* 81–95.

Bell, R.Q. (1979). Parent, child, and reciprocal influences. *American Psychologist, 34,* 821–826.

Borkowski, J.G., & Cavanaugh, J.G. (1979). Maintenance and generalization of skills and strategies by the retarded. In N.R. Ellis (Ed.), *Handbook of mental deficiency: Psychological theory and research* (pp. 569–617). Hillsdale, NJ: Erlbaum & Associates.

Brown, A.L., Campione, J.C., & Barclay, C.R. (1979). Training self-checking routines for estimating test readiness: Generalization from list learning to prose recall. *Child Development, 50,* 501–512.

Brown, A.L., & French, L. (1979). The zone of proximal development: Implications for intelligence testing in the year 2000. *Intelligence, 3,* 253–271.

Bruner, J.S. (1981). The social context of language acquisition. *Language and Communication, 1,* 155–178.

Campione, J.C., Brown, A.L., & Ferrara, R.A. (1982). Mental retardation and intelligence. In R.J. Sternberg (Ed.), *Handbook of human intelligence,* (pp. 392–490). Cambridge, England: Cambridge University.

Cazden, C.B. (1981). Performance before competence: Assistance to child discourse in the zone of proximal development. *The Quarterly Newsletter of the Laboratory of Comparative Human Cognition, 3,* 5–8.

Cazden, C.B., Cox, M., Dickinson, D., Steinberg, Z., & Stone, C. (1979). "You all gonna hafta listen": Peer teaching in a primary classroom. In W.A. Collins (Ed.), *The Minnesota symposia on child psychology,* Vol. 12 (pp. 183–231). Hillsdale, NJ: Erlbaum & Associates.

Childs, C.P., & Greenfield, P.M. (1980). Informal modes of learning and teaching: The case of Zinacanteco weaving. In N. Warren (Ed.), *Studies in cross-cultural psychology,* Vol. 2 (pp. 269–316). London: Academic.

Cicirelli, V.G. (1967). Sibling configuration, creativity, IQ and academic achievement. *Child Development, 38,* 481–490.

Cicirelli, V.G. (1972). The effect of sibling relationships on concept learning of young children taught by child teachers. *Child Development, 43,* 282–287.

Cicirelli, V.G. (1973). Effects of sibling structure and interaction on children's categorization style. *Developmental Psychology, 9,* 132–139.

Cicirelli, V.G. (1976). Sibling interaction and cognitive development. In K.F. Rigel & J.A. Meacham (Eds.), *The developing individual in a changing world* Vol. 2. *Social and environmental issues* (pp.715–722). Chicago: Aldine.

Cohen, J. (1981). Primer in causal analysis. [Review of *Correlation and causality.*] *Contemporary Psychology, 26,* 15–16.

Day, J.D. (1983). The zone of proximal development. In M. Pressley & J. Levin (Eds.), *Cognitive strategy research* Vol. 1. *Psychological foundations* (pp. 155–175). New York: Springer-Verlag.

Day, J.D., French, L.C., & Hall, L.K. (1985). Social influences on cognitive development. In D.L. Forrest-Pressley, G.E. MacKinnon, & T.G. Waller (Eds.), *Metacognition, cognition, and human performance* Vol. 1. *Theoretical perspectives* (pp. 33–56). New York: Academic.

DeLoache, J.S. (1984). What's this? Maternal questions in joint picture book reading with toddlers. *Quarterly Newsletter of the Laboratory of Comparative Human Cognition, 6,* 87–95.

Frankel, M.T., & Rollins, H.A. (1983). Does mother know best? Mothers and fathers interacting with preschool sons and daughters. *Developmental Psychology, 19,* 694–702.

Gardner, W., & Rogoff, B. (1982). The role of instruction in memory development: Some methodological choices. *Quarterly Newsletter of the Laboratory of Comparative Human Cognition, 4,* 6–12.

Gelzheiser, L.M. (1984). Generalization from categorical memory tasks to prose by learning disabled adolescents. *Journal of Educational Psychology, 76,* 1128–1138.

Greenfield, P.M. (1984). A theory of the teacher in the learning activities of everyday life. In B. Rogoff & R. Lane (Eds.), *Everyday cognition* (pp. 117–138). Cambridge, MA: Harvard University Press.

Hartup, W.W. (1985). Relationships and their significance in cognitive development. In R.A. Hinde, A. Perret-Clermont, & J. Stevenson-Hinde (Eds.), *Social relationships and cognitive development* (pp. 66–82). New York: Oxford University Press.

Heckhausen, J. (1987). Balancing for weaknesses and challenging developmental potential: A longitudinal study of mother-infant dyads in apprenticeship interactions. *Developmental Psychology, 6,* 762–770.

Hess, R.D., & McDevitt, T.M. (1984). Some cognitive consequences of maternal intervention techniques: A longitudinal study. *Child Development, 55,* 2017–2030.

Hess, R.D., & Shipman, V.C. (1965). Early experience and the specialization of cognitive modes in children. *Child Development, 36,* 869–886.

Hess, R.D., & Shipman, V.C. (1967). Cognitive elements in maternal behavior. In J.P. Hill (Ed.), *Minnesota symposia on child psychology,* Vol. 1 (pp. 57–81). Minneapolis: University of Minnesota.

Hodapp, R.M., Goldfield, E.C., & Boyatzis, C.J. (1984). The use and effectiveness of maternal scaffolding in mother-infant games. *Child Development, 55,* 772–781.

Kerwin, M.L., & Day, J.D. (1987). *Advantages of joint over individual problem solving for independent performance on cognitive tasks.* Paper presented at the Society for Research in Child Development, Baltimore.

Kerwin, M.L., Day, J.D., & Maxwell, S. (in preparation). *Relation between maternal teaching and children's learning to solve balance scale tasks.* University of Notre Dame.

Koester, L.S., & Bueche, N.A. (1980). Preschoolers as teachers: Where children are seen but not heard, *Child Study Journal, 10,* 107–118.

Ling, R.F. (1982). [Review of *Correlation and causality.*] *Journal of the American Statistical Association, 77,* 489–491.

Ludeke, R.J., & Hartup, W.W. (1983). Teaching behaviors of 9- and 11-year-old girls in mixed-age and same-age dyads. *Journal of Educational Psychology, 75,* 909–914.

Luria, A.R. (1928). The problem of the cultural development of the child. *Journal of Genetic Psychology, 36,* 493–506.

Luria, A.R. (1961). An objective approach to the study of the abnormal child. *American Journal of Orthopsychiatry, 31,* 1–14.

McGillicuddy-DeLisi, A.V. (1982). The relationship between parents' beliefs about child development and family constellation, socioeconomic status, and parents' teaching strategies. In T.M. Laosa & I.E. Sigel (Eds.), *Families as learning environments for children* (pp. 261–299). New York: Plenum.

McGillicuddy-DeLisi, A.V. (1985). The relationship between parental beliefs and children's cognitive level. In I.E. Sigel (Ed.) *Parental belief systems: The psychological consequences for children* (pp. 7–24). Hillsdale, NJ: Erlbaum & Associates.

McGillicuddy-DeLisi, A.V., DeLisi, R., Flaugher, J., & Sigel, I.E. (1987). Familial influences on planning. In S.L. Friedman, E.K. Scholnick, & R.R. Cocking (Eds.), *Blueprints for thinking* (pp. 395–427). Cambridge, England: Cambridge University Press.

McGillicuddy-DeLisi, A.V., Sigel, I.E., & Johnson, J.E. (1979). The family as a system of mutual influences: Parental beliefs, distancing behaviors, and children's representational thinking. In M. Lewis & L. Rosenbaum (Eds.), *The child and its family* (pp. 91–106). New York: Plenum.

McNamee, G.D. (1979). The social interaction origins of narrative skills. *Quarterly Newsletter of the Laboratory of Comparative Human Cognition, 1,* 63–68.

Mehan, H. (1979). *Social organization in the classroom.* Cambridge, MA: Harvard University Press.

Nelson, K. (1980). *Characteristics of children's scripts for familiar events.* Paper presented at the annual meetings of the American Psychological Association, Montreal.

Nelson, K., & Gruendel, J.M. (1981). Generalized event representations: Basic building blocks of cognitive development. In M. Lamb & A.L. Brown (Eds.) *Advances in developmental psychology*, Vol. 1 (pp. 131–158).Hillsdale, NJ: Erlbaum & Associates.

Ninio, A., & Bruner, J.S. (1978). The achievement and antecedents of labelling. *Journal of Child Language*, 5, 1–15.

Palincsar, A.M., & Brown, A.L. (1984). Reciprocal teaching of comprehension-fostering and monitoring activities. *Cognition and Instruction*, 1, 117–175.

Petitto, A.L. (1983). *Long division of labor: In support of an interactive theory of learning.* Unpublished manuscript, University of Rochester, Rochester, NY.

Pressley, M. Borkowski, J.G., & O'Sullivan, J. (1985). Children's metamemory and the teaching of memory strategies. In D.L. Forrest-Pressley, G.E. MacKinnon, & T.G. Waller (Eds.) *Metacognition, cognition, and human performance.* Vol. 1 *Theoretical perspectives* (pp. 111–153). Orlando, FL: Academic Press.

Pressley, M., & Dennis-Rounds, J. (1980). Transfer of a mnemonic keyword strategy at two age levels. *Journal of Educational Psychology*, 72, 575–582.

Reilly, J., Zukow, P.G., & Greenfield, P.M. (1978). *Facilitating the transition from sensorimotor to linguistic communication.* Paper presented at International Congress of Child Language, Tokyo.

Renshaw, P.D., & Gardner, R. (1987). *Parental goals and strategies in teaching contexts: An exploration of "activity theory" with mothers and fathers of preschool children.* Paper presented at the Society for Research in Child Development, Baltimore.

Rogoff, B. (1986). Adult-assistance of children's learning. In T.E. Raphael (Ed.), *Contexts of school-based literacy* (pp. 27–40). New York: Random House.

Rogoff, B., Ellis, S., & Gardner, W. (1984). Adjustment of adult-child instruction according to child's age and task. *Developmental Psychology*, 20, 193–199.

Rogoff, B., Malkin, C., & Gilbride, K. (1984). Interaction with babies as guidance in development. In B. Rogoff, & J.V. Wertsch (Eds.), Children's learning in the "zone of proximal development." *New Directions for Child Development*, Vol. 23 (pp. 31–44). San Francisco: Jossey-Bass.

Schumaker, J.B., Deshler, D.D., & Ellis, E.S. (1986). Intervention issues related to the education of LD adolescents. In J.K. Torgesen & B.Y.L. Wong (Eds.) *Psychological and educational perspectives on learning disabilities* (pp. 329–365). Orlando, FL: Academic Press.

Schunk, D.H., & Hanson, A.R. (1985). Peer models: Influence on children's self-efficacy and achievement. *Journal of Educational Psychology*, 77, 313–322.

Schunk, D.H., Hanson, A.R., & Cox, P.D. (1987). Peer-model attributes and children's achievement behaviors. *Journal of Educational Psychology*, 79, 54–61.

Siegler, R. (1976). Three aspects of cognitive development. *Cognitive Psychology*, 4, 481–520.

Sigel, I.E. (1982). The relationship between parental distancing strategies and the child's cognitive behavior. In L. M. Laosa and I.E. Sigel (Eds.), *Families as learning environments for children* (pp. 47–86). New York: Plenum.

Snow, C.E. (1979). Conversations with children. In P. Fletcher & M. Garmon (Eds.), *Language acquisition* (pp. 69–89). New York: Cambridge University Press.

Tizard, B. (1985). Social relationships between adults and young children and their impact on intellectual functioning. In R.A. Hinde, A. Perret-Clermont, & J. Stevenson-Hinde (Eds.), *Social relationships and cognitive development* (pp. 116–130). New York: Oxford University Press.

Tizard, B., & Hughes, M. (1984). *Young children learning: Talking and thinking at home and at school*. London: Fontana.

Tizard, B., Hughes, M., Carmichael, H., & Pinkerton, G. (1983a). Children's questions and adults' answers. *Journal of Child Psychology and Psychiatry, 24*, 269–281.

Tizard, B., Hughes, M., Carmichael, H., & Pinkerton, G. (1983b). Language and social class: Is verbal deprivation a myth? *Journal of Child Psychology and Psychiatry, 24*, 533–542.

Tizard, B., Hughes, M., Pinkerton, G., & Carmichael, H. (1982). Adults' cognitive demands at home and at nursery school. *Journal of Child Psychology and Psychiatry, 23*, 105–116.

Vygotsky, L.S. (1929). The problem of the cultural development of the child. *Journal of Genetic Psychology, 36*, 415–434.

Vygotsky, L.S. (1978). *Mind in society: The development of higher psychological processes*. M. Cole, V. John-Steiner, S. Scribner & E. Souberman (Eds.), Cambridge, MA: Harvard University Press.

Wertsch, J.V. (1979). From social interaction to higher psychological processes: A clarification and application of Vygotsky's theory. *Human Development, 22*, 1–22.

Wertsch, J., McNamee, G., Budwig, N., & McLane, J. (1980). The adult-child dyad as a problem-solving system. *Child Development, 51*, 1215–1221.

Wood, D., Bruner, J.S., & Ross, G. (1976). The role of tutoring in problem-solving. *Journal of Child Psychology and Psychiatry, 17*, 89–100.

Wood, D., Wood, H., & Middleton, D. (1978). An experimental evaluation of four face-to-face teaching strategies. *International Journal of Behavioral Development, 1*, 131–147.

Wozniak, R.H. (1975). Psychology and education of the learning disabled child in the Soviet Union. In W. Cruikshank & D.P. Hallahan (Eds.), *Perceptual and learning disabilities in children*, Vol. 1. *Psychoeducational practices* (pp. 407–479). Syracuse, NY: Syracuse University.

Zukow, P.G., Reilly, J., & Greenfield, P.M. (1982). Making the absent present: Facilitating the transition from sensorimotor to linguistic communication. In K. Nelson (Ed.), *Children's language*, Vol. 3 (pp. 1–90). New York: Gardner.

5
Domain-Specific Knowledge, Metacognition, and the Promise of Instructional Reform

WILLIAM D. ROHWER, JR. AND JOHN W. THOMAS

Advancements on two major fronts in cognitive and developmental psychology provide a foundation for reforming the character of academic instruction. Advancements on one front, sometimes referred to as domain-specific cognition, promise to identify the structures of content knowledge students need in order to become proficient in particular subject-matter domains. Advancements on the second front, sometimes referred to as metacognition, promise to specify the knowledge of their own cognitive procedures students need in order to acquire and deploy these procedures effectively. Even if both of these promises are fulfilled, however, their impact on the outcomes of education may be negligible unless major changes are made in certain features that typify instruction in academic courses.

Our aims in this chapter are to describe the implications of these advancements for instructional reform, identify impediments to such reform, and examine possible ways of overcoming the impediments. We begin with a brief and selective summary of research on the roles of domain-specific and metacognitive knowledge in the three areas where such research has made notable progress to date, namely, problem solving, reading comprehension, and memory. Then we describe the results of research on those features of academic courses that influence the character of the cognitive and self-management activities engaged in by students. Finally, we explore the implications of these results for the kinds of instructional reforms suggested by the work on domain-specific cognition and metacognitive knowledge.

Domain-Specific and Metacognitive Knowledge

Several lines of research have converged to produce two propositions. The first is that the structures of content knowledge necessary for proficiency in a given intellectual domain are distinctive to that domain. The second is that such proficiency also requires metacognitive knowledge, knowledge of effective means of acquiring, retrieving, and manipulating content knowledge. The lines of research responsible for these propositions have addressed both individual and developmental differences in performance on problem-solving, comprehension, and memory tasks. In each of these task areas, much of the progress made has come from comparative analyses of cognition in experts and novices. Two classes of experts have been subjected to these analyses.

In one class are those who are truly expert in a field such as professional physicists (e.g., Chi, Glaser, & Rees, 1982). Analyses of the cognition of such persons furnish potential models of the ultimate goals of instruction, but only, perhaps, for the select population of persons who will become true experts, as in the case of future physicists, for example. Thus, the utility of these analyses for the reform of instruction may be limited, for the most part, to the upper reaches of education, that is, to the upper-class college and graduate-school years when students major in specialized fields.

In the other class are those who are unusually effective novices. Some fifth-grade students, for example, even though they have not yet developed reading expertise to the level of an accomplished adult, make much more progress in that direction than many of their fifth-grade peers (see Stein et al., 1982). In effect, some students are much more expert at being novices than are other students. Comparative analyses of the cognition of more and less expert novices are of great importance for instructional reform because the vast majority of students are perpetual novices. Virtually every time students enroll in a new course, they are novices with respect to the subject matter to be mastered. Analyses of expert students, then, can furnish models of the objectives of instruction for almost the entire population.

PROBLEM SOLVING

The distinguishing feature of problem solving is that learners are faced with some difficult situation, some barrier to progress that will not yield to the automatic application of some single, instantly accessible algorithm. Domain-specific knowledge has been shown to be a major determinant of proficiency in dealing with such situations. The role of domain-specific knowledge in problem-solving proficiency has been investigated in a number of domains, including mathematics (Derry, this volume, chap. 11; Gallini, this volume, chap. 10; Greeno, 1986; Schoenfeld, in press a, in press b), physics (Chi et al., 1982; Glaser, 1987; Larkin, 1985), radiology (Lesgold, Rubison, Feltovich, Glaser & Klopfer, 1988), and social science (Voss, Greene, Post, & Penner, 1983).

Expert-novice comparisons in these domains seem to indicate that experts differ from novices not only in the amount of knowledge they possess, but also in the organization and accessibility of that knowledge, that is, in their knowledge structures. Expert-novice differences in knowledge structures are of at least three principal kinds (see, e.g., Chi et al., 1982). (a) Whereas the knowledge of novices is structured around the main phenomena in a domain, that of experts represents these phenomena in relation to higher-order principles. The knowledge of novices in physics, for example, appears to be organized around such concrete phenomena as the behavior of entities on inclined planes. In contrast, the knowledge of experts is organized around fundamental principles, such as Newtonian laws of force. (b) For the expert, but not the novice, these principles are represented in the form of procedures for solving relevant problems as well as in the form of propositions, that is, declarative knowledge. (c) Moreover, such procedural representations include specifications of the conditions under which the principles are applicable, for example, the kinds of inclined plane phenomena that are accountable in terms of a particular law of force. Thus, the principles are connected with the phenomena to which they can be applied and even with the concrete components of the phenomena (e.g., a block on an inclined plane).

These expert-novice differences in knowledge structures, according to investigators cited previously, lead to differences in the ways problems are represented, and these differences, in turn, are mainly responsible for expert-novice differences in problem-solving proficiency. Differences in problem representation are of two principal kinds. The first is that experts frequently spend far more time than novices constructing representations of the problems that confront them (Schoenfeld, in press a, in press b). Whereas novices typically read a problem statement, embark immediately on a course of action, and persist on that course, experts spend the bulk of their time analyzing the problem and planning their attack, but relatively little time implementing their approach. The second difference lies in the kind of representation constructed. For experts, the givens in the statement of a problem serve as cues that provide access to the procedural principles in their knowledge structures. They represent problems, then, in terms of these principles (e.g., this is a problem that can be solved using Newton's second law). Novices, in contrast, tend to represent problems in terms of the concrete components of the phenomena described in problem statements (e.g., this is an inclined plane problem) (Chi et al., 1982).

Expert-novice differences in problem-solving proficiency stem not only from differences in content knowledge structures, but also from differences in metacognitive knowledge. Research on metacognitive factors in problem-solving proficiency has focused on superordinate or "executive" processing functions that organize and orchestrate basic information-processing mechanisms. The hallmark of metacognitive proficiency is the organization and combination of individual operations or strategies into a larger sequence of operations. In other words, the essence of metacognitive proficiency at problem solving is planning: the coordination of goal-specific strategies and the monitoring of progress toward some end(s). Schoenfeld (1983), for example, describes some of the strategic misfunctions of college students engaged in mathematical problem solving, misfunctions that are primarily failures of goal setting, monitoring, and the evaluation of plans. The majority of students so engaged embark on a course of action that can be described as "'read a problem, pick a direction, and then work on it until you run out of time'"

(Schoenfeld, 1985, p. 366). Experts, by contrast, have metacognitive knowledge that leads them to pose to themselves and to answer three kinds of questions: (a) what (precisely) are you doing, (b) what is the reason for doing it, and (c) how will the result be used later in the solution.

Implications for Instructional Reform

With respect to problem solving, these advances in the areas of domain-specific and metacognitive knowledge have at least four implications for instructional reform that promise to increase student proficiency. (a) Instruction should be designed to facilitate students' construction of knowledge bases that are structured in terms of higher-order principles. (b) These knowledge structures should include not only propositional or declarative knowledge of principles, but also procedural knowledge of them, that is, knowledge of how to use the principles to solve problems. (c) Furthermore, the structures should include knowledge of the conditions of the applicability of the principles, a specification of the kinds of problems to which they should be applied. (d) Instruction should be designed to explicitly assist students in acquiring metacognitive knowledge of how to plan their problem-solving efforts, how to set goals and subgoals for these efforts, and how to monitor their progress towards their goals. In Schoenfeld's terms, instruction needs to foster the acquisition of the "basics" of a domain, domain-relevant problem-solving strategies or heuristics, and metadomain understanding or "sense-making."

COMPREHENSION

Current theorizing about reading comprehension (e.g., Mandl, Stein, & Trabasso, 1984) bears striking resemblances to the preceding analyses of problem solving. Like the research on problem solving, much of the current evidence about comprehension comes from expert-novice comparisons, but in this case the comparisons are between more and less accomplished readers. Also like the problem-solving case, investigators interpret the available evidence as suggesting that differences in content knowledge structures and in metacognitive knowledge are major sources of differences in skillfulness.

One of the kinds of content knowledge structures posited as important for skillful reading comprehension, namely, domain-specific knowledge, appears to be identical to that specified in the problem-solving case. In the comprehension case, domain-specific knowledge refers to knowledge of the content treated in the text material (Resnick, 1984).

Another kind of knowledge structure, however, distinguishes the two cases. This second kind consists of rhetorical knowledge, knowledge of the forms and conventions of various genres. Like the knowledge structures of expert problem solvers, the rhetorical knowledge of expert readers is procedural as well as declarative. This procedural knowledge enables readers to construct representations of text structure. Brown and Smiley (1978), for example, found that older (and presumably more skilled) readers are better able to discriminate more from less important ideas presented in texts. Similarly, Meyer (1984) has shown that expert readers detect differential levels of importance in the information presented in texts and form relationships between important informational units.

Investigators generally agree on the proposition that skillful comprehension depends on knowledge structures and the procedures embedded in them. They disagree, however, about the role of processing strategies in expert comprehension. Two categories of such strategies have been investigated.

Strategies in the first category, internal, are largely directed toward information that is presented within the text to be read. According to the analysis provided by Palincsar and Brown (1984), for example, skillful reading involves the deployment of strategies such as those of summarizing, posing questions about author intent, and anticipating questions that could be asked about the information presented. These strategies, from the viewpoint of Brown, Palincsar, and Armbruster (1984), are generalizable skills that foster proficient comprehension across domains. This position has been disputed by Resnick (1984), however, who contends that expert comprehension is not characterized by the deliberate deployment of strategies but by automated processing. In her view, those who engage in deliberate strategy deployment are those who are in the transition from novice to expert comprehender. Moreover, such deliberate deployment facilitates their transition through this period.

Strategies in the second category, external, contrast with those in the first in that they are directed toward the formation of links between internal text information and extra-text information in the form of prior knowledge. Mayer (1987) takes the position that the formation of such connections characterizes skillful reading. Similarly, Ballstaedt and Mandl (1984) contend that the deliberate elaboration of connections between prior knowledge and text information enhances comprehension. Furthermore, such elaboration of connections with prior knowledge can serve not only to enhance comprehension but also to elaborate and enlarge the related prior knowledge structures (Resnick, 1984).

These internal and external elaboration strategies are, in the view of some investigators, applicable across a wide variety of subject matter domains and, in this sense, are not domain-specific (Weinstein & Mayer, 1986). Nevertheless, it is plausible to suppose that the probability that such connections will be evoked varies with the amount and organization of prior knowledge possessed by the reader. Moreover, these elaboration strategies are specific in another sense; their effectiveness varies depending on the specific capability required by the task to be performed. An accurate rendering of the information internal to a text, for example, might be impeded by the elaboration of external connections (cf. Mayer, 1987). Additional research indicates that expert and novice comprehenders differ in metacognitive knowledge as well as in content knowledge and the processing strategies they deploy. Most of the research on metacognitive factors in comprehension has focused on the reading and prose-learning behaviors of novice learners and on explaining these behaviors in terms of deficiencies in metacognitive knowledge.

In addition to rhetorical knowledge, Brown, Armbruster, and Baker (1986) identify three major kinds of metacognitive knowledge with skilled comprehension: knowledge of task factors, strategies, and learner characteristics. Task factors refer to the general goals of reading and studying as well as to the criterion objectives specific to a particular reading or studying task. Novice readers do not tend to read for meaning, nor do they adjust their reading behavior to match different kinds of content or reading contexts (Franks et al., 1982). Unlike expert readers, they do not slow down when they encounter difficult passages, for example (Brown et al., 1986).

Metacognitive knowledge appropriate to proficient reading and studying also includes knowledge of strategies. Novice readers often do not know how to "fix up" the situation when comprehension fails (Garner & Reis, 1981). In addition, although they may be able to use strategies such as the use of context clues to assist in comprehension when directed to do so, they do not know when, where, and how to use these strategies spontaneously (Bransford, Stein, Shelton, & Owings, 1981).

Finally, with respect to metacognitive knowledge of learner characteristics, novice readers do not assess and take into account their own strengths and weaknesses as learners, nor are they aware of the general principles of learning and memory that apply to learning and studying (Pressley, Borkowski, & Schneider, 1987).

Implications for Instructional Reform

Thus, theory and research on comprehension, like that on problem solving, imply a number of instructional reforms. These reforms include providing students with systematic assistance in acquiring (a) prior knowledge of specific relevance to the information presented in text form; (b) rhetorical knowledge structures, including embedded procedures for detecting and representing the structures of texts, for discriminating more and less important information, and for integrating or building internal connections among text information; (c) deliberate strategies of summarizing and questioning; and (d) strategies that build external connections between text information and prior knowledge. In addition, according to proponents of the importance of metacognitive factors in comprehension proficiency; (e) instruction should incorporate what Brown and her colleagues call "cognitive training with awareness" or "informed training" as opposed to "blind training." (f) Students should also be made aware of the differing demands of tests to which their knowledge might be put (Brown et al., 1986). Moreover, according to Borkowski and Krause (1985), deficiencies in comprehension can be due to deficiencies in attributional beliefs. Carr and Borkowski (1987), in a study of underachieving elementary school students, report the superiority of strategy training plus attribution training over strategy training alone on measures of reading comprehension and on grades in school. Although there is need for additional research to determine the extent to which attributional training in addition to specific strategy and strategy-control training is beneficial or necessary for different populations, its value facilitating the learning behavior of educationally handicapped students appears to be significant (Borkowski, Weyhing, & Turner, 1986).

MEMORY

Expert-novice comparisons have also been used in attempts to explicate student differences in memory proficiency. Chiesi, Spilich, & Voss (1979), for example, found that baseball experts, in comparisons with novices, exhibit superior memory for baseball-relevant information. A large share of the research on differences in memory proficiency, however, has involved expert-novice comparisons of a different kind, namely, comparisons between older and younger students. For a wide variety of materials and tasks, memory performance has been shown to increase as a function of age up to at least adulthood. Most theorists agree that such age differences are associated with corresponding differences in both knowledge and processing strategies. Theorists divide, however, on the issue of whether or not effective strategy deployment is contingent on the possession of domain-specific knowledge.

Some theorists (e.g., Bransford, Sherwood, Vye, & Reiser, 1986; Chi, 1985) contend that age differences in memory proficiency, like individual differences in problem solving and comprehension proficiency, stem from an increasing correspondence between the content of the information to be remembered and the content of the rememberer's knowledge structures. According to this view, strategies are either a virtually automatic consequence of more advanced knowledge structures or are more effective if they are tied to the specifics of domain knowledge. Thus, for example, Lindberg (1980) found that children deploy the organizational strategy of clustering more frequently than college students when the information to be recalled is more congruent with the knowledge structures (cf. Rohwer, Rabinowitz, & Dronkers, 1982).

Other theorists (e.g., Borkowski, 1985; Brown et al., 1986; Pressley, Borkowski, & O'Sullivan, 1985; Rohwer, 1980), while admitting the importance of knowledge-task congruence, content that age differences in memory performance stem primarily from corresponding differences in the kinds of processing strategies deployed. Indeed, according to this view, at least in the early stages of constructing a knowledge base, content knowledge itself is acquired through effective strategy deployment. Nevertheless, a kind of specificity has a place in this view as well, although the kind of specificity involved is not necessarily of the subject-matter domain variety. Instead, the effectiveness of strategies is held to be specific to the kind of task or criterion performance to be given (Rohwer & Thomas, 1987). Summarization, for example, might be quite effective in fostering the recall of gist information, but might impede the recall of verbatim information.

These apparently divergent view of the roots of memory proficiency need not be mutually exclusive. The memory strategies learners deploy when they are novices with respect to a body of information may be domain-free (though task-specific). In contrast, the strategies of those who are expert with respect to such information may be procedural in character and embedded in relevant, domain-specific knowledge structures. In Anderson's (1982) terms, general strategies may typify the declarative stages of knowledge acquisition whereas domain specificity may be characteristic of the procedural stages.

In addition to domain-specific knowledge and processing strategies, metacognitive factors have also been shown to influence memory proficiency. Such metacognitive factors are similar to those linked to proficient comprehension performance. Similar to the distinctions offered by Brown et al. (1986) in relation to comprehension, Flavell and Wellman (1977), for example, distinguish between sensitivity factors, that is, knowledge of the need for mnemonic behavior, and knowledge of the variability of memory performance given differences in and interactions among task demand factors, learner factors, and strategies.

Research on metacognitive factors in memory, or metamemory, has led to several multiple-component models of proficient performance. Pressley, Borkowski, et al. (1985) and Borkowski and Krause (1985) conceptualize metamemory in terms of four components: specific strategy knowledge, relational strategy knowledge, general strategy knowledge, and metamemory acquisition procedures. Specific strategy knowledge refers to knowing when, why, where, and how to use memory strategies. This knowledge of the range of applicability of strategies is assumed to be central to transfer effects. Relational strategy knowledge has to do with knowledge of the strengths and weaknesses of different kinds of strategies. General strategy knowledge refers to the understanding that effort is required to apply strategies and that effortful strategic approaches are often beneficial. Finally, differences among students in metamemory performance require that an additional component, metamemory acquisition procedures, be specified to account for the mechanisms by which new strategies are acquired and by which existing strategies are selected, implemented, and modified. These procedures help to account for the tailoring of strategies to fit variations in tasks and the self-regulation that is required while strategies are being used and modified.

Metamemory researchers claim that many of the memory and strategy production deficiencies characteristic of young and developmentally retarded children revealed by previous research can be explained by deficiencies in metamemorial knowledge. The validity of this claim has been established by means of meta-analyses of past research and training studies. Schneider (1985) conducted a meta-analysis of 47 of these studies and obtained an average correlation of 0.41, leading to the conclusion that metamemory and memory performance are substantially and significantly related.

Implications for instructional reform

Research on domain-specific and metacognitive factors in memory proficiency suggests that there are three kinds of prerequisites for facilitating memory proficiency in instructional settings. (a) The first, shared with both problem-solving and comprehension proficiency, is the acquisition and structuring of content knowledge. (b) The second kind of prerequisite is the acquisition and deployment of task-appropriate processing strategies which, according to the preceding view, can themselves foster knowledge acquisition. The transformation of this second prerequisite into an explicit objective of academic instruction raises the issue of how the acquisition and skillful use of strategies can best be fostered. Thus, (c) the third prerequisite consists of metacognitive factors that assist students to become proficient in memory performance. Supplementing training in memory strategies with information about the specific utility of that strategy (where, when, how, and why it is useful) has been offered as a prerequisite for both strategy maintenance and transfer, at least with young children (Pressley, Borkowski, et al., 1985). The results of such research on the role of metacognitive factors in memory have led to a renewed interest in teaching cognitive strategies with "awareness," and in the establishment of guidelines concerning how metamemorial knowledge and strategy monitoring might be fostered in the classroom (Duffy & Roehler, this volume, chap. 6; Pressley, Forrest-Pressley, Elliott-Faust, & Miller, 1985; Pressley, Goodchild, Fleet, Zajchowski, & Evans, 1987; Symons, Snyder, Cariglia-Bull, & Pressley, this volume, chap. 1).

Features of Academic Courses that Influence Engagement in Strategic Activities

Advancements in research and theory concerning both metacognition and domain-specific knowledge have progressed to the point that proposals for instructional reforms are beginning to be made. Nevertheless, much remains to be specified, through careful theoretical and empirical analysis, about the particular objectives to be set in a number of subject matter areas. These objectives must be indexed to a variety of strategies and a variety of knowledge structures to form a graduated series of proficiency levels ranging from primary school through college. As the preceding review indicates, this work is proceeding. Accordingly, it is not premature to examine existing conditions of instruction in naturally occurring educational settings to determine how congenial they are for the kinds of reforms envisioned.

Instructional reform requires not only a principled basis for prescribing instructional objectives, but also the design of instructional conditions that effectively foster students' attainment of those objectives. We have suggested elsewhere (Rohwer & Thomas, 1987; Thomas & Rohwer, in press) that at least three classes of such conditions may be critical.

One class consists of the *demands* instruction makes for students to engage in various kinds of cognitive activities, especially as embodied in the performance criteria instructors use to evaluate student achievement. The items on teacher-made tests, for example, can vary in terms of their demands, ranging from verbatim memory for facts or propositions to the integration of disparate propositions to answer a novel question or solve a novel problem.

A second class of conditions consists of the *supports* instructors provide for meeting instructional demands. We conceive of supports as conditions intended to prompt students to engage in cognitive activities. For example, instructors might or might not provide metacognitively based training in processing strategies that serve to integrate disparate information. The procedures for teaching summarization strategies from a metacognitive perspective as described by Brown, Campione, and Day (1981) are examples of highly supportive conditions in that a cognitive demand is accompanied by instruction in an appropriate strategy for meeting that demand, the provision of feedback concerning the significance of the strategy for successful task completion, and training in self-control techniques for monitoring and evaluating strategy use.

The third class of conditions consists of *compensations*. Compensations are defined as instructional conditions that decrease the demand for cognitive activities, typically by providing students with the end products of those activities. The demand for selective reading and notetaking activities, for example, can be nullified effectively when an instructor provides a list of key terms or an outline of a chapter. Similarly, an instructor might compose test items that ostensibly demand integrative processing, but furnish students with review materials that explicitly contain the integrated propositions called for by the test items. Instructor-provided handouts and text-embedded aids can play either a compensatory or a supporting role then, depending on whether they supply students with the end product of cognition or facilitate students' construction of these products.

According to this analysis, then, recent advancements in theory and research can lead to instructional reform only if instructors demand that students attain the newly identified instructional objectives, provide support for constructing knowledge structures and for acquiring and deploying productive strategies, and avoid furnishing compensations that mitigate the need for these structures and strategies. The issue examined in this section is the extent to which current instructional practices meet these specifications in courses where either problem solving, comprehension, or memory are central to the subject matter being taught.

PROBLEM SOLVING

While problem solving may be important in virtually any subject-matter domain, it should surely be of central importance in mathematics (see Van Haneghan & Baker, this volume, chap. 9), science, and computer programming (see Lehrer, this volume, chap. 12). The question is whether courses in these domains make demands for the knowledge structures and procedures prerequisite for problem solving, and if they provide support for acquiring these structures and procedures.

In the case of mathematics curricula, Schoenfeld (in press a), for example, notes the prevalence and importance of "word problems" as well as the difficulties students have in learning to solve them. He then characterizes the response of instructors to these difficulties:

Teachers give you the rules for solving problems, which you memorize and use. Those rules don't have to make sense, and they may not — but if you do what you're told, you'll get the right answer, and then everybody's happy. The result in the short term is that some students manage to "solve" word problems that they might not otherwise be able to solve. (p. 21)

Instructors impose performance criteria that nominally demand of students that they construct a knowledge structure of mathematical modeling that contains procedures for solving word problems such as, "13 passengers boarded the bus at its first stop. At the next stop, 7 passengers got off. How many passengers were left on the bus?" The instructors compensate for this demand by providing rules of thumb for dealing with the problems. With reference to the preceding example, students are taught to apply a routine: circle the numbers in the problem; then look for the word "left"; if you find it, subtract the second number from the first. The result, according to Schoenfeld, is that students ostensibly succeed, but without understanding the problem described, without modeling the problem mathematically, and without acquiring the procedural knowledge intended.

The picture is no more encouraging in the sciences. Mergendoller, Marchman, Mitman, and Packer (1987), for example, analyzed the character of the problems posed by the laboratory exercises, worksheets, and tests given by 11 seventh-grade science teachers. Laboratory exercises were classified as either explicit, implicit, or integrative. Explicit exercises posed a problem, prescribed the methods to be followed in solving it, and specified the solution to be obtained. Implicit exercises posed a problem and prescribed the methods to be followed, but omitted specification of the solution. Integrative exercises posed the problem to be solved only. Exercises in the explicit category accounted for 45% of all of those assigned, and those in the implicit category accounted for an additional 55%. Thus, none of the exercises examined demanded one of the core components of problem-solving proficiency, namely, the capability of classifying problems with reference to relevant knowledge structures and their embedded problem-solving procedures.

Furthermore, 84% of the questions posed on worksheets and 82% of those on examinations in these courses required only verbatim recall of information from texts and other course documents.

Similar results have been reported by Fleming and Chambers (1983) in their analysis of the teacher-developed tests administered in the Cleveland public schools. These investigators reviewed over 300 tests and 8,800 items from kindergarten through the twelfth grade in core subject-matter areas. Each item was classified into one or another of three knowledge categories or three appliction or skill categories. In science courses, 85% of the items at the junior-high-school level and 89% at the senior-high-school level required only recall of terms, facts, or principles. Thus, less than 20% of the items at either level even posed a problem to be solved.

It might be supposed that the central objective of courses in computer programming would be students' acquisition of knowledge and procedures for problem solving. Yet, preliminary evidence suggests that this supposition is far from reality. As part of a larger project (Linn, Sloane, & Clancy, 1986) conducted in 15 senior-high-school courses in Pascal programming, students were asked to assess a variety of course features. One such feature is indexed by responses to six questionnaire items that make up the scale, demand for planning. Each of the items asks students to indicate how frequently their teachers required them to provide evidence of planning activities (e.g., ". . . design part of the program") before entering code at the computer. Across courses, the mean score on this five-point scale, ranging from "never" to "always" was 2.1, nearly on the point designated by the term "rarely."

In each of these subject-matter domains, then, the evidence is that few demands are made for the kinds of knowledge structures and procedures that research has shown to be characteristic of expert problem solvers. Indeed, it appears that genuine problems, as such, are rarely posed. Test items and exercises do not demand that students call on declarative and procedural knowledge organized around higher-order principles in the given subject-matter domain, nor that they apply this knowledge in discriminating ways across different kinds of novel problems. The performance criteria imposed in actual secondary-school courses in mathematical and the sciences are far removed from the knowledge-structure objectives implied by advancements in cognitive and developmental psychology. These criteria rarely include any demands for problem solving, and even when they ostensibly do, instructors compensate for these demands by furnishing students with algorithms that compensate for the demands.

COMPREHENSION AND MEMORY

Just as acquisition of problem-solving procedures might be expected to be central to courses in mathematics and the sciences, the acquisition of strategies for comprehending, remembering, and integrating information might be expected to be central to courses in English and the social sciences. Thus, it is appropriate to examine such courses for evidence that they make demands and provide support for comprehension, memory, and integration.

Relevant evidence is reported in the previously cited paper by Fleming and Chambers (1983), in that English and social studies courses were among those they examined. Their classification of items on the tests given in these courses revealed that the average percentage of the total items that required only knowledge and memory of terms and facts was 83% at the junior-high-school level and 92% at the senior-high-school level. In these courses, then, very little demand is made for either knowledge of rhetorical structures or for the deployment of the integrative processing strategies. It is plausible to suppose that students faced with demands such as these would be unlikely to build such structures or to deploy constructive processing strategies to enhance memory, comprehension, and integration of information.

This supposition can be tested against the results of research we conducted recently in junior-high-school, senior-high-school, and college courses. Students from two universities, four high schools, and three junior high schools participated in the study. A total of 22 courses and 1,240 of the 1,586 students enrolled in these courses were surveyed. At the college level, two courses were sampled, one in American history and one in European history (two instructors and 284 student participants). At the high school level, the participants were 536 students from 11 American history or government courses (nine instructors). At the junior high school level, there were nine American history courses (eight instructors) and 420 students. The high schools sampled were known feeder schools for the universisites included in the study. Wherever possible, a feeder relationship was maintained between the participating senior high schools and junior high schools as well. Where the relationship could not be maintained, an attempt was made to substitute a junior high school that matched the high school demographically. In each of these samples, information was obtained about course features, students' study activities, and achievement. (A more complete description of the methods used in this investigation may be found in Christopoulos, Rohwer, & Thomas, 1987; Strage, Tyler, Rohwer, & Thomas, 1987.)

Course Features

Information regarding course features was derived from two sources: analyses and ratings of classroom observations and of all course documents pertaining to the instructional unit examined.

Classroom Observations

Project staff observed classroom events and recorded them on audio tape in each course on three occasions. Two of these observations were made on days of routine instruction, no less than two weeks preceding the end-of-marking-period examination. The third observation was made on the last class day before the test. For one of the routine sessions and for the session immediately preceding the test, independent observations were made by two members of the project staff.

Field notes from these observations were transposed onto summary log sheets on which observers rated overall class sessions and individual instructional topics covered during the session. Overall ratings included: (a) availability of the instructor to students, (b) instructor's responsiveness to students' questions, (c) the degree to which the instructor encouraged student comprehension, (d) the degree to which the instructor encouraged students to integrate material, and (e) the amount of advance notice the instructor gave students about the end-of-unit test. Each instructional topic was rated along 10 dimensions: (a) whether material presented was new or had already been covered elsewhere in the course; (b) the number of sources where that information was covered; (c) whether or not organizational frameworks were provided for the lecture and, if so, what types (e.g., outlines, advance organizers); (d) numbers of cues introduced to highlight important information (flags for key points); (e) the manner in which topics were treated (integrative or factual); (f) the number of examples provided; (g) whether and how the instructor checked on students' comprehension or entertained students' questions; (h) whether the instructor provided summaries, transitions, or recontextualizations for topics; (i) whether the instructor suggested methods for completing assignments or reviewing particular topics for the test and, if so, what sorts of methods were offered; and finally (j) the amount of time devoted to each topic.

Additionally, transcripts of 5 to 7 minutes of the second routine observation were prepared. These transcripts consisted of verbatim records of instructors' lectures covering two or three instructional topics, prepared using standard orthographic conventions. These transcripts were then rated along three dimensions: (a) pace of information presentation (number of teacher words per minute), (b) familiarity of vocabulary (indexed by the Carroll, Davies, and & Richman, 1971, word frequency norms), and (c) comprehensibility (concreteness of a sample of nouns drawn from the transcripts as well as overall comprehensibility) as rated independently by three raters who had not been present at the class session itself. These transcripts were used only for the purpose of producing ratings on the preceding three dimensions to augment the more comprehensive sets of variables drawn from the observations themselves.

Document Analyses

All assigned readings, handouts, and tests pertaining to the marking period in question were collected for each course. Readings were rated along the following seven dimensions: (a) number of sources from which readings were drawn, (b) average number of words assigned per day, (c) familiarity of vocabulary (word frequency for a sample of nouns, verbs, and adjectives; indexed by the Carroll et al., 1971, word frequency norms), (d) cues for selection of important content (presence and adequacy of previews, summaries, and adjunct questions for selecting important points), (e) comprehensibility of readings (concreteness of a sample of nouns and t-units drawn from each reading assignment, and presence and adequacy of previews, summaries, adjunct questions, examples, and definitions as supports for comprehension), (f) presence and adequacy of mnemonic aids (charts, tables, lists, etc.), and (g) extent and manner of integration (explicit vs. implicit) of material within and between sources.

Tests were rated by two independent raters as to the proportion of the possible points that required the student to have encoded each of three kinds of information: verbatim, comprehended, and integrated.

Additionally, information was obtained from teachers about the weight of the exam in determining the final course grade and whether grading criteria were absolute or competitive.

Readings and tests, taken together, were then rated along five dimensions to measure the congruence between the content and presentation of material in the readings and on the test: (a) number of details in the readings appearing or called for on the test; (b) proportion of answers to test questions provided in the readings; (c) proportion of test questions that paraphrased material presented in the readings; (d) predictions, for a random sample of details drawn from the readings, of the likelihood that each would appear on test covering the particular chapter; and (e) ratings, for each test item, of whether answers had been covered in the readings, and if so, whether the test item used the same wording as the readings, a paraphrase of that wording, or inferences from the reading.

Similarly, handouts and tests, taken together, were rated along three dimensions: (a) whether test items or their answers had been mentioned on the handout; (b) how the test item material had been treated in the handout (factual, comprehension, integration); and (c) the similarity in treatment of the material on handouts and in test questions.

The preceding instruments and procedures yielded scores on a total of 14 course features, 7 demand features, 5 support features, and 2 compensation features. Of these, four of the demand features and four of the support features are of special relevance to the current discussion.

One of these demand features, demand for selection, indexes the amount of information and the amount of detail presented per unit of time in assigned readings and course meetings. Our presumption was that, other things being equal, the larger the amount of information to be dealt with in a course, the greater the need for students to selectively allocate processing time to more important information. Such selective processing, according to Brown et al. (1986), for example, presupposes knowledge of rhetorical structures as well as strategies for using this knowledge to discriminate between more and less important information. Three additional demand features are demands for verbatim, comprehended, and integrated information. Each of these features is indexed by the proportion of the total point value of examinations devoted to items that call for the given kind of information. Thus, the higher these demands, the greater the premium on deployment of verbatim, comprehension, and integration processing strategies.

Matched to these demand features are four support features. These support features reflect the extent to which instructors or text materials provide specific encouragement or suggestions to students about how to select important information (selection support); remember it (verbatim support); understand it (comprehension support); or form internal or external connections among facts, concepts, or principles (integration support).

The scales used to score the demand features differed from those used to score the support features. For the purpose of comparing the outcomes for the two kinds of features, then, it is convenient to standardize the scores of each kind across the 22 courses. The results are shown in Figure 5.1. Analyses of variance in these features scores (treating courses as the unit of analysis) indicated that selection demand increases significantly as a function of educational level, but selection support does not. Indeed, descriptively speaking, such support appears to decrease across levels. In contrast, verbatim demand remains relatively constant across junior and senior high school, but decreases dramatically between senior high school and college. Descriptively, verbatim support also decreases significantly across levels. Neither comprehension demand nor support, varies significantly across levels. In marked contrast, both integration demand and support remain constant from junior to senior high school, but increase sharply and significantly from senior high school to college.

An alternative way of viewing these results is to examine the mean raw scores for the demand features as a function of educational level. For example, the difference across levels in selection demand stems from an increase in the amount of reading assigned from an average of 263 words per day in junior high school to 1,623 words per day in senior high school, to 4,815 words per day in college. As for the three demands that relate to specific processing strategies, the current results are consistent with those reported by Fleming and Chambers (1983). At the junior- and senior-high-school levels, the overwhelming majority of examination items demand verbatim information, 72% and 74% respectively, whereas at the college level none of the items are of this type. The percentages of items demanding comprehension are relatively constant across levels, 9%, 11%, and 1%. In contrast, the percentages of items demanding integration increase dramatically between the secondary-school and college levels, from 18% in junior high school and 14% in senior high school to 99% in college.

Evidently, then, throughout the secondary-school years, there is comparatively little demand for knowledge of rhetorical structures in that the volume of information to be processed is small, and few examination items demand comprehension. Moreover, there is slight demand or support for processing strategies that produce either comprehension of integration of information, much less for procedurally powerful knowledge structures. The next

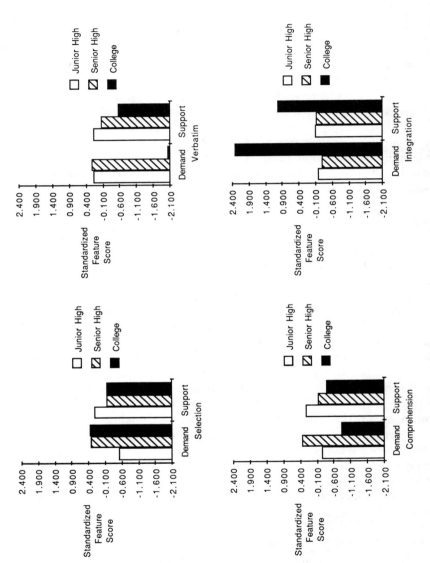

FIGURE 5.1. Standardized demand and support feature scores as a function of educational level.

question, then, is whether the kinds of studying students engage in parallel the character of these demands.

Study Activities

Study activities were indexed by students' responses to the items on a self-report instrument, the Study Activity Survey. For each of the 190 items on the survey, student responses reflect self-reported frequencies of engaging in the activity described, ranging from "never" (1), through a midpoint of "sometimes" (3), to "always" (5). Each of the items is associated with one or another of 15 scales. A student's score on a given scale is the average of the scores of the responses made to the component items.

Eight of the scales are pertinent here. A representative item from each of these scales is shown in Table 5.1. Three of the scales pertain to general study allocation activities, two of which are selective in character and one of which is nonselective. The selective scales reflect the allocation of processing based on estimated difficulty of understanding or remembering material (difficulty), and estimated likelihood that material would appear on examinations (exam). The nonselective scale reflects intense but equal attention to all assigned material (uniform). The other five scales index classes of specific processing strategies. Three of these scales reflect constructive processing strategies, that is, the use of memory strategies such as mnemonic elaboration (mnemonic), comprehension strategies such as questioning and summarizing (comprehension), and strategies for forming internal and external connections (integration). The other two scales reflect superficial processing as in merely reading through assignments (receptive), or repetitiously rehearsing material to be remembered (duplicative).

As the results displayed in the top panel of Figure 5.2 suggest, self-reported engagement in selective allocation activities, those that reflect an emphasis on both difficult and exam-relevant material, increase significantly across educational level. This outcome is consistent with the previously noted increase in demand for selection (see Figure 5.1), and occurs despite the descriptive decrease in selection support. Unexpectedly, however, uniform processing remains comparatively constant across levels, with the average scores being about midway between "sometimes" and "often." Moreover, engagement in such nonselective allocation activities is reported to be at least as frequent (except perhaps at the college level) as engagement in the more selective activities.

Displayed in the lower panel of Figure 5.2 are the results for the specific processing scales. In a number of respects, the trends across educational level in self-reported strategy deployment parallel the relevant trends in demand and support features (cf. Figure 5.1). For example, as demand and support for integration increases between senior high school and college, (a) the frequency of deployment of integrative processing strategies also increases, and (b) deployment of the superficial strategies of duplicative and receptive

TABLE 5.1. Characterization of Processing Scales of the Study Activity Survey

Scale	Characterization	Example items
	Study allocation activities	
	Selective allocation according to	
Difficulty	Self-initiation of extra processing of information that is anticipated to present comprehension or memory difficulties.	"(In class) I make an effort to pick out the important points."
Exam relevance	Self-initiated investigation, identification, and processing of information that is likely to be important for a test.	"(While reading) I identify points that might be on the test."
	Nonselective processing activities	
Uniform processing	Nonselective processing of all the information at hand, voluntarily, intensely, or earnestly.	"(While attending the last class before the test) I took notes on every point that came up."
	Specific processing activities	
	Constructive processing activities	
Mnemonic processing	Elaborating or transforming mental modality of target information to enhance memorability.	"(While studying for the test) I made up a mental picture to represent important ideas."
Comprehension processing	Explicating, investigating, or inquiring into the meaning of information to enhance comprehension or memory.	"(While studying) I tried to explain important ideas to someone else."
Integrative processing	Elaborating, reorganizing, contrasting, integrating, or summarizing newly encountered or previously recorded information.	"(While reading) I write down the specific similarities between topics."
	Superficial processing activities	
Receptive processing	Reception of information given in texts or by instructor without implication of further processing.	"(While doing the assigned reading) I just read."
Duplicative processing	Unaltered re-encoding or mental recycling of previously encountered information.	"(While studying) I repeated specific facts over and over."

processing decreases. Similarly, as demand and support for verbatim processing decreases across levels, so too does deployment of mnemonic strategies. Even the comparative constancy of demand for comprehension is matched by a similar constancy in the deployment of comprehension strategies. Thus, as would be expected almost nonexistent demands for comprehension and integration at the secondary-school levels are associated with superficial processing instead of the constructive integration strategies that are more characteristic of the college level.

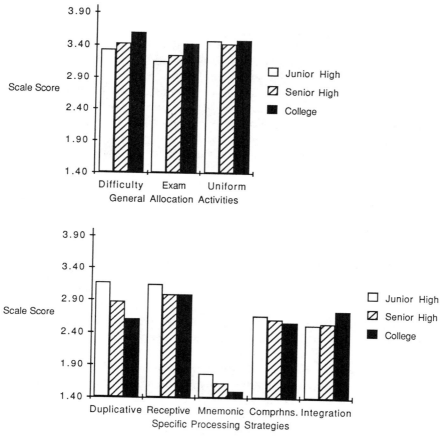

FIGURE 5.2. General allocation and specific processing scale scores as a function of educational level.

Other aspects of these results, however, are not explicable solely in terms of levels of demand. In particular, as noted previously, there is great demand at the junior- and senior-high-school levels on memory for verbatim information. Yet, as Figure 5.2 shows, students report that they deploy mnemonic strategies only rarely. Instead, they elect to use duplicative strategies despite the fact that in controlled research investigations, such strategies are dramatically less effective than mnemonic ones (e.g., Jones & Hall, 1982; Rohwer, 1980).

A possible interpretation of this outcome calls attention to the potential role of support features. Note that the increase at the college level in demand for integration is coupled with an increase in support (see Figure 5.2), and deployment of integrative strategies also increases. In contrast, the heavy demands at the junior- and senior-high-school levels for verbatim information are not accompanied by high levels of support for using mnemonic strategies, and their reported frequency of use is rare.

The low incidence of support, in turn, may stem from the difficulties associated with providing it. As Pressley, Goodchild, et al. (1987) note, the provision of support for the acquisition and appropriate use of strategies is a complex matter; (a) numerous strategies are needed, for their effectiveness is specific classes of tasks; (b) they are best acquired when instruction is reciprocal, in the manner developed by Palincsar and Brown (1984), and assists students to monitor the comparative outcomes that result from different strategies; and (c) their appropriate use depends on their internalization (cf. Brown, 1987) and the concurrent acquisition of metacognitive knowledge. As noted previously, the research of Borkowski and his colleagues (e.g., Borkowski & Krause, 1985; Borkowski et al., 1986; Carr & Borkowski, 1987) suggests that such knowledge may also need to include students' own attributions of their performance capabilities to the kinds of strategies they deploy. The rationale for this proposition is that students are unlikely to adopt and deploy a strategy unless they are convinced that by doing so they can better achieve the goals they seek. Strategy support that incorporates all or even a substantial subset of these components was not in evidence in any of the social studies courses sampled in our research and, according to Pressley, Goodchild, et al. (1987), it is equally rare in elementary-school classrooms.

Thus, a number of features of existing academic courses constitute impediments to the instructional reforms implied by research on domain-specific and metacognitive knowledge. As noted previously, instruction in disciplines that place a premium on problem solving should assist students in building structures of domain-specific knowledge organized around higher-order principles. Moreover, this knowledge should be compiled into problem-solving procedures. In physics, for example, students should be assisted to acquire problem-solving procedures and to organize these procedures in relation to physics principles. Whereas current theory and research results provide strong endorsement for these instructional reforms, their institution will be impeded by certain features of existing courses. Principal among these features, as described in the current section, is the character of the performance demands made in secondary-school courses that would be expected to emphasize problem solving, that is, courses in mathematics, the sciences, and computer programming. In these courses, instructors rarely pose genuine problems in the examinations they construct. Thus, the goal structures in these courses make superfluous the kinds of proceduralized knowledge structures that constitute true proficiency in problem solving.

Analogous impediments stand in the way of instituting instructional reforms suggested by research on metacognitive knowledge. These reforms, especially applicable in disciplines that ostensibly emphasize comprehension, memory, and integration of information, center on designing instruction to foster students' acquisition and use of strategies for detecting text structures, identifying important information, comprehending this information, building internal and external connections involving the information, and for making the information memorable and accessible. The effective acquisition and deployment of such strategies, research indicates, requires instruction that assists students in constructing relevant metacognitive knowledge. Instruction must aid students in appreciating the utility of each kind of strategy; the comparative effectiveness of different strategies for different tasks; and, thus, when, where, and how to use them. In existing junior- to senior-high-school courses, however, such metacognitive knowledge appears to be unnecessary, for these courses make little demand for the use of the kinds of strategies such knowledge would foster. As shown in this section, instructors rarely construct test items that call for the kind of subject matter knowledge that results from the comprehension and integration of information, but instead test mainly for the retrieval of verbatim information. Moreover, they rarely provide support for the acquisition and use of efficient processing strategies. The research reviewed here indicates that even when instructors impose performance criteria that demand verbatim information, they do not support students' acquisition and deployment of constructive mnemonic strategies. Moreover, students appear to respond by relying heavily on superficial processing strategies.

IMPEDIMENTS TO EDUCATIONAL REFORM

We have suggested that there are at least three classes of instructional conditions necessary for students to acquire and use domain-specific and metacognitive knowledge in educational settings. First, instructors must design tasks, both in class and out of class, and set criteria for evaluting achievement that place *demands* on students' knowledge and capabilities. Second, the instructional environment must provide students with sufficient *supports* to ensure that students are able and willing to acquire and use the requisite knowledge and skills. Third, instructional environments must be free of the kind of *compensations* that reduce or eliminate demands.

Consider, again, a typical social studies or science course at the secondary-school level. In such a course, textbooks are relied upon as the principal means of assisting students to acquire content knowledge. Although students may take part in other activities in class and in homework assignments, these textbooks typically contain all that one needs to know to do well in the course. Although the central role of the textbook is well known to students, their teachers complain that students tend to complete reading assignments without comprehending what they read; that is, when asked to state the main ideas in a particular section or explain the significance of some event or information they have just read about, students are often unable to produce meaningful interpretive summaries.

However, this apparent student deficiency becomes understandable when other relevant factors are taken into account. It is often the case in secondary-level courses that students are called upon to read material (a) with no indication of how the reading assignment fits in with what they have learned up to that time in the course (lack of support); (b) with no instruction, either in general or specific to the subject matter or structure of the text, in how to summarize or select out important information (lack of support); (c) with no external requirement to read for meaning or to be selective (lack of demand); and (d) with no expectation that they will be responsible for demonstrating their knowledge of the main ideas of the passage either in class or on a test (lack of criterion demand). Moreover, these students often have every indication that (e) ultimately, satisfactory achievement in the course rests on their ability to recognize items of information on a future test (a different demand) and (f) they will have the meaning of the chapter explained to them and the criterial items of information provided to them, prior to the test, in some future class presentation or handout (compensation). In this example, each of these conditions represents an impediment to students' acquisition of metacognitive knowledge or use of strategies associated with reading for meaning and with the differentiation of important from less important information.

Removing impediments such as these as well as the kinds of impediments that hinder the acquisition of domain-specific knowledge will not be an easy task. We have already noted the complexity and difficulty of providing effective instructional support for the acquisition and appropriate deployment of constructive processing strategies. No less complex and difficult is the instructor's task in designing performance criteria that pose genuine problems or that demand comprehension and integration of knowledge. Our conjecture is that the instructional reform efforts intended to fulfill the promises of recent research are themselves impeded by a number of gaps in knowledge on the part of both practitioners and the research community, as well as by certain dilemmas that affect instructional practice.

First, we are impeded by a lack of knowledge. We lack accepted instructional design principles for specifying how the acquisition of metacognitive and domain-specific knowledge can be effectively fostered. The analyses necessary to product such accepted principles have been conducted with respect to only a few, mostly high-level mathematical and physical science content areas.

With regard to our understanding of how best to facilitate the acquisition and use of such knowledge, we are hampered also by the current state of teacher training. It seems reasonable to believe that the majority of instructors have never acquired the kind of proceduralized knowledge that would be required to provide effective support or to construct demanding performance criteria for their students. These kinds of capabilities have not been prominent among the objectives of teacher education, in part because subject matter experts have had little influence on the education of teachers, and in part because the knowledge of how to structure instruction in a subject matter area has rarely been explicitly specified.

We also lack the knowledge of when and how to incorporate instruction in metacognitive strategies into the curriculum. To return to the example of the reading assignment given earlier, we know that summarizing paragraphs is a complex skill that involves, at the least, knowledge of text structures, the differentiation of information according to some criteria such as importance to the author's central message or criterion relevance, the identification of superordinate and subordinate categories and exemplars, and the selection or generation of topic sentences (Brown & Day, 1983). Summarizing across multiple paragraphs can introduce additional subskills when the relationships between these paragraphs are not explicit. With the exception of very recent work published in journals and books that are largely inaccessible to teachers (e.g., Armbruster & Anderson, 1984; Brown & Day, 1983; Mayer, 1987), there are no guidelines available for teachers, or for teacher-training institutions, that would help them to assist their students to use these and other metacognitive strategies. An obvious potential source of such support, perhaps delivered through institutions of teacher education or through the design of instructional materials in different subject-matter areas, is the educational research community.

The process of removing impediments to the acquisition and use of domain-specific and metacognitive knowledge is hampered by a second class of factors: the dynamics of classroom practices. Many of the impediments currently in place exist and are sustained because they have value for teachers and students. That is, although current practices may impede student learning, they serve to support some other objective of equivalent or perhaps greater value in the educational setting. As a consequent, educational reform efforts focused on removing impediments of the kind discussed herein must be carried out with an appreciation of some of the dilemmas that face practitioners.

One such dilemma concerns the avoidance of risk in the classroom. As Doyle (1983) has pointed out, teachers and students maintain an implicit agreement to keep down the risks associated with teaching and learning. High demands can mean increasing the probability of student failure, which, in turn can mean increasing the chances that teachers are regarded as incompetent or unfair. Low-level repetitive tasks and reproductive criterion demands combined with compensatory practices insures that the risk of failure is low. Attempts to change this system by increasing the cognitive demands of reading assignments or by requiring that students demonstrate their procedural knowledge on criterion tasks, for example, would no doubt be met with resistance by participants in educational settings, at least until they were able to adjust the new requirements to low-risk activities.

The solution to the dilemma of how to increase cognitive demands without increasing student failure is to couple these demands with frequent, accessible supports in the form of training, guidance materials, and individual assistance. However, as Pressley, Goodchild, et al. (1987) have pointed out, the support that is often required is very time consuming and requires considerable expertise. It is clear that providing for the acquisition of procedural and metacognitive knowledge could not be accomplished without sacrificing, to some degree, the extent of content coverage currently associated with courses at the secondary-school level. The choice might have to be between covering a few things in depth versus covering many topics superficially.

In addition, students must be provided with opportunities that enable them to appreciate, by means of feedback events incorporated into different tasks, the effectiveness of differential strategy use. Students need to be aware of the connection between different task outcomes and the quality and quantity of strategic effort they put into the task. Although testing and grading is an established aspect of schooling, feedback of the kind necessary to acquire strategic knowledge is not typically provided. Providing for informative feedback relative to the use of varieties of strategies would not only be a major unprecedented innovation, it would be required by different students in different amounts and kinds and thus would need to be individualized. The requirement for individualization may be yet another impediment to instructional reforms of the kind discussed here, at least for schools that rely mainly on group instruction.

Finally, there has been increasing interest in recent years in describing the links among strategy acquisition and use, feelings of self-efficacy, and the opportunity to engage in self-directed, self-regulated learning. Among the implications of this research is that the most effective to teach and encourage the use of the kinds of domain-specific and metacognitive strategies we have described is to combine instruction in the use of the strategy with instruction in self-monitoring, self-regulation, and attributions of success and failure to personal effort and efficacy (Carr & Borkowski, 1987; Short & Weissberg-Benchell, this volume, chap. 2). A further implication is that strategy acquisition and use is best facilitated in situations where students have some control over and responsibility for their own learning (Corno & Rohrkemper, 1985).

To the extent that the acquisition of metacognitive and domain-specific knowledge and the use of associated strategies is dependent on the presence of learner control in the instructional and learning process, yet another dilemma arises. Schools have little experience, or at least, little positive experience in giving students responsibility over their own learning. Moreover, there may be significant resistance on the part of teachers and administrators to relinquish control in schools and classrooms. It is interesting to note that computer programming courses constitute one of the few contexts at the secondary-school level in which students have a measure of control over their own learning, engage in legitimate problem solving, receive feedback to enhance learning rather than for assessment purposes, and work with their instructors as colleagues. Courses that have these characteristics are typically taught by instructors who have been recently drafted out of other subject matter areas and who are operating at a level of expertise just months ahead of their students. Thus, rather than assuming the more typical role of established oracle, they join with their students in the process of intellectual development. The challenge, then, is to find ways of inducing such role changes in traditional subject-matter domains.

Acknowledgments. Preparation of this chapter and the original research reported herein were supported by grants from the National Institute of Child Health and Human Development (HD17984-03) and the National Science Foundation (DPE 84-70364).

REFERENCES

Anderson, J.R. (1982). Acquisition of cognitive skill. *Psychological Review, 89,* 369–406.

Armbruster, B.B., & Anderson, T.H. (1984). Mapping: Representing informative text diagrammatically. In C.D. Holley & D.F. Dansereau (Eds.), *Spatial learning strategies* (pp. 189–212). New York: Academic Press.

Ballstaedt, S. & Mandl, H. (1984). In H. Mandl, N.L. Stein & T. Trabasso (Eds.), *Learning and comprehension of text. Elaborations, assessment and analysis.* pp. 331–353. Hillsdale, NJ: Erlbaum & Associates.

Borkowski, J.G. (1985). Signs of intelligence: Strategy generalization and metacognition. In S.R. Yussen (Ed.), *The growth of reflection in children* (pp. 105–144). Orlando, FL: Academic Press.

Borkowski, J.G., Krause, A.J. (1985). Metacognition and attributional beliefs. In G. d'Ydewalle (Ed.), *Cognition, information processing, and motivation,* (pp. 557–567). North Holland: Elsevier Science Publishers.

Borkowski, J.G., Weyhing, R.S., & Turner, L.A. (1986). Attributional retraining and the teaching of strategies. *Exceptional Children, 53,* 130–137.

Bransford, J.D., Sherwood, R., Vye, N., & Reiser, J. (1986). Thinking, teaching and problem solving: Suggestions from research. *American Psychologist, 41,* 1078–1089.

Bransford, J.D., Stein, B.S., Shelton, T.S., & Owings, R.A. (1981). Cognition and adaptation: The importance of learning to learn. In J.H. Harvey (Ed.), *Cognition, social behavior, and the environment* (pp. 92–110). Hillsdale, NJ: Erlbaum & Associates.

Brown, A. (1987). Metacognition, executive control, self-regulation, and other more mysterious mechanisms. In F.E. Weinert & R.H. Kluwe (Eds.), *Metacognition, motivation and understanding* (pp. 65–117). Hillsdale, NJ: Erlbaum & Associates.

Brown, A.L., Armbruster, B.B., & Baker, L. (1986). The role of metacognition in reading and studying. In J. Orasanu (Ed.), *Reading comprehension: From research to practice* (pp. 49–75). Hillsdale, NJ: Erlbaum & Associates.

Brown, A.L., Campione, J.C., & Day, J.D. (1981). Learning to learn: On training students to learn from texts. *Educational Researcher, 10,* 14–21.

Brown, A.L., & Day, J.D. (1983). Macrorules for summarizing texts: The development of expertise. *Journal of Verbal Learning and Verbal Behavior, 22,* 1–16.

Brown, A.L., Palincsar, A.S., & Armbruster, B.B. (1984). Instructing comprehension-fostering activities in interactive learning situations. In H. Mandl, N.L. Stein, & T. Trabasso (Eds.), *Learning and comprehension of text* (pp. 255–286). Hillsdale, NJ: Erlbaum & Associates.

Brown, A.L., & Smiley, S.S. (1978). The development of strategies for studying texts. *Child Development, 49,* 1076–1088.

Carroll, J.B., Davies, P., & Richman, B. (1971). *American heritage word frequency book.* New York: American Heritage.

Carr, M.M., & Borkowski, J.G. (April 1987). *Underachievement: The importance of attributional retraining of comprehension strategies.* Paper presented at the annual meeting of the American Educational Association, Washington, DC.

Chi, M.T.H. (1985). Changing conception of sources of memory development. *Human Development, 28,* 50–56.

Chi, M.T.H., Glaser, R., & Rees, E. (1982). Expertise in problem solving. In R.J. Sternberg (Ed.), *Advances in the psychology of human intelligence,* Vol. 1 (pp. 7–75). Hillsdale, NJ: Erlbaum & Associates.

Chiesi, H., Spilich, G.J., & Voss, J.F. (1979). Acquisition of domain-related information in relation to high and low domain knowledge. *Journal of Verbal Learning and Verbal Behavior, 18,* 257–273.

Christopoulos, J., Rohwer, W.D., Jr., & Thomas, J.W. (1987). Grade level differences in students' study activities as a function of course characteristics. *Contemporary Educational Psychology, 12,* 303–323.

Corno, L., & Rohrkemper, M.M. (1985). The intrinsic motivation to learn in classrooms. In C. Ames & R. Ames (Eds.), *Research on motivation in education,* Vol. 2, *The classroom milieu* (pp. 53–92). New York: Academic Press.

Doyle, W. (1983). Academic work. *Review of Educational Research, 53,* 159–199.

Flavell, J.H., & Wellman, H.M. (1977). Metamemory. In R. Kail, Jr., & J. Hagen (Eds.), *Perspectives on the development of memory and cognition* (pp. 3–33). Hillsdale, NJ: Erlbaum & Associates.

Fleming, M., & Chambers, B. (1983). Teacher-made tests: Windows on the classroom. In W.R. Hathway (Ed.), *Testing in the schools.* San Francisco: Jossey-Bass.

Franks, J., Vye, N.J., Auble, P.M., Mezynski, K.J., Perfetto, G.A., Bransford, J.D., Stein, B.S., & Littlefield, J. (1982). Learning from explicit versus implicit texts. *Journal of Experimental Psychology: General, iii,* 414–422.

Garner, R., & Reis, R. (1981). Monitoring and resolving comprehension obstacles: An investigation of spontaneous lookbacks among upper-grade good and poor comprehenders. *Reading Research Quarterly, 16,* 569–582.

Glaser, R. (1987). Thoughts on expertise. In C. Schooler & W. Schaie (Eds.), *Cognitive functioning and social structure over the life course* (pp. 81–94). Norwood, NJ: Ablex.

Greeno, J.G. (April 1986). *Mathematical cognition: Accomplishments and challenges in research.* Paper presented at the annual meeting of the American Educational Research Association, San Francisco.

Jones, B.F., & Hall, J.W. (1982). School application of the mnemonic keyword method as a study strategy by eighth graders. *Journal of Educational Psychology, 74,* 230–237.

Larkin, J.H. (1985). Understanding, problem representations, and skill in physics. In S.F. Chipman, J.W. Segal, & R. Glaser (Eds.), *Thinking and learning skills,* Vol. II (pp. 141–159). Hillsdale, NJ: Erlbaum & Associates.

Lesgold, A.M. Rubison, H., Feltovich, P., Glaser, R., & Klopfer, D. (1988). Expertise in a complex skill: Diagnosing x-ray pictures. In M.T.H. Chi, R. Glaser, & M. Farr (Eds.), *The nature of expertise.* Hillsdale, NJ: Erlbaum & Associates.

Lindberg, M. (1980). The role of knowledge structures in the ontogeny of learning. *Journal of Experimental Child Psychology, 30,* 401–410.

Linn, M.C., Sloane, K.D., & Clancy, M. (1986). Ideal and actual outcomes of Pascal programming instruction. *Journal of Research in Science Teaching, 24,* 467–490.

Mandl, H., Stein, N.L., & Trabasso, T. (Eds.). (1984). *Learning and comprehension of text.* Hillsdale, NJ: Erlbaum & Associates.

Mayer, R.E. (1987). Instructional variables that influence cognitive processes during reading. In B. Britton & S. Glynn (Eds.), *Executive control processes in reading* (pp. 201–216). Hillsdale, NJ: Erlbaum & Associates.

Mergendoller, J., Marchman, V.A., Mitman, A.J., & Packer, M.J. (1987). Task demands and accountability in middle-grade science classes. *The Elementary School Journal, 3,* 251–265.

Meyer, B.F. (1984). [Text dimensions and cognitive processing.] In H. Mandl, N.L. Stein, & T. Trabasso (Eds.), *Learning and comprehension of text* (pp. 3–51). Hillsdale, NJ: Erlbaum & Associates.

Palincsar, A.S., & Brown, A.L. (1984). Reciprocal teaching of comprehension-fostering and comprehension-monitoring activities. *Cognition and Instruction, 1,* 117–175.

Pressley, M., Borkowski, J.G., & O'Sullivan, J. (1985). Children's metamemory and the teaching of memory strategies. In D.L. Forrest-Pressley, G.E. MacKinnon, & T.G. Waller (Eds.), *Metacognition, cognition, and human performance: Theoretical perspectives,* Vol. 1 (pp. 111–154). New York: Academic Press.

Pressley, M., Borkowski, J.G., & Schneider, W. (1987). Good strategy users coordinate metacognition, strategy use and knowledge. In R. Vasta & G. Whitehurst (Eds.), *Annals of child development,* Vol. 4 (pp. 89–129). Greenwich, CT: JAI Press.

Pressley, M., Forrest-Pressley, D.L., Elliot-Faust, D., & Miller, G. (1985). Children's use of cognitive strategies, how to teach strategies, and what to do if they can't be learned. In M. Pressley & C.J. Brainerd (Eds.), *Cognitive approaches to memory development* (pp. 1–47). New York: Springer-Verlag.

Pressley, M., Goodchild, F., Fleet, J., Zajchowski, R., & Evans, E.D. (April 1987). *What is good strategy use and why is it hard to teach?: An optimistic appraisal of the challenges associated with strategy instruction.* Paper presented at the annual meeting of the American Educational Research Association, Washington, DC.

Resnick, L.B. (1984). Comprehending and learning: Implications for a cognitive theory of instruction. In H. Mandl, N.L. Stein, & T. Trabasso (Eds.), *Learning and comprehension of text* (pp. 431–443). Hillsdale, NJ: Erlbaum & Associates.

Rohwer, W.D., Jr. (1980). An elaborative conception of learner differences. In R.E. Snow, P.A. Federico, & W.E. Montague (Eds.), *Aptitude, learning and instruction: Cognitive process analyses of aptitude, learning and problem solving,* Vol. 1. Hillsdale, NJ: Erlbaum & Associates.

Rohwer, W.D., Jr., Rabinowitz, M., & Dronkers, N.F. (1982). Event knowledge, elaborative propensity, and the development of learning proficiency. *Journal of Experimental Child Psychology, 33,* 492–503.

Rohwer, W.D., Jr., & Thomas, J.W. (1987). The role of mnemonic strategies in study effectiveness. In M.A. McDaniel & M. Pressley (Eds.), *Imaginal and mnemonic processes* (pp. 428–450). New York: Springer-Verlag.

Schneider, W. (1985). Developmental trends in the metamemory-memory behavior relationship: An integrative review. In D.L. Forrest-Pressley, G.E. MacKinnon, & T.G. Waller (Eds.), *Metacognition, cognition, and performance* (pp. 57–110). Orlando, FL: Academic Press.

Schoenfeld, A.H. (1983). On failing to think mathematically: Some kinds of mathematical malfunctions in college students. *Focus on Learning Problems in Mathematics*, 5, 93–104.

Schoenfeld, A.H. (1985). Metacognitive and epistemological issues in mathematical understanding. In E.A. Silver (Ed.), *Teaching and learning mathematical problem solving: Multiple research perspectives* (pp. 361–379). Hillsdale, NJ: Erlbaum & Associates.

Schoenfeld, A.J. (in press a). On mathematics as sense-making: An informal attack on the unfortunate divorce of formal and informal mathematics. In D.N. Perkins, J. Segal, & J. Voss (Eds.), *Informal reasoning and education*. Hillsdale, NJ: Erlbaum & Associates.

Schoenfeld, A.H. (in press b). Teaching mathematical thinking and problem solving. In L.B. Resnick & L.E. Klopfer (Eds.), *Cognitive research in subject matter learning.* (1989 Yearbook of the ASCD) Alexandria, VA: Association for Supervision and Curriculum Development.

Stein, B.S., Bransford, J.D., Franks, J.J., Owings, R.A., Vye, N.J., & McGraw, W. (1982). Differences in the precision of self-generated elaborations. *Journal of Experimental Psychology: General*, *111*, 399–405.

Strage, A., Tyler, A.B., Rohwer, W.D., Jr., & Thomas, J.W. (1987). An analytic framework for assessing distinctive course features with and across grade levels. *Contemporary Educational Psychology*, *12*, 280–302.

Thomas, J.W., & Rohwer, W.D., Jr. (in press). Studying across the lifespan. In S.R. Yussen and M.C. Smith (Eds.), *Reading across the lifespan*. New York: Springer-Verlag.

Voss, J.F., Greene, T.R., Post, T.A., & Penner, B.C. (1983). Problem-solving skill in the social sciences. In Bower, G.H. (Ed.), *The psychology of learning and motivation*, Vol. 17 (pp. 165–213). New York: Academic Press.

Weinstein, C.F., & Mayer, R.E. (1986). The teaching of learning strategies. In M.C. Wittrock (Ed.), *Handbook of research on teaching*, third edition (pp. 315–327). New York: Macmillan.

6
Why Strategy Instruction Is So Difficult and What We Need to Do About It

Gerald G. Duffy and Laura R. Roehler

Reading strategy instruction has recently received much research attention. Typical of this research are laboratory studies such as those by Miller (1985, 1987) and classroom studies by Palincsar (Palincsar & Brown, 1984), Paris (Paris, Cross, & Lipson, 1984), Pearson (1985), and ourselves (Duffy, Roehler, Sivan, et al., 1987). This instructional research is based on what researchers have learned about how expert readers use strategies (Pressley & Brainard, 1985; Segal, Chipman, & Glaser, 1985). Strategies are defined as cognitive activities readers engage in as they construct meaning from text (Paris, Lipson, & Wixson, 1983). Unlike routine procedures associated with skills, strategies are flexible plans that readers adapt to the comprehension demands of the text.

While research establishes that expert readers use strategies and that instruction results in improved strategy use, the difficulties inherent in successfully teaching reading strategies have received little attention. This chapter describes what makes reading strategy instruction difficult, describes an instructional theory that accounts for these difficulties, and makes recommendations for improving research and practice regarding reading strategy instruction.

Background

This chapter is based on our findings about (a) explicit teacher explanations to low-aptitude students regarding the reasoning used when employing reading strategies and (b) subsequent exploratory research about the relationship between teachers' knowledge structures and the explanations they provide during instruction. The focus in all studies is (a) the mental processes involved in using reading strategies, (b) at-risk students, and (c) implementation of strategy instruction in the context of normal classroom conditions. We describe this research in three stages.

The first stage, initiated in 1981, consisted of a series of pilot studies and subsequent experiments involving a total of 53 third- and fifth-grade teachers and their low-reading groups. The first experimental study was conducted in 1982–83 with low-group fifth graders (Duffy, Roehler, Meloth, et al., 1986) and the second experimental study was conducted in 1984–85 with a low group of third graders (Duffy, Roehler, Sivan, et al., 1987). In both studies the curricular focus was repair strategies—those strategies readers use during reading to remove blockages to comprehension (e.g., using context clues to figure out the meaning of an unknown word in a text). The hypothesis was that low-group students who receive explicit explanations of what repair strategies are (declarative knowledge), when to use them (conditional knowledge), and how to use them (procedural knowledge) will demonstrate high levels of metacognitive awareness regarding what the teacher was teaching and, ultimately, high levels of reading achievement. In these studies, teachers were randomly assigned, and we observed both control-group and treatment-group teachers periodically throughout the year as they taught their low-reading groups. In treatment classrooms, teachers were trained by researchers to recast prescribed basal reading textbook skills as repair strategies and to explicitly explain these strategies. Explanations began with brief discussions of the selection to be read and explicit introductory statements about when the repair strategy would be used in that selection. It then progressed to teacher modeling of reasoning used when employing the strategy, to guided student practice, and to student application while reading the previously discussed selection. Control teachers, in contrast, followed standard basal reading textbook procedures and prescriptions emphasizing routine skills rather than strategies, and drill and practice rather than explicit explanations. Audio tapes of both treatment and control teachers' explanations were rated for explicitness of explanation, and low-group students in both groups were interviewed following lessons to determine their metacognitive awareness of lesson content and tested to determine their conceptual understanding and reading achievement. These studies established (a) that classroom teachers, working in the context of normal curricular and instructional constraints, can learn to explain mental processes involved in using reading strategies; (b) that low aptitude students who receive such instruction demonstrate more metacognitive awareness of lesson content and of the need to employ repair strategies than students of teachers who do not provide such instruction; and (c) that such students then demonstrate greater achievement on a variety of traditional and nontraditional reading achievement measures than students of teachers who do not provide such instruction.

The second stage of this line of research was a series of post hoc studies of relationships suggested by the experiments. One set of such studies was quantitative. For instance, Meloth (1987) reanalyzed the data from the second experiment and established that student awareness of lesson content mediated between teacher explanation and student achievement, with highly aware students having high achievement. Similarly, a discriminant analysis indicated that students' awareness of conditional and procedural knowledge as reflected in post-lesson interviews accounted for a majority of variance in achievement favoring treatment-group students (Meloth & Roehler, 1987), and a correlational analysis of teacher statements during instruction revealed high correlations between teacher statements about when a strategy will be used (conditional knowledge) and student achievement (Sivan & Roehler, 1986).

Another set of post hoc studies was qualitative, examining teachers' explanations during lessons about the use of reading strategies and their reactions to such instruction. The data consisted of lesson transcripts and transcripts of teacher interviews conducted periodically to assess teachers' understanding of how to explain strategies. The usual procedure was to select a sample of effective and less effective teachers (based both on the explicitness of their explanations and on their students' achievement) and to analyze the transcripts of these teachers' lessons and their interviews using modified microethnographic techniques (see, for example, Green & Wallat, 1981). These descriptive studies led to hypotheses regarding the importance of substantive teacher statements during instruction (Duffy, 1983), the need for teachers to make such statements not only when providing initial explanations but also when responding to students' emerging understandings (Roehler, Duffy, & Tiezzi, 1987), that teachers differ greatly in their ability to provide substantive explanations (Duffy, Roehler, & Rackliffe, 1986), and that certain conceptual and contextual conditions constrain teachers in their attempts to provide such explanations (Duffy & Roehler, 1986).

The third stage of this line of research explored why some teachers are able to provide substantive explanations despite environmental constraints while others apparently cannot. We turned to the expert-novice literature and considered the possibility that expert-like teachers organize information about explaining reading strategies into coherent knowledge structures; less effective teachers, in contrast, make few meaningful ties between what they are told about explaining and the specific situations they encounter in their classrooms. For instance, while some teachers selectively applied our suggestions to their specific classroom situations, others routinely and rigidly followed our directives regardless of conceptual and contextual constraints. In short, some of our teachers integrated our intervention training into coherent knowledge structures and, because they networked these suggestions with other professional and situational knowledge, they were able to apply them flexibly as conditions demanded; other teachers interpreted what we said as "rules" to be followed without adaptation or variation. These observations led us to hypothesize that teachers' classroom actions may be tied to how they organize (or fail to organize) what they are taught about how to teach. Subsequently, we initiated exploratory descriptive work on relationships between teachers' knowledge structures and their instructional practice (Duffy, Roehler, Conley, Herrmann, & Johnson, 1988; Roehler, Duffy, Conley, Herrmann, Johnson, & Michelsen, 1987) and on the relationship between knowledge structures students develop during lessons and knowledge structures teachers possess (Roehler, Duffy, & Warren, 1987). Early results suggest that the most effective teachers possess coherent knowledge structures, that they are metacognitively aware of their knowledge, that their instructional actions suggest that they exert regulatory control over instruction, and that they are more successful in developing student outcomes than teachers who do not exhibit these characteristics.

In attempting to help teachers (a) organize their knowledge about explaining reading strategies and (b) improve their reading strategy instruction, we have become more and more sensitive to how difficult it is for teachers to teach reading strategies. The subtleties that account for this difficulty must be considered when researching reading strategy instruction and when helping teachers improve such instruction.

Subtleties of Reading Strategy Instruction

Three subtleties make reading strategy instruction difficult. The first is learning-oriented, focusing on how students learn reading strategies; the second is curricular in nature, focusing on what we teach when we teach reading strategies; and the third is instructional, focusing on both direct and less direct teacher actions associated with effective strategy instruction. Each category is described herein.

SUBTLETIES RELATED TO LEARNING

To learn how to use reading strategies, students combine new experiences with their older understanding about how reading works and about the social rules that form the instructional context (Mayer & Greeno, 1972). In effect, they filter instructional information through their current understanding of the topic at hand and, during this filtering process, restructure the instructional message to make it compatible with their existing conceptions (Winne & Marx, 1982). For instance, a student who moves from one school, where mastery of sequential reading skills was the criteria for classroom success, to a new classroom where strategy use is valued will try to understand strategies in terms of previous experiences with drill and practice of skills. In a sense, students negotiate meanings for instruction that fit their prior understandings of both the topic of instruction and the existing social system in the classroom, a process sometimes referred to as the cognitive mediational paradigm (Winne, 1985). This restructuring process often results in student understandings that are different in important ways from what the teacher intended.

Two important subtleties result from this student mediation of instructional information. The first focuses on the length of time it takes students to learn to use reading strategies and the second focuses on the consistency of instructional messages about strategies.

The Longitudinal Nature of Strategy Learning

Because students gradually restructure instructional information in terms of their existing schemata, strategies are not learned immediately. Instead, strategy learning is longitudinal. This is particularly so regarding what has come to be called the metacognitive aspects of strategy use, in which teachers develop students' conscious awareness of what they know so they can exert regulatory control over that knowledge (Baker & Brown, 1984).

Data from our experimental studies of teacher explanation of reading strategies (Duffy, Roehler, Sivan, et al., 1987) are illustrative. One of the outcome measures was student metacognitive awareness of lesson content, as determined by interviewing students following six lessons observed across the academic year. It was hypothesized that students' metacognitive awareness, as revealed by rating the post-lesson interviews, would be high whenever teachers were sufficiently explicit in explaining lesson content. This was not the case. Treatment teachers provided highly explicit explanations beginning in October; however, their students did not demonstrate significant metacognitive awareness of lesson content until February. For instance, the following is typical of student interview responses in October following explicit explanations of strategy use[1]:

I. What was your lesson about this morning?
S: It was about words—the teacher wanted us to learn about words.
I: When would you use this information?
S: Well, I would use it—I'm not certain—I guess I'd use it in junior high.
I: If you were going to tell our friend how to do what you learned what would you say?
S: It's important to read the paragraph carefully and reread it enough to get the answer. Rereading is important.

In February, the same student typically responded to explicit explanations of strategy use as follows:

I: What was your lesson about this morning?
S: It was about finding the meaning of words that we don't know in a sentence and using the context to help you.
I: Okay, when would you use this information?
S: You could use it anywhere, from a cereal box—you see the word "nutrition" and you could do it there—or else in your math book or in this social studies book, any old . . . anyplace you could use it.
I: Okay, well, why would it be useful for you when you are reading? What would you do with it?

---

[1]All interview excerpts used in this paper are taken from (or adapted from) transcriptions of reading strategy lessons taught by teachers in our second experimental study (Duffy, Roehler, Sivan, et al., 1987).

S: When you come to a word when you're reading you would use that skill to find out that word you don't know, if you don't know it. If you do know it, you don't have to use it.

I: If your friend was absent today, what would you tell him about how to do it?

S: Well, the strategy is to find the clues in the context or the surrounding sentences. Then you . . . once you have all the clues you think there are in that sentence . . . you put them together with what you already know about that word — that one word that you don't know. Then you see if it makes sense with those meanings that you put together. And that is the strategy.

Students' delay in demonstrating metacognitive awareness is explained by the fact that they do not immediately replace one schema with another following initial strategy instruction but, rather, modify instructional information to fit old schemata and thereby create restructured understandings. For instance, in October the student whose interview was just transcribed had less information to work with and tried to make the teacher's instructional message about strategies fit old conceptions about reading (e.g., what is learned in reading is not immediately useful); by February, the message about immediate strategy use is incorporated into the student's growing schema about strategies and how they are used. Hence, students do not replace old reading concepts with new concepts about strategy use in the first lesson but rather, gradually restructure their concepts as teachers present successive lessons.

From teachers' perspectives, this is a discouraging phenomenon. They frequently complain early in the academic year that "I'm providing explicit explanations but the kids aren't getting it." In the face of evidence that seems to say students are not learning, teachers want to try a different approach. However, such rapid tactical change makes learning even more difficult, since student restructuring is aided when instructional messages are consistent over time but is impeded when restructuring must begin from scratch because tactics are changed.

The subtlety for teachers is distinguishing real student failure from restructuring. If students are really failing, alternative instructional approaches are called for. However, if teachers are observing restructuring, they must persist in providing the instructional message (i.e., persist in their explicit explanations), even though students seem to be failing. It requires instructional sensitivity and patience to distinguish these differences, and it requires good judgment to know when to continue developing specific conceptual understandings in the face of few signs of learning. Additionally, teachers must be instructionally creative to provide students with successive opportunities to restructure their understandings about strategies without simply teaching the same strategy over and over again with deadening regularity. However, such teacher sensitivity, patience, judgment, and creativity in response to students' longitudinal restructuring is crucial to successful strategy instruction.

Consistent Instructional Messages

A second learning subtlety is the provision of consistent instructional messages. Because students mediate instructional information in light of both of their prior knowledge about the topic and the "rules of the game" in the classroom, *all* the messages conveyed in the total instructional environment — not just those conveyed during specific strategy lessons — must support strategic reading. Two examples are illustrative.

First, consider how direct instruction of strategies interacts with the more general activities of the classroom. For instance, in a literate classroom environment (Duffy & Roehler, 1987a) in which general activities focus on opportunities to read selections of personal choice, on exchange of written messages, and on using written text to solve meaningful problems, teachers provide students with tangible experiences demonstrating that literacy is worth pursuing. However, teachers familiar with direct instruction find it difficult to see what such environments have to do with effective strategy instruction, feeling that because literate environment activities do not normally include explicit mention of strategies, time would be better spent on specific strategy lessons. In actuality, however, literate environments support strategy instruction because they consistently provide meaningful evidence about what reading is. That is, the general classroom activities provide evidence that reading (and reading strategy use) is worthwhile. From this understanding flows motivation, or what Paris and his colleages (Paris et al., 1984) call "the will" to learn the skill. The evidence of reading's meaningfulness during general activities makes learning strategies worthwhile. In this sense, instructional messages conveyed by general activities and by specific strategy lessons are mutually supportive, not contradictory.

Second, consider the sequence in which strategies are usually presented to students. In standard basal reading textbooks, instruction typically begins by reading a selection and answering associated questions; it then moves to a specific skill lesson. No clear connection is established between reading selection and subsequent skill. This sequence contradicts the idea that skills and strategies are to be used in reading. Teaching a strategy separately from a selection leaves its usefulness unclear, and there is no compelling reason to learn it. The message that strategies are useful when reading is consistently communicated, however, if strategy lessons *precede* the reading of the selection. By altering the sequence in this way, students directly experience the usefulness of the skill or strategy because they immediately see an instance where the strategy is applied. The message about strategy use is consistent.

Summary

Learners, particularly unmotivated learners, need both time to successively restructure their instructional experiences and a rich context in which to build a meaningful conceptual mosaic for why strategies are useful.

Unfortunately, teachers tend to expect immediate evidence of learning and tend to put their effort into direct instruction of strategy lessons rather than also expending energy on supportive activities that demonstrate why strategies are worth learning (see, for instance, Duffy & Roehler, 1986).

SUBTLETIES RELATED TO CURRICULUM

Curriculum refers to what is to be taught. During strategy instruction, strategies are taught. However, it is not as simple as that.

Curriculum guides and school goal statements are "official" statements of what is to be taught. However, what students actually learn is often something else. Why is this so? Because students interpret their academic work and conclude that one thing is really important when the teacher actually meant for something else to be important.

Academic work is the most prevalent cue students use to make sense of the curriculum (Doyle, 1983). This term is used broadly to mean the conceptual sum of the meaning students get from tasks completed during instruction. Tasks are defined by students' answers and by the way in which they arrive at these answers. As such, tasks have both cognitive characteristics (what cognitive operations are required to carry out the task?) and form characteristics (what procedures and social skills must be employed to carry out the task?) (Blumenfeld, Mergendoller & Swarthout, 1987). For instance, if the teacher teaches a main idea strategy using worksheets that require students to choose the best title for short paragraphs from among four choices, the cognitive and form characteristics of the task encourage students to identify best titles in artificial texts; if the teacher teaches main idea by having students use the strategy to retrieve a temporarily lost central thread of a passage in self-selected recreational reading, the cognitive and form characteristics of the task encourage students to construct the gist of passage encountered while reading real text. Hence, students make sense of the curriculum by reference to academic work. They interpret the meaning of their academic work and, in the process, decide what they must do to be successful with that work in that particular classroom environment. The academic work causes them to ask themselves: What do I have to do here and how must I do it?

Consequently, teachers determine what students will learn by deciding what tasks they will have students do and what they will count as satisfactory performance of those tasks. In making verbal statements to students during lessons, teachers further define tasks for students. One kind of academic work leads students to one interpretation of what is important; other kinds lead them to other interpretations. Consequently, the teacher's perception of the curricular task is crucial. The following section is illustrative. It describes three curricular distinctions which, when teachers translate them into academic work and present them to students, cause students to interpret strategy instruction differently and to develop substantially different understandings.

Skills Versus Strategies

Most of today's teachers were taught that reading is a set of discrete skills that expert readers employ automatically and routinely. A skill can be isolated, its components discretely described, and the steps in performing it routinized. The curriculum, in this view, is an identified set of skills to be taught as routinized, memorized procedures that are employed automatically as needed.

Teachers often think strategies are the same as skills. In fact, in some cases, the skill labels and strategy labels are the same (e.g., context has long been taught as a "skill" and is now commonly described as a "strategy"). Consequently, many teachers talk about teaching strategies when in actuality the academic work they assign sets expectations more appropriate for skills. For instance, note the skill-oriented description of a context "strategy" that the following teacher provides for students (Duffy, Roehler, & Rackliffe, 1986):

T: Okay, on the board I've listed the strategy, on the board behind you. Okay? The first step is to read the sentence. The second thing?
S: Look for the underlined word.
T: The third thing?
S: Reread the sentence.
T: And then you . . .
S: Look for the clue words.
T: Now, what did I just do? Tell me.
S: (In chorus) Read the sentence. Look for the underlined word. Reread the sentence and look for the clue words.
T: Excellent.

Given such academic work, students conclude the curricular goal is to memorize the steps involved. However, an important difference between skills and strategies is that strategies cannot be proceduralized. Strategic thinking is a reasoning process, and individuals reason with their own storehouse of background knowledge. Consequently, unlike skills for which a "right way" for doing it can be proceduralized and applied in virtually all situations, strategies often have an idiosyncratic flavor. Second, specific strategies are not always applied in the same way. For instance, how a reader activates background knowledge depends upon the textual situation, and how a reader uses a strategy such as context depends upon the available semantic clues and the syntactical arrangement of those clues. Consequently, while skills are uniformly applied in all situations, strategies may be applied procedurally in highly familiar text situations but are more often reflectively adapted to fit situations. Finally, unlike skills, strategies are seldom applied individually. Instead, expert readers typically apply strategies in combination. That is, expert readers are as likely to figure out the meaning of an unknown word by combining a context strategy with a phonics strategy, or an inferencing strategy, or a predicting strategy, or some other kind of strategy as to use context alone. These subtle distinctions between skills and strategies are reflected in substantially different kinds of instructional exchanges in lessons taught by teachers sensitive to these subtleties. These exchanges, in turn, set different expectations for students (Roehler & Duffy, 1986). For instance, note that the teacher in the following example presents a context strategy in a way that encourages students to conclude that it is related in important ways to other strategies.

> T: We have been reading stories and when you are going through a story you quite often find words that you don't know the meaning of. We've talked about different strategies that we can use when we come to a word in a story we don't know. We can divide it up into two words (compound words). We can look in the word and recognize a root word and then recognize a suffix. There is another way that we are going to learn today. You look at other words around the unknown words for hints to what the word means. We use these clues to guess what might fit and, as always we always ask ourselves, "Does it make sense?"

Distinctions between skill and strategy become even more subtle when the tension between conscious awareness and automatic use is considered. Unlike skill instruction, where the goal is a relatively uncomplicated development of automatized responses, strategy instruction involves the development of metacognitive awareness of strategies *and* the expectation that strategies will eventually be applied automatically (Baker & Brown, 1984; Pressley, Snyder, Symons, & Cariglia-Bull, in press). That is, strategy instruction develops expert readers who (a) routinely and automatically use strategies in familiar reading situations and (b) metacognitively regulate strategy use when unfamiliar reading situations are encountered. This curricular duality makes strategy instruction all the more difficult for teachers. While they may be able to handle teaching students to be either automatic or aware, they have difficulty developing both simultaneously.

In sum, if teachers think they are teaching skills, the academic work they assign will cause students to think that they should memorize something for immediate recall rather than developing plans to be applied adaptively and flexibly. This distinction is important, yet subtle. It is even more subtle and difficult to create academic work that sets expectations that strategies should be automatic when comprehension is going smoothly and consciously applied when comprehension is difficult.

Content Focus Versus Direct Strategy Instruction

Another curricular subtlety is the distinction between the direct development of strategies and text comprehension (with strategies learned incidentally). Readings' historical emphasis on decoding has resulted in a backlash against direct emphasis on direct development of strategies in favor of focusing on text content. Content approaches assume that individuals possess inherent ability to comprehend, and that reading strategies are learned "naturally" if appropriate environmental conditions exist (Tierney & Cunningham, 1984). Hence, teachers are frequently urged to teach reading by asking students questions before, during, and after reading a selection (Ogle, 1986), on the apparent assumption that "good" questions trigger students' inherent comprehension processes and produce good readers. Not surprisingly, teachers are frequently observed "teaching" comprehension by asking students to answer comprehension questions about text content (Durkin, 1978–79). Recent emphasis on strategies has not altered this situation. The expectation is that students will learn to be strategic even though strategies are not directly taught. Consequently, the academic work emphasizes story content, not strategies. For instance, the following teacher's instructional talk focuses students on content, not on the strategic process employed to comprehend the content (Roehler & Duffy, 1986):

T: Number 5, Annie.
S: (Student reads sentence).
T: Very good, Tell me what you know about the sentence, Annie?
S: (inaudible).
T: Tell me—look at the sentence and tell me what they are talking about in the sentence. They are talking about something . . .
S: The clubs.
T: What kind of club is it?
S: Secret.
T: A secret club. And they also have something else that is secret. What is it?
S: Password.

In contrast, the following teacher uses the same story to provide different academic work that focuses on learning strategies, not content.

T: Today we are going to learn how to tell what is being talked about in a sentence. For instance, in the story we are going to read today, there are lots of complicated sentences about a secret club. You may find that they are difficult to figure out. If that happens to you, you can use this strategy to help you as you read today's story.

Advocates of direct strategy instruction argue that students must be cued to what strategy is being taught, when it would be useful, and how to apply it in an appropriate situation because strategic processes are not inherent in all students. Students with rich language backgrounds may learn to use some cognitive strategies fairly easily, not because the strategies are lying dormant but, rather, because their language experiences provide them with the raw materials to build an organized schema for reading. Such students may even look like they are learning strategies "naturally" because the teacher needs only provide a minimum of instruction for the student to "catch on." However, low-aptitude students with sparse language experiences have either disorganized or inaccurate schemata for reading, and they have difficulty learning to be strategic without explicit instructional cues. Consequently, the academic work must focus on the strategy itself as it is applied in content, not the story content alone.

There are two subtleties here. The first is that reading always involves content. That is, readers read to understand the content of a message. In this sense, process can never be separated from content. The subtlety, therefore, is to be able to place a relatively heavier emphasis on the strategy for purposes of making students aware of how to employ strategies while simultaneously not losing sight of the ultimate goal of understanding the content of the passage. Second, a content emphasis works with good readers; a process emphasis is particularly effective with low ability readers (Doyle, 1983; Roehler, Duffy, & Meloth, 1986). Consequently, teachers whose academic work focuses students on answering questions before, during, and after reading may get the upper half of the class to be strategic but not low-ability students. They find it difficult to understand why instruction that works with "good" students does not work for all students. That good students construct schemata about strategy use with minimal cues while poor readers require explicit assistance is a subtle distinction that teachers find difficult to discern.

Conceptualizing Strategic Reading

Various forms of academic work encourage different understandings about what strategic readers really do. Deciding what conceptualization of strategic reading to emphasize in academic work requires subtle distinctions by teachers.

For instance, the academic work in our studies (Duffy, Roehler, Sivan, et al., 1987) focused students on identifying blockages to anticipated meaning, identifying an appropriate repair strategy, and then reasoning in flexible ways to repair the blockage. Miller (1987) also provided academic tasks that focused students on being aware of text meaning as they read but then had students follow an established set of self-questions as a means for maintaining meaning. These are two different messages about what students do to monitor meaning getting. The cognitive operations required to carry out the two tasks are different, and students therefore learn different things. An even greater difference is seen in the research of Palincsar and Brown (1984). They do not explicitly teach or measure student self-monitoring during reading but, instead, emphasize post-reading activities of summarizing, questioning, predicting, and clarifying in the context of a reciprocal teacher-student dialogue. The cognitive demands focus on the four activities and the form limits these to group situations (as opposed to independent reading). Similarly, Paris (Paris et al., 1984) does not explicitly teach students to self-monitor but, instead, provides a series of lessons in which strategies are presented as metaphors. Again, the cognitive and form characteristics of the task convey a different message about what strategic readers do. Teachers must distinguish between these subtly different conceptualizations of what strategic reading is. Do they want students to conclude that strategic reading is listening for meaning and applying repair strategies? Or listening for meaning and asking a fixed set of questions? Or engaging in summarizing, questioning, predicting, and clarifying in post-lesson discussions? Or thinking in terms of specific metaphors that serve as mnemonic cues for strategies? While the difference from one to another is subtle, the curricular outcome in each is different. Teachers must make these subtle distinctions and choose academic work designed to promote development of the desired concept (or combination of concepts) about what strategic readers do.

Summary

The curriculum is what students conclude they are supposed to learn. They decide this by reference to their academic work. Distinctions between skill and strategy, between incidental strategy development and an explicit focus, and between various interpretations of what strategic reading involves result in different kinds of academic work and, ultimately, in major differences in what students learn.

SUBTLETIES RELATED TO INSTRUCTION

Instruction is defined here as the actions teachers engage in during lessons to help students learn strategies. The subtleties associated with such actions are described in the following.

Modeling and Other Overt Forms of Information Giving

Modeling is what teachers do to show novice learners how to do something they do not know how to do. It is a particularly important instructional action because by modeling the teacher reduces the ambiguity associated with tasks and, in the process, reduces the inferencing students must do to figure out what the curricular goal is. In short, modeling and other forms of overt instructional information-giving by the teacher reduces the guesswork in students' attempts to learn, thereby helping them restructure what the teacher says in the intended way.

Modeling itself is not a new instructional technique, nor is it particularly subtle in its usual form. For instance, reading stories to students is a relatively common and uncomplicated way to model the physical act of reading. Similarly, various approaches to scaffolding (Langer & Applebee, 1986; Vygotsky, 1978; Wood, Bruner, & Ross, 1976) recommend a gradual process of social mediation in which the instructor models expected language outcomes and gradually transfers the learning to the student (see Day, Cordon, & Kerwin, this volume, chap. 4, for ideas regarding information instruction approaches). However, reading strategy instruction demands two particular qualities of modeling, and therein lies the subtlety.

First, when we teach cognitive strategies we are teaching reasoning, and reasoning is invisible to observers. Further, strategic reasoning cannot be proceduralized because readers adapt strategies to particular textual situations. To cope with these difficulties, a type of modeling called "mental modeling" (Duffy, Roehler, & Herrmann, 1988) is needed to provide students with substantive information about how to be strategic. When providing mental modeling, teachers describe their own thinking as they use strategies to make visible to students the invisible mental processing involved in strategy use. It is a subtle distinction between mental modeling and other forms of scaffolded assistance to learners. For instance, in the following example the teacher makes visible her invisible mental processing when using a reading strategy:

T: I want to show you what I look at when I come across a word I don't know the meaning of. I'll talk out loud to show you how I figure it out. Then I will help you do this. [reading] "The cocoa steamed fragrantly." Hmm, I've heard that word "fragrantly" before, but I don't really know what it means here. I know one of the words right before it though — "steamed." I watched a pot of boiling water once and there was steam coming from it. That water was hot so this must have something to do with the cocoa being hot. Okay, the pan of hot cocoa is steaming on the stove. That means steam is coming up and out, but that still doesn't explain what "fragrantly" means. Let me think again about the hot cocoa on the stove and try to use what I already know about cocoa as a clue. Hot cocoa bubbles, steams and . . . smells! Hot cocoa smells good. [reading] "The cocal steamed fragrantly." That means it smelled good! [addressing the students] Thinking about what I already knew about hot cocoa helped me figure out what that word meant.

In another example, however, the teacher gives directions that appear to be scaffolded support but does not describe the reasoning she engages in:

T: The first thing you do is try to guess from your own experience what the word is. Do you know what experience means? If you can predict what the word is, then fit the word into the sentence to see if it makes sense. Secondly, if you can't guess, ask yourself this: Is the word defined in the passage? Look before and after the word. If it is, then see if the word makes sense. Third, ask yourself this: Is there a synonym for the word before or after the word? Do you know what a synonym is? It's when the words have the same meaning like "big" and "large." Fourth, ask yourself if you can guess what the word is by the general mood or feeling of the passage. Using these steps will help you predict what the word might mean and it's faster than going to a dictionary.

This subtle difference is difficult for teachers to discern. However, substantial differences in student performance result because, in mental modeling such as that provided by the first teacher, students receive substantive information about how to reason as they use the strategy. Thus, ambiguity is reduced and student restructuring is more likely to resemble the intended outcome. In contrast, students in the second teacher's classroom receive little information about how a reader actually reasons in the process of using the strategy. Because the teacher does not reduce ambiguity about how expert readers reason with strategies, students must infer more and, as a result, are less likely to create schemata consistent with the intended curricular outcome.

A second subtlety when modeling strategies relates to metacognitive control. Hopefully, strategy instruction puts students in conscious control of strategy use so they can recognize the need for a strategy in similar future situations and, at those times, access and use similar reasoning. To accomplish this, students (particularly at-risk students) must be explicitly informed (a) that they should be in conscious control of the strategy they are being taught and (b) that they need to recognize situations where the strategy will be needed and search their mental repertoire of strategies to access an appropriate one. Traditional reading instruction does not do this. For instance, the traditional practice of asking comprehension questions following the reading of selections puts the teacher in control of deciding what strategy is needed and of accessing it; the student simply follows the teacher's lead. Because the teacher does not inform the student that a particular strategy should be used, how to access it, or how to use it, it is doubtful whether metacognitive control results.

In sum, teachers must be explicit when modeling mental processing involved in strategy use even though no two people engage in precisely the same reasoning when using a strategy, and they must be explicit about putting students in metacognitive control.

Responding to Students' Developing Understandings

As important as modeling is, it is only the beginning of an instructional cycle. Once students receive information contained in teachers' models, they mediate what they hear and create restructured understandings. While teachers sometimes think that provision of the "perfect model" will eliminate student restructuring entirely, this is not the case. No matter how well a teacher models, students restructure that information in light of their background experiences and the social rules of the classroom. Consequently, teachers must be prepared to continue their instructional actions beyond modeling.

Post-modeling teacher action is characterized as "alternative representations" by Wilson, Shulman, and Richert (1987). That is, mental modeling is an initial effort by teachers to transform their understanding of the strategy and how it is used into a form students can learn. When students restructure this information, teachers provide additional information (or alternative representations) designed to move students gradually toward a construction of the intended outcome.

Such "responsive elaboration" (Duffy & Roehler, 1987b) requires teachers to monitor students' evolving understandings and to respond to these understandings with appropriate statements, cues, prompts, analogies, metaphors, or other forms of assistance designed to refine students' understanding of the intended outcome. Contrary to modeling, which can be planned ahead of time, this assistance cannot be formulated until the situation arises. The necessary spontaneous decision making is difficult and involves two subtleties. First, because publishers and curriculum developers cannot anticipate responsive elaborations in advance, teachers must create them themselves. Second, teachers must gradually diminish the amount of assistance provided in these responsive elaborations, with students receiving more assistance early in the instructional sequence and less assistance as they develop schemata for a strategy. The progression, referred to as fading by psychologists, as movement from "other-directed to self-directed" by Vygotsky (1978), and as "a gradual release of responsibility" by Pearson (1985), requires high levels of teacher sensitivity to students' individual progress. This is yet another instructional subtlety.

Summary

Teachers' instructional actions during strategy instruction are not "cut and dried." Teachers must distinguish between modeling generally and modeling invisible reasoning to put students in metacognitive control of comprehension processes, and they must respond spontaneously to student understandings or misunderstandings during post-modeling instructional interactions. These actions require subtle distinctions.

Discussion

While cognitive strategies are an integral part of expert readers' repertoires, *teaching* strategies is a very complex business. Effective classroom strategy instruction requires changes in how we think about instruction itself, and how we think about research and the practice of reading strategy instruction particularly.

An Instructional Model

Given the complexities and subtleties of strategy instruction, it is clear that current instructional models do not suffice. They do not account for student restructuring of academic work and the resulting instructional fluidity, for the awareness, which is the essence of student control of strategy application, nor for the flexible adaptiveness that teachers must possess if they are to respond effectively to students' emerging understandings.

Our research, as well as our experience in teaching teachers to apply findings of our research, suggests a particular instructional model (Roehler, Duffy, & Tiezzi, 1987). As shown in Figure 6.1, instructional effectiveness begins with teacher metacognitive control both of what is taught (curriculum) and of how it is taught (instruction). Only if teachers are in metacognitive control of their own professional knowledge can they simultaneously provide substantive instructional information and spontaneously modify that information to fit students' restructurings both within specific lessons and across series of lessons. Effective instruction requires that teachers tailor

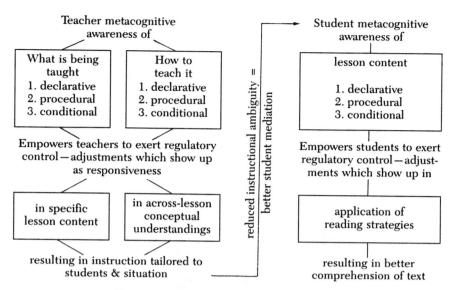

FIGURE 6.1. Model of effective instruction.

information to students' backgrounds and situations. This adaptiveness cannot be scripted or proceduralized. It comes only from teachers' rich conceptual understandings about what they are trying to do, the ability to exert regulatory control over that knowledge and the application of that knowledge to specific instructional situations.

When teachers are in metacognitive control of their professional knowledge, they can reduce instructional ambiguity inherent in the instructional enterprise. That is, because students mediate instructional information as they try to make sense of academic work, they often misinterpret what is intended; the inferences they draw result in restructured understandings different from those intended by the teacher. However, when instructional information is tailored to students' backgrounds and situations, the size of students' inferential leap is reduced, and they are more likely to conclude what the teacher intends. Hence, teachers not only attempt to be explicit in presenting initial information but tailor the explicitness of subsequent information to particular students and groups of students.

Such explicitness helps students interpret academic work in ways consistent with teachers' intentions. That is, they not only become metacognitively aware of lesson content, they also become aware that they are in charge of accessing and applying what is taught. In strategy instruction, for instance, they are aware of what strategies they have learned, when to use them, and how to use them. Consequently, when faced with a difficult reading situation, they can consciously think about what needs to be done and make necessary adjustments for constructing an author's intended meaning. This regulatory control allows them to selectively and appropriately apply their knowledge which, in turn, results in improved reading ability and, ultimately, expertise as a reader.

While this instructional theory is presented here in the context of reading strategy instruction, it can be applied to all instruction in which the goal is student regulatory control. Its significance lies in acknowledgment of the complexity and fluidity of teaching for cognitive processing, particularly as it relates to subtleties associated with learning how to be in metacognitive control of one's cognition, with providing academic work that reflects that goal and with instruction that provides students with substantive assistance in achieving that goal.

IMPLICATIONS FOR RESEARCH AND TEACHING

The complexity and fluidity of strategy instruction and the associated subtleties have implications beyond instructional theory. There are also implications for researchers, curriculum developers, and teacher educators (see also Rohwer & Thomas, this volume, chap. 5; for other instructional reform suggestions).

First, let's consider research. Strategy instruction must be more frequently researched in the natural environment of classrooms. While laboratory studies were useful in establishing that strategies can be taught and continue to be useful as pilot studies for subsequent field work, they do not meet the test of reality. They examine what happens when researchers teach strategy lessons to small numbers of select students or what happens when strategies are taught as a temporary adjunct to the "real" curriculum. In short, they eliminate many of the naturally occurring conditions that produce the subtleties described in this chapter. For instance, laboratory studies are so short that (a) longitudinal student restructuring is not evident, (b) real-world application of the academic work is virtually impossible, and (c) teachers' actions are so isolated from actual classroom constraints that they do not reflect what real teachers do. Consequently, laboratory studies offer few implications for real teachers working in real classrooms. To help these teachers, research must account for the complex problems associated with long-term classroom teaching of large numbers of students simultaneously under mandated conditions that constrain teachers' instructional actions. This is the context of the real world. This context, and how to teach cognitive strategies in this context, must become the research focus if we are to understand how strategy instruction can be effectively implemented in real school situations.

Second, curriculum developers must create instructional materials that take into account the learning, curricular, and instructional subtleties described in this chapter. Current instructional materials, as represented by standard basal reading textbooks, do not provide for cohesive longitudinal development of strategies, do not promote orderly student restructuring, and do not provide substantive assistance to teachers about how to create environmental conditions that promote conditional knowledge. Further, the basal textbook's academic work typically emphasizes a narrow view of question answering, routinized skills, and automaticity rather than a broader emphasis on strategy use, reasoning, and metacognitive awareness. These shortcomings may have been understandable in light of recent eductional demands for "quick fix" instructional procedures to meet accountability demands based on skill models of reading acquisition. However, they are not appropriate for developing strategic readers. To develop strategic readers, curriculum developers must create instructional materials that provide structure and guidance while simultaneously supporting teacher decision making about instructional interactions, as opposed to script following (see also Duffy, Roehler, & Putnam, 1987). Gallimore and Tharp (as cited in Palincsar, 1986) suggest that curriculum developers can do this through the use of metascripts, which provide a general format and general guidelines suggestive of particular strategy but are not so highly prescriptive that there is no room for responsive teaching.

Finally, teacher education must become much more sophisticated in training teacher to teach strategies. The usual short-term, campus-based methods courses emphasizing declarative and procedural knowledge measured by midterm and final examinations cannot develop teachers who understand cognitive strategies and who can deal with the subtleties involved in teaching them. Instead, methods courses must last long enough to allow prospective teachers to do the extensive restructuring demanded when their own past reading experiences encounter the new concept of strategies. Additionally, methods courses must be integrated with extensive supervised field experiences in real classrooms so prospective teachers receive both models of how to conduct strategy instruction and extended experience in dealing directly with the various instructional subtleties in the context of real classrooms (see also Pressley, Goodchild, Fleet, Zajchowski, & Evans, in press; Symons, Snyder, Cariglia-Bull, & Pressley, this volume, chap. 1).

Conclusion

Cognitive strategies can be effectively taught. However, it is a complex and difficult process involving many subtleties. Consequently, achieving wide implementation of such instruction will not be easy. To achieve it, we need a theory of instruction that accounts for the subtleties and a concerted, longitudinal effort by researchers, curriculum developers, and teacher educators to meet the challenges the subtleties pose. It involves an evolutionary shifting of concepts of instruction and an openness between educators having diverse perceptions of learning, curriculum, and instruction. However, it is an effort that must be made if what we know about reading strategies is to be incorporated into classroom practice.

Acknowledgments. The authors gratefully acknowledge the assistance of Beth Ann Herrmann of the University of South Carolina and Janet Johnson of Michigan State University in critiquing earlier versions of this paper.

REFERENCES

Baker, L., & Brown, A.L. (1984). Metacognitive skills and reading. In P.D. Pearson, R. Barr, M. Kamil, & P. Mosenthal (Eds.), *Handbook of reading research* (pp. 353–394). New York: Longman.

Blumenfeld, P., Mergendoller, J., & Swarthout, D. (1987). Task as a heuristic for understanding student learning and motivation. *Journal of Curriculum Studies, 19,* 135–148.

Doyle, W. (1983). Academic work. *Review of Educational Research, 53,* 159–199.

Duffy, G. (1983). From turn-taking to sense-making: Broadening the concept of reading teacher effectiveness. *Journal of Eductional Research, 76,* 134–139.

Duffy, G., & Roehler, L. (1986). Constraints on teacher change. *Journal of Teacher Education, 37,* 55–59.

Duffy, G., & Roehler, L. (1987a). Building a foundation for strategic reading. *California Reader, 20,* 6–9.

Duffy, G., & Roehler, L. (1987b). Improving classroom reading instruction through the use of responsive elaboration. *Reading Teacher, 40,* 514–521.

Duffy, G., Roehler, L., & Herrmann, B.A. (1988). Modeling mental processes helps poor readers become strategic readers. *The Reading Teacher.*

Duffy, G., Roehler, L., Meloth, M., Vavrus, L., Book, C., Putnam, J., & Wesselman, R. (1986). The relationship between explicit verbal explanation during reading skill instruction and student awareness and achievement: A study of reading teacher effects. *Reading Research Quarterly, 21,* 237–252.

Duffy, G., Roehler, L., & Putnam, J. (1987). Putting the teacher in control: Instructional decision making and basal textbooks. *Elementary School Journal, 87,* 357–366.

Duffy, G., Roehler, L., & Rackliffe, G. (1986). How teachers' instructional talk influences students' understanding of lesson content. *Elementary School Journal, 87,* 3–16.

Duffy, G., Roehler, L., Sivan, E., Rackliffe, G., Book, C., Meloth, M., Vavrus, L., Wesselman, R., Putnam, J., & Bassiri, D. (1987). Effects of explaining the reasoning associated with using reading strategies. *Reading Research Quarterly, 22,* 347–368.

Durkin, D. (1978–79). What classroom observation reveals about reading comprehension instruction. *Reading Research Quarterly, 14,* 481–533.

Green, J., & Wallat, C. (1981). Mapping instructional conversations. In J. Green & C. Wallat (Eds.), *Ethnography and language in education settings.* Norwood, NJ: Ablex.

Langer, J., & Applebee, A. (1986). Reading and writing instruction: Toward a theory of teaching and learning. In E. Rothkopf (Ed.), *Review of research in education,* vol. 13. Washington, DC: American Educational Research Association.

Mayer, R., & Greeno, J. (1972). Structural differences between learning outcomes produced by different instructional methods. *Journal of Educational Psychology, 63,* 165–173.

Meloth, M. (1987). *The improvement of metacognitive awareness and its contribution to reading performance of third grade low group readers who receive explicit reading instruction.* Unpublished doctoral dissertation, Michigan State University, East Lansing.

Meloth, M., & Roehler, L. (April 1987). *Unpacking the impact of various instructional components during explanation lessons of reading for low group students.* Paper presented at the annual conference of the American Educational Research Association, Washington, DC.

Miller, G. (1985). The effects of general and specific self-instruction training in children's comprehension monitoring performances during reading. *Reading Research Quarterly, 20,* 616–628.

Miller, G. (1987). The influence of self-instruction on the comprehension monitoring performance of average and above average readers. *Journal of Reading Behavior, 19,* 303–318.

Ogle, D. (1986). The K-W-L: A teaching model that develops active reading of expository text. *The Reading Teacher, 39,* 564–570.

Palincsar, A.M. (1986). The role of dialog in providing scaffolded instruction. *Educational Psychologist, 21,* 73–98.

Palincsar, A.M., & Brown, A. (1984). Reciprocal teaching of comprehension-fostering and monitoring activities. *Cognition and Instruction, 1,* 117–175.

Paris, S., Cross, D., & Lipson, M. (1984). Informal strategies for learning: A program to improve children's reading awareness and comprehension. *Journal of Educational Psychology, 76,* 1239–1252.

Paris, S., Lipson, M., & Wixson, K. (1983). Becoming a strategic reader. *Contemporary Educational Psychology, 8,* 663–672.

Pearson, P.D. (1985). Changing the face of reading comprehension instruction. *Reading Teacher, 38,* 724–738.

Pressley, M., & Brainard, C. (Eds.). (1985). *Cognitive learning and memory in children.* New York: Springer-Verlag.

Pressley, M., Goodchild, F., Fleet, J., Zajchowski, R., & Evans, E. (in press). The challenge of classroom strategy instruction. *Elementary School Journal.*

Pressley, M., Snyder, B., Symons, S., & Cariglia-Bull, T. (in press). Strategy instruction research is coming of age. *Learning Disability Quarterly.*

Roehler, L., & Duffy, G. (1986). Why are some teachers better explainers than others? *Journal of Education for Teaching, 12,* 273–284.

Roehler, L., Duffy, G., Conley, M., Herrmann, B., Johnson, J., & Michelsen, S. (April 1987). *Exploring preservice teachers' knowledge structures.* Paper presented at the annual conference of the American Educational Research Association, Washington, DC.

Roehler, L., Duffy, G., Herrmann, B., Conley, M., & Johnson, J. (in press). Knowledge structure as evidence of "personal": Bridging the gap from thoughtto practice. *Journal of Curriculum Studies, 20*(2)59–165.

Roehler, L., Duffy, G., & Meloth, M. (1986). What to be direct about in direct instruction in reading. In T. Raphael (Ed.), *Contexts of school-based literacy* (pp. 79–96). New York: Random House.

Roehler, L., Duffy, G., & Tiezzi, L. (December 1987). *Teachers' instructional expertise and the role of situational knowledge.* Paper presented at the National Reading Conference, St. Petersburg Beach, FL.

Roehler, L., Duffy, G., & Warren, S. (December 1987). *Characteristics of instructional responsiveness associated with effective teaching of reading strategies.* Paper presented at the National Reading Conference, St. Petersburg Beach, FL.

Segal, J., Chipman, S., & Glaser, R. (Eds.). (1985). *Thinking and learning skills*, Vol. 1, *Relating research to instruction*. Hillsdale, NJ: Erlbaum & Associates.

Sivan, E., & Roehler, L. (1986). Motivational statement in explicit teacher explanations and their relationships to student metacognition in reading. In J.A. Niles & R.V. Lalik (Eds.), *Thirty-fifth yearbook of the national reading conference: Solving problems in literacy: Learners, teachers & researchers* (pp. 178–184). Rochester, NY: National Reading Conference.

Tierney, R., & Cunningham, J. (1984). Research on teaching reading comprehension. In P.D. Pearson, R. Barr, M. Kamil, & P. Mosenthal (Eds.), *Handbook of reading research* (pp. 609–656). New York: Longman.

Vygotsky, L.S. (1978). *Mind in society: The development of higher psychological processes*. In M. Cole, V. John-Steiner, S. Scribner, & E. Souberman (Eds. & trans.). Cambridge, MA: Harvard University Press.

Wilson, S., Shulman, L., & Richert, A. (1987). '150 different ways' of knowing: Representations of knowledge in teaching. In J. Calderhead (Ed.), *Exploring teacher thinking* (pp. 104–124). London: Cassell.

Winne, P. (1985). Steps toward promoting cognitive achievements. *Elementary School Journal*, 85, 673–693.

Winne, P., & Marx, R. (1982). Students' and teachers' views of thinking processes for classroom learning. *Elementary School Journal*, 82, 493–518.

Wood, D., Bruner, J., & Ross, G. (1976). The role of tutoring and problem solving. *Journal of Child Psychology and Psychiatry*, 17, 89–100.

Part II
Educational Applications

In Part II of this volume, issues related to the application of cognitive strategy research in specific content domains (i.e., reading, writing, math, and science) are discussed. In general, many of these chapters pursue related lines of reasoning as reflected by similar organizational schemes. First of all, the ways in which experts differ from novices are explored for the particular content domain. Then, it is argued, either implicitly or explicitly, that it is ultimately not productive to conceptualize expert-novice distinctions as being dichotomous. Instead, it is important to realize that novices and experts can be considered ends of a continuum of competence. Instructional interventions designed to further the progress of novices along the continuum to expertise are described or suggested. The realistic goal of public education may well be the search for competent as opposed to expert performance.

The first two chapters consider cognitive strategy research applications for competent performance in reading and writing. Reynolds, Wade, Trathen, and Lapan (Chapter 7) focus on one specific strategy for processing prose information—the selective attention strategy (SAS). First, Reynolds et al. report evidence indicating that the reader's perception of text-element importance is determined by the interaction of external variables (such as text or learning task) with internal variables (such as prior knowledge or interest). Next, the role of SAS in mediating the relationship between importance and learning is carefully assessed. It is concluded that SAS plays a causal role when text elements are primarily affected by external variables. In general, however, effective use of SAS has only been demonstrated in highly skilled college readers. Three critical components of such expert strategy use are described—efficiency, adaptability, and sophistication. Reynolds et al. describe a study designed to determine if these three aspects of strategy complexity account for performance differences and to assess whether competent readers exhibit all three components. A model detailing how selective attention interacts with other cognitive components to produce skilled reading performance is presented.

In Chapter 8, Carole Beal describes the development of communication skills in children and speculates on the implication of this research for understanding the development of writing skills. Beal analyzes expert and novice performance in three general skills of the writing process—content generation, text planning and organization, and text revision. Beal also describes some successful techniques for teaching students to employ retrieval cues during content generation and evaluative questions during text revision.

Similarly, Van Haneghan and Baker (Chapter 9) also explore the relevance of an established body of knowledge to another content domain. Specifically, Van Haneghan and Baker consider the impact of cognitive monitoring, which has been a central theme in cognitive strategy research in reading, communication, and memory skills, upon skilled mathematical thinking and problem solving. Three levels of cognitive analysis that may be employed by students are described. The student can evaluate the results of arithmetic procedures as well as the correctness of the chosen procedure. In addition, the sensibility (logical consistency and real-world applicability) of the problem itself can also be evaluated. Appropriate use of evaluation standards is required at all three levels. A three-component model of monitoring is presented, with a discussion of how to encourage monitoring during instruction in mathematics curricula.

Joan Gallini (Chapter 10) details important expert-novice differences in performance on problem-solving tasks for a variety of content domains including reading, social studies, science, and math. In general, experts are characterized as being more capable than novices, of recognizing patterns of relationships and organizing ideas into a conceptual network or schema. Gallini presents empirical validation of an instructional intervention designed to foster the development of schema-based strategies in novices. Sharon Derry (Chapter 11), focusing on expert versus novice differences in solving mathematical word problems, argues that expertise results from domain-specific systems of thought that are largely procedural in nature. Expert performance is facilitated by knowledge of domain-specific schemata and by strategies for combining schemata. The emphasis on the acquisition of procedural knowledge has implications for instruction, specifically for the facilitation of skills in pattern-recognition and action sequences. In the final section of the chapter, Derry describes an intelligent computer-based system designed to promote the development of expertise in problem-solving skills.

Finally, Richard Lehrer (Chapter 12) presents arguments for the use of a computer programming language, Logo, as a medium for strategy instruction and for the transfer of skills to other contexts. Lehrer describes specific empirical evidence supporting the contention that Logo instruction helps children decipher problem constraints in nonprogramming contexts. Finally, Lehrer emphasizes that the strength of interactive computer-based instruction lies in the ability to utilize one type of understanding—the narrative world of intuitive thought—for the development of mathematical and scientific reasoning.

In summary, it must be recognized that the development of competent strategy use is a complex process. Clearly, expertise in a content domain is characterized by skills that cannot be taught quickly or easily, or even by direct instruction alone. The integration of knowledge generated in studies of cognition with advances in instructional technology can lead to interventions that promote competence in a wide variety of educational contexts.

7
The Selective Attention Strategy and Prose Learning

RALPH E. REYNOLDS, SUZANNE E. WADE,
WOODROW TRATHEN, AND RICHARD LAPAN

Introduction

For more than a century, educators and psychologists have sought to understand how readers learn and recall text information. Early models of the learning process relied on almost mechanical explanations for how prose material was learned and recalled. For example, Frase (1969) described ways in which inserted questions might "shape" reading behaviors to promote greater learning. Thus, the reader was seen as passive and without any real input into the learning process. More recently, cognitive psychologists such as Anderson (1970), Brown (1980), and Flavell (1979) have proposed that readers are really active, strategic participants in the learning situation. This recent approach has encouraged prose learning researchers to investigate the types of strategies that learners employ in different contexts, particularly as they attempt to learn and recall information from long, expository texts.

The purpose of this chapter is to identify and delineate a number of processes that make up one prose-learning strategy—the selective attention strategy (SAS)—that might help us to understand how readers learn and recall text information. Anderson (1982) has suggested a simple formulation of how the SAS might work in a prose-learning situation and, in doing so, has identified the following processes that together constitute the SAS:

1. Text elements are initially processed to some minimal degree and graded for importance.
2. Extra attention is devoted to elements in proportion to their importance.
3. Because of the extra attention, or a process supported by the extra attention, important text elements are learned better than other elements.

Thus, if Anderson's formulation is correct, readers must engage several different processes if they are to use the SAS. First, they must determine which text elements are important and which are not. Second, they must be able to focus their attention on those important text elements. Third, they must be able to do so effectively. In this chapter we present evidence to support the notion that the SAS is a viable explanation for how readers learn and retain prose information.

The chapter is divided into five sections. In the first section, we discuss how different text elements become important to individual readers. Second, we review previous research concerning the role of selective attention as a mediator between importance and learning (see Dufresne & Kobasigawa, this volume, chap. 3). The third section describes the role of metacognition as an important enabling variable for the SAS. Fourth, we present the results of a recent study of the relationship among importance, selective attention, metacognition, and learning. Finally, we propose a framework for understanding how the SAS works in prose-learning situations.

Determining Importance

Readers tend to learn and recall more of what they perceive as important than unimportant information (Brown, 1980; Brown & Smiley, 1977, 1978; Johnson, 1970; Reynolds & Shirey 1988). Thus, to understand the role of the SAS in learning, it is necessary to first understand how importance is determined in a reading situation. Three distinct variables have been identified as influencing the perceived importance of individual text items: characteristics of the text; characteristics of the task, or the purpose for reading; and characteristics of the individual readers (Reynolds & Shirey, 1988). The locus of control for the task and text variables is considered to be primarily *external* to the reader and beyond his or her direct control. The locus of control for the reader variable is primarily *internal*. This distinction will become significant later in the chapter when we discuss differences in the allocation of selective attention across internal and external variables.

A good deal of empirical evidence supports the notion that the importance of individual text elements is determined by the interaction of external and internal variables. For example, many researchers have investigated the effect of text structure on the reader's perception of importance. Cirilo and Foss (1980) manipulated text element importance as follows: In one story, a sentence appeared as an insignificant detail that neither subsumed nor was subsumed by other propositions. In a second story, the same sentence appeared as a central idea that was well integrated into the text structure. The sentence was seen as more important when it was integrated into the text structure than when it was not. Other studies have manipulated importance by structural means. These have included investigations of the effect of topic setting, summary, and supporting ideas on importance in narratives and other prose materials (Duffy & Waller, 1985; Reynolds, 1988); highlighting text elements in some way such as side headings (Wilhite, 1986); and altering the density and complexity of the text in which the item occurs (Rothkopf & Kaplan, 1972).

A number of researchers have investigated the effect of task characteristics on what is identified as important. Wade and Trathen (in press) found that subjects who were given prereading, main-idea questions perceived a clearer boundary between important and unimportant information than did subjects who received no questions. They also found that this information about the task significantly increased the recall of important information for lower-ability but not higher-ability subjects. In a different type of study, Pichert and Anderson (1977; Anderson & Pichert, 1978) asked subjects to read a story from one of two possible perspectives and then rate the importance of individual text elements. Assigning a perspective can be seen as an external variable similar to assigning an objective in a reading situation. Pichert and Anderson found that subjects rated as more important those text items that related to their assigned perspectives. They also learned and recalled those items better than other story elements.

Other researchers have investigated the effect of reader characteristics on what is perceived as important. These characteristics include interest (Shirey & Reynolds, 1988), cultural background knowledge (Reynolds, Taylor, Steffensen, Shirey, & Anderson, 1982), and occupational knowledge (Goetz, Schallert, Reynolds, & Radin, 1983). Goetz et al. had police officers, real estate agents, and education majors read an experimental passage containing text items that were judged important to either burglars or home buyers. It was expected that the police officers would rate the burglar items as most important, whereas the real estate agents would rate the home buyer items as most important. The education majors served as controls. The results were as expected for the police officers, but the real estate agents did not rate the home buyer items as the most important. This study suggests that background knowledge, an internal variable, can affect the importance ratings of text elements; however, the effect is not as pronounced or pervasive as the influence of an assigned task since it works for some types of occupational knowledge but not for others. A likely explanation for this result has to do with the complexity of the schemata in which the occupational knowledge is stored (for a more complete discussion of this issue, see Reynolds, 1980).

In summary, the importance of individual text elements is the result of the interaction between external variables (text and task) and internal variables (the reader's background knowledge, interest, etc.). Since prose learning is largely the act of learning and retaining important text elements, no explanation of how successful prose learning works or how to improve students' reading behavior can be complete without an understanding of the process by which learners identify what is and is not important. Figure 7.1 illustrates some possible types of internal and external variables that might help to determine which text elements readers perceive as important.

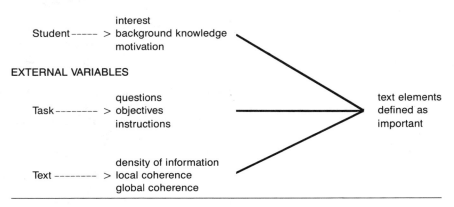

FIGURE 7.1. Some factors used to determine text element importance.

Selective Attention

Once important information has been identified, there must be some mechanism by which it its learned. The selective allocation of cognitive resources to important text elements is one way in which such information might become better learned and recalled than less important information (Reynolds & Anderson, 1982).

Numerous researchers have investigated the relationship between selective attention and learning. The studies generally use the same research method—the presentation of text on a computer in order to record measures of attention allocation—and the same subject population, adults.

Two measures of attention are frequently used—duration and intensity. Duration of attention reflects how long readers process information, and is measured by recording how much time subjects spend reading various text segments. Intensity of attention is seen as the amount of available cognitive resources that individuals engage to process information, and is measured using the secondary task methodology. The basic principle behind the secondary task methodology is the notion of distractibility. If readers are intensely involved in attempting to understand, they tend to be less distractible than if they are less intensely involved. This idea is operationalized by sounding a tone when students are reading. When they hear the tone, the students press a key on a computer console as quickly as they can. If they are intensely involved when the tone is sounded, it takes longer for them to respond to the tone than if they are only superficially involved.

As mentioned earlier, a variable of concern in the current discussion is how text item importance is determined in the various studies. Therefore, the studies reviewed will be grouped according to whether importance was determined by manipulating external variables such as assigned tasks and structural importance or by internal variables such as background knowledge and interest.

Importance Determined by External Variables

A study typical of this genre was conducted by Reynolds, Standiford, and Anderson (1979). Students were asked to read a long passage from a computer screen and were told that they would be tested on the contents when they had finished. Students' perceptions of the importance of text elements were manipulated by using the inserted-question paradigm (Rothkopf, 1966). This involves asking subjects to answer questions inserted into the text at intervals to highlight particular types of information such as proper names or technical terms. The passage was divided into segments that contained information that was either related or unrelated to the questions the students were asked. The results showed that students learned the informaiton made important by the questions better than the control information. Also, students took longer to read text segments containing question-relevant information than text segments that contained control information. These results were seen as supporting the SAS, at least as far as attention duration was concerned, since the students spent more time reading the information on which they demonstrated better learning and recall.

Similar results were obtained for the attention intensity notion in several studies using the secondary task methodology (Britton, Piha, Davis, & Wehausen, 1978; Reynolds & Anderson, 1982; Reynolds & Shirey 1988; Rothkopf & Billington, 1979). Subjects' reaction times indicated that they were more intensely involved when they read important rather than unimportant information; subjects also learned and recalled important information better than unimportant information.

Importance Determined by Internal Variables

Goetz, et al. (1983) reported a second experiment, similar to the one reported earlier, in which they had police officers, real estate agents, and education majors read the burglar/home buyer passage on a computer so that their reading times could be recorded. Results showed that police officers spent more time reading the burglar segments and learned more burglar information than either of the other two groups. Real estate agents spent more time reading the home buyer segments but did not show a comparable increase in learning the home buyer information. These results partially support the use of the SAS in the learning of text elements made important by internal variables; however, more research must be conducted before any firm conclusions can be drawn.

In summary, the research literature supports the selective allocation of attention as the likely processing mechanism in the SAS. Strong empirical support was noted for the SAS when text elements were made important by external variables. The support for the SAS was less strong when text elements were made important by internal variables. In other words, the studies cited show that important text elements receive more attention and are better learned than are unimportant text elements. Thus, text element importance has been shown to be related to learning and to attention; however, it has not yet been demonstrated that attention mediates the relationship between importance and learning in a *causal* fashion. Anderson (1982) argues that proving causality is necessary for the utility of the SAS to be supported. In the research just reviewed, the notion that attention plays a causal role in facilitating the learning of important text elements has been only assumed, not demonstrated.

Stated another way, if the SAS is to be supported, researchers must demonstrate that a causal relationship exists among importance, attention, and learning. This relationship is illustrated in the following diagram in which the plus signs (+) indicate a positive, linear relationship between the two factors involved. Thus, if attention were removed, the relationship between importance and learning would either disappear entirely or at least be significantly reduced.

IMPORTANCE---(+)--->ATTENTION---(+)--->LEARNING

Previous research has demonstrated only that importance is related to attention and to learning, not that the learning of important information is dependent on attention. Indeed, Rothkopf and Billington (1979) suggested that the results of the research just reviewed could describe the following relationship as easily as the one developed by Anderson:

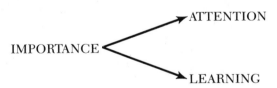

In the model formulated by Rothkopf and Billington, attention is an epiphenomenon that occurs in the vicinity of important text information but does not affect how, or if, it is learned. In order for the SAS to be useful as an explanation for how important text elements are learned, it must be demonstrated that attention plays a causal, not an epiphenomenal, role in the process.

CAUSAL ANALYSIS

Anderson (1982) suggested that the two competing models of the role of selective attention in prose learning could be tested by using a conceptually driven path analysis. Much of the selective attention research is based on the following premise: An independent variable (importance) causes changes in a dependent variable (learning) because of an influence on a mediating variable (attention). Causality for this type of argument can be claimed only if all of the following entailments are met:

1. Importance is related to learning at traditional level of significance [Importance---(+)--->Learning].
2. Importance is related to attention at traditional level of significance [Importance---(+)--->Attention].
3. Attention is related to learning at traditional level of significance [Attention---(+)--->Learning].
4. When the relations of importance to attention and attention to learning are removed, the relationship between importance and learning will have been significantly reduced [Importance---> (–Attention)--->Learning].

Causal Analysis: External Variables

Reynolds and Anderson (1982) investigated the relationship between importance and attention using the causal analysis just described. Their subjects read a 36-page passage concerning marine biology. The text was presented on a PLATO computer terminal one segment (about 33 words) at a time. As in the previous studies, each segment contained information that pertained to a specific category of information (e.g., names, technical terms, or filler). Subjects were told to read the text in preparation for a test to be given at the end of the session. Using the inserted-question paradigm, different categories of text elements were made important by asking the subjects sets of questions that dealt with specific types of information. Data were collected on reading times, secondary task reaction times, the learning of question-relevant information (information of the same category as that needed to answer the inserted questions), and the learning of question-incidental information (information not related to the inserted questions).

Text-element importance was shown to be related to the learning of both types of information and to attention allocation, thereby supporting the first two of Anderson's four causal entailments. For the third entailment, attention was shown to have a significant relationship with learning. Attention accounted for 7.7% of the variance in question-incidental learning and 23.8% of the variance in question-relevant learning. Most important, when the effect of attention was removed, the relationship between importance and learning was reduced for both question-relevant and question-incidental learning. The proportion of learning variance accounted for by importance dropped from a significant 8.3% to a nonsignificant 2.4% for question-incidental learning and from a significant 63.6% to a still significant 39.9% for question-relevant learning. In both cases, the reduction in variance was statistically significant. In the case of the question-relevant learning, it appears that, in addition to selective attention, another process was involved because of the still significant relationship between importance and learning that remained after attention was removed.

Reynolds and Anderson (1982) concluded that attention, or a process supported by attention, causally mediated the relationship between text-element importance and learning. Thus, as far as external variables are concerned, it is unlikely that selective attention is an epiphenomenon as suggested by Rothkopf and Billington (1979).

Causal Analyses: Internal Variables

Anderson, Shirey, Wilson, and Fielding (1984) investigated how fourth graders used selective attention to learn information made important by an internal variable—reader interest. Subjects read a series of sentences that had been previously rated for interest. It was expected that the subjects would learn more of the interesting sentences and that selective attention—measured by both reading time and probe reaction time—would mediate between interest and learning. They found that fourth graders did indeed learn more of, and allocated more attention to, the interesting material; however, no causal relationship was found to exist among the three variables.

The results of the Anderson et al. study can be interpreted in one of two ways: (a) It could be that the SAS does not mediate the relationship between importance and learning when importance is determined primarily by internal variables such as interest, or (b) it could be that fourth graders do not use the SAS as effectively as adults. Implicit in the second statement is the assumption that if adults were given a task similar to the one used by Anderson et al., they would use the SAS to causally mediate the relationship between importance and learning.

To determine which of these two possible explanations is correct for the Anderson et al. results, Shirey and Reynolds (1988) had 25 college students read 72 sentences that had been previously rated for interest. Reading times and secondary task reaction times were collected as measures of attention allocated to the various sentences. The measure of learning was a cued recall test administered after each block of 24 sentences. The data were analyzed using Anderson's causal analysis approach, described earlier. The results showed that interest was positively related to learning, thus supporting the first entailment of the causal model. However, contrary to expectations, interest was not positively related to either measure of attention in the second set of analyses. This lack of support for the second causal entailment made further analysis unnecessary. Shirey and Reynolds suggested that the SAS does not mediate between importance and learning when text elements are made important by internal variables such as interest.

In summary, the SAS plays a causal role when readers attempt to learn text elements made important by external variables such as assigned tasks and inserted questions. It plays a minimal role when readers attempt to learn text elements made important by internal variables such as interest. Nonetheless, even though the SAS can no longer be considered a general explanation for all types of prose learning, it merits further investigation because external variables are prominent in almost all "reading to learn" situations such as studying.

EMERGENCE OF THE SELECTIVE ATTENTION STRATEGY

Since the SAS seems to be a basic mediator between importance, as determined by external variables, and learning, questions of when readers begin to use it and how well they use it become significant. To find out, Bliss (1984) constructed a story about a hike through a forest to a campsite. The story contained numerous references to the colors of the various flora and fauna encountered on the hike. She had good and poor sixth-grade readers study the story using one of two sets of instructions. In the first set, subjects were told to read the story and prepare for a test. The second set was the same as the first except that the students were told that the colors described in the story would be very important on the test. In other words, the subjects were asked to determine text-element importance in relation to the assigned task—an external variable. All subjects were interviewed to determine what strategies they were using to learn the material after they had completed the post-test.

The results showed that both the good and poor readers who received the "color" instructions spent more time reading, and recalled more from, text segments that contained colors. Although the good readers learned more information and read more quickly, the pattern of the results was the same for both ability groups; however, because the results were not causally analyzed, the precise role of attention could not be determined.

Reynolds, Goetz, and Kreek (1984) conducted a study with good and poor 10th-grade readers to find out when attention begins to act as a causal mediator between importance and learning. They used the same questioning paradigm—that is, inserting questions periodically throughout the text—that Reynolds and Anderson (1982) used to demonstrate the causal role of attention with college students. They also interviewed all subjects upon completion of the post-test. The quantitative data showed that both good and poor readers learned more and allocated more resources to important text elements. The interview data revealed two interesting findings: First, virtually all of the subjects stated that they had figured out that all of the inserted questions they received related to the same type o;f information. The good readers came to this conclusion after receiving an average of five questions; the poor readers came to the same conclusion after receiving eight questions. Second, virtually all of the subjects reported using the SAS after they became aware of the implicit task. However, a causal role for using the SAS was not established because there was no reduction in the relation between importance and learning when attention was removed (see Table 7.1).

TABLE 7.1. Test of the Entailments for the Causal Model Among Importance, Attention, and Learning

Entailment	Beta	Significance level
Good readers		
Importance------> learning	0.23	$F(2, 794) = 44.52, p < 0.01$
Importance------> attention	0.14	$F(2, 794) = 21.64, p < 0.01$
Attention--------> learning	0.07	$F(2, 794) = 4.27, p < 0.05$
Import-->(-Att)--> learning	0.22	$F(2, 794) = 40.92, p < 0.01$
Poor readers		
Importance------> learning	0.15	$F(2, 680) = 14.90, p < 0.01$
Importance------> attention	0.15	$F(2, 680) = 22.15, p < 0.01$
Attention--------> learning	0.06	$F(2, 680) = 2.55,$ NS
Import-->(-Att)--> learning	0.14	$F(2, 680) = 13.99, p < 0.01$

Note. Results are for repeated questions only. Table adopted from Reynolds, Goetz, and Kreek (1984).

In summary, it seems that the ability to use the SAS to causally mediate learning has not been demonstrated in any subject population except highly skilled college readers. Although even sixth graders demonstrate the behaviors associated with successful use of the SAS—that is, most can identify important text elements and focus attention on at least a subset of those text elements—not even good 10th-grade readers exhibit a causal relationship between the SAS and learning. Thus, all groups except skilled college readers seem to be using the SAS ineffectively. One reason for this lack of effective functioning might be that the younger students had not yet developed an awareness of when and how the SAS should be used. In other words, they may not have attained the level of metacognitive ability necessary to monitor their use of the SAS and thus use it effectively.

Metacognition

Metacognition—a concept first introduced by Flavell (1979); Flavell & Wellman, 1977) and later expanded by Brown (1980, 1981; Baker & Brown, 1984)—refers to knowledge about and control of certain cognitive processes such as attention, memory, and comprehension. The knowledge component of metacognition implies, among other things, that learners know about strategies and skills necessary to perform tasks effectively. This includes the recognition that the internal and external variables previously discussed (person, task, and text) interact to affect the importance of incoming information. The knowledge component also includes the understanding that certain strategies, such as the SAS, are available and can be used to facilitate learning.

The second component, control of cognition, means that learners are able to use this metacognitive knowledge to monitor and regulate the success of their strategies for learning. In terms of the central issues in this chapter, the ability to carry out and monitor the cognitive processes of identifying important information and focusing attention on specific text elements is an example of metacognitive control.

A number of researchers have provided empirical support for the powerful role that metacognition plays in different learning situations (Ghatala, 1986; O'Sullivan & Pressley, 1984; Pressley, Levin, & Ghatala, 1984). Impressive though this work is, there are still some difficulties with the concept of metacognition that could benefit from additional research (Reynolds & Wade, 1986). The difficulties relevant to our discussion center on identifying valid and reliable indices of metacognition and establishing a clear causal relationship between metacognition and cognitive performance.

Identifying Indices of Metacognition

To be more useful as a psychological construct, the effect of metacognition on cognitive behavior and performance must be understood. This requires a precise definition of metacognition with valid and reliable ways to measure it. Unfortunately, there is some disagreement among researchers as to what metacognition is or how it can be operationalized (Reynolds & Wade, 1986). From a meta-analysis and review of the literature on metamemory, Schneider (1985) concluded that one reason the research in this area has been somewhat inconsistent is that different definitions of metamemory as well as different indices of it have been used. For example, studies that focus on metacognitive knowledge have found that metamemory is not a good predictor of actual memory performance. However, when metamemory is operationalized in terms of on-line memory, a relatively strong correlation between meta-memory and memory behavior occurs.

In an effort to respond to these difficulties, Schneider argues for a more precise definition of exactly what metacognitive ability is, clearer methodologies concerned with identifying instances of metacognitive behavior, and the use of multiple methods for isolating it. Unfortunately, metamemory is the only aspect of metacognition that has been reviewed in sufficient detail to identify specific problems and judge the nature of the relationship between metacognitive ability and cognitive behavior.

Another major concern is the validity and reliability of the means by which researchers have attempted to measure metacognitive ability and behavior. One of the most frequently used methods is the verbal report. One advantage of this method is its open-endedness, subjects can respond in their own words and at any depth or length they feel is appropriate. A second advantage is the ease of data collection because only a list of questions and a tape recorder are normally required. On the other hand, verbal responses may be ambiguous and may be edited by the respondent to conform to his or her expectations about what the experimenter wants to hear. In addition, interview procedures that involve interrupting students in the process of performing a learning task have the potential of interfering with their concentration or affecting their study behaviors. Indeed, Wade and Trathen (in press) show that asking questions during reading does change the way in which subjects process the text and, in addition, interacts with other variables to affect recall.

Another difficulty with verbal reports is that they may not reflect what students are really doing—that is, they may be engaged in metacognitive strategy but not report it, or they may report it inaccurately (Reynolds & Wade, 1986; Schneider, 1985). As an explanation for such anomalies, Flavell (1979) notes that metacognitive knowledge can be either conscious or automatic. If the activity has reached the stage of automaticity, it is unlikely that children will be able to report its occurrence. Brown (1981) suggests that the same claim can also be made about monitoring activities since they are likely to be "overlearned" in skilled readers. Furthermore, children may not always use the strategies that they have in their repertoires. Finally, even if subjects use the "correct" strategy and are able to verbalize it, they may not use it effectively, thereby reducing any possible correlation with performance (Reynolds & Shirey, 1988). Consequently, even though several researchers have obtained interesting insights into metacognition using verbal reports, the difficulties outlined earlier might help to explain why metacognitive activities, as measured by verbal report data, are not consistently correlated with the performance of cognitive behaviors (Baker, 1985).

A second method employed to identify metacognitive behavior is the forced-choice task. In this type of experiment, students are interrupted during reading and asked specific questions about what cognitive processes they are using. However, instead of describing the nature of these processes as in verbal reports, subjects simply select one of several descriptions provided by the experimenter. This approach has certain advantages: Student responses are neither limited by an inability to verbalize nor are they prone to the types of editing behaviors associated with verbal reports. In addition, ease of scoring enables the experimenter to provide feedback during the task. The major disadvantage is that the meaning of the subject's response is only implied in the data and must be induced by the experimenter.

Baker (1985; Baker & Brown, 1984) and Markman (1979, 1981) have suggested a third approach to gathering data on metacognitve processes. Their technique involves altering texts to include impediments to comprehension and then seeing if students notice them. The assumption is that if students are engaging in monitoring activities, they will notice the inconsistency and take some corrective action. In some studies, reading time was recorded to see if subjects spent more time reading the text segments that contained the inconsistent text (Baker & Anderson 1982). Results indicated that many subjects failed to notice the inconsistencies while they were reading. Upon interviewing them, Baker discovered that some of the subjects had indeed noted the inconsistency but had changed their understanding of the story in order to make it fit meaningfully into the scenario they were creating. As a result of her extensive work, Baker concluded that even with careful analysis of on-line data, errors in identifying metacognitive abilities are frequent (Baker, 1985).

Still another method of identifying metacognitive behavior is the one used in the reading-time studies reviewed earlier—analyzing subjects' reading patterns in terms of attention allocation to certain text elements. The rationale for this approach is as follows: Find a concrete measure that will accurately reflect an underlying cognitive process, manipulate task demands so that changes in the underlying process are likely to occur, and determine if the on-line measure varies in the predicted text segments and in predicted ways. The advantages of this method correspond to the disadvantages identified in the methods previously discussed. For example, it eliminates the need for subjects to describe verbally the processes in which they are engaged and requires no interruption of the assigned task. The primary disadvantage is having to induce underlying processes from an indirect measure.

In summary, there seem to be difficulties with all of the indicators of metacognitive functioning discussed. Verbal report, forced choice, and interview data are easy to obtain but they can be unreliable and ambiguous. Data obtained from inserting inconsistencies into texts do not seem to encourage the types of metacognitive responses expected. On-line indicators of processing, such as attention allocation, are difficult to obtain and, as yet, have not predicted causal changes in learning with any population except skilled adult readers. The only possible solution to these difficulties seems to be the use of multiple indicators of metacognition as well as sensitivity to different levels of strategy proficiency (Campbell & Fiske, 1959; Schneider, 1985). In the studies discussed in the next section, both verbal reports and on-line indicators are used in an attempt to identify the metacognitive component of the SAS.

Selective Attention and Metacognition

The equivocal results obtained in the 10th-grade selective attention study described previously may be due, in part, to the failure to consider metacognitive ability. For instance, Hale (1983) suggests that the discrepancies among research findings in the area of study skills may be due to students not having a clear understanding of the effectiveness of the study strategies they employ. Thus, it appears that metacognitive development might be as important to effective learning as building background knowledge and learning specific cognitive strategies (Baker & Brown, 1984).

In an attempt to determine why the 10th graders in the Reynolds et al. (1984) study were unable to use the SAS effectively, Reynolds, Goetz, Lapan, and Kreek (1988) had 45 10th-grade students—25 good readers and 20 poor readers—read a long, technical passage on an Apple II Plus computer. Subjects were instructed to read the passage and prepare to take a test on the material. Text segments contained information related to either proper names or technical terms. The importance of this information was manipulated by using the inserted-question paradigm. The subjects were not told that the inserted questions targeted a particular type of information, that all of the questions would be of one type, or that the post-test was related to the questions; consequently, they had to deduce this knowledge during the reading process. Once they figured out the task, the subjects had to adjust their strategies or adopt new ones in order to learn the targeted information.

Measures of attention allocation, question-relevant learning, and question-incidental learning were collected for all subjects. Two methods were used to determine subjects' awareness of any strategies they might be using while they read: (a) On-line data were collected to see if attention allocation varied in the predicted areas, and (b) interview data was collected after subjects had completed the short-answer post-test. As part of the interview, subjects were shown a hard copy of the experimental text and asked to indicate the point at which they became aware that the inserted questions were all of the same type. This was considered to be a measure of *task awareness*. Those who indicated that they had been aware of the similarity among the questions at some point in their reading were then asked to describe the strategies, if any, they had employed in order to learn information that related to the questions. If subjects mentioned the SAS in the interview and if reading and probe reaction time data indicated that they had focused their attention on important text segments, they were considered to be exhibiting *strategy awareness*.

The data were analyzed separately for good and poor readers, with each group further divided along the dimension of task awareness. This resulted in four groups of subjects: good readers before task awareness was manifested, good readers after task awareness was manifested, poor readers before task awareness was manifested, and poor readers after task awareness was manifested. Separate causal analyses were performed for each of these groups (see Table 7.2). The results showed that the good readers demonstrated a trend toward a causal relationship among importance, attention, and learning, but only after thy became aware of the true nature of the task. Close perusal of Table 7.2 reveals other interesting patterns of results as well. For example, before they became aware of the optimal strategy, the good readers exhibited no strategy whatsoever in their reading pattern. That is, they did not differentiate between important and unimportant text information in terms of attention allocation or learning. However, after they became aware of the task, they demonstrated the beginnings of effective use of the SAS to improve their learning. In contrast, before the poor readers became aware of the task, they did attend to and learn important information, although there is no evidence that attention was causally related to learning. After becoming aware, the poor readers continued to use the SAS, but they still did not do so effectively since removing attention from the causal path did not significantly reduce the relationship between importance and learning.

TABLE 7.2. Test of the Entailments for the Causal Model Among Importance, Awareness, Attention, and Learning

Entailment	Beta	Significance level
Good readers		
Before strategy awareness		
Importance------> learning	0.09	$F(2, 143) = 1.13$, NS
Importance------> attention	0.03	$F(2, 143) = 2.68$, NS
Attention--------> learning	0.03	$F(2, 143) = 0.09$, NS
Import-->(-Att)--> learning	0.01	$F(3, 142) = 1.08$, NS
After strategy awareness		
Importance------> learning	0.26	$F(2, 648) = 48.32, p < 0.01$
Importance------> attention	0.15	$F(2, 648) = 22.14, p < 0.01$
Attention--------> learning	0.09	$F(2, 648) = 5.07, p < 0.01$
Import-->(-Att)--> learning	0.21	$F(3, 647) = 36.99, p < 0.01$
Poor readers		
Before strategy awareness		
Importance------> learning	0.16	$F(2, 174) = 4.28, p < 0.01$
Importance------> attention	0.12	$F(2, 174) = 3.83, p < 0.05$
Attention--------> learning	0.07	$F(2, 174) = 0.84$, NS
Import-->(-Att)--> learning	0.16	$F(3, 173) = 4.13, p < 0.01$
After strategy awareness		
Importance------> learning	0.13	$F(2, 503) = 8.29, p < 0.01$
Importance------> attention	0.17	$F(2, 503) = 20.86, p < 0.01$
Attention--------> learning	0.06	$F(2, 503) = 2.34$, NS
Import-->(-Att)--> learning	0.12	$F(3, 502) = 7.46, p < 0.01$

Note. Results are for repeated questions only. Table adopted from Reynolds, Goetz, Lapan, and Kreek (1988).

The interview data were used to corroborate and further understand what these results might mean. Good readers reported that before they became aware of the similarity in the questions, they relied on a default strategy of "general learning." However, once they became aware of the task, as revealed by the inserted questions, they reported using the SAS almost exclusively. In contrast, poor readers reported adopting the default strategy of attending to long, unusual words and people's names. Since the experimental materials contained both technical terms and proper names, this strategy was reasonably successful. After they became aware that the questions targeted either technical terms or proper names, the poor readers reacted like the good readers by attempting to use the SAS; however, they did not do so as effectively as the good readers.

These results reveal some interesting insights into how metacognitive ability might affect the effective use of the SAS. Metacognitive awareness of different aspects of the SAS seems to emerge at different times. Initially, students seem to develop an awareness of the relationship of understanding the task to successful learning—regardless of whether it is explicitly stated by means of objectives or implied with inserted questions. Most sixth graders and virtually all 10th graders in previous studies showed evidence of task awareness (Bliss, 1984; Reynolds, Goetz, et al., 1988). Next to emerge seems to be a sense that certain strategies can be applied to help the reader learn the information highlighted by the task. Good readers at the sixth-grade level and virtually all 10th graders exhibited this strategy awareness when they read; however, good 10th-grade readers exhibited both strategy and task awareness before poor 10th-grade readers did. Finally, of all the groups tested, only good 10th-grade readers and adults demonstrated the existence of a causal relationship between using the SAS and improved learning, which we will refer to as *performance awareness*. This level of effective strategy use seems to represent a level of metacognitive ability beyond either task or strategy awareness.

In summary, three points emerge from the research to date: (a) Readers can report using a strategy, reveal on-line measures that verify their verbal report, and still not use the strategy effectively—as was the case for poor 10th-grade readers (see Table 7.2). Therefore, it is necessary to perform some type of causal analysis before effective strategy use can be inferred. (b) Metacognitive ability is not monolithic. It is made up of many different levels and types of abilities. With reference to the SAS, three different levels of metacognitive functioning were identified—task awareness, strategy awareness, and performance awareness. (c) Metacognitive awareness, at least as it pertains to the SAS, seems to evolve gradually. Task awareness emerges first. Readers begin to move from allowing internal variables to predominate in determining importance to a greater reliance on external variables (Myers & Paris, 1978; Shirey & Reynolds, 1988). Strategy awareness emerges next. Both good and poor sixth-grade readers demonstrated a knowledge of the SAS in both on-line data and verbal reports; however, neither they nor poor-reading 10th graders were able to use the strategy effectively (Bliss, 1984; Reynolds, Goetz, et al., 1988). Last to emerge is performance awareness, which is evident only when readers demonstrate a causal relationship between strategy use and increased learning (Reynolds & Anderson, 1982).

Since metacognitive ability can be manifested on a number of different levels and in a number of different ways, it seems likely that strategies can be used with varying degrees of effectiveness and manifested with different levels of complexity. For example, even strategies that are being used effectively may vary in terms of efficiency of use, sophistication of conception, and adaptability. In other words, mature strategy use likely has several levels of proficiency. In the next section, this issue of strategy complexity will be discussed and a study addressing the issue will be presented.

The SAS: Indices of Strategy Complexity

A strategy can be considered effective when a strong, positive influence on the learning and retention of information is noted as a result of its use. Causal analysis has been used to differentiate effective from ineffective use of the SAS. Much of the research that has been described in this chapter attests to the utility of the notion of effectiveness as a descriptor of strategic functioning. Young children have been shown to use strategies when trying to learn from text but they seem to use them ineffectively (Bliss, 1984). Indeed, in all of the research previously discussed, only skilled college readers have demonstrated effective use of the SAS. Tenth-grade, good readers come close but do not demonstrate the same degree of effectiveness as do the college students.

A possible problem with some of the previous reading research concerning metacognitive ability is the dichotomous way in which strategy use has been conceptualized (c.f., Gordon & Braun, 1985; Mason, 1985; Wellman, 1985). For the most part, strategies are viewed as either being there or not being there. There seems to be an implicit assumption that if students say they are using a strategy or exhibit behaviors that are seen as reflecting a strategy, then they must be using the strategy effectively. Also, little concern seems to have been given to differences in the complexity of individual strategies or the sophistication of strategy use. This may be because the primary purpose of much of the early work concerning strategies was to show that strategies existed and that they were in some way related to success in learning. Since the notion of metacognition now has a relatively long history of credibility in the literature (Forrest-Pressley, MacKinnon, & Waller, 1985), it seems appropriate to shift the focus from showing that strategies are either used or not used to showing that readers can display different levels of skill in using strategies.

To understand why strategies can be used with differing degrees of effectiveness, we examine in this section three possible components of effective strategy use: efficiency, adaptability, and sophistication. The *efficiency* component of a strategy is defined as the marshalling of cognitive resources such as time and effort toward only those text elements that need to be learned to accomplish the criterion task successfully. For example, efficient use of the SAS would be reflected by a pattern of increased attention to important information and decreased attention to unimportant information in the latter parts of a text without a decrease in learning. In other words, the reader would be maximizing the SAS by focusing more and more precisely on important information as the benefits of that approach become increasingly apparent. There is evidence to support the notion of efficient strategy use. Reynolds and Anderson (1982) showed that college students increased their reading speed almost 50% from the beginning to the end of a 36-page text with no loss of learning. Although these students read all types of text segments faster, they

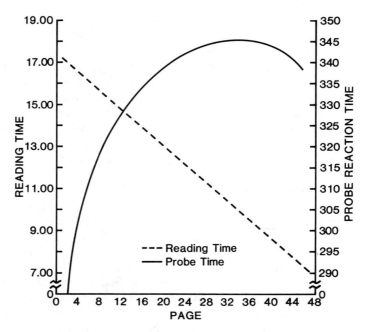

FIGURE 7.2.

almost eliminated attention to text segments containing unimportant information and focused almost solely on important information. These same students also increased the intensity of their attention as their duration of attention decreased (see Figure 7.2). Reynolds and Anderson suggested that learning continued at the same pace because the subjects were compensating for the loss of duration with the increase in intensity; consequently, it might be that a second aspect of efficient strategy use involves moving from duration to intensity as the operative mode of attention focusing.

The *adaptability* of a strategy refers to how quickly it can be engaged and disengaged. For example, adaptable strategy users would be expected to identify the appropriate strategy very quickly and disengage and move onto a new strategy if and when that strategy is perceived as ineffective. Nonadaptable strategy users would be expected to identify a new strategy less quickly and to persist in using a familiar strategy even after it has become ineffective. Two diverse sets of data support the notion of strategy adaptability. First, Reynolds et al. (1984) and Reynolds, Goetz, et al. (1988) noted that good, 10th-grade readers began to use the SAS long before the poor readers did. Second, many researchers involved in concept-learning research have suggested that the ability to quickly abandon an unsuccessful strategy is highly correlated to success in concept learning (Driver, Guesne, & Tiberghien, 1985; Reif, 1987).

Strategy *sophistication* is defined as the depth to which a strategy is understood, the degree to which it becomes more effective over time, and the nature in which it is applied. This aspect of strategy use is the most difficult to measure because it is the most difficult to define. In terms of the SAS, sophistication might be manifested in higher-order reading patterns that go beyond the straightforward pattern of more attention to important versus less attention to unimportant information, which represents our current understanding of how the SAS works. In other words, the sophisticated SAS user might look at the text in larger chunks than just the segments presented on the screen, or he/she might develop a higher level of efficiency over time. However, in order for the notion of sophistication—even as vaguely as it is defined here—to have any validity, it must demonstrate increased effectiveness of learning. To date, there is no evidence in the selective attention literature that higher-order reading patterns exist or that increased learning can be predicted from them.

In summary, it seems reasonable to expand the notion of strategy as it has been conceptualized in some of the previous reading research. In the next section, we describe a study that was designed to test the notions of efficiency, adaptability, and sophistication as they pertain to the SAS in order to determine whether or not they have empirical validity as predictors of successful learning.

Strategy Complexity: Empirical Support

Reynolds, Wade, Trathen, and Lapan (1988) designed a study intended to test the indicators of strategy complexity listed in the previous section. A key aspect of the study was that strategies used by the same subjects were investigated in two different reading situations. In one session subjects read a lengthy text for factual information, such as names and dates (Session 1); in the second session they read a second lengthy text for conceptual information, such as higher-order relationships (Session 2). Data for the two study situations were gathered over a one-month interval. The subjects were 77 college students who voluntarily participated for class credit. To insure a wide range of reading skill, approximately half of the subjects were recruited from remedial-study-skill classes and half were recruited from an upper-level education class. Of these 77 subjects, 47 received various forms of treatment instructions and 30 served as controls.

The research method used in Session 1 was similar to that of previous selective attention studies. Students read a technical text presented in short segments on a computer terminal. Both attention duration and attention intensity were measured using reading times and secondary task reaction times. After reading, the students took a 40-question, short-answer test concerning factual information in the passage. For all treatment subjects, one-half of the questions were addressed to important information and one-half were addressed to unimportant information. As in the previous research, text-item importance was manipulated by using the inserted-question paradigm. All of the subjects were interviewed after completing the post-test.

Session 2 more closely reflected a normal study situation. The subjects were asked to read a printed version of a different passage from the same text. The chapter was about 15 pages long and contained information on the effects of the tides. Text elements in the passage had been previously rated for structural importance using a method similar to that of Johnson (1970).

Subjects were told to study the passage using any technique or strategy they chose. They were provided with pencils, pens, highlighters, note cards, and paper for this purpose. While the subjects were reading, an experimenter inconspicuously recorded their overt study behaviors. Any notes, underlinings, or highlightings were collected before the subjects began the post-test—again, a 32-question, short-answer test that addressed information from all the importance levels previously identified in the passage.

The major purpose of this study was to discover major differences between those subjects who did well on the post-tests given after each reading session and those who did not do well; consequently, the regression analyses reported here include only those subjects who scored greater than 70% correct on the combined score of the two session post-tests and those who scored less than 35% correct (leaving 29 subjects in the analysis). There were no significant differences between the grade-point averages of individuals in these two groups. It was expected that the indicators of strategy complexity, calculated from data gathered in Session 1, would account for some of the variance between the scores of the two groups on the Session 2 post-test, after ability had been factored out.

In order to see if the three aspects of strategy complexity accounted for any of the difference in success demonstrated by the subjects, methods by which to operationalize each construct were developed. Strategy adaptability was operationalized as the number of inserted questions that subjects saw before they discerned the category of information to which their attention needed to be allocated. This information was obtained in the interview that followed the Session 1 post-test. As in the study by Reynolds, Goetz, et al. (1988) described earlier, subjects were given a hard copy of the text to read and asked to indicate the place at which they became aware of the similarity in the questions they were being asked. They were also asked where they began to focus their attention on information of the same type as required to answer the questions.

Strategy efficiency was computed for each subject by subtracting the average reading time on unimportant text segments from the average reading time on important text segments after the subject became aware of the nature of the questions, and dividing the result by the same calculation for segments before awareness occurred. The following formula was used to calculate strategy efficiency:

$$\text{Efficiency} = \frac{\text{Differential focusing after awareness}}{\text{Differential focusing before awareness}}$$

This calculation produced an indication of the degree to which subjects used the SAS. It was expected that efficient strategy users would show an increasingly greater difference between important and unimportant text segment reading times as they progressed through the text. It was also expected that there would be no corresponding reduction in learning as reading time decreased.

Strategy sophistication was calculated by using both univariate and bivariate spectral analyses to analyze the reading patterns and learning patterns of the subjects. Spectral analysis is useful as a way to identify higher-order reading patterns that explain variance in an observed time series. Gottman (1981) used the example of a prism breaking light into its basic color spectrum as an analogy to what spectral analysis does to time-series data. Univariate spectral analysis decomposes a unidimensional time series into a spectrum of significant wave patterns. Wave patterns represent hidden, yet repetitive, patterns embedded in the time series. This analytic tool offers a unique way to examine the SAS as a time-dependent phenomenon. Components of the SAS such as emergence over time, differentiation between text segments, and commitment to the strategy can be effectively identified using invariate spectral analysis. Potential differences between effective and ineffective readers might be represented in univariate spectral analysis as frequency waves indicating different strategy-acquisition techniques and different use of the strategy over time. Bivariate spectral analysis was used to determine when learning and attention were in close coherence — that is, in close positive relationship with one another. For example, if strategy users were indeed sophisticated, we would assume that they would become more effective if the strategy they were using met with continuing success as they moved through the text. This would be reflected by an increasing coherence between attention and learning.

An additional advantage of using both types of spectral analysis accrues from the way in which the data are aggregated. One possible reason why previous researchers have found few instances of high correspondence between measures of metacognitive behavior and measures of learning is that they frequently used single indicators of each in their analyses. Rushton, Brainard, and Pressley (1983) suggest that aggregation of the data across subjects will increase the reliability of the measure involved and will present "a more accurate picture of the relationships in the population" (p. 19). In both univariate and bivariate spectral analysis, attention and learning data were aggregated across groups of subjects to ensure greater reliability of both the predictor and criterion variables. Specifically, the data were arranged as follows: 60 data points were arranged chronologically in order of appearance in the text for each subject. Thirty of these were reading times for important text segments and 30 were reading times for unimportant segments. Important and unimportant segments appeared in alternating fashion throughout the text. Inserted questions appeared after every sixth segment for a total of 10 questions in all. For purposes of graphic representation, every six segments is referred to as a zone of text.

The basic pattern of results replicated previous work (Reynolds, Goetz, et al., 1988) in that both good and poor readers generally learned more important than unimportant information and both groups paid more attention to important information. In order to determine if strategy sophistication represented a way in which successful readers outperformed less successful readers, the univariate and bivariate spectral analyses were performed. For both sets of analyses, the data were separated into four groups: good readers' data from the first half of the experimental text, good readers' data from the second half," poor readers' data from the first half; and poor readers' data from the second half. The univariate test revealed different reading patterns over time for all four of these groups. For the good readers, the pattern for the first half of the text was characterized by two waves — one that repeated every two segments and one that repeated every six to seven segments. The pattern for the second half was characterized buy three waves — one that repeated every two segments, one that repeated every three segments, and one that repeated every 12–15 segments. For the poor readers, their reading pattern for the first half was characterized by a wave that repeated every two segments. Their pattern for the second half was characterized by two waves — one that repeated every two segments and one that repeated every three segments.

Exactly what do these reading patterns mean? A wave that repeats every two segments suggests a dramatic shift in attention as the reader moves from an important to an unimportant text segment. As expected, both good readers and poor readers showed this pattern on both halves of the text. In the second half of the text, both good and poor readers revealed a reading pattern that repeated every three segments. Again as expected, this represents an attention pattern moving from important-to-unimportant-to-important text segments.

The poor readers showed no other significant patterns, whereas the good readers demonstrated two more: (a) In the first half of the text, they showed a pattern that repeated approximately every six segments. We suggest that this represents good readers treating each incidence of encountering an inserted question as a time to pause and reestablish the external criterion for text-element importance — in effect, almost "resetting" their reading strategy and essentially repeating it between occurrences of the inserted questions. The poor readers did not reveal this pattern, apparently only continuing the back-and-forth oscillations indicative of moving from important to unimportant text segments and perhaps revealing a very constrained conception of the SAS. (b) In the second half of the text, good readers showed a reading pattern

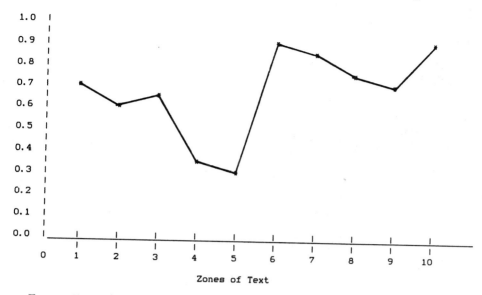

FIGURE 7.3. Coherence between pattern of reading times and learning for good readers.

that repeated every 12–15 segments. This pattern is easily interpreted because it occurs approximately every two inserted questions. We speculate that this pattern might represent an extended resetting and reverifying pattern similar to the one that the good readers demonstrated when they encountered the inserted questions.

The bivariate spectral analysis also revealed interesting differences between good and poor readers. Recall that this analysis charts the coherence of the relationship between reading patterns and learning as they occur over time. Figures 7.3 and 7.4 show the results for the good and poor readers, respectively. Note that as the good readers progress through the text, the coherence, or positive relationship between their reading pattern and their learning, increases. This suggests that good readers become increasingly effective at using the SAS as they progress through the text. The poor readers do not show a similar increase.

In order to determine the relative degree to which strategy adaptability, efficiency, and sophistication represent ways in which successful readers outperform unsuccessful readers, two regression analyses were performed. In the first regression, two measures—a vocabulary test and an analogies test—were entered first to remove between-subject variance due to ability. The three indices of strategy complexity were entered next as predictor variables. The post-test score from Session 1 served as the criterion measure. The second regression used the same measures of ability and the same three predictors but used the post-test score from Session 2 as the criterion.

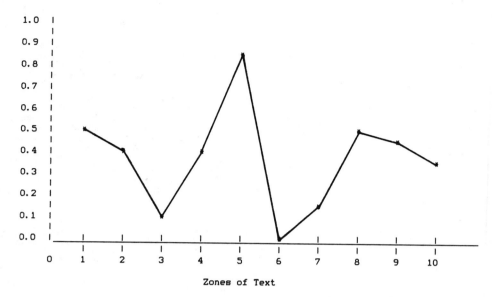

FIGURE 7.4. Coherence between pattern of reading times and learning for poor readers.

Using the score from the first post-test as the criterion measure, strategy sophistication and adaptability accounted for significant amounts of variation. Strategy sophistication proved to be the best predictor of successful reading followed by strategy adaptability. The total variance accounted for by strategy sophistication and strategy adaptability was approximately 43%.

Using total learning on the second post-test as the criterion, strategy adaptability and strategy efficiency accounted for significant variance in the post-test scores. Strategy adaptability was the first variable entered, followed by strategy efficiency. The total amount of variance accounted for by all three variables was approximately 57%.

Two additional regression analyses were performed to see if the relationship between any of the three aspects of strategy complexity was changed when the importance of the information learned was taken into account. Again, scores on the vocabulary test and the analogies test were entered into

TABLE 7.3. Results of Regression Analysis with Session 1 Post-Test Scores as the Criterion Measure

Predictor	R^2 change	Beta	Significance level
Sophistication	0.28	0.55	$F(2, 27) = 10.50, p < 0.01$
Adaptability	0.15	0.41	$F(3, 26) = 6.89, p < 0.05$

Note. Variables appear in order of entry into regression equation.

TABLE 7.4. Results from Regression Analysis with Session 2 Post-Test as the Criterion Measure

Predictor	R^2 change	Beta	Significance level
Adaptability	0.43	0.67	$F(2, 27) = 22.91, p < 0.01$
Efficiency	0.14	0.39	$F(3, 26) = 10.32, p < 0.01$

Note. Variables appear in order of entry into regression equation.

the equation first to remove variance due to ability. In addition to the three strategy complexity variables, whether or not subjects noted (underlined, highlighted, or written as notes) target information was used as a fourth predictor. For the learning of important information, strategy adaptability, strategy efficiency, and noting each accounted for a significant amount of variance—the noting variable being *negatively* related to improved learning of important information. Strategy adaptability accounted for about 8% of the total variance. For the learning of unimportant information, three predictors were significant: adaptability, noting and efficiency. Together they accounted for better than 13% of the total variance (see Tables 7.3, 7.4 and 7.5).

Taken together these results suggest the following: The notion of strategy complexity—operationalized by the measures of strategy sophistication, strategy adaptability, and strategy efficiency—is a potentially powerful way of looking at differences between successful and unsuccessful readers. Successful readers used all three of the methods to improve their post-test performance in both reading sessions. Strategy sophistication was of particular importance because it could be seen as reflecting a higher-order manifestation of the SAS. The spectral analyses revealed that successful readers consistently showed two patterns of selective attention use in their reading behavior. The first will be called a micro-strategy and was reflected by a

TABLE 7.5. Results from Regression Analysis with Session 2 Important and Unimportant Post-Test Responses as the Criterion Measures

Predictor	R^2 change	Beta	Significance level
	Important text elements		
Adaptability	0.08	0.29	$F(2, 477) = 41.75, p < 0.01$
Efficiency	0.03	0.18	$F(3, 476) = 15.65, p < 0.01$
Noting	0.01	−0.09	$F(4, 475) = 3.94, p < 0.01$
	Unimportant text elements		
Adaptability	0.07	0.28	$F(2, 477) = 38.02, p < 0.01$
Noting	0.04	0.19	$F(3, 476) = 19.16, p < 0.01$
Efficiency	0.02	0.16	$F(4, 475) = 13.22, p < 0.01$

Note. Variables appear in order of entry into regression equation.

simple up-and-down oscillation in reading times. In other words, the successful readers showed high points of attention on important text elements and low points on unimportant text elements.

The second pattern will be called a macro-strategy and was reflected by two patterns of ready times that repeated themselves every 6 and every 12–15 segments respectively. These macro-strategy waves seem to represent a second level of the SAS. They indicate that after the successful readers became aware of the strategy, they used it with increasing efficiency over the second half of the text. The unsuccessful readers demonstrated only the micro-strategy in their reading-time data.

Looking at these data in terms of the discussion of metacognition, the spectral analyses might have revealed two of the types of awareness previously discussed. The micro-strategy might reflect strategy awareness. These readers seem to possess the prerequisite skills needed to attend selectively to important information, but they do not possess the ability to monitor their learning. The macro-strategy might reflect performance awareness in that the higher-order wave pattern seems to show an occasional rechecking of the appropriateness of the strategy.

Clearly, extensive interview data, as well as a number of replication studies, are needed before the speculations about micro- and macro-strategies can be either confirmed or refuted. Although the notions are intriguing and have some face validity, they could be nothing more than "time phantoms"— fluctuations in reading-time data that seem important but stubbornly resist understanding and replication (E.Z. Rothkopf, personal communication, April, 1987). However, since the spectral analysis variable accounted for almost 28% of the variance in the scores on the first post-test, the notion of strategy sophistication certainly seems worth pursuing.

The strategy adaptability variable accounted for the most variance—almost 43%—in the scores from the second post-test as well as 15% of the variance of the scores from the first post-test. This is an impressive finding because of the differences in the tasks assigned in the two reading sessions. The task in Session 1 was to learn factual information while the task in Session 2 focused more on learning higher-order, conceptual information. Given this difference, it is not surprising that the ability to quickly identify the appropriate strategy for use in Session 1 should be related to success on a second task since that task likely required the use of a different strategy for success.

The strategy efficiency variable accounted for the second most variance in the learning of information in Session 2— about 14%. This result is not surprising since strategy efficiency should be successful with any text in which important and unimportant information can be identified and delineated.

The final result was the relationship of noting information (noting was defined as using any study method such as underlining, highlighting, or notetaking) to subsequent learning. The noting variable was negatively related to differences in the learning of important information and positively related to differences in learning unimportant information. It seems that successful readers tended to note less material than did unsuccessful readers. Also, both groups seemed to note only that material they felt they would not remember by just attending to it. For the most part, that material tended to be unimportant.

In summary, the Reynolds, Wade, et al. (1988) study seems to show that the notion of strategy complexity is powerful in predicting success in learning from text. The result cannot be attributed solely to ability differences between the two groups of subjects analyzed because two measures of ability—verbal ability and analogical reasoning—were entered first into the regression equation, thereby removing variance due to ability alone before the measures of strategy complexity were entered. Even with this control in place, the indices of strategy complexity accounted for almost 43% of the variance in the first post-test and as much as 57% of the variance in the second post-test scores. Consequently, it seems that measures of metacognitive functioning beyond determining whether or not subjects are using a strategy are necessary if strong relationships between metacognitive functioning and cognitive performance are to be isolated.

Conclusion

This chapter started with a simple notion of how information was learned in prose-learning situations. Understanding the processes that underlay traditional reading behavior—identifying important text elements and selectively attending to them—is a necessary step in understanding why readers learn and recall certain information from texts. This notion, operationalized as the SAS, was represented as follows:

IMPORTANCE---(+)--->ATTENTION---(+)--->LEARNING

Research reviewed by Reynolds and Shirey (1988) showed that this model is useful in explaining the results of only a small number of the studies conducted to test it. In response to this lack of success, research was reviewed in this chapter, which showed that an understanding of metacognition and strategy complexity is necessary to understand how the SAS works. The SAS seems to begin with ineffective use of the strategy and progress to effective used as metacognitive ability develops (see also Short & Weissberg-Berchell, this volume, chap. 2, for implications with a special population). Metacognitive ability also seems to develop in phases, beginning with task awareness, progressing to strategy awareness and culminating in performance awareness. The major signpost of each of these changes is greater effectiveness in reading.

Taking these new insights into account, it is possible to construct a new model of how identifying important text elements, selective attention, and metacognitive ability interact to produce optimal learning of information made important, or salient, by both internal and external variables. The model would look as follows:

EXTENDED
VARIABLES ---(+)--->SALIENCE---(+)--->ATTENTION---(+)---->LEARNING$_1$

INTERNAL
VARIABLES ---(+)--->SALIENCE---(+)--->LEARNING$_2$

The basic idea behind this model is that two separate types of learning take place in reading situations. The first is the learning of text elements made important primarily by external variables—assigned or personal tasks and text structure (LEARNING$_1$). The SAS plays a causal role in the learning of this type of information. The second type is the learning of text elements made important primarily by internal variables such as interest and background knowledge (LEARNING$_2$). Selective attention plays a minimal role in this type of learning. Research findings suggest that successful, efficient readers use both approaches. In contrast, ineffective, inefficient readers seem less able to use both approaches, usually selecting one or the other (Shirey & Reynolds, 1988).

In the proposed model, the term "salience" is used instead of the term "importance" because it is more general and because it better captures the intent of the various research arguments. Salience means "the property of standing out." Importance means "indicative of significant worth. . . ." When Pichert (1979) argued that children chose interesting information as important, he did not mean to imply that they saw significant worth in that information. He meant that those items stood out for the children. In the same way, importance as defined by external variables refers more to identification of those text elements as relevant to fulfilling some task rather than to any intrinsic worth in the material. Another reason for using "salience" instead of "importance" is to widen the scope of the model. It is reasonable to argue that salience is a superordinate term that encompasses both importance and interest; however, it is more difficult to argue that importance is superordinate to interest.

As used in the model, the term "attention" refers to selective attention and implies that both attention duration and attention intensity are included. Selective attention seems to develop beginning with ineffective and progressing to effective use of strategy (Reynolds et al., 1984). Also, it might be that as attention allocation becomes more efficient, readers employ more intense concentration for shorter periods of time (Reynolds & Anderson, 1982); however, more research is needed before this last claim can be considered to be more than speculation.

One of the first phases in metacognitive awareness is task awareness. Task awareness is characterized by the ability to understand the implicit and explicit demands of a given task but does not include the knowledge of how to use the appropriate strategy. Students are said to be at the task-awareness phase of metacognitive development when they understand the implied task demand of the inserted question paradigm but do not apply the SAS. This was the case with some of the subjects in the Reynolds, Goetz, et al. (1988) study.

Readers who are able to infer task requirements as in the inserted question paradigm and are able to employ appropriate strategies such as the SAS but without evidence that this causally affects learning represent the strategy-awareness phase of metacognitive development. Reynolds, et al. (1984) found that most 10th-grade subjects were at this phase.

At the highest level of learning in this model are readers who use the SAS in a causal fashion to learn information made important primarily by external variables — they exhibit performance awareness. Reynolds and Anderson (1982) found readers at this level in the college populations they studied. In addition, Shirey and Reynolds (1988) showed that the same type of readers could learn information important to internal variables without focusing extra attention on it. To date, only skilled college readers have represented this level of functioning, although 10th-grade good readers exhibit the initial stages of it.

Once strategy awareness is achieved, students seem to be able to expand their repertoires to include more complex manifestations of various strategies in order to be more effective. For the SAS, these include strategy adaptability, strategy efficiency, and strategy sophistication. Reynolds, Wade, et al. (1988) showed that all three of these indices of strategy complexity account for significant differences in how successful and unsuccessful readers approach reading situations.

Given the basic framework outlined in this chapter, there seem to be at least two areas in which future research is indicated. First, research needs to be conducted into the developmental aspects of effective strategy use for strategies other than the SAS. As Schneider (1985) has argued, relationships between metacognitive strategies and cognitive performance must be made if metacognition is to continue as a viable concept. Second, the findings of Reynolds, Wade, et al. (1988) certainly seem to suggest that one major difference between successful and unsuccessful readers is the ability to use very complex manifestations of the SAS. Research needs to be conducted to investigate why differences exist in the complexity of individual readers' repertoire of strategies. It is hoped that this chapter has provided a framework that can be used as a starting point for conceptualizing and interpreting some of this future work.

REFERENCES

Anderson, R.C. (1970). Control of student mediating processes during verbal learning and instruction. *Review of Educational Research, 40*, 349–369.

Anderson, R.C. (1982). Allocation of attention during reading. In A. Flammer & W. Kintsch (Eds.), *Discourse processing* (pp. 292–305). New York: North Holland Publishing Company.

Anderson, R.C., & Pichert, J.W. (1978). Recall of previously unrecallable information following a shift in perspective. *Journal of Verbal Learning and Verbal Behavior, 17,* 1–12.

Anderson, R.C., Shirey, L.L., Wilson, P.T., & Fielding, L.G. (1984). *Interestingness of children's reading material* (Tech. Rep. No. 323). Urbana-Champaign, IL: University of Illinois, Center for the Study of Reading.

Baker, L. (1985). How do we know when we don't understand? Standards for evaluating text comprehension. In D.L. Forest-Pressley, G.E. MacKinnon, & T.G. Waller (Eds.), *Metacognition, cognition, and human performance,* Vol. 1 Theoretical perspectives (pp. 155–205). Orlando, FL: Academic Press.

Baker, L., & Anderson, R.I. (1982). Effects of inconsistent information on text processing: Evidence for comprehension monitoring. *Reading Research Quarterly, 17,* 281–294.

Baker, L., & Brown, A.L. (1984). Metacognitive skills and reading. In R. Barr, M.L. Kamil, & P. Mosenthal (Eds.), *Handbook of reading research* (pp. 353–394). New York: Longman.

Bliss, S. (1984). *The allocation of attention by sixth grade, good and poor readers.* Unpublished master's thesis, University of Utah, Salt Lake City.

Britton, B.K., Piha, A., Davis, J., & Wehausen, E. (1978). Reading and cognitive capacity usage: Adjunct question effects. *Memory and Cognition, 6,* 266–273.

Brown, A.L. (1980). Metacognitive development and reading. In R.J. Spiro, B.B. Bruce, & W.F. Brewer (Eds.), *Theoretical issues in reading comprehension* (pp. 453–481). Hillsdale, NJ: Erlbaum & Associates.

Brown, A.L. (1981). Metacognition: The development of selective attention strategies for learning from texts. In M.L. Kamil (Ed.), *Directions in reading: Research and instruction,* Thirtieth Yearbook of the National Reading Conference (pp. 21–43). Washington, DC: National Reading Conference.

Brown, A.L., & Smiley, S.S. (1977). Rating the importance of structural units of prose passages: A problem of metacognitive development. *Child Development, 48,* 1–8.

Brown, A.L., & Smiley, S.S. (1978). The development of strategies for studying texts. *Child Development, 49,* 1076–1088.

Campbell, D.T., & Fiske, D.W. (1959). Convergent and discriminant validation by the multitrait-multimethod matrix. *Psychological Bulletin, 56,* 81–105.

Cirilo, R.K., & Foss, D.J. (1980). Text structure and reading time for sentences. *Journal of Verbal Learning and Verbal Behavior, 19,* 96–109.

Driver, R., Guesne, E., & Tiberghien, A. (Eds.). (1985). *Children's ideas in science.* Philadelphia: Open University Press.

Duffy, T.M., & Waller, R. (Eds.). (1985). *Designing usable texts.* Orlando, FL: Academic Press.

Flavell, J.H. (1979). Metacognition and cognitive monitoring: A new area of cognitive-developmental inquiry. *American Psychologist, 34,* 906–911.

Flavell, J.H., & Wellman, H.M. (1977). Metamemory. In R.V. Kail, Jr., & J.W. Hagen (Eds.), *Perspectives on the development of memory and cognition.* Hillsdale, NJ: Erlbaum & Associates.

Forrest-Pressley, D.L., MacKinnon, G.E., & Waller, T.G. (Eds.). (1985). *Metacognition, cognition, and human performance*, Vols. 1–2. Orlando, FL: Academic Press.

Frase, L.T. (1969). Cybernetic control of meaning while reading connected discourse. *Journal of Educational Psychology, 60*, 49–55.

Ghatala, E.S. (1986). Strategy-monitoring training enables young learners to select effective strategies. *Educational Psychologist, 21*, 43–54.

Goetz, E.T., Schallert, D.L., Reynolds, R.E., & Radin, D.I. (1983). Reading in perspective: What real cops and pretend burglars look for in a story. *Journal of Educational Psychology, 75*, 500–510.

Gordon, C.J., & Braun, C. (1985). Metacognitive processes: Reading and writing narrative discourse. In D.L. Forest-Pressley, G.E. MacKinnon, & T.G. Waller (Eds.), *Metacognition, cognition, and human performance*, Vol. 2, *Instructional practices* (pp. 1–75). Orlando, FL: Academic Press.

Gottman, J.M. (1981). *Time series analysis*. Cambridge, MA: Cambridge University Press.

Hale, G.A. (1983). Students' predictions of prose forgetting and the effects of study strategies. *Journal of Educational Psychology, 75*, 708–715.

Johnson, R.E. (1970). Recall of prose as a function of the structural importance of the linguistic units. *Journal of Verbal Learning and Verbal Behavior, 9*, 12–20.

Markman, E.M. (1979). Realizing that you don't understand: Elementary school children's awareness of inconsistencies. *Child Development, 50*, 643–655.

Markman, E.M. (1981). Comprehension monitoring. In W. P. Dickson (Ed.), *Children's oral communication skills*. New York: Academic Press.

Mason, J.M. (1985). Cognitive monitoring and early reading: A proposed model. In D.L. Forest-Pressley, G.E. MacKinnon, & T.G. Waller (Eds.), *Metacognition, cognition, and human performance*, Vol. 2, *Instructional practices* (pp. 77–102). Orlando, FL: Academic Press.

Myers, M., & Paris, S.G. (1978). Children's metacognitive knowledge about reading. *Journal of Educational Psychology, 70*, 68–69.

O'Sullivan, J.T., & Pressley, M. (1984). Completeness of instruction and strategy transfer. *Journal of Experimental Child Psychology, 38*, 275–288.

Pichert, J.W. (1979). *Sensitivity to what is important in prose* (Tech. Rep. No. 149). Urbana-Champaign, IL: University of Illinois, Center for the Study of Reading.

Pichert, J.W., & Anderson, R.C. (1977). Taking different perspectives on a story. *Journal of Educational Psychology, 69*, 309–315.

Pressley, M., Levin, J.R., & Ghatala, E.S. (1984). Memory strategy monitoring in adults and children. *Journal of Verbal Learning and Verbal Behavior, 23*, 270–288.

Reif, F. (1987). Instructional design, cognition, and technology: Applications to the teaching of scientific concepts. *Journal of Research in Science and Teaching, 24*, 309–324.

Reynolds, R.E. (April 1980). *Cognitive capacity usage in prose learning*. Paper presented at the meeting of the American Educational Research Association, Boston.

Reynolds, R.E. (1988). *Metaphors in text: Implications for theories of prose learning*. Manuscript submitted for publication.

Reynolds, R.E., & Anderson, R.C. (1982). Influence of questions on the allocation of attention during reading. *Journal of Educational Psychology, 74*, 623–632.

Reynolds, R.E., Goetz, E.T., & Kreek, C. (April 1984). *Metafocusing: The role of metacognitive awareness in the focusing of attention.* Paper presented at the meeting of the American Educational Research Association, New Orleans.

Reynolds, R.E., Goetz, E.T., Lapan, R., & Kreek, C. (1988). *Attention allocation and awareness as components of efficient comprehension.* Manuscript submitted for publication.

Reynolds, R.E., & Shirey, L.L. (1988). The role of attention in studying and learning. In E.T. Goetz, C.E. Weinstein, & P. Alexander (Eds.), *Learning and study strategies: Issues in assessment, instruction and evaluation.* Washington, DC: Academic Press.

Reynolds, R.E., Standiford, S.N., & Anderson, R.C. (1979). Distribution of reading time when questions are asked about a restricted category of text information. *Journal of Educational Psychology, 71,* 183–190.

Reynolds, R.E., Taylor, M.A., Steffensen, M.S., Shirey, L.L. & Anderson, R.C. (1982). Cultural schemata and reading comprehension. *Reading Research Quarterly, 17,* 353–366.

Reynolds, R.E., & Wade, S.E. (1986). Thinking about thinking about thinking: Reflections on metacognition. *Harvard Educational Review, 56,* 307–317.

Reynolds, R.E., Wade, S.E., Trathen, W., & Lapan, R. (1988). *Components of effective strategy use in prose learning situations: Adaptability, efficiency, and sophistication.* Manuscript submitted for publication.

Rothkopf, E.Z. (1966). Learning of written instructive materials: An exploration of the control of inspection behavior by test-like events. *American Education Research Journal, 3,* 241–249.

Rothkopf, E.Z., & Billington, M.J. (1979). Goal-guided learning from text: Inferring a descriptive processing model from inspection times and eye movements. *Journal or Educational Psychology, 71,* 310–327.

Rothkopf, E.Z., & Kaplan, R. (1972). Exploration of the effect of density and specificity of instructional objectives on learning from text. *Journal of Educational Psychology, 63,* 295–302.

Rushton, J.P., Brainard, C.J., & Pressley, M. (1983). Behavioral development and construct validity: The principle of aggregation. *Psychological Bulletin, 94,*18–38.

Schneider, W. (1985). Developmental trends in the metamemory-memory behavior relationship: An integrative review. In D.L. Forest-Pressley, G.E. MacKinnon, & T.G. Waller (EDs.), *Metacognition, cognition, and human performance.* Vol. 1, *Theoretical perspectives* (pp. 57–109). Orlando, FL: Academic Press.

Shirey, L.L., & Reynolds, R.E. (1988). The effect of interest on attention and learning. *Journal of Educational Psychology.*

Wade, S.E., & Trathen, W. (in press). The effect of self-selected study methods on learning. *Journal of Educational Psychology.*

Wellman, H.M. (1985). The origins of metacognition. In D.L. Forest-Pressley, G.E. MacKinnon, & T.G. Waller (Eds.), *Metacognition, cognition, and human performance,* Vol. 1, *Theoretical perspectives* (pp. 1–31). Orlando, FL: Academic Press.

Wilhite, S.C. (1986). The relationship of headings, questions, and locus of control to multiple-choice test performance. *Journal of Reading Behavior, 18,* 23–40.

8
Children's Communication Skills: Implications for the Development of Writing Strategies

CAROLE R. BEAL

Several recent national studies have shown that students in the United States perform at a remarkably low level on writing tasks (Boyer, 1983; National Assessment of Educational Progress, 1986; National Commission on Excellence in Education, 1983). The 1986 NAEP "Writing Report Card" surveyed the writing skills of 55,000 students from 4th to 11th grade across the country. Children in this project completed assignments that assessed their informative, persuasive, and imaginative writing skills. After reviewing the children's work, the authors' conclusion was that "most students . . . are unable to write adequately except in response to the simplest of tasks. . . . Performance in writing in our schools is, quite simply, *bad*" (NAEP, 1986, pp. 3, 9). There are clearly many factors that contribute to this situation. However, one important factor is that when children first begin to learn to write, their understanding of the requirements of the writing task is limited, and they lack many of the comprehension and memory strategies that expert writers use to cope with the cognitive demands of the writing task.

Much research has shown that when children enter school their understanding of the requirements for effective communication is quite limited: Children first tend to overestimate message quality and to believe that they and others can comprehend messages that are in fact inadequate. Such findings can shed light on the difficulties that elementary-school children have in learning to communicate effectively through written text. Characteristics of the typical classroom writing task may also tax children's fragile understanding of strategies for effective communication. Writing is a highly skilled activity that requires the retrieval of information from memory, the organization of material in light of a particular goal, and the evaluation and revision of the text as it is produced. Research showing that children in the early grades have only limited knowledge about memory and comprehension processes can help us to understand their difficulties with these steps in the writing process, and can suggest procedures that can help them acquire these important skills. In addition, research on the strategies used by skilled writers to allocate their attention efficiently while writing can suggest interventions to help elementary school children cope with the demands of the writing task.

This chapter will first review research on elementary-school children's developing knowledge about oral communication and will suggest implications of this research for writing development. Second, this chapter will review expert and novice writers' performance in three general skills defined by models of the writing process: generating content, planning and organizing the information, and revising (Bereiter & Scardamalia, 1986; Collins & Gentner, 1980; Flower & Hayes, 1980). Research on the effects of strategy intervention training in these three skills will also be reviewed (see Derry, this volume, chap. 11; Gallini, this volume, chap. 10; Rohwer & Thomas, this volume, chap. 5).

The Transition from Oral to Written Communication

When children first enter school, they must acquire a new understanding of the communication process. In particular, they must learn to consider the role of the message in effective communication (Dickson, 1981). Children need to learn that the information provided in the message can determine their own comprehension or that of a listener. That is, if the message does not provide enough information the listener will not be able to understand what the speaker intended, even though both parties might be cooperative and trying to understand one another. The development of knowledge about effective oral communication in the early grades may therefore be a prerequisite for the acquisition of written communication skills.

CHILDREN'S ORAL COMMUNICATION SKILLS

Much of the research on children's oral communication skills has been conducted with the referential communication task. In this task, the child and a partner sit on opposite sides of the table. They each have a matching set of referents that differ on several dimensions. The speaker selects one referent and describes it verbally to the listener, who must try to select the matching referent from his or her own set. The task is constrained so that the *message* must convey the information necessary for the listener to choose the correct referent. The speaker cannot gesture and the listener cannot use contextual cues to try to guess what the speaker means. Many studies have shown that in the early grades children lack important knowledge about how to communicate effectively in this constrained task situation (Dickson, 1981). When they are in the speaker role, children often produce messages that are too general, so that the listener cannot be sure which referent is correct. For example, children might describe a picture as "the red one" when there are actually two referents that are red. When children are in the listener role they often guess when the message does not provide enough information, and they generally overestimate how informative the message was.

Recent studies have suggested several reasons why elementary school children perform inefficiently as speakers and listeners in the referential communication task. Speer (1984) has found that children rely on their knowledge about ordinary conversation in the referential communication task. They assume that the speaker will be cooperative and will provide additional information if a misunderstanding occurs. Whitehurst and Sonnenschein (1978, 1985) have shown that children do not know what makes an informative message, namely, that they should describe the *differences* between the referents. There is also evidence that children do not understand the role of the message as a representation of the speaker's meaning, a representation that may be adequate or inadequate. Several researchers (Beal & Flavell, 1984; Bonitatibus, 1988; Bonitatibus & Flavell, 1985; Robinson, Goelman, & Olson, 1983) have found that children confuse the words of the message with what the speaker actually meant. Olson (1977; Olson & Hildyard, 1983) has argued that children need to distinguish between the information available in the message itself (its "literal meaning") and the meaning that the speaker may have intended to convey by means of the message (see Nystrand, 1986 for a contrasting view). In some cases the message may express that intended meaning accurately, but in other cases it may be too brief, ambiguous, or confusing for the listener to infer accurately the speaker's intended meaning. Children need to learn to recognize the distinction between what one says and what one means, and to deal with communication failures by improving the communicative quality of the message (Peterson, Danner, & Flavell, 1972).

By the time children reach second or third grade, their performance has improved significantly in the referential communication task. They are able to provide more informative messages for a listener and are more likely to monitor accurately their own comprehension of a message. They will also blame the speaker when communication failure occurs, because they understand that the listener is dependent on the information available in the message itself. Much of the knowledge about effective oral communication that is acquired in the early grades is also relevant to written communication. In fact, the text becomes even more important as the vehicle for the writer to convey his or her meaning to the reader, because the two parties are generally not in the same place at the same time. The writer must anticipate possible confusions and try to revise the text ahead of time to avoid them, because there may not be an opportunity later for the reader to question the writer about his or her intended meaning. An understanding of the role of the message is therefore critical to effective written communication as well as oral communication.

THE WRITING TASK

Although children in the early grades perform well in referential communication tasks, their performance is much less impressive on typical classroom writing assignments because the characteristics of the writing task place new demands on children's developing communication skills. The differences between referential communication and writing are captured by a distinction articulated by Simon (1973; also see Bereiter & Scardamalia, 1986). The referential communication tasks used to study children's oral communication skills tend to be "well-structured," in that they have a clear objective that is known to both the speaker and the listener and there is one solution that is easily recognized when it is achieved. In contrast, writing is an "ill-structured" problem. The exact form of the final text—what information will be included, how it will be organized, how long it will be, etc.—is often not clearly defined when the writer begins to work, and may actually be altered several times during the writing process. There may be also several texts that would all be reasonably good solutions, and it may be difficult for the writer to determine when the goal has been achieved satisfactorily. In addition, while it is relatively easy to evaluate the communicative quality of the message in a referential communication task, it is considerably more difficult to evaluate the quality of a piece of writing and the effects of revisions (Applebee, 1984; Bridwell, 1980; Coop, White, Tapscott, & Lee, 1983; Diederich, 1974; Faigley & Witte, 1981, 1984). Highly skilled writers develop their own style and standards, and a text that strikes one reader as disorganized and fragmented may be found intriguing and exciting by another reader. It is not even clear that agreement on a universal standard for "good writing" would be desirable. Of course, the difficulty in assessing the quality of writing has implications for writing instruction. Without a clearly defined goal state it is hard to develop a plan for teaching children the components of good writing or to assess their progress.

Another important difference between referential communication and writing tasks is their relative demands on the young communicator's attention and processing capacity. Models of adult writing suggest that writing requires the simultaneous coordination of several subprocesses at different levels of complexity (Collins & Gentner, 1980; Hayes & Flower, 1980). The writer must generate a plan for the composition, retrieve content information from memory, formulate sentences, select individual words, and engage in ongoing revision, all the while monitoring the lower-level processes of spelling, handwriting or typing quality, and punctuation. Most models of skilled writing stress that writing is not done in a direct linear fashion from one process to another. Rather, writers seem to alternate between these processes in an interactive fashion. For example, sometimes an initial "bit" of text in a draft may push the writer into revision, or trigger the addition of new information that had not been part of the original plan (Humes, 1983). The many processes that must be executed and controlled place heavy demands on the writer's limited attentional resources. Flower and Hayes (1980) use the metaphor of a busy switchboard operator to describe the multiple and simultaneous demands on the writer's attention. Given these demands, successful writing appears to require a high level of control and planning so that attentional resources can be allocated to different processes.

In addition to coordinating the many processes involved in writing, children have the additional burden of monitoring their new routines for handwriting, spelling, and the placement of text on the page. Mechanical impediments may certainly contribute to the difficulties that children have in learning to write, by limiting their ability to consider higher-order goals while writing. However, such problems do not seem to account entirely for children's low level of writing skill. Scardamalia and Bereiter (1979) found that although children produced more text when they dictated their compositions to a scribe, the *quality* of their work was not significantly higher than when they wrote by hand (also see Cioffi, 1984; Gould, 1980; Hidi & Hildyard, 1983). Teaching children in the early grades to type and use a computer text editor also does not necessarily result in superior performance unless children are also provided with instruction in the writing process itself (Beal & Griffin, 1987; Daiute, 1985; Gerlach, 1987; Kurth & Kurth, 1987). Freeing children from the mechanical burdens of writing by hand does not seem to automatically increase their ability to consider higher-order goals such as planning and revision of their work.

THE ROLE OF STRATEGIES

Models of the activity of expert writers generally characterize three general stages in the writing process — text production, planning, and revision — although activity in these stages can overlap in a recursive and interactive fashion (Bereiter & Scardamalia, 1986; Flower & Hayes, 1980). A critical difference between the novice and expert writer may be in the use of strategies for managing the attentional demands of these stages. Experts use high-level metacognitive strategies that involve the selection and execution of cognitive actions, such as focusing on one subprocess at a time rather than trying to tackle everything at once. For example, an expert writer may decide to postpone revision until a first draft has been produced, or may focus on the development of a solid outline before actually producing any prose. Experts also rely on metacognitive strategies that involve assessments of their cognitive state in order to make appropriate decisions about what to do next (Bereiter & Scardamalia, 1986; Flower & Hayes, 1980, 1981). For example, the writer may assess what he or she knows about several topics in order to decide which one to write about, or may assess his or her comprehension level while reviewing the text in order to decide whether a reader would understand what has been produced so far. Studies of children's writing suggests that they lack many of the strategies that expert writers use to generate information, plan and organize their material, and evaluate and revise their text. Research on children's performance at each of these steps in the writing process will be reviewed herein, along with research on interventions designed to help children cope with demands of the writing task through the use of memory, communication, and comprehension strategies.

Content Generation and Text Production

One of the first steps in the writing process is to generate information that can be included in the text. Young writers often panic when they are given free choice about what to write, since information that might be used in a composition does not automatically come to their minds (Bereiter & Scardamalia, 1986; D.H. Graves, 1983; Humes, 1983). Even when the topic is assigned by the teacher the child must retrieve relevant content information from memory before he or she can even begin to plan and organize the material. Children tend to write a sentence or two and then say that they cannot think of anything else to include. Sentences that make the same point several times may be observed when children feel they should keep writing but cannot think of new material. For example, Figure 8.1 shows a fourth grader's composition about penguins. Jeannie's goal was to fill up the page, so she repeated the same point about how much people like penguins several times until she reached the last line on the paper.

Although children often say that they cannot think of anything more to write, they often do have more knowledge about the topic in memory. If they are asked questions about what they have written they will generate more information that can then be included in the composition (Bereiter & Scardamalia, 1982, 1986). Bereiter and Scardamalia account for this by suggesting that when children first begin to write they rely on a conversational model of communication, where the response from the partner serves as an automatic retrieval cue for new topic information. However, when they are writing, children must learn to retrieve content from memory without the assistance of a communication partner. Efficient content generation requires the use of strategies for assessing the availability of content in memory and for retrieving content from memory.

About Penguins

Penguins are very pretty. They are white and black. Penguins wiggle wogle when they walk. Finnie's favorite animal is a penguin to. A penguin is a neat animal to have for a pet to look at. I would like to have a penguin for a pet. I bet if you went all around the world you wouldent belive *howe many peopole like penguins. Peopole just love penguins. It is increatable how many peopol like penguins.* The End. By Jeannie.

FIGURE 8.1. Example of a fourth grader's difficulty with new content generation, resulting in the repetition of an idea (italics added) to fill up the page.

Strategies for Generating Content: Selecting Familiar Topics

One strategy for solving the content generation problem is to assess one's knowledge base and select a familiar topic. Expert writers know on what topics they can write easily, and they tend to specialize in particular domains (Stein, 1986). Bos (1988) gives the example of a student who avoided writing about certain topics because he "didn't know enough about that." However, Scardamalia, Bereiter, and Woodruff (1980) found that many elementary children were unable to give examples of topics that they knew a lot about versus those that they did *not* know much about. In addition, research on comprehension-monitoring skills suggests that children generally overestimate how much they know about various subjects (Flavell, Speer, Green, & August, 1981; Markman, 1977, 1979). This suggests that children may sometimes have trouble generating sufficient content because they have selected an inappropriate topic, one that they did not actually know much about.

Strategies for Generating Content: Prewriting Activities

Children also have problems in generating content about familiar topics, suggesting that they lack strategies to retrieve information stored in memory. Prewriting activities can be used to help children activate the relevant content information in memory. For example, children write more if the teacher has selected topics that are exciting or emotionally arousing, or has kept notes about each child's special interests, or has scheduled writing early in the morning so that greetings and initial conversations between children as they enter the classroom can help them generate material to write about (A. Graves, 1983; Pekala, 1983). Activities such as discussions of the topic or brainstorming are also helpful, and many teachers spend a large percentage of classroom writing time on such "orienting" activities (Beach, 1983; Shaw, Pettigrew, & van Nostrand, 1983; Whitt, Paul, & Reynolds, 1988). However, there is no evidence that children themselves recognize the utility of such prewriting activities as a strategy for solving the content-generation problem.

While children may be able to satisfy some writing tasks by using information already stored in memory, other writing tasks may require them to retrieve additional information from external sources, such as books, encyclopedias, and other people (Bos, 1988). Expert writers often must research their topics to gather additional information before they begin to write. D.H. Graves (1983) recommends that teachers help children set up a "future topics" file, to help children store information that is not appropriate for a current piece but that might be retrieved and used in a subsequent composition. Similarly, Scardamalia, Bereiter, and their colleagues (Scardamalia, 1986) are developing a computer-based system for prospective information storage and retrieval. The system will allow children to read and summarize points of information in a large data base on a regular basis. Children could then use the data base to retrieve information while working on their writing assignments.

SELF-PROMPTING STRATEGIES

Many of the prewriting activities that are used to help children retrieve content from memory can be quite effective. However, they have the long-term drawback that children can continue to take a relatively passive approach to the content-retrieval problem. What children need to learn to do is to set up memory retrieval aids on their own, such as self-prompting strategies. Several researchers have found that training children to use such strategies helps them to write more. Anderson, Bereiter, and Smart (1980) found that training children to list single words on a topic increased their output because the words seemed to act as automatic retrieval aids when children ran out of things to write. Sager (1973) found that training sixth-grade children to ask questions about very brief stories helped them to generate additional details to include and fill out the stories. Similarly, Bereiter and Scardamalia (1986) have found that the use of "contentless prompts" increased the amount that children wrote. Children were given cards with sentence openers such as "For example" or "Also" or "That's why" to use as they began each sentence. The prompts did not provide any specific content information but they seemed to serve as "conversational partners" to get the child going again. Children wrote more varied compositions when using the prompts and reported that the cards "help[ed] them think of things to write" (Bereiter & Scardamalia, 1986, p. 62). Graham, Harris, and Sawyer (1987) also found that learning-disabled students could be trained to prompt themselves with questions to produce additional story content.

A related approach is to have children write in a style that will allow them to utilize the knowledge that they have about conversational communication. Andrews, Beal, and Corson (1988) found that sixth-grade students wrote significantly longer stories when they used a "dialogue" style of writing than when they wrote stories in narrative form. In dialogue writing, the characters tell the story through conversation, without narration or descriptions. Each character's remark then serves as a prompt for the next sentence. Children also seem to have less trouble with the content-generation problem when working with familiar formats, such as story writing. Stein (1986) has proposed that children write better when using such well-known forms because they know how to begin, and each segment then automatically prompts ideas for the subsequent sections.

SUMMARY

Young writers often have great difficulty in generating content during the writing process, even when they choose their own topics. Several researchers have suggested that children rely on a conversational model of communication when they first begin to write, and that without the support of a communication partner they cannot retrieve sufficient information on a particular topic from memory. In addition, they lack strategies for estimating how much they know about different topics and so may not always choose subjects about which they can easily write. Procedures that encourage children to use self-prompting strategies, and prewriting exercises that activate information in memory make it easier for children to generate content during the writing process.

Text Planning and Organization

After the child selects a topic and retrieves information from memory or other sources, he or she must decide how to organize the material and structure the text in light of an overall goal. Simply writing down the information as it first comes to mind will probably not produce an effective composition. The order of presentation must be considered and the needs of potential readers should be assessed. Flower and Hayes (1981) found that adult writers devoted considerable time to deciding what approach to take to a topic, considering the information requirements of potential readers, and selecting among different ways to present the subject matter. Skilled adult writers may consider and discard several presentation ideas during the planning stage (Bereiter & Scardamalia, 1986).

In contrast to the skilled writer's assessment and selection of material in light of an overall goal, children simply include everything that they can think of. The content-retrieval problem is so great that they can pay relatively little attention to the organization of their work, and because an overall goal is not kept in mind they often have trouble staying on the topic (Bruce, Collins, Rubin, & Gentner, 1982; Rubin, 1983). Bereiter and Scardamalia (1986) and Heap (1986) describe children's disorganized texts as resulting from the use of a "what next" strategy, where children produce one sentence after another without trying to interrelate them. McCutchen and Perfetti (1983) have shown that children's ability to create locally coherent text increases steadily from second through eight grade. Younger children's sentences tend to be unrelated to one another, while older children begin to use connectives such as "but" and "also" to relate each new sentence to the one preceding it. Younger children also find it particularly difficult to *exclude* material on the grounds that it does not fit an overall plan. The idea that one might consider a piece of information and then decide not to include it is almost inconceivable to a novice writer, who is generally worried that he or she will not have enough to say in the first place.

STRATEGIES FOR TEXT ORGANIZATION

Skilled writers often use strategies such as making an outline and listing key points as they develop an organization for the text. Bereiter and Scardamalia

(1986) found that older children and adults used code words and brief phrases to represent their main points, and experimented with different orders and sequences in order to find an effective structure for their text. In contrast, elementary-school children did not use such strategies; their "outlines" were almost identical to their final drafts. Children also did not take advantage of extra time provided during the writing session in order to plan their work before they began to write.

One reason that elementary-school children do not use organizational strategies is that they do not yet have a model of the text as a structure that provides main points along with supporting arguments. That is, children may not prepare outlines of key ideas in advance because they do not know what their main points and ideas *are*. Brown and her colleagues found that most elementary-school children could not select the most important text units when asked to summarize stories, while older students were able to select or highlight the topic sentences and main conclusions (Brown & Smiley, 1977, 1978; Brown, Day, & Jones, 1983). While these studies focused on children's developing ability to use attentional and self-questioning strategies to *acquire* knowledge from prepared texts, the results suggest that children may also lack the skills required to *present* information to the reader in a well-organized fashion when they are producing texts.

TRAINING IN TEXT STRUCTURE AND ORGANIZATIONAL STRATEGIES

There has been relatively little research on the effects of training children to use organizational strategies before they begin to write. Several studies have found that training children about the components of a well-formed text helped them to produce more coherent stories and essays (Fitzgerald & Teasley, 1985; Graham & Harris, 1986, 1988). Humes (1983) also suggests strategies that teachers might use in the classroom to help children structure their information as they write. For example, the teacher might display a poster that says "when you write a story, arrange your ideas into sentences that show the time order of the beginning, the middle [and] the end." Similarly, Wheeler (1985) suggests that teachers provide students with prepared "templates" for different text structures, with slots that can be filled in by the children. For example, a "class news" article might have slots for the title, and for who, where, and when the event took place, and for how the reporter or audience felt about the event.

Another intervention to help children produce more organized text is to provide them with part of a narrative and ask them to complete it. The existing text acts as a restriction on what can be added next and may therefore help children stay on the topic. Several researchers have designed computer-based story-completion games to help children learn to write well-structured stories. The computer guides children through the process of completing a story, allowing them to select from among several options, advising them to write the next part in light of the overall goal, and alerting them when the story deviates from the original plan (Levin, Boruta, & Vasconcellos, 1983; Rubin, 1983). One limitation on such interventions is that if too much information is presented in the initial text, children may include new information that is inconsistent with the existing text. For example, Tetroe (1984) gave students story endings that contained up to seven pieces of information. The students had to write stories that would lead up to the prepared endings. The quality of the students' stories declined as the amount of information that had to be considered increased beyond their memory capacity, which had been estimated independently. Lehrer and Comeaux (1987) also found that third and fifth graders had difficulty in generating stories to satisfy multiple constraints, although the older children performed better than the younger ones.

WRITING FOR THE READER

When skilled writers decide what information to include and how to organize it, they assess who their potential readers are likely to be and what knowledge they might already have on the topic. Writers must sort out their own knowledge and continually monitor whether the text will make sense to the reader. Assumptions about the prior knowledge of the reader may have an important effect on the form of the text. For example, the writer may decide to use code words or dispense with detailed introductions of key concepts if he or she expects the reader will already possess a basic understanding of the topic. Little information is available about expert writers' decision-making processes. For example, how do skilled science writers translate technical material into articles that represent the main thrust of the research accurately while conveying its importance to novice readers? (On the other hand, experts who try to write for novice readers without developing the necessary *writing* skills may not succeed; a favorite example is computer documentation, which is often notoriously unhelpful because it is written by expert users.)

Relatively little is known about children's ability to adjust their writing for different purposes or for readers with different backgrounds (Hillocks, 1986). Kroll (1978) argues that writing requires the author to "decenter" and take the reader's point of view, and that well-developed perspective-taking skills should therefore be a prerequisite to effective writing. Research by Rubin and his colleagues provides some initial evidence that children with better social cognitive skills may be more advanced writers than their agemates. Rubin, Piche, Michlin, and Johnson (1984) found that fourth graders who scored higher on several role-taking tests received higher wholistic quality scores on their written work than other children. Rubin (1982) also found that children's ability to adjust the complexity of their language for readers whom they knew well or not well was related to their social cognitive ability. There is some evidence that older elementary-school students can simplify their writing for readers who are younger than they are (Bracewell, Scardamalia, &

Bereiter, 1978; Prentice, 1980), but we know little about their ability to write for readers with different kinds of knowledge.

Several researchers have suggested that persuasion tasks might be particularly difficult for novice writers, because persuasion depends on the author's ability to anticipate and counter the reader's potential objections to the message in advance (Bereiter, 1978; Crowhurst, 1987). Studies of the development of *oral* persuasion skills suggest that the ability to consider a particular listener's point of view and adjust a message accordingly may be a relatively late acquisition. For example, Flavell, Botkin, Fry, Wright, and Jarvis (1968) asked children in elementary and high school to imagine that they were a salesperson trying to sell a customer a tie. The protocols illustrate the tremendous development in children's ability to tailor arguments to the other person and present them in an effective manner. The elementary-school children simply stated their goal ("Here's a tie. Buy it.") while the high-school students flattered their customer and appealed to his skill as a careful consumer. Kroll (1984) and Edmunds, Cameron, and Eglington (1988) found that elementary-school writers showed some adaptation to different types of readers in their written persuasive letters. However, the 1986 National Assessment of Educational Progress study found that only about one-quarter of their secondary-school subjects could write adequate responses on persuasion writing assignments such as "Select a school rule and convince the principal that it needs changing." Most of the unsatisfactory responses described how the change would benefit the *writer*, without also providing arguments that would address the potential concerns of the person to be persuaded.

A critical issue for future research is when and to what extent children can consider the prior knowledge and information needs of the listener when they are writing. Tasks might involve asking children to insert additional information for novice readers or to delete superfluous details for knowledgeable readers. In addition, research is needed to develop methods that might help novice writers consider the information requirements of the reader (Crowhurst, 1987). One possibility is that increasing the child's sense of audience or awareness of the reader might be beneficial. Several researchers have pointed out that in the classroom children rarely write for a real audience other than a teacher who only has time to comment on the mechanics of the piece rather than its content (Cohen & Reil, 1986; D.H. Graves, 1983; Levin et al., 1983; Riel, 1986). These researchers recommend activities such as group sharing of work in progress, electronic networks and paper mail exchanges, and the publishing of children's best work so that their writing will be read by others.

SUMMARY

While studies of expert writers show that they plan extensively, elementary-school children rarely attempt to organize their material in advance. There seem to be three reasons for children's failure to plan: First, the content-generation problem is so great that children may not initially have enough information to develop a plan, and they may be reluctant to exclude information even if it does not fit with their topic. Second, children do not have an understanding of how the structure of text can be used to support an overall goal. Finally, children tend not to consider the reader's perspective while writing, so they do not include and organize information to meet the reader's information requirements. There has been relatively little research on training children to use organizational strategies such as outlining when writing.

Text Evaluation and Revision

Skilled writers are rarely satisfied with their first drafts. The process of crafting words to express one's meaning is so demanding that revisions are generally required before all the necessary information is included in the text. Studies of expert writers show that they consider revision to be a critical part of the writing process and devote considerable time and attention to it. In contrast, children rarely revise their work, and when they are required to revise, their performance suggests that they assess their writing at the most local level: Are the words spelled properly, and are there enough sentences? Considerations of overall coherence and communicative intent are infrequent (Calkins, 1980). For example, Figure 8.2 shows an example of the changes made by a sixth grader when he was required to revise his first draft. He switched the order of two sentences, but the change does not expand the topic or integrate the sentences with the other paragraphs (e.g., explain what the twin dogs have to do with the dog contest).

The Dog Contest

Once there was a girl named Julie. She had four dogs, *and* eight cats. She loved them all.

Two of the dogs were twins. They looked *ate* all the same. They ate *looked* all the same.

One day Julie saw in the newspaper that there was going to be a dog race. Suddenly she thought "maybye Snowflake would like it. If not there was Beauty too. She ran down to the cellar (Where the dogs were kept) she ran over to snowflake. She started barking. But Julie kept her down. *The next day* When they got back from the contest Snowflake had won! They were both proud! The End.

FIGURE 8.2. Example of a sixth grader's prompted revision. Italicized words were added to the second draft; underlined words were deleted.

Evaluating the Text

Several researchers have suggested that the demands of producing a *first* draft are so great that children do not have enough attention remaining to review and revise their work (Bruce et al, 1982). However, research on children's comprehension-monitoring skills suggests that another factor is that children cannot evaluate accurately the communicative quality of their own text even when they attempt to revise. The first step in the revision process must be to evaluate the text and to try to assess its communicative quality in light of the overall goal and the characteristics of potential readers (Beal, 1987). If a problem is detected the writer would then try to locate the words or sentences that were unclear and generate a new version of the text to repair the problem. While these steps can occur in an interactive manner, it is clear that text evaluation skills are of critical importance in the revision process.

Elementary-school children generally find it difficult to evaluate the communicative quality of messages. They tend to assume that a message is clear and that they or another person understood messages that actually did not provide enough information or contained inconsistencies. For example, when Markman (1979) asked children for advice on improving essays that contained logical contradictions, she found that while the children were flattered and quite eager to suggest changes, most of their revisions did not address the overall coherence of the essays. Children suggested changing individual words or complained that the topic was not sufficiently interesting, but did not point out that readers would not be able to understand the material. Bartlett (1982) also found that when children recognized that there were problems with passages that were not cohesive they often could not identify exactly what was wrong and so could not revise them appropriately. Olson (1977) has suggested that children must acquire the concept of the "very words" or literal meaning of the text before they can assess the communicative informativeness of a message. If children do not distinguish clearly between what the text actually says and what they would like the reader or listener to know, they will find it difficult to accurately assess the communicative quality of their written work. This may account for the seemingly random appearance of some changes; when children are told that they should make changes to their work they may not be able to tell what parts of the text should be changed.

Text Repair

Several studies have shown that children's revision is limited primarily by their poor message-evaluation skills, but that once children detect that a message is not actually clear they are often able to locate and repair the problem (Beal, 1987, 1988; Beal, Bonitatibus, & Garrod, 1988; see Van Haneghan & Baker, this volume, chap. 9, for repair strategies in the math domain). In one study, second, third, and fourth graders were asked to help the experimenter evaluate and then "fix up" (revise) problematic instructions for making simple block buildings or following roads on a board game (Beal, 1987). The results showed that while third graders revised more of the problematic messages than the younger children, the performance differences were due primarily to the older children's ability to detect the message problems, rather than to their ability to locate and repair the problems. Once a problem had been detected younger and older children were equally likely to make an adequate repair to the words of the message. Similarly, when fourth and sixth graders were asked to evaluate and revise stories and essays containing several types of text problems, children in both grades could make appropriate revisions once they had detected the text problems (Beal, 1988). Problem detection again seemed to be the limiting factor on the younger children's ability to revise.

These results imply that children's limited revision activity may be due primarily to poor message-evaluation skills. It may be particularly difficult for novice writers to evaluate the clarity of their own work because their intended meaning is clear to them (Kroll, 1978). Beal and Flavell (1984) found that children were more likely to overlook problems in short written messages when they knew what the author actually meant than when they did not know. The "decentration" required while writing may be difficult even for advanced writers. Perl (1979) found that college writers often reread what they thought they had written, rather than what they had actually put on the page. Many skilled writers recognize this problem and develop strategies for increasing their ability to evaluate their work, such as setting the text aside for a few days, reading it backwards, or (in the age of word processors) printing the draft in a new font so that it has a fresh appearance.

Training in Revision Strategies: Procedural Facilitation

How can we help children evaluate and revise their written work? Procedures that walk the young writer through the revision process step by step appear to be particularly helpful. Bereiter, Scardamalia, and their colleagues have developed a "procedural facilitation" method to help children revise by using advice printed on index cards that tell the child to first review a sentence and then to select an appropriate action. For example, the child might write a sentence, select a card that says "People won't understand what I mean here," and then select a card that says "Try saying it a different way." Children reported that this procedure was very helpful and that it made them review and think about their work more than they would have on their own. They also made evaluations of their work that corresponded reasonably well to those made by an expert writer (Bereiter & Scardamalia, 1986). These results suggest that providing a guide to tell children precisely what to do while revising seems to be helpful. Hillocks (1986) suggests that the classroom researchers in the New Hampshire writing project (D.H. Graves, 1983) may also have provided this type of procedural guidance to their young subjects as they questioned the children about what they were writing and why they were making certain revisions.

TRAINING IN TEXT-EVALUATION STRATEGIES

One limitation to procedural facilitation procedures is that they may only increase the frequency of revision activity without necessarily increasing children's awareness of the information needs of the reader or improving the communicative quality of the text (Bracewell et al., 1978; O'Looney & Rubin, 1896; Perl, 1979). Training in comprehension-monitoring strategies may provide a method to help children revise more *effectively* as well as more *frequently*, since recent research has shown that children's revision is limited primarily by their problem-detection skills (Beal, 1987, 1988). Several researchers have found that children can be taught to question themselves about the comprehensibility and meaning of written material, and that such strategies help children locate problematic sections of text (Capelli, 1985; Miller, 1985; Miller, Giovenco, & Rentiers, 1987). Beal et al. (1988) hypothesized that training in a comprehension-monitoring strategy might therefore also help children to revise problematic texts. To evaluate this hypothesis, third and sixth graders were trained to use a self-questioning strategy to help themselves detect inconsistencies in prepared texts (Capelli, 1985). Children were later asked to revise problematic texts. The results showed that both the third and sixth graders revised more effectively after training in the self-questioning strategy, and that the training generalized to texts with different types of problems.

PROVIDING CRITERIA FOR EVALUATING WRITING QUALITY

Research on comprehension monitoring also suggests that an additional approach for improving revision skills might be to provide information about the criteria for writing quality, including what types of text problems should be revised. Markman and Gorin (1981) found that providing children with examples of specific types of text problems helped them locate such problems in other texts. Fitzgerald and Markham (1987) gave sixth graders an extensive series of group lessons about the process of revision. The lessons involved modeling by the teacher of the revision process, including specific examples of additions, deletions, substitutions, and text rearrangement (Faigley & Witte, 1984). The results showed that the children wrote stories that were rated of higher overall quality than control children, suggesting that the examples may have helped the children to make changes that actually improved their stories.

In addition to providing children with information about different types of text problems, children might also be taught strategies for deciding when the revision process has been completed and the text has reached its final polished form. D.H. Graves (1983) has proposed as part of his "process writing" approach that children write regularly and be given the responsibility of deciding when they have completed a piece and are ready to publish their work. However, research on children's text-evaluation skills suggests that children may use inappropriate criteria in deciding whether a piece has been completed. Sonnenschein (Whitehurst, Sonnenschein, & Ianfolla, 1981) has found that children use a "longer is better" criterion in assessing the quality of oral messages. Children also use the length of their text to decide when they have finished writing: they count sentences or say that a piece is "not good" because it does not fill up the page (Englert & Raphael, 1988). Therefore, procedures to help children with the evaluation process might also stress that overall coherence and adequate comprehensibility to the reader should be used as criteria for completion, rather than length.

Having children review one another's written work is sometimes suggested to develop children's awareness of the information requirements of the reader, and as a way to reduce the burden on the classroom teacher of reviewing each child's work several times during the writing process (D.H. Graves, 1983; Humes, 1983; Tompkins & Friend, 1988). However, the research on children's comprehension-monitoring skills suggests that peer review may not be very effective unless children are taught specific strategies for reviewing the other person's work, including information about the criteria to be used in the evaluation process (Potter, Busching, McCormick, Wilkes, & Slesinger, 1987). My own observations in the classroom are that children need considerable direction for peer review to be successful, because they do not appear to know how to evaluate the other child's text without some guidance. Part of the problem may be that children do not understand the relationship between the quality of the message and the reader or listener's comprehension; they tend to believe that the listener is responsible for comprehension failures rather than the poor quality of the message or text (Beal & Flavell, 1982; Peterson et al., 1972; Robinson, 1981). Perl (1983) suggested that students should be taught the strategy of "saying back" what they thought the writer was trying to convey, to help the writer detect misunderstandings. A. Graves (1983) has also proposed that the classroom teacher should model active listening and questioning behaviors when children read their work to the class, so that children know exactly what they should do as reviewers.

Summary

Research on children's message-evaluation skills has fairly direct implications for the revision process. Children who do not yet distinguish their own intended meaning from the actual words that they write will overlook discrepancies and fail to revise the text to better express their meaning. They may also be unable to analyze the reader's information requirements and determine precisely what information the text should encode for the reader to understand their intended meaning. On the other hand, recent studies suggest that children can often revise texts surprisingly well once they have figured out that a communication problem exists (Beal, 1987, 1988). Thus, a primary goal for current research should be the development of methods to train text-evaluation skills and to encourage children to utilize these skills in the classroom.

Conclusions

There has been a great deal of research on elementary-school children's knowledge about communication, but there has been relatively little consideration of the implications of the results for young children's writing. As concern about students' poor writing skills increases, more attention is being focused on the early stages of writing development. As discussed in this chapter, research on children's communication skills may lead to specific techniques for diagnosing children's difficulties in learning to write and to effective instructional methods. Knowledge such as this can enable researchers to examine instructional techniques designed to encourage children to engage in the strategic activities of expert writers. For example, teaching children to use "cue cards" to help themselves retrieve information on a topic can help them overcome their dependence on a conversational partner to provide retrieval cues. Methods to train children to ask evaluative questions about the comprehensibility of texts also appear to hold promise for improving revision skills. However, a critical component of these procedures is that the child is taught to focus on one step of the writing process at a time, such as generating content *or* rereading and revising the first draft. Thus, it remains to be seen whether memory and communication strategies can help children in the typical classroom writing task where they may be required to produce a final version of their work in one writing session. It is also not yet clear whether children will benefit most from instruction that encourages them to continue to work through the steps of the writing process in a linear manner (text production, organization, and revision) or whether children would benefit most from learning to coordinate multiple strategies and to write in the more interactive and recursive manner of expert writers. Finally, some caution is in order before recommending the use of writing tools such as text editors and planners for young writers. They may be of enormous benefit to relatively skilled writers who have already automatized much of their writing and can accommodate the mastery of a new skill into their writing process, but the introduction of such tools may not necessarily benefit novices unless they are also taught to use effective writing strategies.

When children first begin to write in the classroom, they must master skills in three areas: generating content, organizing their text, and revising it in light of the reader's information requirements. At first, children find it difficult to think of things to write about because they cannot easily assess the availability of content in memory and they lack strategies for retrieving information from memory. They also find it difficult to consider the reader's information requirements when selecting the information to be included and organizing the material in light of a particular goal. Finally, their limited knowledge about the communication process limits their ability to evaluate and revise their work, because they do not understand the role of the message in determining the reader's comprehension. Models of the writing process emphasize the high demands of allocating attention to these steps in the task and suggest that expert writers use strategies to help themselves generate and organize their material, and to evaluate and revise their work. Recent research suggests that children can be taught to use memory and comprehension-monitoring strategies, and that such interventions may help them learn to write more effectively in the classroom.

REFERENCES

Anderson, V.A., Bereiter, C., & Smart, D. (1980). *Activation of semantic networks in writing: Teaching students how to do it themselves.* Paper presented at the annual meeting of the American Educational Research Association, Boston.

Andrews, P., E. Beal, C.R., & Corson, J. (1988). *Talking on paper: Dialogue as a writing task for sixth graders.* Unpublished manuscript, Dartmouth College, Hanover, NH.

Applebee, A.N. (1984). Writing and reasoning. *Review of Educational Research, 54,* 577–596.

Bartlett, E.J. (1982). Learning to revise: Some component processes. In M. Nystrand (Ed.), *What writers know: The language, process, and structure of written discourse* 345–363. New York: Academic Press.

Beach, J.D. (1983). Teaching students to write informational reports. *Elementary School Journal, 84,* 213–220.

Beal, C.R. (1987). Repairing the message: Children's monitoring and revision skills. *Child Development, 58,* 401–408.

Beal, C.R. (April 1988). *The development of text evaluation and revision skills.* Paper presented at the annual meeting of the American Educational Research Association, New Orleans, LA.

Beal, C.R., Bonitatibus, G., & Garrod, A. (1988). *The effect of training in comprehension monitoring on children's ability to evaluate and revise problematic texts.* Unpublished manuscript, Dartmouth College, Hanover, NH.

Beal, C.R., & Flavell, J.H. (1982). Young speakers' evaluations of their listener's comprehension in a referential communication task. *Child Development, 54,* 148–153.

Beal, C.R., & Flavell, J.H. (1984). Development of the ability to distinguish communicative intention and literal message meaning. *Child Development, 55,* 920–928.

Beal, C.R., & Griffin, E.A. (March 1987). *Learning to use a text editor.* Paper presented at the annual meeting of the American Educational Research Association, Washington, DC.

Bereiter, C. (1978). *Discourse type, schema and strategy—A view from the standpoint of instructional design.* Paper presented at the annual meeting of the American Educational Research Association, Toronto.

Bereiter, C., & Scardamalia, M. (1982). From conversation to composition: The role of instruction in a developmental process. In R.Glaser (Ed.), *Advances in instructional psychology*, Vol. 2, pp. 1–64. Hillsdale, NJ: Erlbaum & Associates.

Bereiter, C., & Scardamalia, M. (1986). *The psychology of written composition*. Hillsdale, NJ: Erlbaum & Associates.

Bonitatibus, G.J. (1988). Comprehension monitoring and the apprehension of literal meaning. *Child Development, 59*, 60–70.

Bonitatibus, G.J., & Flavell, J.H. (1985). Effect of presenting a message in written form on young children's ability to evaluate its communication adequacy. *Developmental Psychology, 21*, 455–461.

Bos, C.S. (1988). Process-oriented writing: Instructional implications for mildly handicapped students. *Exceptional Children, 54*, 521–527.

Boyer, E.L. (1983). *High school: A report on secondary education in America*. New York: Harper & Row.

Bracewell, R.J., Scardamalia, M., & Bereiter, C. (1978). *The development of audience awareness in writing*. (ERIC Document Reproduction Service No. ED 154–443)

Bridwell, L.S. (1980). Revising strategies in twelfth grade students' transactional writing. *Research in the Teaching of English, 14*, 197–222.

Brown, A.L., Day, J.D., & Jones, R.S. (1983). The development of plans for summarizing texts. *Child Development, 54*, 968–979.

Brown, A.L., & Smiley, S.S. (1977). Rating the importance of structural units of prose passages: A problem of metacognitive development. *Child Development, 48*, 1–8.

Brown, A.L., & Smiley, S.S. (1978). The development of strategies for studying texts. *Child Development, 49*, 1076–1088.

Bruce, B.C., Collins, A., Rubin, A.D., & Gentner, D. (1982). Three perspectives on writing. *Educational Psychologist, 17*, 131–145.

Calkins, L.M. (1980). Children's rewriting strategies. *Research in the Teaching of English, 14*, 331–341.

Capelli, C.A. (April 1985). *Improving comprehension monitoring through training in hypothesis testing*. Paper presented at the biennial meeting of the Society for Research in Child Development, Toronto.

Cioffi, G. (1984). Observing composing behaviors of primary-age children: The interaction of oral and written language. In R. Beach & L.S. Bridwell (Eds.), *New directions in composition research* pp. 171–190. New York: Guildford Press.

Cohen, M., & Riel, M. (1986). *Computer networks: Creating real audiences for students' writing* (Report No. 15). San Diego: University of California, Interactive Technology Laboratory, Center for Human Information Processing.

Collins, A., & Gentner, D. (1980). A framework for a cognitive theory of writing. In L.W. Gregg & E.R. Steinberg (Eds.), *Cognitive processes in writing* pp. 51–72. Hillsdale, NJ: Erlbaum & Associates.

Coop, R.H., White, K., Tapscott, B., & Lee, L. (1983). A program to develop basic writing skills in grades 4–9. *Elementary School Journal, 84*, 76–87.

Crowhurst, M. (March 1987). *The effect of reading instruction and writing instruction on reading and writing persuasion*. Paper presented at the annual meeting of the American Educational Research Association, Washington, DC.

Daiute, C. (1985). *Writing and computers*. Reading, MA: Addison-Wesley.

Dickson, W.P. (1981). *Children's oral communication skills*. New York: Academic Press.

Diederich, P.B. (1984). *Measuring growth in writing*. Urbana, IL: National Council of Teachers of English.

Edmunds, G.A., Cameron, C.A., & Eglington, K. (April 1988). *Audience adaptation in persuasive letters of elementary school children*. Paper presented at the annual meeting of the American Educational Research Association, New Orleans.

Englert, C.S., & Raphael, T.E. (1988). Constructing well-formed prose: Process, structure and metacognitive knowledge. *Exceptional Children, 54*, 513–520.

Faigley, L., & Witte, S.P. (1981). Analyzing revision. *College Composition and Communication, 32*, 400–414.

Faigley, L., & Witte, S.P. (1984). Measuring the effects of revisions on text structure. In R. Beach & L.S. Bridwell (Eds.), *New directions in composition research* pp. 95–108. New York: Guildford Press.

Fitzgerald, J., & Markham, L.R. (1987). Teaching children about revision in writing. *Cognition and Instruction, 4*, 3–24.

Fitzgerald, J., & Teasley, A. (1985). *Effects of instruction in narrative structure on children's writing*. Unpublished manuscript, University of North Carolina, Chapel Hill.

Flavell, J.H., Botkin, P.T., Fry, C.L., Wright, J.W., & Jarvis, P.E. (1968). *The development of role-taking and communication skills in children*. New York: John Wiley.

Flavell, J.H., Speer, J.R., Green, F.L., & August, D.L. (1981). The development of comprehension monitoring and knowledge about communication. *Monographs of the Society for Research in Child Development, 46*, (5, Serial No. 192).

Flower, L.S., & Hayes, J.R. (1980). The dynamics of composing: Making plans and juggling constraints. In L.W. Gregg & E.R. Steinberg (Eds.), *Cognitive processes in writing* pp. 31–50. Hillsdale, NJ: Erlbaum & Associates.

Flower, L.S., & Hayes, J.R. (1981). Plans that guide the composing process. In C.H. Frederiksen & J.F. Dominic (Eds.), *Writing: The nature, development and teaching of written communication* pp. 39–58. Hillsdale, NJ: Erlbaum & Associates.

Gerlach, G.J. (March 1987). *The effect of typing skill on using a word processor for composition*. Paper presented at the annual meeting of the American Educational Research Association, Washington, DC.

Gould, J.D. (1980). Experiments on composing letters: Some facts, some myths and some observations. In L.W. Gregg & E.R. Steinberg (Eds.), *Cognitive processes in writing* pp. 97–127. Hillsdale, NJ: Erlbaum & Associates.

Graham, S., & Harris, K. (April 1986). *Improving learning disabled students' compositions via story grammar training: A component analysis of self-control strategy training*. Paper presented at the annual meeting of the American Educational Research Association, San Francisco.

Graham, S., & Harris, K. (April 1988). *Improving learning disabled students' skills at generating essays: Self-instructional strategy training*. Paper presented at the annual meeting of the American Educational Research Association, New Orleans.

Graham, S., Harris, K.R., & Sawyer, R. (1987). Composition instruction with learning disabled students: Self instructional strategy training. *Focus on Exceptional Children, 20*, 1–11.

Graves, A. (1983). Sharing as a motivation for writing. *Elementary School Journal, 84*, 33–35.

Graves, D.H. (1983). *Writing: Teachers and children at work*. Portsmouth, NH: Heinemann Educational Books.

Hayes, J.R., & Flower, L.S. (1980). Identifying the organization of writing processes. In L.W. Gregg & E.R. Steinberg (Eds.), *Cognitive processes in writing* pp. 3–30. Hillsdale, NJ: Erlbaum & Associates.

Heap, J.L. (April 1986). *Collabrative practices during computer writing in a first grade classroom.* Paper presented at the annual meeting of the American Educational Research Association, San Francisco.

Hidi, S., & Hildyard, A. (1983). The comparison of oral and written productions of two discourse types. *Discourse Processes, 6*, 91–105.

Hillocks, G. (1986). *Research on written composition: New directions for teaching.* Urbana, IL: ERIC clearinghouse on reading and communication skills.

Humes, A. (1983). Putting writing research into practice. *Elementary School Journal, 84*, 3–17.

Kroll, B.M. (1978). Cognitive egocentrism and the problem of audience awareness in written discourse. *Research in the Teaching of English, 12*, 269–281.

Kroll, B.M. (1984). Audience adaptation in children's written persuasive letters. *Written Communication, 1*, 407–427.

Kurth, R.J., & Kurth, L.M. (March 1987). *A comparison of writing instruction using word processing, word processing with voice synthesis, and no word processing in kindergarten and first grade.* Paper presented at the annual meeting of the American Educational Research Association, Washington, DC.

Lehrer, R., & Comeaux, M. (March 1987). *A developmental study of the effects of goal constraints on composition.* Paper presented at the annual meeting of the American Educational Research Association, Washington, DC.

Levin, J.A., Boruta, M.J., & Vasconcellos, M.T. (1983). Microcomputer-based environments for writing: A Writer's assistant, In A.C. Wilkinson (Ed.), *Classroom computers and cognitive science* pp. 219–232. New York: Academic Press.

Markman, E.M. (1977). Realizing that you don't understand: A preliminary investigation. *Child Development, 48*, 986–992.

Markman, E.M. (1979). Realizing that you don't understand: Elementary school children's awareness of inconsistencies. *Child Development, 50*, 643–655.

Markman, E.M., & Gorin, L. (1981). Children's ability to adjust their standards for evaluating comprehension. *Journal of Educational Psychology, 73*, 320–325.

McCutchen, D., & Perfetti, C.A. (1983). Local coherence: Helping young writers manage a complex task. *Elementary School Journal, 84*, 71–75.

Miller, G.E. (1985). The effects of general and specific self-instruction training on children's comprehension monitoring performances during reading. *Reading Research Quarterly, 20*, 616–628.

Miller, G.E., Giovenco, A., & Rentiers, K.A. (1987). Fostering comprehension monitoring in below-average readers through self-instruction training. *Journal of Reading Behavior, 19*, 379–393.

National Assessment of Educational Progress. (1986). *The writing report card: Writing achievement in American schools.* Princeton, NJ: Educational Testing Service.

National Commission on Excellence in Education. (1983). *A nation at risk.* Washington, DC: U.S. Government Printing Office.

Nystrand, M. (1986). *The structure of written communication: Studies in reciprocity between writers and readers.* Orlando, FL: Academic Press.

O'Looney, J., & Rubin, D. (April 1986). *Procedural facilitation of audience awareness in the revision processes of basic writers.* Paper presented at the annual meeting of the American Educational Research Association, San Francisco.

Olson, D.R. (1977). From utterance to text: The bias of language in speech and writing. *Harvard Educational Review, 47*, 257–281.

Olson, D.R., & Hildyard, A. (1983). Writing and literal meaning. In M. Martlew (Ed.), *Psychology of written language: A developmental and educational perspective* pp. 41–65. New York: John Wiley.

Pekala, R. (1983). By popular demand. *Elementary School Journal, 84,* 25–27.

Perl, S. (1979). The composing process of unskilled college writers. *Research in the Teaching of English, 13,* 317–336.

Perl, S. (1983). How teachers teach the writing process. *Elementary School Journal, 84,* 19–24.

Peterson, C.L., Danner, F.W., & Flavell, J.H. (1972). Developmental changes in children's responses to three indications of communicative failure. *CHild Development, 43,* 1463–1468.

Potter, E.F., Busching, B.A., McCormick, C.B., Wilkes, V., & Slesinger, B.A. (March 1987). *Criteria children use to evaluate their own and others' writing.* Paper presented at the annual meeting of the American Educational Research Association, Washington, DC.

Prentice, W.C. (1980). The effects of intended audience and feedback on the writings of middle grade pupils. *Dissertation Abstracts International, 41,* 943A.

Riel, M.M. (April 1986). *The educational potential of computer networking.* Paper presented at the annual meeting of the American Educational Research Association, San Francisco.

Robinson, E. (1981). The child's understanding of inadequate messages and communication failure: A problem of ignorance or egocentrism: In W.P. Dickson (Ed.), *Children's oral communication skills* pp. 167–188. New York: Academic Press.

Robinson, E., Goelman, H., & Olson, D.R. (1983). Children's understanding of the relation between expressions (what was said) and intentions (what was meant). *British Journal of Developmental Psychology, 1,* 75–86.

Rubin, A. (1983). The computer confronts language arts: Cans and shoulds for education. In A.C. Wilkinson (Ed.), *Classroom computers and cognitive science* pp. 201–217. New York: Academic Press.

Rubin, D.L. (1982). Adapting syntax in writing to varying audiences as a function of age and social cognitive ability. *Journal of Child Language, 9,* 497–510.

Rubin, D.L., Piche, G.L., Michlin, M.L., & Johnson, F.L. (1984). Social cognitive ability as a predictor of the quality of fourth-graders' written narratives. In R. Beach & L.S. Bridwell (Eds.), *New directions in composition research* pp. 297–307. New York: Guilford Press.

Sager, C. (1973). Improving the quality of written composition through pupil use of rating scale. *Dissertation Abstracts International, 34,* 1496A.

Scardamalia, M. (August 1986). *Designs for fostering expertise.* Paper presented at the annual meeting of the Cognitive Science Society, Amherst, MA.

Scardamalia, M., & Bereiter, C. (April 1979). *The effects of writing rate on children's composition.* Paper presented at the annual meeting of the American Educational Research Association, San Francisco.

Scardamalia, M., Bereiter, C., & Woodruff, E. (1980). *The effects of content knowledge on writing.* Paper presented at the annual meeting of the American Educational Research Association, Boston.

Shaw, R.A., Pettigrew, J., & van Nostrand, A.D. (1983). Tactical planning of writing instruction. *Elementary School Journal, 84,* 45–51.

Simon, H.A. (1973). The structure of ill-structured problems. *Artificial Intelligence, 4,* 181–201.

Speer, J.R. (1984). Two practical strategies young children use to interpret vague instructions. *Child Development, 55,* 1811–1819.

Stein, N. (1986). Knowledge and process in the acquisition of writing skills. In E.Z. Rothkopf (Ed.), *Review of research in education,* Vol. 13. Washington, DC: American Educational Research Association.

Tetroe, J. (1984). *Information processing demand of plot construction in story writing.* Paper presented at the annual meeting of the American Educational Research Association, New Orleans.

Tompkins, G.E., & Friend, M. (1988). After your students write: What's next? *Teaching Exceptional Children, 20,* 4–9.

Wheeler, F. (1985). Can word processing help the writing process? *Learning: The magazine for creative teaching, 13,* 54–62.

Whitehurst, G.L., & Sonnenschein, S. (1978). The development of communication: Attribute variation leads to contrast failure. *Journal of Experimental Child Psychology, 25,* 454–490.

Whitehurst, G.L., & Sonnenschein, S. (1985). The development of communication: A functional analysis. *Annals of Child Development, 2,* 1–48.

Whitehurst, G.L., Sonnenschein, S., & Ianfolla, B.J. (1981). Learning to communicate from models: Children confuse length with information. *Child Development, 52,* 507–513.

Whitt, J., Paul, P.V., & Reynolds, C.J. (1988). Motivate reluctant learning disabled writers. *Teaching Exceptional Children, 20,* 37–39.

9
Cognitive Monitoring in Mathematics

JAMES P. VAN HANEGHAN AND LINDA BAKER

The role of cognitive monitoring has been a dominant theme in cognitive strategy research in recent years. Cognitive monitoring can be defined as any activity aimed at evaluating or regulating one's own cognitions (Flavell, 1979). Examples of cognitive monitoring include planning, checking, self-testing, assessing one's progress, and correcting one's errors. Researchers have come to recognize that cognitive monitoring plays a vital role in virtually any cognitive endeavor and thus has important implications for instructional intervention. Accordingly, cognitive monitoring has received a substantial amount of attention in the reading, communication, and memory literatures (e.g., Baker, 1985; Baker & Brown, 1984a, 1984b; Beal, this volume, chap. 8; Brown, 1978; Flavell, 1979; Markman, 1981).

Somewhat surprisingly, cognitive monitoring has received little attention in research on mathematical thinking and problem solving, despite the applicability of the construct to many important theoretical and practical issues. For example, the debate over the relationship between conceptual knowledge (e.g., knowledge of the base-ten system) and procedural knowledge (e.g., algorithms) is really an issue of whether conceptual standards can be used to judge the sense of procedural results (see Hiebert, 1986; Nesher, 1986; Resnick & Omanson, 1987). By examining this issue in light of current theorizing about cognitive monitoring, perhaps some progress can be made in understanding and closing the gap between children's use of procedures and their understanding of concepts. Research on cognitive monitoring would be valuable from a practical standpoint as well, given that cognitive monitoring is actually an explicit part of the mathematics curriculum. For example, teachers routinely tell their students to check their answers, and mathematics texts often present heuristics for answer checking. In addition, students are frequently taught specific ways to judge the sensibleness of answers, using procedures such as estimation.

In this chapter we establish the relevance of the concept of cognitive monitoring in mathematics, drawing parallels where appropriate to cognitive monitoring research in other domains. The relative paucity of empirical research on cognitive monitoring in mathematics necessitates that our discussion involve a certain degree of theoretical speculation. We will begin by clarifying what it is we mean by cognitive monitoring in the domain of mathematics. We will then go on to review existing research and theory, focusing primarily on elementary-school children's work with word problems. We will discuss how children are taught to monitor their work in mathematics classes and some of the problems with current practices. We will present some of our own research which examines children's abilities to detect errors in word problems and will then sketch a model of cognitive monitoring in mathematics based on the research. Finally, we will discuss existing instructional interventions and will offer suggestions for designing curricula that are more apt to enhance students' monitoring skills.

What is Cognitive Monitoring in Mathematics?

We use the term cognitive monitoring in the domain of mathematics to refer to students' attempts to determine whether they have given a correct answer, chosen a correct strategy for solving a problem, or understood a problem or concept. We are particularly interested in children's judgments of their understanding, an aspect of cognitive monitoring known as comprehension monitoring (Baker & Brown, 1984a; Flavell, 1979). Like much of the work on comprehension monitoring in the domain of reading, we emphasize children's evaluation of their understanding rather than their regulation of understanding (Baker, 1985). That is, we focus on children's discoveries of incorrect or nonsensical aspects of word problems rather than on their resolution of their misunderstandings or errors. This focus in no way implies that regulation is less important than evaluation, nor does it imply that these are the only aspects of cognitive monitoring worthy of investigation. It is simply that the length constraints of the chapter require selectivity of coverage. (See Pressley, 1986, for discussion of other relevant aspects of the literature.)

Our theoretical orientation is that there are multiple levels at which cognition can be monitored in mathematics, just as there are multiple levels at which comprehension can be monitored in reading (Baker, 1985). We see at least three levels at which children need to evaluate their cognition in solving mathematics word problems. First, there is the need to evaluate the results of arithmetic procedures carried out to get an answer. Such monitoring could occur simply by checking the arithmetic involved (e.g., adding in the other direction, subtracting an addition result, dividing a multiplication result). Second, there is the need to evaluate whether the procedure one has chosen is correct. To do this, one would have to carry out some level of semantic analysis of the text, whether that involves rereading the entire text or simply finding a key word. Finally, there is the need to evaluate the sensibleness of the problem itself. Such an evaluation would involve looking at the semantic relationships expressed in the text and making a decision about whether those relationships make sense. Each of these three levels of analysis will be considered individually in the sections that follow. However, this is an expository convenience; in practice the various levels are interdependent. For example, if a child monitors at the calculational level and realizes that the result is outlandish, this realization may signal to the child that there is something wrong with his or her comprehension of the text, thus triggering monitoring at the level of semantic sensibleness.

Herein, we will consider research that has addressed either directly or indirectly these three levels of analysis. First, we will examine children's checking of calculations. Second, we will consider children's judgments of whether they have chosen the correct operation. Next, we will explore how children judge the sensibleness of a problem, considering their sensitivity to the logical consistency of the problem (internal consistency) and their application of real-world standards to the circumscribed world of word problems (external consistency). Finally, we will consider children's use of standards at all three levels of analysis as examined in recent research by the first author (Van Haneghan, 1986).

Children's Checking of Their Calculations

Children's checking of their calculations has received the most attention of any of the three levels of analysis. A major issue in this literature has been the relationship between children's use of procedures and their understanding of the number system. Much of the research in this vein has centered around children's "subtraction bugs," that is, subtraction errors children make consistently when learning to borrow (Van Lehn, 1983). In the first part of this section, we will consider research pertaining to children's monitoring of the relationship between their conceptual and procedural knowledge about mathematics. Relatively few studies have been conducted with an explicit focus on cognitive monitoring and metacognition in mathematics, but those studies that have had such a focus will be considered in the second part. Finally, we turn to an examination of current instructional practices designed to foster checking strategies.

MONITORING THE RELATIONSHIP BETWEEN PROCEDURAL AND CONCEPTUAL KNOWLEDGE

As noted earlier, much of the research on this issue has been designed to induce children to recognize errors due to "buggy algorithms." These errors can lead to answers that differ substantially from the correct answer, yet the errors still go undetected (e.g., giving the answer of 5,984 to the problem 7,002 − 28; Davis & McKnight, 1980). Relevant studies of children who use buggy algorithms have been conducted by Davis and McKnight (1980) and by Resnick (1982, 1983; Resnick & Omanson, 1987).

Davis and McKnight (1980) presented third-grade children with problems involving cashier exchanges and other everyday embodiments of number, reasoning that such exposure might help them recognize their subtraction errors. They thought that helping children to see that, for instance, $7,000 − $25 would not yield an answer under $6,000 might lead them to reconsider their buggy answers to the decontextualized subtraction procedures. However, children did not notice the relationship between their errors and the meaningful embodiments of number. In light of what we know about the importance of informed strategy training (e.g., Brown, Bransford, Ferrara, & Campione, 1983), it is not surprising that the children failed to make the connection. However, for theoretical reasons, the authors chose not to make the connection explicit.

Resnick (1982, 1983; Resnick & Omanson, 1987) also gave third-grade children concrete embodiments of number, using Dienes blocks to represent the base-ten system. Children were taught to map the results of their work with blocks onto their work with traditional subtraction algorithms. Resnick (1982, 1983) initially reported some improvement in children's use of traditional subtraction algorithms resulting from learning the correspondences between the blocks and the algorithms. Resnick and Omanson (1987) recently reported, however, that the long-term effects of teaching children to map their written work onto concrete embodiments were negligible. Resnick and Omanson suggested, in retrospect, that perhaps the instruction had little effect because children's subtraction algorithms are so highly automated that they do not access a semantic representation to check their work.

Failures to connect procedures to concepts also occur in children's work with fractions, as Lesh, Landau, and Hamilton (1983) demonstrated. Lesh et al. gave children in grades four through eight a word problem involving the addition of 1/4 and 1/5 of a pizza, first in written form and then in concrete form (i.e., children were given sections of a clay "pizza"). Of relevance here is that a number of children gave different answers to the concrete and written forms of the problem and did not view the discrepancies as problematic. They made the somewhat startling claim that there was no necessary correspondence between the real world and the world of numbers.

One additional effort aimed at inducing children to use conceptual knowledge to check their algorithmic work was undertaken by DeCorte and Vershaffel (1981). These researchers attempted to teach first- and second-grade children verification skills when solving open-sentence problems (e.g., _____ − 7 = 8). The children were taught to use a part-whole schema for conceptualizing the problems. That is, they were taught to recognize the relationship between the parts (the smaller numbers in the problems) and the whole (the largest number). They were also explicitly taught how to verify their answers. Despite the fairly extensive training, there were no differences in subsequent checking behaviors between the experimental group and a control group, although the trained subjects had better overall performance.

Cognitive Monitoring and Metacognitive Knowledge

As noted earlier, only a few studies of calculational checking have been explicitly concerned with cognitive monitoring and metacognitive knowledge. In a study of cognitive monitoring, Slife, Weiss, and Bell (1985) compared normal and learning-disabled elementary-school children's abilities to differentiate correct from incorrect answers. This approach is analogous to comprehension monitoring research that requires students to assess the accuracy of their responses to comprehension questions (e.g., Forrest-Pressley & Waller, 1984; Maki & Berry, 1984). The children were matched on mental age, mathematics achievement, and their performance on the mathematics problems they were to check. That is, each learning-disabled child was matched with a normal child who missed the same problems he or she did. The learning-disabled children were much less successful in differentiating the problems they solved incorrectly from those they solved correctly.

Slife et al. interpret their results as evidence of a cognitive monitoring deficit in learning-disabled children that is independent of their knowledge base (see also Short & Weissberg-Benchell, this volume, chap. 2). This claim of independence is based on the belief that the children must have had comparable knowledge because they were matched on performance. However, it may be that the learning-disabled children had to put much more effort into completing the problems and were therefore less confident in the accuracy of their responses than their normal counterparts. Thus, not only must children have relevant knowledge, they also must have fluent knowledge (i.e., knowledge that can be accessed easily; Bransford et al., in press). Without information as to whether knowledge fluency was the same for both groups, we cannot conclude that they had equivalent knowledge of the problems. Hence, although it is appropriate to conclude that the learning-disabled children in the study were deficient monitors, it is unclear whether their monitoring difficulties were independent of their knowledge base.

Children's metacognitive knowledge about checking has been examined by Lester and Garafolo (1982), who used the interview approach characteristic of research on metacognition in other domains such as memory (Kreutzer, Leonard, & Flavell, 1975) and reading (Myers & Paris, 1978). Lester and Garafolo interviewed third- and fifth-grade children and, somewhat surprisingly, found virtually no developmental differences in responding. Most children reported that they checked their calculations when they had time. However, calculations were usually the only level of analysis children considered, even when checking word problems. In other words, children did not evaluate their work with respect to operational choice, semantic sensibleness, or any other standard.

An examination of both cognitive monitoring and metacognitive knowledge was undertaken by Van Haneghan in some preliminary unpublished work. Children in first, third, and fifth grades were asked to prove, by checking, that their answers to simple grade-appropriate open-sentence problems and word problems were correct. Even some of the first graders demonstrated knowledge of checking. They usually appealed to memorized addition and subtraction facts or counted on their fingers or with objects to show how they would prove they were correct. Third and fifth graders usually checked their work against a computational standard, adding the column back up in the opposite direction, redoing the calculations, or using the inverse operation. Interestingly, most third- and fifth-grade children who solved a problem incorrectly did not benefit from checking. That is, the computational check frequently did not lead them to change the answer to a correct one. This was particularly true when children made conceptual errors. For example, when answering an open-sentence problem of the form "____ $- Y = X$," children unclear about what other strategy to use would subtract X from Y. These children would then perform that operation again to reconfirm their answers, or they would add X to their answer to get Y. Children who used "buggy" procedures for borrowing also had problems discovering their errors because they had difficulty dissociating their check from their original procedures.

CURRENT INSTRUCTIONAL PRACTICES

Although most of the research on children's checking of their calculations does not involve word problems, it is the checking of answers to word problems that gets most attention in school mathematics texts. We learned from an informal survey of elementary mathematics texts that most of them provide heuristics for solving word problems that have as their last step checking the answer (see e.g., May, Frye, & Jacobs, 1981; Merrill Publishing Company, 1987). Some give specific ways to check answers (e.g., telling the student to check a subtraction calculation by adding). Others emphasize the sensibleness of the answers, but they offer no assistance in helping children understand what a sensible answer is or is not. This is unfortunate, because some children view instructions to find a sensible answer as a cue to check their calculations rather than to evaluate their answer with respect to the story problem (Trafton, 1986). Finally, textbooks often teach children to use estimation or approximation strategies to check their work, but the strategies are rarely linked to word problems. A typical strategy might be for the child to round to a certain place value and compare the rounded result with his or her answer.

The instructional emphasis on estimation as a means of checking has been attacked in the literature. For example, Trafton (1986) argues that estimation strategies are cumbersome to apply, requiring almost as much time as redoing the problem. Consequently, children do not use them, and so their work is left unchecked.

Nevertheless, there are situations where estimation is useful, as in working with fractions. However, it appears that children do not learn estimation strategies very well. For example, the National Assessment of Educational Progress (NAEP) found that a surprisingly small number of children (24% of the 13-year-olds tested) could correctly pick the answer 2 as a reasonable estimate for the problem $^{12}/_{13}$ + $^{7}/_8$. The most common choices out of the four presented were 19 and 21 (Post, 1981).

Many mathematics educators believe estimation is becoming an increasingly important checking strategy as computers and calculators simplify the task of calculating (Hope, 1986; Reys, 1984). Students need to be able to determine if what comes up on the calculator makes sense. Unfortunately, there is little research exploring how children can be taught this skill or how they acquire it informally. However, Reys, Rybolt, Bestgen, and Wyatt (1982) found that students in seventh grade through college who were proficient estimators used several effective strategies involving mental calculation. For example, they reformulated numbers (e.g., changing them into multiples of 5 and 10). They also changed the problems by translating them into easier ones (e.g., changing problems involving addition of several numbers to the multiplication of a single number that is a rough average of all the numbers). Such mental calculation seems to be just the skill needed to judge the sensibility of answers that come up on calculators and computers. Certainly one would not want to lose the advantage of the new technology by using time-consuming hand calculations to check one's answers!

Children's Evaluation of Operation Choice

As children learn how to use several different arithmetic operations, it becomes increasingly important that they learn when they should use a particular operation in solving a word problem. In practice, however, elementary school children are not often asked to evaluate operation choice. Although some mathematics texts (e.g., May et al., 1981) do include exercises in which children are asked to find the correct operation, and word problem sets that mix up the operations to help children learn to differentiate them, most texts present blocks of problems that vary little in the operation required (at least in grades one through three; Stigler, Fuson, Ham, & Sook Kim, 1986). In this section we first consider how children make their initial selection of an operation, focusing on their use of the "key word" strategy and on the inappropriate generalizations children make about when particular operations are applicable. We next consider how limitations in the way children choose an operation impact on their ability to evaluate their choice.

CHILDREN'S USE OF THE "KEY WORD" STRATEGY

On those occasions when children are asked to choose among operations, they often adopt a "key word" strategy. This strategy is frequently explicitly taught, although sometimes children devise it on their own. Children might learn, for example, that the key word "all together" means to add, and so if they encounter this phrase, they will automatically add. We should note that there is evidence that the key word approach can be useful. For example, Schoenfeld (1982) reports that the majority of elementary word problems in some texts can in fact be solved by this method. However, we believe that excessive reliance on the key word strategy for choosing the correct operation may create difficulties.

One of the difficulties is that key words can take on different meanings in different contexts. Van Haneghan (1986) found, for example, that some children interpreted the word "more" in a problem as a signal for addition when in fact the problem involved subtraction. This is an error that is fairly common (Briars & Larkin, 1984); the word "more" tends to be seen as indicating the addition of something (e.g., he received 10 more) rather than as a comparative term (e.g., John had 11 more than Pat). The children in Van Haneghan's study who made this kind of error tended to be lower achievers. Their inability to differentiate different meanings of the word "more" led them to choose the inappropriate operation. Thus, instead of providing a useful shortcut for these children, the key word approach, combined with semantic deficits, led them to further failure and confusion.

Even when the issue is not one of multiple meanings, there are other common types of problems where the key word could be seriously misleading. Consider the following problem:

John has 27 apples. He has 3 times as many apples as Frank. How many apples does Frank have?

If a child attended only to the key word "times" he or she might end up multiplying when the problem calls for division. Thus, misunderstanding of the key word, or failure to take into account its context, can and does lead to an incorrect choice of operation.

INAPPROPRIATE GENERALIZATIONS REGARDING OPERATION CHOICE

Research has shown that children tend to have an incomplete picture of the applicability of particular operations, limited by rules of thumb that work with some numbers but not others and by gaps in their experience with certain applications of an operation. To illustrate, consider what happens when children first encounter fractions and decimals. Greer (1987) found that children who are given word problems that include decimals less than one and integer numbers greater than one have difficulty choosing the correct operation. For example, if a problem asked the cost of 0.70 pounds of roast beef given that it cost $2.40 per pound, the child might think division is necessary lest the answer be too large. In other words, the child believes that multiplication always gives larger answers and division smaller answers, a belief fostered in elementary school through work with whole numbers.

Another common limitation is that children are often taught operations in one context and have difficulty using them in another. For example, Silver

(1986) discusses a word problem that children mishandled surprisingly often on the NAEP. The problem dealt with 130 students who were waiting to go on a field trip. Children from grades five and up were asked how many buses would be needed to take the students on the field trip if each bus can hold 50 students. A number of children, failing to recognize the absurdity involved, chose a number with a fraction or a number with a remainder as their answer. Because the children were more interested in the calculation of the answer than the sensibleness of the answer, they failed to think about the question they were asked. Silver found that with explicit clues about the question, some children who previously failed to understand were able to do so, but even then there were children who still did not give the correct answer. Silver attributes part of the difficulties children have with this kind of problem to the types of division word problems they are exposed to across the grades. Most of the problems involve situations that require *partitioning* a number into groups of a particular size. They do not require *quotitioning*, which concerns the number of sets of a certain size that will be needed.

This same tendency to favor certain uses of an operation over others was also noted by Bell, Fischbein, and Greer (1984). When children were given multiplication or division problems in algorithmic form and were asked to make up story problems surrounding them, they tended to construct proto-typical kinds of stories, even when they were inappropriate. Consider the following problem one child made up:

Emma had 0.74 sweets. She want (sic) to share them out so each doll got the same. There was 0.21 dolls. How many did each doll have? (p. 141)

Although this problem is answerable, it makes little sense. It is the result of a child's limited understanding of the applications of an operation to certain situations. In this case, the child made up a problem involving *partition* when the numbers, two decimals, would make more sense if used in a problem involving *quotition*.

PROBLEMS CHILDREN FACE IN EVALUATING OPERATION CHOICE

Based on what we know about how children choose operations initially, we suspect that many children lack the necessary skills to evaluate their choice of an operation. Consider first how use of a key word strategy impacts upon subsequent evaluation. Children who use the key word strategy may believe that an effective way to evaluate their operation choice is to look back at the key word chosen. However, this would be of little help, given that the key word provided the basis for the initial selection of an operation. A good approach would be to (re)read the text and then evaluate the operation chosen, but given that children using the key word strategy typically do not read the text during initial operation selection, they are unlikely to do so later. Finally, if children use only key words and do not read the problem text, they will not be able to evaluate the result of their calculation with respect to the sense of the problem as a way of examining their operation choice.

A second difficulty children face in evaluating their choice of operations is that the standards they may select often do not generalize to every application. For example, the common belief that multiplication leads to bigger numbers and division to smaller numbers holds for whole numbers but not for fractions and decimals. Thus, children make errors because they overgeneralize their use of a strategy.

Finally, the limited applications of operations children typically see in word problems they receive in school may limit their ability to evaluate the operation they have chosen in more naturalistic contexts.

CHILDREN'S USE OF SEMANTIC STANDARDS

The word problem example featuring 0.21 dolls and 0.74 candies also illustrates a monitoring failure at the final level of analysis we will consider: the comprehensibility of the problem. Research on comprehension monitoring has shown that children frequently fail to evaluate the semantic aspects of texts they read (Baker & Brown, 1984b). We would expect, therefore, to find similar evaluation failures when children deal with word problems in mathematics. The limited evidence available suggests that this is indeed the case. In this section we will examine the evidence, beginning with a consideration of children's use of specific semantic standards. We then turn to an examination of factors influencing children's failures to adopt semantic standards, and we conclude with an evaluation of current instructional practices.

CHILDREN'S USE OF SPECIFIC SEMANTIC STANDARDS

Baker (1985) identified a number of semantic standards that ought to be applied when evaluating one's own comprehension. Two of these standards are particularly relevant to our current purposes. One is an internal consistency standard, which involves examining the text for facts that are logically inconsistent with one another (Baker, 1984a, 1984b; Markman, 1979). Internal inconsistencies can be created in mathematics word problems by providing numbers that are inconsistent with statements concerning, for example, which character had more of something. Van Haneghan (1986), in research to be discussed further in the following section, has shown that children are quite unlikely to adopt an internal consistency standard in solving word problems.

The second semantic standard important to mathematics is an external consistency standard, which involves judging sensibleness according to one's general knowledge of the world (Baker, 1984a, 1984b; Markman & Gorin, 1981). For example, the existence of 0.21 dolls does not make any sense in light of one's knowledge about dolls, nor does the existence of a fractional bus. Thus, we know from studies discussed in the preceding section that children frequently fail to evaluate the external consistency of word problems.

Factors Influencing children's Failures to Use Semantic Standards

To some extent it is not surprising that children seldom evaluate the sensibleness of problem texts. From the very beginning of their work with word problems children have to learn to suspend reality (DeCorte & Verschaffel, 1985; Nesher & Katriel, 1977). DeCorte and Verschaffel (1985) suggest that children develop a "word problem schema," a set of assumptions about how word problems differ from real-world problems. They found that some first-grade children believed word problems were unanswerable because they did not meet a real-world standard of sensibility. For example, one child stated that the problem, "Pete had 3 apples; Ann gave him 5 more apples; how many apples does Pete have now?" (p. 10) was unanswerable because "Ann doesn't have any apples" (p. 10). Thus, part of learning to do word problems is learning to suspend reality, learning how to play the word problem game.

Expectations about problem comprehensibility, like expectations about operations, also suffer from a limited understanding of the nature of a legitimate word problem. Mayer (1982) found that college students have such strong expectations about what a prototypical word problem should be that, when asked to recall word problems, they transformed infrequently encountered problems into more common ones. Van Haneghan (1986) found that children's expectations about problems influenced not only their comprehension, but their monitoring of their comprehension. He found that a group of third- and fifth-grade children said that a perfectly answerable word problem was unanswerable and made no sense simply because it differed from prototypical word problems. The problems were like the following:

Sam had 28 cookies. He had 13 more than John. How many cookies did John have?

Children explained that problems of this type were unanswerable for two reasons: (a) "They never tell you how much John has"; and (b) "First they tell you Sam has 28, then they tell you he has 13; this problem makes no sense." Both of these explanations reflect children's expectations for receiving problems with assignment propositions (e.g., Sam had 28 cookies) rather than relational propositions (e.g., He had 13 more than Tom) (Mayer, 1982). The first explanation reflects an unsuccessful search for the quantity to assign to John. The second reflects the confusion that occurs when the second sentence is misinterpreted as an assignment proposition rather than a relational proposition.

In summary, what many children appear to lack is what Greeno, Riley, and Gelman (1984) and Gelman and Meck (1986) label utilization competence. That is, they are not aware of when or where to put their plans for particular types of problems into action. Thus, they mistakenly develop a limiting standard for judging the sensibility of problems.

CURRENT INSTRUCTIONAL PRACTICES

Children's analysis of the sensibleness of problem texts in mathematics curricula is largely limited to exercises that ask whether there is enough information presented in the problem text to get an answer. Moreover, as noted earlier, those textbooks that do stress the importance of monitoring for comprehensibility typically provide no assistance in helping children do so effectively.

There are many common instructional practices we believe *discourage* active analysis of problem texts. One example is the key word strategy. First, as noted earlier, the key word strategy can be misleading, and it may compound problems for children who have not differentiated the meanings key words can take on. Second, we believe that the use of the key word strategy may inhibit or delay the growth of more active problem-solving strategies (e.g., drawing diagrams, using analogous problems). For example, Lester (1985) found that third-, fourth-, and fifth-grade children, when given a problem that could not be solved by simply finding the key words and carrying out an operation on two numbers, had no alternative but to give up once the key word method failed to help them solve the problem. Schoenfeld (1983) reports similar problems in getting college students to use active rather than passive strategies (see also Day, Cordon, & Kerwin, this volume, chap. 4).

Another problematic common practice involves the way word problems are presented in textbooks (see Rohwer & Thomas, this volume, chap. 5, for a general discussion). They tend to be presented with work on particular operations, such that the word problems seem to be a simple extension of drill with a particular operation. Such presentation suggests to the child that what is important is the operation and not the underlying meaning of the story problem. Thus, he or she may have difficulty differentiating various problem types, unless mixed problem types are presented together (Mayer, 1985). Finally, the lack of more complex problems in American textbooks (c.f., Stigler et al., 1986), means that children will have few school mathematics contexts to develop active strategies for comprehending word problems.

Cognitive Monitoring Using Multiple Standards

The majority of studies discussed in this chapter were not designed to study cognitive monitoring per se, although they offer suggestive evidence that most children are ineffective at monitoring their performance in mathematics. Moreover, the majority of the studies were not concerned with developmental differences. The one exception, the study by Lester and Garafolo (1982) cited earlier, examined children's metacognitive knowledge about when they should monitor rather than their actual monitoring. Although the authors found that third and fifth graders responded similarly to the interview questions, it would certainly be premature to conclude that cognitive monitoring skills remain unchanged throughout the middle elementary-school years. Finally, the studies address one level of analysis or another but do not consider the fact that monitoring ought to occur at multiple levels. In this section we will consider in detail Van Haneghan's (1986) recent research, which is perhaps the first to examine cognitive monitoring in mathematics per se, with a developmental emphasis, and with regard to multiple standards of evaluation.

Van Haneghan (1986) conceptualized children's detection of errors in word problems as a simple form of comprehension monitoring. Accordingly, he adapted the error-detection paradigm frequently used in studies of comprehension monitoring in reading (Baker & Brown, 1984b) to study cognitive monitoring in mathematics. The errors children were expected to find corresponded to the three levels of analysis discussed earlier. Thus, they were expected to use standards sensitive to calculational accuracy, operation choice, and semantic sensibleness. The rationale for studying multiple standard use was based on Baker's (1984a, 1984b, 1985) view of comprehension monitoring as a multilayered set of abilities rather than a single ability. She argues that comprehension-monitoring competence is a function not only of age but also of the kinds of standards children are expected to use and the instructions they are given.

Description of the Research Method

The errors children were expected to find were embedded in "compare" problems (Riley, Greeno, & Heller, 1983). Compare problems require children to contend with "more than" and "less than" relations between quantities and are somewhat more difficult than problems that explicitly require the child to put two sets together or pull them apart. The problems vary in difficulty such that there are some that even first graders can solve, but others with which even fifth graders have difficulty. In our work we used what Riley et al. considered simple (Level I) and difficult (Level III) compare problems. Problems 1a and 1b in Table 9.1 illustrate the two difficulty levels. Level I problems provide the amounts in each set to be compared and ask the child to find who has more (or less). Level III problems give the child the amount of one set and the amount by which that set is greater or less than the second set. The child has to find the amount of the second set.

The sample problems in Table 9.1 also illustrate each error type. Note that the problems include not only the text but also an algorithmic form of the problem and a solution provided by "another child." As can be seen, some of the problem solutions contained simple calculational errors that did not involve borrowing; some of the problem solutions contained errors in operation choice (the child who solved the problem added instead of subtracted); some of the problem texts were inconsistent and thus unanswerable (e.g., the person who was said to have more actually had less); and some of the problems contained no errors either in the text or in the solution. Altogether, there were three problems of each type at each difficulty level.

Participants in the study were 78 third graders and 77 fifth graders from two middle-class public schools. All children were tested individually. They were presented with the set of word problems and were asked to check them

TABLE 9.1. Examples of "Compare" Problems of Each Difficulty Level and Error Type

Error type	Difficulty Level	
	Level I	Level III
Correctly solved	1a. Ruth has 66 pieces of gum. Rich as 34 pieces of gum. How many more pieces of gum does Ruth have than Rich? 66 − 34 32	1b. Rita has 32 cookies. She has 11 more cookies than Tom. How many cookies does Tom have? 32 − 11 21
Solved with cal- culational errors	2a. George had 36 balls. Jerry has 12 balls. How many more balls does George have than Jerry? 36 − 12 23	2b. Bob has 52 cards. He has 21 more cards than Robin. How many cards does Robin have? 52 − 21 33
Solved with the wrong opera- tion	3a. Chris has 44 buttons. Beth has 22 buttons. How many more buttons does Chris have than Beth? 44 + 22 66	3b. Terry has 32 toys. He has 12 more toys than Mark. How many toys does Mark have? 32 + 12 44
Solved but actu- ally unan- swerable	4a. Matt has 22 cents. Ken has 69 cents. How many more cents does Matt have than Ken? 69 − 22 47	4b. Ann has 25 chicks. She has 37 more chicks than Sally. How many chicks does Sally have? 37 − 25 12

over to see if they had been solved correctly. Whenever they identified an error they were asked to explain what was wrong with the problem; this step was taken to determine whether they actually spotted the intended errors.

Comprehension-monitoring research using the error-detection paradigm has shown that children typically benefit from being given specific information about the kinds of errors they are to find (e.g., Baker, 1984b; Markman & Gorin, 1981). To determine whether this effect also holds for cognitive monitoring in mathematics, children received one of two sets of instructions. One group was simply told that some of the answers to the problems were wrong and that some of the stories did not make sense. A second group was told specifically about the nature of the errors they were to find and were given examples of each using problems intermediate in difficulty to those used in the task itself.

Finally, children's emerging competencies in the absence of explicit instruction were examined by providing hints upon completion of the task. Those children who initially failed to notice any errors of a particular type were given an opportunity to reexamine a problem containing an error of that type. Children were instructed to look at the problem again and see if anything was wrong. If they still failed to find the error, they were given an obvious hint about the locus of the error and another chance to examine the problem and identify the error.

Comprehension-monitoring research has shown that children's achievement levels in reading account for substantial variance in their performance (Baker, 1985; Garner, 1986). In order to determine whether mathematics achievement similarly predicts cognitive monitoring in mathematics, children's performance was analyzed in relation to their mathematics achievement stanine scores on the California Achievement Test.

A SUMMARY OF THE RESULTS

The results of the study revealed the expected developmental differences in cognitive-monitoring performance. The older children, the fifth graders, outperformed the younger children, the third graders. In addition, the nature of the errors affected detection probability, also as expected. Thus, calculational errors were most likely to be found and unanswerable problems were least likely. This outcome is compatible with comprehension-monitoring research in showing that standards involving more superficial levels of analysis are more likely to be applied than those involving deeper levels of analysis (e.g., Baker, 1984b; Garner, 1981). Problem difficulty effects were also evident, with children generally doing better on Level I than on Level III problems, thus confirming the differences observed by Riley et al. (1983).

The study also revealed a limited effect of the instructional manipulation. Third graders who received general instructions performed more poorly on operation errors than on calculation errors, whereas those who received explicit instructions performed about as well on the two types of errors. This suggests that although third graders are capable of monitoring their choice of operation, they have not internalized this standard very well. Thus, these results are consistent with comprehension-monitoring research by Baker (1984b) and Markman and Gorin (1981) showing that children are more likely to adopt a particular standard if they are explicitly instructed to do so.

ACHIEVEMENT-RELATED DIFFERENCES IN MONITORING

Also as in research on comprehension monitoring (e.g., August, Flavell, & Clift, 1984; Baker, 1984b; Miller, 1987), ability level was reliably related to children's error-detection skills. Higher achievement was associated with better error detection for all error types at both difficulty levels. Additionally, lower achievers were more likely to need a second reading or a clue to find an error. Finally, lower achievers were more likely than higher achievers to adopt incorrect or inadequate strategies.

For example, some of these children thought the problems were addition problems. Most used key word strategies inappropriately; they thought that the word "more" meant that they were to add. A few others were convinced by the presence of the addition sign in the algorithm that it was okay to add instead or subtract; they ignored the goal of finding the answer to the question from the story.

Children who were lower achievers were also more likely to adopt just one standard of evaluation. This was evidenced by the fact that they were more likely to detect only calculational errors. This focus on a low level of analysis parallels the tendency of children who are lower achievers in reading to focus on word-level problems at the expense of higher-level semantic problems (e.g., Baker, 1984b; Garner, 1981).

Also related marginally to ability level was the tendency of some children to respond that the Level III "compare" problems were unanswerable (regardless of the error type) because, "they did not tell you how much [the second character in the story] had." As mentioned earlier, this response seems to be a function of a limited conception of the nature of a legitimate word problem. It is as if a problem were legitimate only if it contained two quantities and some action on those quantities.

We will now offer some tentative explanations as to why lower achievement was associated with these various response patterns. Consider first the observation that a number of lower achievers used only a calculational standard. This may reflect the fact that lower achievers view calculations as the only important element of the problem. There are at least two reasons why they might hold this view. One has to do with the automaticity of their knowledge of basic facts. Children who are not fluent in their knowledge of basic addition and subtraction facts may allocate more of their attention to the calculations, perhaps forgetting to scrutinize the problem text. The other possibility is that the lower achievers believe that the most important goal in doing mathematics is to calculate answers rather than to understand problems. Their word problem schema may have suspended reality to such an extent that they no longer use their real-world knowledge or intuitive mathematical knowledge when they do word problems.

Consider next the observation that a number of lower achievers stated that subtraction problems were actually addition problems. Probably the most parsimonious explanation for the children who appeared to base their judgments on the inappropriate use of the key word "more" is, as noted previously, that they have not clearly differentiated the comparative use of "more". Their semantic misunderstanding led them to incorrectly evaluate the choice of operation. The children who were distracted by the addition sign seem to have a very weakly regulated set of procedures for solving word problems. Instead of being driven by the overall goal of solving the word problem, they got bogged down in figuring out whether the calculation was correct. They resolved their concern about the calculation by noting the addition sign, forgetting that the story indicated they were supposed to subtract.

Finally, consider the tendency of lower achievers to declare that answerable problems were actually unanswerable. This seems to have its source in some sort of response set that children develop when doing word problems.

Because problems like the more difficult compare problems are rarely presented in textbooks, nor are problem sets with much variation, it is likely that the children who gave this response simply did not invoke a different plan or solution strategy when they first received the difficult problems. That they actually had the necessary competence, however, was revealed by the fact that in all but two cases they eventually recognized the problems as answerable prior to the phase of the study where they were given hints.

A Sketch of a Model of Cognitive Monitoring in Mathematics

Our review of the literature and the results of Van Haneghan's research suggest a three-component model of cognitive monitoring in mathematics. We offer a brief sketch here. First, children must have an adequate procedural and conceptual knowledge base. Otherwise, they will not be fluent enough to check their work. For example, children who spend much of their time trying to work out calculations by counting on their fingers may not allocate attention to examining the semantics of the problem text or the operation they choose. Likewise, children who are having difficulty conceptualizing a problem may not spot a simple calculational error.

Second, children must be able to coordinate their procedural knowledge base with their conceptual knowledge and must link their knowledge of school mathematics to mathematics outside the classroom. The studies reviewed earlier indicate that less-successful mathematics students frequently fail to consider the relation between these two sources of knowledge. Such coordination is clearly essential to effective cognitive monitoring.

Third, children must have knowledge about the standards that are relevant in monitoring their performance, and they must be able to apply them. We can hardly expect children to monitor at a particular level of analysis unless they understand that that level is relevant. We have seen, for example, that the meaning of the problem text is not important to many children and so they tend to ignore that level of analysis.

This model of cognitive monitoring can be compared to Hiebert and Lefevre's (1986) explanation for why children fail to coordinate their procedural and conceptual knowledge. Hiebert and Lefevre suggest that three factors are important: (a) deficits in the knowledge base; (b) difficulties in encoding relationships between concrete embodiments and algorithmic work and between arithmetic operations and semantic concepts in word problems; and (c) compartmentalization of knowledge. Compartmentalization is the result of children's failures to link up their various representations of math knowledge. Thus, it results from failures of coordination (our second component), and it is responsible for children's inabilities to regard certain standards as relevant (our third component). Children compartmentalize their knowledge of word problems from their knowledge of the real world; consequently, the meaning of a problem is evaluated superficially if at all.

IMPLICATIONS FOR INSTRUCTION AND INTERVENTION

The available research suggests that many children are poor monitors of their mathematical problem solving. They have a difficult time recognizing the link between concrete embodiments and algorithmic work. They overgeneralize some of the standards they use to judge their work by applying them in situations where they do not make sense. Finally, they learn that the world of word problems is very different from the real world, and so they do not judge that world with the same standards they use in the outside world. We know, however, that not all children are poor monitors. This raises the questions of how we can enhance the cognitive monitoring skills of those students in whom they are deficient. In this section, we will consider some of the curriculum approaches designed to help children monitor their performance and we will conclude with some recommendations for developing more effective intervention methods (see also Duffy & Roehler, this volume, chap. 6; Symons, Snyder, Cariglia-Bull, & Pressley, this volume. chap. 1).

CURRENT INSTRUCTIONAL PRACTICES

In previous sections, we discussed some commercial mathematics curriculum materials intended to foster cognitive monitoring skills at particular levels of analysis. We also found commercial materials focusing on more general cognitive strategy training. For instance, the Merrill series (Merrill Publishing Company, 1987) gives children a flow chart directing them to *read* the problem, *decide* how to solve it, *solve it*, and *examine* it to see if the answer is sensible. In addition to these step-by-step instructions, children are also given strategies for checking their answers. For example, to check addition problems, they are told to add numbers in the opposite direction or to subtract; to check subtraction problems, they are told to add. They are also taught to use estimation for checking.

This type of curriculum would probably be successful in helping children develop the ability to check their calculations. However, it probably would not succeed in providing children with a systematic way of evaluating when an answer makes sense. Moreover, it is unclear that children would actually use the step-by-step rules when they are doing word problems on their own. There is, for example, evidence that children often do not even read problem texts, as was apparent in Van Haneghan's (1986) research.

Training of general strategies such as those presented in the Merrill series has become popular in cognitive intervention research, but there has not been much work in the domain of mathematics. An exception is a study by Leon and Pepe (1983) that drew upon the work of Meichenbaum in its emphasis on the use of self-statements for self-regulation. Learning-disabled children were taught to ask themselves a series of self-monitoring questions, such as whether they were on task and whether they had chosen the correct procedures. This very general strategy training was effective for these children, perhaps because it helped them overcome their impulsive tendencies.

RECOMMENDATIONS FOR CHANGES IN INSTRUCTIONAL PRACTICE

Although general strategy training appears to be effective in some situations, it is usually necessary to provide more specific and thorough strategy training to help children overcome their difficulties and to promote transfer to new situations (Pressley, 1986). For example, children might need to be taught special strategies for determining a sensible answer for problems involving comparisons and relationships, strategies that are not applicable to problems involving putting together or taking apart sets. Children need to know more about what is or is not sensible. It does little good to ask children to evaluate the sensibility of an answer unless we provide them with the skills necessary to differentiate what makes sense from what fails to make sense.

A recent comprehension-monitoring training study by Elliott-Faust and Pressley (1986) demonstrates the importance of teaching children *how* to *judge* whether a particular standard has been met. Elliott-Faust and Pressley found more durable gains in children's abilities to detect internal inconsistencies when they taught children strategies for determining if passages did not make sense than when they simply gave them an illustration of the standard. Such an approach merits further investigation with mathematics word problems given Van Haneghan's (1986) failure to find instructional effects for internal inconsistencies when instruction involved illustrations only.

Not only do we need to help children understand what is or is not sensible, we need to give them problems where sensibility is an issue. As the research discussed earlier reveals, children treat word problems as if they were just calculational problems, the only difference being that one has to figure out the operation. Thus, if children are to monitor their work, they need problems where monitoring is important not only after the answer is found but also en route to the answer (Lester, 1985). This recommendation is supported by Charles and Lester (1984), who found that a program for fifth and seventh graders that emphasized reflection on one's work led to improvements in problem-solving performance. As our previous discussion suggests, children must perceive the relevance of monitoring at multiple levels of evaluation or they will not do so. It is unlikely, for example, that children will consider semantic elements of texts if they believe the only real requirement is to find a key word and then add or subtract.

It is also important to provide problems that tie into the real world, so that children can build links between their mathematical and real-world knowledge. As Davis (1986) notes, real-world mathematics bears little resemblance to the mathematics children learn in school. If our ultimate goal is for the development of mathematical skill in the everyday world, then it is imperative we find a match between that world and the world of school mathematics by presenting more applied sorts of problems. Applied problems have the added advantage of being more motivating and exciting, an important consideration for children numbed by the mundane problems in mathematics texts (Lesh, 1981). Applied problems also differ from traditional textbook problems in that they present a broader "macro-context" (Bransford et al., in press); that is, the answers to one problem may give rise to other problems or may give clues as to plausible answers to other problems. Finally, applied problems require one not only to figure out the answer but also to figure out what the problem is. Thus, problem definition, an important real-world skill, might be better inculcated by using problems that better fit real-world criteria.

Computers and interactive videodiscs facilitate the presentation of real-world problems and make it possible to remove mathematics from the confines of paper-and-pencil tasks so characteristic of school. For example, Papert's (1980) computer language LOGO illustrates how the new technology can engage children in interesting mathematical problems (see Lehrer, this volume, chap. 12). Similarly, Bransford et al. (in press) present promising evidence of the effectiveness of interactive videodisc technology. Problems involving simple ratios were devised from scenes in *Raiders of the Lost Ark* and were presented on videodisc to children with mathematical learning difficulties. These children, who also received intensive one-on-one tutoring for several days, showed more improvement in problem-solving performance than a control group.

CONCLUSIONS

Our recommendations for improving children's cognitive-monitoring skills may seem extreme in their call for what essentially is a revamping of the mathematics curriculum. It certainly would be simpler to teach monitoring strategies within the context of the current curriculum, but the evidence suggests such interventions would not be effective. The difficulty that many children have in debugging their answers, even after a well-conceived intervention (e.g., Resnick & Omanson, 1987), and the tendencies of children to compartmentalize their mathematical knowledge makes a less radical solution unsatisfactory.

As our simple model of cognitive monitoring suggests, there are multiple levels of evaluation that must be considered. These multiple levels require training beyond a knowledge-free monitoring capability. They require knowledge of what to monitor, how to monitor, and when to monitor. Thus, monitoring cannot be separated from children's mathematical knowledge base. This is not to say, however, that proficient monitoring is a natural outgrowth of an improved knowledge base. Monitoring strategies must be taught explicitly, and students must be taught to recognize when particular strategies are appropriate and when they are not. Thus, we share the consensual view in the current literature that direct instruction in cognitive monitoring is crucial to strategy acquisition (e.g., Baker & Brown, 1984b; Brown et al., 1983; Paris, Wixson, & Palincsar, 1987; Pressley, Goodchild, Fleet, Zajchowski, & Evans, in press).

In summary, this chapter has applied and extended current theory and research about cognitive monitoring to children's performance on mathematics word problems. Our review of the literature indicated that various elements of cognitive monitoring are lacking, at least for some children. Our research has indicated that, as in reading, cognitive monitoring in mathematics occurs at many levels and arises from a complex interaction of factors associated with the child and the context in which he or she learns mathematics. We make the somewhat radical claim that simply adding more tasks meant to inculcate cognitive monitoring in mathematics will not substantively change children's monitoring behavior. What is needed is not only a revamping of the curriculum on monitoring, but also a different approach to teaching mathematical knowledge. We need an approach that does not simply emphasize rote calculation, but also provides students with meaningful materials and contexts.

Acknowledgment. The first author's contribution to this chapter was supported by NIH, National Science Award, HD-07226 from NICHD.

References

August, D.L., Flavell, J.H., & Clift, R. (1984). Comparison of comprehension monitoring of skilled and less skilled readers. *Reading Research Quarterly, 20,* 39–53.

Baker, L. (1984a) Children's effective use of multiple standards for evaluating their comprehension. *Journal of Educational Psychology, 76,* 588–597.

Baker, L. (1984b). Spontaneous versus instructed use of multiple standards for evaluating comprehension: Effects of age, reading proficiency and type of standard. *Journal of Experimental Child Psychology, 38,* 289–311.

Baker, L. (1985). How do we know when we don't understand? Standards for evaluating text comprehension. In D.L. Forrest-Pressley, D.L. MacKinnon, & T.G. Waller (Eds.), *Metacognition, cognition, and human performance* (pp. 155–205). New York: Academic.

Baker, L., & Brown, A.L. (1984a). Cognitive monitoring in reading. In J. Flood (Ed.), *Understanding reading comprehension* (pp. 21–44). Newark, DE: International Reading Association.

Baker, L., & Brown, A.L. (1984b). Metacognitive skills and reading. In P.D. Pearson (Ed.), *Handbook of research in reading* (pp. 353–393). New York: Longman.

Bell, A., Fischbein, E., & Greer, B. (1984). Choice of operation in verbal arithmetic problems: The effects of number size, problem structure, and context. *Educational Studies in Mathematics, 15,* 129–147.

Bransford, J., Hasselbring, T., Barron, B., Kulewicz, S., Littlefield, J., & Goin, L. (in press). Use of macrocontexts to facilitate mathematical thinking. In R. Charles & E. Silver (Eds.), *Teaching and evaluating mathematical problem solving.* Reston, Va: National Council of Teachers of Mathematics.

Briars, D.J., & Larkin, J.H. (1984). An integrated model of skill in solving elementary word problems. *Cognition and Instruction, 1,* 245–296.

Brown, A.L. (1978). Knowing when, where, and how to remember: A problem of metacognition. In R. Glaser (Ed.), *Advances in instructional psychology* (pp. 77–165). Hillsdale, NJ: Erlbaum & Associates.

Brown, A.L. Bransford, J.D., Ferrara, R.A., & Campione, J.C. (1983). Learning, remembering and understanding. In J.H. Flavell & E.M. Markman (Eds.), *Handbook of child psychology, Vol. III, Cognitive development* (pp. 77–166). New York: Wiley.

Charles, R.I., & Lester, F.K. (1984). An evaluation of a process-oriented mathematical problem solving instruction program in grades five and seven. *Journal for Research in Mathematics Education, 15,* 15–34.

Davis, R.B. (1986). Conceptual and procedural knowledge in mathematics: A summary analysis. In J. Hiebert (Ed.), *Conceptual and procedural knowledge: The case of mathematics* (pp. 265–300). Hillsdale, NJ: Erlbaum & Associates.

Davis, R.B., & McKnight, C. (1980). The influence of semantic content on algorthmic behavior. *Journal of Mathematical Behavior, 3,* 167–201.

DeCorte, E., & Verschaffel, L. (1981). Children's solution processes in elementary arithmetic problems. *Journal of Education Psychology, 73,* 765–779.

DeCorte, E., & Verschaffel, L. (1985). Beginning first graders' initial representation of arithmetic word problems. *Journal of Mathematical Behavior, 4,* 3–21.

Elliott-Faust, D.J., & Pressley, M. (1986). How to teach comparison processing to increase children's short- and long-term listening comprehension monitoring. *Journal of Educational Psychology, 78,* 27–33.

Flavell, J.H. (1979). Metacognition and cognitive monitoring: A new area of cognitive-developmental inquiry. *American Psychologist, 34,* 906–911.

Forrest-Pressley, D., & Waller, T.G. (1984). *Cognition, metacognition and reading.* New York: Springer-Verlag.

Garner, R. (1981). Monitoring of passage inconsistency among poor comprehenders: A preliminary test of the "piecemeal processing" explanation. *Journal of Educational Research, 74,* 159–162.

Garner, R. (1986). *Metacognition and reading comprehension.* Hillsdale, NJ: Ablex.

Gelman, R., & Meck, E. (1986). The notion of principle: The case of counting. In J. Hiebert (Ed.), *Conceptual and procedural knowledge: The case of mathematics* (pp. 29–57). Hillsdale, NJ: Erlbaum & Associates.

Greeno, J.G., Riley, M.S., & Gelman, R. (1984). Conceptual competence and children's counting. *Cognitive Psychology, 16,* 94–134.

Greer, B. (1987). Nonconservation of multiplication and division involving decimals. *Journal for Research on Mathematics Education, 18,* 37–45.

Hiebert, J. (Ed.). (1986). *Conceptual and procedural knowledge: The case of mathematics.* Hillsdale, NJ: Erlbaum & Associates.

Hiebert, J., & Lefevre, P. (1986). Conceptual and procedural knowledge in mathematics: An introductory analysis. In J. Hiebert (Ed.), *Conceptual and procedural knowledge: The case of mathematics* (pp. 1–27). Hillsdale, NJ: Erlbaum & Associates.

Hope, J.A. (1986). Mental calculation: Anachronism or basic skill. In H.L. Schoen, & M.J. Zweng (Eds.), *Estimation and mental computation* (1986 yearbook of the National Council of Teachers of Mathematics, pp. 44–54). Reston, VA: National Council of Teachers of Mathematics.

Kreutzer, M.A., Leonard, C., & Flavell, J.H. (1985). An interview study of children's knowledge about memory. *Monographs of the Society for Research in Child Development, 40,* (1, Serial No. 159).

Leon, J.A., & Pepe, H.J. (1983). Self-instructional training: Cognitive behavior modification for remediating arithmetic deficits. *Exceptional Children, 50,* 54–60.

Lesh, R. (1981). Applied mathematical problem solving. *Educational Studies in Mathematics, 12*, 235–264.

Lesh, R., Landau, M., & Hamilton, E. (1983). Conceptual models and applied mathematical problem-solving. In R. Lesh & M. Landau (Eds.), *Acquisition of mathematical concepts and processes* (pp. 264–343). New York: Academic.

Lester, F.J. (1985). Methodological considerations in research on mathematical problem-solving. In E.A. Silver (Ed.), *Teaching and learning mathematical problem solving* (pp. 41–69). Hillsdale, NJ: Erlbaum & Associates.

Lester, F.J., & Garafolo, J. (April 1982). *Metacognitive aspects of elementary school students' performance on arithmetic tasks.* Paper presented at the annual meeting of the American Educational Research Association, New York.

Maki, R.J., & Berry, S.L. (1984). Metacomprehension of text material. *Journal of Experimental Psychology: Learning, Memory, and Cognition, 10*, 663–679.

Markman, E.M. (1979). Realizing that you don't understand: Elementary school children's awareness of inconsistencies. *Child Development, 50*, 643–655.

Markman, E.M. (1981). Comprehension monitoring. In W.P. Dickson (Ed.), *Children's oral communication skills* (pp. 61–84). New York: Academic.

Markman, E.M., & Gorin, L. (1981). Children's ability to adjust their standards for evaluating comprehension. *Journal of Educational Psychology, 73*, 320–325.

May, L.J., Frye, S.M., & Jacobs, D.C. (1981). *HBJ mathematics* (teacher's ed., grade 3). New York: Harcourt, Brace, Jovanovich.

Mayer, R.E. (1982). Memory for algebra story problems. *Journal of Educational Psychology, 74*, 199–216.

Mayer, R.E. (1985). Implications of cognitive psychology of instruction in mathematical problem solving. In E.A. Silver (Ed.), *Teaching and learning mathematical problem solving: Multiple research perspectives* (pp. 123–138). Hillsdale, NJ: Erlbaum & Associates.

Merrill Publishing Company. (1987). *Merrill mathematics* (teacher's ed., grade 3). Columbus, OH.

Miller, G. (1987). The influence of self-instruction on the comprehension monitoring performance of average and above average readers. *Journal of Reading Behavior, 19*, 303–317.

Myers, M., & Paris, S.G. (1978). Children's metacognitive knowledge about reading. *Journal of Educational Psychology, 70*, 680–690.

Nesher, P.A. (1986). Are mathematical understanding and algorithmic performance related. *For the Learning of Mathematics, 6*, 2–9.

Nesher, P.A., & Katriel, T.A. (1977). A semantic analysis of addition and subtraction word problems in arithmetic. *Educational Studies in Mathematics, 8*, 251–270.

Papert, S. (1980). *Mindstorms: Children, computers, and powerful ideas.* New York: Basic Books.

Paris, S.G., Wixson, K.K., & Palincsar, A.M. (1986). Instructional approaches to reading comprehension. In E. Rothkopf (Ed.), *Review of research in education* (Vol 13, pp. 91–128). Washington, DC: American Educational Research Association.

Post, T.R. (1981). Fractions: Results and implications from national assessment. *Arithmetic Teacher, 28*, 26–31.

Pressley, M. (1986). The relevance of the good strategy user model to teaching of mathematics. *Educational Psychologist, 21*, 139–161.

Pressley, M., Goodchild, F., Fleet, J., Zajchowski, R., & Evans, E.D. (in press). The challenges of classroom strategy instruction. *The Elementary School Journal.*

Resnick, L.B. (1982). Syntax and semantics in learning to subtract. In T.P. Carpenter, J.M. Moser, & T.A. Romberg (Eds.), *Addition and subtraction: A cognitive perspective* (pp. 136–154). Hillsdale, NJ: Erlbaum & Associates.

Resnick, L.B. (1983). A developmental theory of number understanding. In H.P. Ginsburg (Ed.). *The development of mathematical thinking* (pp. 110–152). New York: Academic.

Resnick, L.B., & Omanson, S.F. (1987). Learning to understand arithmetic. In P. Glaser (Ed.), *Advances in instructional psychology* (Vol. 3, pp. 41–96). Hillsdale, NJ: Erlbaum & Associates.

Reys, R.E. (1984). Mental computation and estimation: Past, present, and future. *Elementary School Journal, 84,* 547–557.

Reys, R.E., Rybolt, J.F., Bestgen, B.J., & Wyatt, J.W. (1982). Processes used by good computational estimators. *Journal for Research on Mathematics Education, 13,* 183–201.

Riley, M.S., Greeno, J.G., & Heller, J.I. (1983). Development of children's problem-solving ability in arithmetic. In H.P. Ginsburg (Ed.), *The development of mathematical thinking* (pp. 153–196). New York: Academic.

Schoenfeld, A.H. (1982). Some thoughts on problem solving research and mathematics education. In F.J. Lester & J. Garafolo (Eds.), *Mathematical problem solving: Issues in research* (pp. 27–37). Philadelphia: The Franklin Institute Press.

Schoenfeld, A.H. (1983). Beyond the purely cognitive: Belief systems, social cognitions, and metacognitions as driving forces in intellectual performance. *Cognitive Science, 7,* 329–363.

Silver, E.A. (1986). Using conceptual and procedural knowledge: A focus on relationships. In J. Hiebert (Ed.), *Conceptual and procedural knowledge: The case of mathematics* (pp. 181–198). Hillsdale, NJ: Erlbaum & Associates.

Slife, B.D., Weiss, J., & Bell, T. (1985). Separability of metacognition and cognition: Problem solving in learning disabled and regular students. *Journal of Educational Psychology, 77,* 437–445.

Stigler, J., Fuson, K., Ham, M., & Sook Kim, M. (1986). An analysis of addition and subtraction word problems in American and Soviet elementary mathematics textbooks. *Cognition and Instruction, 3,* 153–171.

Trafton, P.R. (1986). Teaching computational estimation: Establishing an estimation mind set. In H.L. Schoen & M.J. Zweng (Eds.), *Estimation and mental computation* (1986 yearbook of the National Council of Teachers of Mathematics, pp. 16–30). Reston, VA: National Council of Teachers of Mathematics.

Van Haneghan, J.P. (1986). *Children's detection of errors in word problems: Evidence for comprehension monitoring in math* (Doctoral dissertation, University of Maryland, Baltimore County 1986). *Dissertation Abstracts International, 47B:* 2650.

Van Lehn, K. (1983). On the representation of procedures in repair theory. In H.P. Ginsburg (Ed.), *The development of mathematical thinking* (pp. 201–253). New York: Academic.

10
Schema-Based Strategies and Implications for Instructional Design in Strategy Training

JOAN K. GALLINI

Introduction

An important hypothesis underlying expert-novice differences is that superior performance is mediated by the use of better strategies (Adelson, 1984; Britton & Glynn, 1987; Pressley, 1986; Pressley, Borkowski, & Schneider, 1987). For example, novices use surface features of concepts to establish relationships (e.g., a square and a rectangle are similar because they have four sides); experts use their executive control system in search of deep-structure principles (e.g., Chi, Feltovich, & Glaser, 1981; Larkin, McDermott, Simon, & Simon, 1980) to formulate relational links among concepts (e.g., a square is viewed as a special case of a rectangle whereby length equals width). A salient hypothesis generated from such observations is that training in the efficient use of strategies demonstrated by expert levels can improve the performance of novices (e.g., Greeno, 1978a, 1978b; Mayer, 1987; Shavelson, 1981; Voss, 1986).

Thus, the first part of this chapter is concerned with the strategies used by experts compared to novices (see also Rohwer & Thomas, this volume, chap. 5). The second part deals with instruction that might foster development of expert strategies in novices. The final section reports an experimental study of instruction to promote expert performance on a math task.

Schema-Based Behaviors

The term *schema* is typically used to refer to a person's knowledge structure for a particular class of concepts. Embedded within a schema is a hierarchy of subschemata. Thus, in the fullest sense, a schema describes the organization of information in human memory in terms of a conceptual network believed to be held among the constituent concepts in question (Rumelhart & Ortony, 1977). Schema-driven strategies, then, involve the use of schemata in performing complex cognitive tasks. These include categorizing information by concept domains, developing conceptual hierarchies for information that is processed, and formulating relationships between concepts. Most learners are likely to engage in strategic behavior involving the use and formulation of schemata, to some extent, especially in situations where a schema is well known and readily suggested. The novice's use of schema is limited, however, to occasions when there are strong cues to activate a particular schema, such as when a conceptual advanced organizer or a thematic synthesizer is supplied.

EXPERT–NOVICE DIFFERENCES: PROBLEM REPRESENTATION

An impressive body of research describes qualitative differences in the expert's and novice's representation of problems in complex content domains (e.g., computer programming, Adelson, 1984; chess, Chase & Simon, 1973; de Groot, 1965; geometry, Greeno, 1980; algebra, Hinsley, Hayes, & Simon, 1977; physics, Chi et al., 1981; social science, Voss, Tyler, & Yengo, 1983). A large part of the differences can be explained by the expert's superior skill in formulating abstract representations of the problem in terms of concepts and principles provided by the knowledge base (Reif, 1980). In essence, the expert searches the context for underlying principles from which relationships among superficially different concepts can be formulated and incorporated into categories of problem types. For illustration, consider two economic problems. One relates to the effects of bad weather on a producer's supply of corn. Another problem relates to the effects of a price increase of green beans, a popular vegetable among consumers, on the demand for peas, a likely substitute for green beans. While each problem appears to address a different dimension of the market (i.e., supply and demand, respectively), the expert tends to search for a relationship between the problems and, consequently, a general principle applicable to their solution (i.e., the law of supply and demand).

By contrast, novice problem representations are simpler and more concrete in nature, with problems decomposed into concrete subproblems (e.g., Voss et al., 1983) such as a list of steps involved in adding and subtracting or in how to conduct a programming task. To illustrate further, consider again the just-described economic situation. Novices would be inclined to search for a separate solution path to each problem. The first problem might be viewed as dealing with the *producer* and the issue of *supply* for a given commodity, corn. On the other hand, novices might classify the second problem in a different category since it deals with the relationship of price between two products, and the consequential effects of consumers' *demand* for the products. In other words, the novice fails to search for a generic principle applicable to both problems (law of supply and demand) and instead tends to represent the first problem as a "producer" or "supply" problem and the second as a "consumer" or "demand" problem. Such an approach results in schemata that are poorly differentiated, imprecise, and situation-specific (Champagne, Gunstone, & Klopfer, 1985, p. 67; diSessa, 1982). Novices do not use deep-structure features to identify the conceptual relationships underlying the list of subproblems/subgoals of the problem context.

Such novice-expert distinctions are illustrated further in the different solution paths described for math word problems such as the following:

1. A distance of 500 miles is represented by 6 inches on a map. One inch represents how many miles?
2. A box is 3 feet in length or 0.9144 meters. A box 1 meter in length equals how many feet?

The novice would approach each problem as a new problem since on the surface they involve very different concepts. One is about distance and the other deals with the metric system. The expert, however, might initially classify both problems as measurement problems, and then search deeper for common dimensions or a common problem schema underlying their solutions. For example, the problems could be categorized as a "direct variation" problem, represented as $A/B = C/D$ where $A = 500$ miles (or 3 feet), $B = 6$ inches (or 0.9144 meters), $C =$ the unknown, and $D = 1$ (Mayer, 1986). A rapid and maybe even automatic production of the problem type suggests the existence of "problem schemata" consisting of interrelated sets of knowledge unifying superficially disparate problems on the basis of common underlying traits.

Voss et al. (1983) evaluated expert-novice differences in approaching an ill-structured problem in the social sciences, a problem of how agricultural productivity in the USSR could be increased, if the problem solver were assuming the position of Head of the Ministry of Agriculture. Protocols were collected from people ranging in expertise, from undergraduates starting a course on the Soviet Union to experts on the Soviet Union.

Novices identified concrete, low-level subproblems (e.g., a shortage of tractors, poor irrigation, a need for crop rotations). Separate solutions were typically proposed for each. With no attempt to describe the overall problem at its top-level structure, responses showed a poorly integrated set of solutions addressing specific subproblems.

In contrast, experts constructed abstract representations of the problems. One expert, for example, analyzed the problem from a historical perspective, identified inadequate technological modernization as the major explanatory factor underlying low productivity, and proceeded to classify the problem as technological in nature. He then proposed a basic solution to this problem type, with subproblems viewed as subordinate to the more general technological issue. The expert apparently used his knowledge base to index the problem as a particular type, from which a hierarchical network of problem solutions appropriate to the identified problem type was generated. In short, the expert's problem representation was guided by the activation of superior, principle-oriented knowledge structures (Adelson, 1984; Chi et al., 1981).

Performances by experts and novices in the more structured domain of physics are similarly described by subjects' use or lack of use of schema-driven strategies. Chi et al. (1981) specifically investigated the nature of categorization in college-level expert problem solvers in physics. Analyses of subjects' verbal protocols while solving problems revealed that novices used surface features of problem statements. Novices typically relied on vocabulary similarities to classify problems. For example, problems were paired together as "conservation of energy" or "center of mass" problems because the physics term "energy" or "mass" was mentioned in both. Expert problem-classification strategies, by contrast, involved the identification of idealized objects and physical concepts as well as the laws of physics governing each problem solution. For instance, problems that could be solved by applying Newton's Second Law ($F = MA$) were grouped together as were those involving principles of angular rotation or momentum.

This general approach of recognizing patterns of relationships and organizing ideas into a conceptual network or schema is reflected in skilled reading as well (Bartlett, 1932; Rumelhart, 1975, 1980; Schank & Abelson, 1977). The surface or novice reader skims the text and retains isolated facts. But the practiced reader recognizes patterns that interrelate text to a coherent representation. The process involves searching the text for its underlying structure to identify the top-level or superordinate text schemata and formulating relational links between superordinate and subordinate ideas (van Dijk & Kintsch, 1983; Voss et al., 1983). Schema-based strategies are used to improve the organization of text memories as well (Meyer, Brandt, and Bluth, 1980).

Expert–Novice Differences: Solution Schemata

Experts' ability to recognize problem types is apparent from their problem representations as well as from their use of a solution schema. The principle-based knowledge guiding their formulation of problem categories includes a hierachy of problem solution sets (action or procedural schemata) appropriate for different problem classes (conceptual schemata). So when the subject encounters a "combination" type problem such as" "Cathy has 10 cents. John has 25 cents. Ellen has twice the amount of money as both her friends. How much money does Ellen have?," the expert will activate the problem solution schema (i.e., the "addition/multiplication" procedural schema) appropriate for this combination problem type. As demonstrated by Larkin et al. (1980), expert solvers discern patterns among problems and are able to store a complete solution schema for similar problem types. Thus, rather than having to execute a sequence of steps as the novice does (i.e., first add together 10 cents and 25 cents; record the sum; next multiply the sum by 2), the expert retrieves the entire sequence as a single step. In essence, the sequence has been stored as the solution schema associated with a combination problem type.

Further support that novices lack solution schemata was provided by Larkin et al. (1980). About 11 equations are involved in solving kinematic problems. Larkin et al. found that novices accumulated lists of information about each equation and apparently stored "bits" and "pieces" of knowledge about how each equation could be used to obtain values of certain variables. Novices lacked the insight to organize problems by problem types or common schemata. This leads to reconstruction of step-by-step solution procedures each time a new problem is encountered (despite the fact some problems are from a common schema). Such an approach relies on the use of inefficient search-based strategies (e.g,. trial and error, means-end analysis) instead of the more efficient schema-driven strategies (see Gick, 1986).

Discussion

High-skilled performance is represented not only by the presence of domain-specific knowledge, but also by the expert's efficient use of it (Chiesi, Spilich, & Voss, 1979; Spilich, Vesonder, Chiesi, & Voss, 1979). Schema development and use, thus, seem to represent a generic type of higher-order strategy manifested especially by experts in complex domains such as reading, physics, social sciences, and problem solving in general.

Experts approach complex tasks by schematically encoding information; that is, they form mental models (Mayer, 1976; Mayer, Dyck, & Cook, 1984), categorize problems by type and solution sets (Greeno, 1978a; Mayer, 1987), establish relational links among concepts within and across different domains (Adelson, 1984), and develop abstract levels of problem representation and solution paths by investigating deep-structure features of the problem space (Greeno, 1976; Hayes & Simon, 1974). While novices manifest some level of schematic processing as in categorizing problems from which problem representations are formulated, there are qualitative differences in the methods of categorization (Chi et al., 1981).

Dreyfus and Dreyfus (1986) describe a "transformation" that occurs among learners classified at higher levels on an expert-novice continuum. The first three levels are distinguished by varying degrees of differences in subjects' use of declarative knowledge and rules in the domain. The so-called transformation that occurs at the upper end of the continuum reflects a type of cognitive processing quite distinct from previous levels. One explanation offered is that subjects developed an abstract representation of the problem consisting of relational networks of knowledge and complex production systems for implementing the problem solution.

The descriptions are consistent with the work presented previously by Voss and his colleagues in the social studies field. Analogous to Dreyfus and Dreyfus's lower-level descriptions are the beginning novices (undergraduates taking a course in Soviet domestic policy) and postnovices (undergraduates after the course) of Voss et al's research. Problem representations at both levels were simple and "embodied in a strategy of isolating possible causes of the problem" (p. 216). Similarities at these novice stages may in part be explained by the subject's treatment of all physical (i.e., surface-structure) problem features of equal importance (Dreyfus & Dreyfus, 1986).

A progression of sophisticated strategies became evident in two groups with greater academic experience: experts in areas besides the Soviet Union (e.g., chemistry), and Soviet experts. Non-Soviet experts approached the problem in a fashion similar to the two groups of novices, but developed greater abstraction in their problem representation. The Soviet experts, however, were most skilled in decomposing the problem into meaningful subproblems, and subgoals that led to general problem solutions. Such findings support domain-specific knowledge as a major discriminating factor contributing to this so-called "transformation" along the expert-novice continuum. However, we know that the knowledge alone does not guarantee strategic expertise. That is, while the postnovice possibly had stored declarative knowledge during the Soviet Union course, he or she portrayed a problem-solving approach similar to the beginning novice stage. By contrast, advanced scholars in other areas demonstrated some degree of schema-driven strategic behavior in formulating more abstract problem representations.

Instruction in Schema-Based Strategies

Strategies involving knowledge and use of schemata are particularly relevant in computational and algebraic problem-solving tasks. A main hypothesis is that the ability to combine a collection of problems into a meaningful representation, or schema (e.g., a combination or comparison/contrast schema), facilitates mathematical learning (e.g., Burton, 1984; Charles & Lester, 1984; National Council of Teachers of Mathematics, 1977). Such a hypothesis is particularly relevant when one considers the conceptual and procedural knowledge structures underlying mathematical learning.

STRUCTURE OF THE MATH DOMAIN

The subject matter structure of mathematics may be described in terms of two components (Greeno, 1978a, 1978b; Shavelson, 1972): (a) a propositional or conceptual structure and (b) a procedural or algorithmic structure. The propositional structure refers to the representations of the meaning of mathematical concepts and operations (Shavelson, 1981). Understanding problems in numerical comparisons, for example, requires knowledge of the semantic relationships among such mathematical concepts as ratio and proportion, as shown in Figure 10.1. In the figure, the top-level structure (Kintsch & van Dijk, 1978; Meyer, 1975) describes the use of numbers to express a correspondence (in contrast to the use of numbers to express a specific value), with ordered pairs, fractions, and proportions representing three different forms of comparisons. To illustrate, in the problem, "Alex bought 4 pens for 65 cents, and Mary bought 6 pens for $1.30. Who purchased the better deal?," the comparison can be expressed as ordered pairs, (4,65) to (6,1.30). In solving the problem the ordered pairs can be converted to fractions, $4/65$ to $6/1.30$,

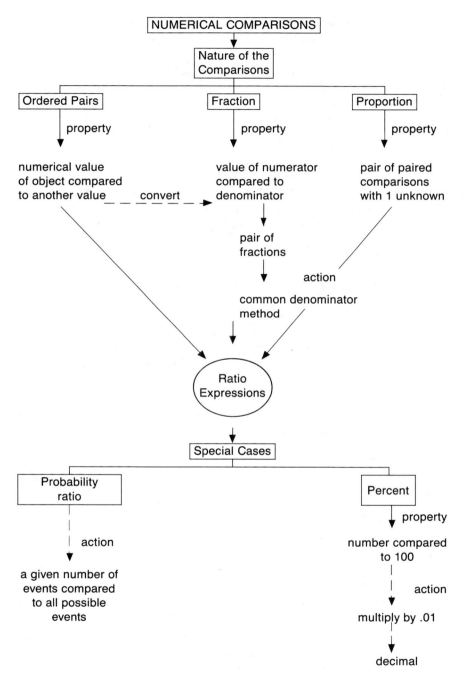

FIGURE 10.1. Conceptual schema for numerical comparisons.

and the common denominator method is applied to find the better sale. In a modified version of the problem, where the number of pens Mary purchased is not given, proportion computation techniques are applied to solve for X, i.e., $4/65 = X/1.30$. Despite differences in the problem sets and relational forms (e.g., (4,65), $4/65$), the concepts of ordered pair, fraction, and proportion are conceptually related. That is, they are ratio expressions.

Percents and probabilities are linked to the same concept of ratio. However, they are represented in the diagram as special cases of ratio because of the specifications of their comparisons. For example, percent involves the correspondence between a number and the constant value, 100.

A procedural structure is similarly represented in a schematic format. But, in contrast, the structure typically describes a hierarchical set of rules or procedures leading to the task solution. Figure 10.2 (Merrill, 1978) portrays a procedural or algorithmic structure for the concept "subtracting a whole number."[1] Unlike the conceptual schema[2] that describes "what the system can do," the procedural schema reflects the operations involved in conducting a particular task.

The new math movement evolved in response to a need to overcome the emphasis on procedural aspects of math. However, a rather extreme shift to the propositional knowledge undermined the importance of performance of procedural goals. Such discrepancies associated with new math made it clear that instruction needs to attend to the reciprocal relation between propositional/conceptual and procedural knowledge. Shavelson (1981) contends that

"an adequate representation of the structure of an area of mathematics would contain components for propositional structure and procedural structure along with the links between the two. Omitting one or the other would produce curricula (and students) strong in one but weak in the other, much like the differences in old and new math." (p. 30)

This view is shared by Mayer (1986), Greeno (1980), and others who espouse the importance of schemata in mathematics training. For example, instruction could include teaching learners mathematical schemata for cause-change problems, metric-conversion problems, "side-angle-side" (Anderson, Greeno, Kline, & Neeves, 1981) or angular rotation problems. Learners should be made to see the link between both the conceptual and the procedural dimensions of the problem sets. In Figure 10.1, for example, relationships between ordered pair and fraction are specified by the "convert" process (i.e., (4,6) can be expressed as $4/6$) as well as by their link to the "ratio" concept. Such an approach focuses on showing learners how to identify underlying

---

[1]Typically there are variations to any one schema. For example, see Merrill (1978) for an alternative "subtracting a whole number" schema.
[2]A conceptual schema describes the relationships among concepts within and across different concept domains. For example, relationships among the concepts of quantity, difference, and reference object are depicted in the comparison schema for addition/subtraction arithmetic problems.

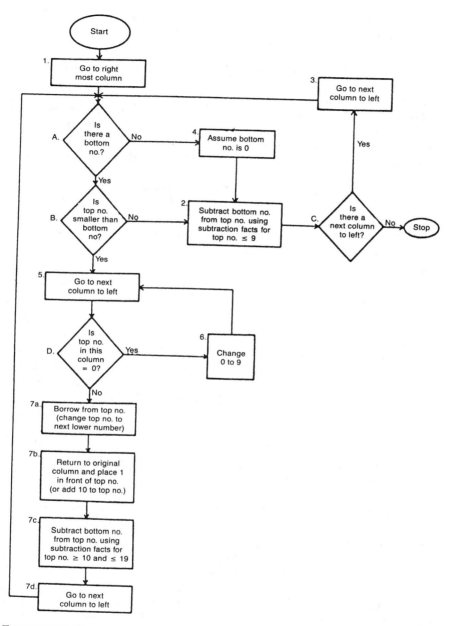

FIGURE 10.2. Representation of a procedural schema or "algorithm" for subtracting whole numbers. (Adopted from P. Merrill, 1978, p. 36, with permission)

relationships among mathematical proposition/concepts and procedures involved in solving problems tied to a common schema.

ROLE OF SCHEMATA IN MATH INSTRUCTION AND LEARNING

Empirical support for the need of more explicit schema-based training in mathematical problem solving is particularly evident among young children in solving addition and subtraction word problems. A main finding from a study by Riley (Riley & Greeno, 1978), for example, indicated that lacking knowledge of semantic schemata predicted problem difficulty for second-grade children. Willis and Fuson (1988) found an overall significant pre-post-test improvement, also among second graders, in solving addition/subtraction word problems of varied types (e.g., "put-together," "change-get-more") under a schema-based instructional intervention. It appeared that using schematic drawings to represent the general story category enhanced learners' selections of an appropriate strategy and correct arithmetic solution procedures.

Mapping Knowledge

Resnick (1979) reported that while elementary-school age children may know a substantial amount about the base [ten] system, they are not necessarily adept in using the conceptual [semantic] knowledge to facilitate their learning the procedures [symbolic] for arithmetic in subtraction and addition tasks (p. 12). Resnick investigated the processes and solutions reached in solving addition/subtraction problems in written form (e.g., $210 - 133 = \_\_\_\_$) and with concrete objects (e.g., blocks). From these observations she assessed whether subjects were able to "map" or establish relationships between the two mathematical forms (i.e., their conceptual knowledge about addition and subtraction in symbolic form and their procedural knowledge in using concrete materials to carry out the arithmetic operations). Three hypothesized types of connections or mappings likely to occur during the math tasks included (a) code mapping, involving the representation of written numbers in concrete form; (b) expectation mapping, described as the projection of equivalent answers from procedures applied to solve the written [symbolic] problems and to solve the problems with concrete materials; and (c) operation mapping, the identification of equivalent operations underlying the written problems and problems using concrete materials.

The verbal protocols reflected prevalence of code mapping. Subjects failed to formulate a connection between problems under the written and concrete forms (i.e, expectation mapping). Furthermore, there was no evidence of operation mapping among the subjects. For example, one student was insensitive to the discrepancy in obtaining a different solution for the same problem conducted with blocks and in symbolic code. In general, subjects appeared to lack skill in integrating the conceptual and procedural knowledge underlying the solution process for problems in written form and those conducted with concrete materials.

Schema Formation

Further reports of difficulty in solving algebra story problems are related to deficits in schema formation and utilization. Both young children (Riley, Greeno, & Heller, 1983) and college students (Soloway, Lochhead, & Clement, 1982) encounter confusion in translating relational propositions of a word problem (e.g., John has three times as many coins as David. John has 9 coins. How many does David have?) into accurate algebraic expressions. This in turn impedes activation of appropriate "action" or procedural schemata for solving the problem.

A series of experiments with college students conducted by Mayer (1982, 1986) confirmed that learning to solve word problems involves more than being able to execute arithmetic operations. Of critical note is that subjects were able to translate the word problems and combine them into a meaningful representation by activating appropriate schematic structures. People skilled in algebra possess schemata for standard algebra story problems, and such schemata guide the encoding and retrieval of information.

Krutetskii (1976) found substantial differences between high- and low-ability students that could be attributed in part to differences in their ability to perceive rapidly and accurately the formal structure of a problem and to generalize across a wide range of mathematically similar problems. Silver's subsequent work (1979, 1982) among junior-high-school students elaborated on Krutetskii's observations and confirmed a significant correlation between the ability of junior-high-school students to sort mathematical problems on the basis of mathematical problem schemata and their problem-solving skills.

The importance of schema knowledge is further substantiated by Kintsch and Greeno's (1985) information-processing model for solving word problems. Kintsch and Greeno integrated principles from a theory of text processing (van Dijk & Kintsch, 1983; Kintsch & van Dijk, 1978) with hypotheses about semantic knowledge for understanding problem texts (Riley et al., 1983) to formulate a model of problem comprehension. The essence of the model is the use of mental representations or schemata and the use of appropriate strategies to solve arithmetic work problems involving a single addition or subtraction operation. Basically three sets of knowledge structures are used in representing and solving problems: (a) a set of proposition frames used for translating sentences of the problem into a conceptual representation of its meaning, or a so-called list of propositions; (b) a set of schemata representing properties and relations of sets in general form and used in constructing macrostructures and problem models (reflecting knowledge of information needed to solve the problem); and (c) a set of schemata representing counting and arithmetic operations in general form, and applied in calculating problem solutions. An important prediction from the model is

Set 1: Albert has five VCR tapes.

P1 X = Albert
P2 HAVE(X$_1$,P3)
P3 FIVE(TAPES)

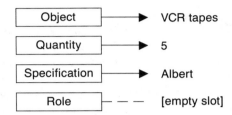

Set 2: Joe has four VCR tapes

P4 X$_2$ = Joe
P5 HAVE(X$_2$,P6)
P6 FOUR(TAPES)

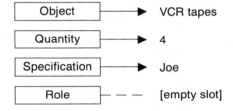

FIGURE 10.3. Representation of "combination" problem type using set schema. Based on a modification from "Understanding and Solving Word Arithmetic Problems" by W. Kintsch and J.G. Greeno, 1985, *Psychological Review*, 92, 1, pp. 113.

that a coordination among the propositional and procedural schemata facilitates successful acquisition of a problem solution.

Set Schema

A central dimension of the Kintsch and Greeno model is the use of "set" schemata for simulating how learners are likely to represent problems. A set is represented with four slots of information as illustrated in Figure 10.3 (adapted with modifications from Kintsch & Greeno, 1985). Each slot contains information related to one of the attributes: (a) an *object* slot consists of a common noun referring to the kind of objects the set contains; (b) a *quantity* slot contains a numerical value that describes how much of something is transferred, taken away, and so forth; (c) a *specification* slot distinguishes the set from others by specifying the owner of the set; and

(d) the *role* slot depicts the relational link of the set with other sets of the problem context.

An example similar to Kintsch and Greeno's (1985) is used for illustration. The learner first identifies the propositions of each set (van Dijk & Kintsch, 1983). As shown in the figure, three propositions are delineated for set 1, "Albert has five VCR tapes"; and three propositions for set 2, "Joe has four VCR tapes." Information from the propositions is appropriately assigned to the slots. The numerical value *five* [VCR tapes] provides the cue for the quantity slot, with *VCR tapes* as the object of reference. *Albert* provides ownership to the set. Similarly, with set 2, *four* is assigned to the quantity slot and *VCR tapes* is the object. The proper name *Joe* distinguishes set 2 from set 1. Since the sets do not contain overlapping elements (i.e., set 2 does not refer to information from set 1) the *role* slots are empty. However, role information is provided in a final set such as, "How many tapes do they have altogether?" In this role set (i.e., set 3), the "have-altogether" proposition specifies a relationship between sets 1 and 2. Since it combines information from both sets (i.e., subsets Albert and Joe), set 3 is referred to as the superset. The superset establishes the ultimate goal of the problem, that is, to determine the total number of tapes.

Identifying relations among the sets is a critical process in solving the problem and requires the use of higher-order schemata. Kintsch and Greeno described higher-order schemata appropriate to solving such problem types. For example, the foregoing problem is referred to as a "combined" problem that is based on a part-whole schema. This schema is cued by the "have-altogether" term of the superset.

The set schema model has particular utility in predicting successful problem-solving behavior. The expert solver is expected to recognize [automatically] text-based cues (e.g., "have-altogether") associated with a particular problem schema. The schema in turn activates an appropriate strategy, such as the count-all strategy, for solving the problem.

In another example, Kintsch & Greeno (1985) describe the use of a difference strategy activated by the more-than and less-than schemata. This strategy in turn assigns appropriate roles. Consider a problem like those used by Kintsch and Greeno: "Mary has 80 penny coins. John has 55 penny coins. How many more coins does Mary have than John?" The difference strategy is cued by the "have-more-than" proposition.

These sample problems are considered one-schema problems because they typically can be solved by accessing a particular schema stored in long-term memory that involves a single operation (addition, subtraction). Propositional cues in the superset activate a particular schema such as the part-whole schema for a combined problem type.

Derry, Hawkes, and Tsai (1987; see Derry, this volume, chap. 11) extended Greeno and Kintsch's one-schema model to multischema problems such as the following: "Joe's age is 9 now. His allowance each week equals out to 5 cents per day. If Joe gets a 20 cents raise each year, how much will he get each week when he is 12 years old?" (p. 60). Propositional information has been assigned to the set slots in Figure 10.4. Overlapping elements imply a relationship between sets. For example, "allowance" describes the object slots of sets 2 through 5, with each new set representing a modified quantity of the object.

The model also contains role slots that are relational links between sets. Information shown in the role slots of sets 2–4 are not considered part of the text base since they are inferred from the problem based on particular schemata (Kintsch & Greeno, 1985). Terms as "now" and "one year later" imply a vary/compare schema; the term "total" of the role slot in the superset (set 5) implies a "combined" schema. That is, set 5 involves combining the weekly earnings of set 2 to the accumulated 20-cent increases (sets 3 and 4) to obtain the total new allowance three years later. Thus, the structure of this problem requires the solver to activate a sequence of schemata in solving the problem, such as the compare, vary/change, and combine schema (see Derry et al., 1987, p. 63). Comprehension of this type of problem requires skill in identifying relations between sets, in activating appropriate schemata representing those relations, and in translating the relational schemata to calculations that yield a problem solution.

IMPLICATIONS FOR SCHEMA-BASED INSTRUCTION

In general, there are three primary sources of expert-novice differences in the use of schema-related strategies. Experts are more likely than novices to (a) translate the propositions in word problems into appropriate mental representations of a problem (Mayer, 1976, 1982); (b) categorize problems by appropriate schema (Mayer, 1986; Riley & Greeno, 1978); and then (c) link that schema to an appropriate problem solution (Vergnaud, 1982). Schema theory (e.g., Anderson, 1977; Minsky, 1975; Rumelhart & Ortony, 1977) implicates the importance of such schema-driven processes in guiding the organization of incoming information and in facilitating the retrieval of prior knowledge during task performance.

Some have suggested direct instruction of domain-based knowledge structures and how they can be used strategically in linking mathematical problem statements with the appropriate procedures (Gagné, 1983; Greeno, 1980, 1983; Mayer, 1986; Nesher, 1986; Shavelson, 1981). Such instruction should include a focus on conceptual definitions and relationships between concepts.

For example, in the problem, "Kathy sold nine tickets. Alice sold four more than Kathy. How many tickets did Alice sell?," key conceptual terms like "more than" can be highlighted to cue a particular schema. The learner can be shown how the components of the problem fit the comparison schema described by Greeno (1980). The problem is analyzed in terms of the components of the schema to include a reference object [Kathy's tickets], the amount associated with the reference [9], the direction of the difference

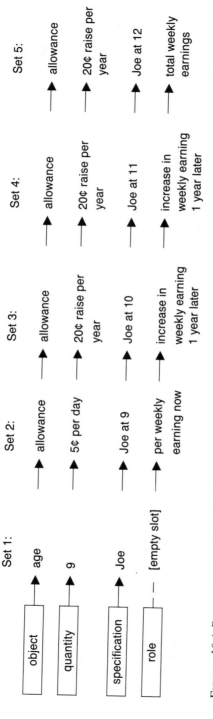

FIGURE 10.4. Representation of a multischema problem using set schemata. Problem example adapted from Derry, Hawkes and Tsai (1987), p. 60.

["more"], and the amount of the difference [4]. Also included is the comparative object [Alice's tickets] and the unknown amount associated with that [unknown number of tickets sold by Alice]. When the difference is known, and the direction of the difference is "more", the solution schema involves adding the amount of the difference to the reference object. A variation to the problem might use the same general schema but require a different procedure to the solution (e.g., subtraction). Instruction might include instances where the direction of the difference is "fewer" (i.e., Alice has four fewer tickets than Kathy. How many tickets does Alice have?), or when the amount of the difference is unknown (i.e., Kathy has nine tickets. Alice has four tickets. How many fewer tickets does Alice have than Kathy?).

DISCUSSION

Typically, the first step in solving a math word problem is translating the verbally described situation into mathematical expressions. How might we approach instruction in this task? As suggested by Gagné (1983), instruction should go beyond simply matching words, such as "more" with "add" and "loss" with "subtract." Teaching learners, instead, how to represent the concepts as schemata gives them a general strategy for problem representation. Thus, there might be a "'linear measuring schema' and an 'area measuring schema' . . . . and many others, each one representing a typical kind of concrete situation that can be translated into the form of a mathematical expression" (p. 12). Schemata provide the structure for interpreting text and representing math problems (Greeno, 1980).

Applications of Instructional Design Principles

Training for "expertise" requires more than selecting the "optimal" strategies that should be taught to students. Consideration must also be given to the high cognitive-resource demands (e.g., working memory; Case, 1985) required of advanced strategic processing, at least in the initial stages (Pressley, Goodchild, Fleet, Zajchowski, & Evans, 1987). Novice performances are controlled in that they are slow, effortful, and capacity limited. This is in contrast to the fast, fairly effortless performance of experts who process automatically (James, 1890; LaBerge, 1975; Schneider & Shiffrin, 1977; Shiffrin & Schneider, 1977). With practice, novice performers become more skilled and "automatic" in their execution of strategies (Logan, 1985; Schneider, Dumais, & Shiffrin, 1984), and thus reduce demands on working memory. For example, consider a novice typist. After much practice, automatic productions develop so that the typist can strike the keys faster with greater accuracy and with less effort expended. Thus, the smaller resource demands of automated typing compared to novice typing permit greater attention to other demands of writing, such as correcting grammar in the typed document.

Development of automaticity is a goal of instruction (e.g., Gagné, 1982, 1983; Landa, 1974, 1983; Lesgold, 1983; Logan, 1985; Resnick & Ford, 1981). It is required for acquisition of complex skills (e.g., Brown, 1985; Lesgold, 1983; Mayer, 1986), with consistent practice of skills the key component (Schneider & Fisk, 1982). A variety of instructional design theories/models (e.g., Gangé, 1977; Gagné & Briggs, 1979; Merrill, 1983) provide recommendations of practice to the point of automaticity, with one of them taken up in detail here.

A SCHEMA-BASED INSTRUCTIONAL DESIGN APPROACH: THE ALGO-HEURISTIC MODEL

Landa (1974, 1983) proposed a theory of performance, learning, and instruction, originally referred to as the Algo-Heuristic Theory (AHT). The objective of the AHT is to accelerate the development of a nonexpert through a special course of instruction in which complex tasks are decomposed into sequences of "elementary component operations."[3] For example, instruction in math word problems belonging to the comparison/contrast schema can be decomposed into instructional components consisting of sets of rules and principles. One instructional component describes the relationship between the reference quantity (Mary has 15 pens), direction of the difference (David has 21 pens), and the unknown difference (How many fewer pens does Mary have than David?). A higher-level instructional component is the algorithmic[4] procedures involved in integrating information about the reference with the known difference to determine the comparative difference. These integration components can be sequenced to facilitate automaticity of the lower-level components (e.g., developing automatic skills in labeling Mary's pens as the reference and David's pens as the comparison set).

Characteristics of the Algo-Heuristic Model

AHT utilizes principles of Gagné's (1977; Gagné & Briggs, 1979) hierarchical learning analysis to describe a systematic instructional approach with focus on (a) common processes underlying a particular set of cognitive tasks and (b) the learner's automatic production of some of these processes. In decomposing the tasks into the "elementary cognitive operations" or schema-

---

[3]Algorithms refer to a definitive set of rules or procedural schemata leading to a solution. Heuristics are abstract sets of rules, or specific conceptual schemata in describing solution paths.

[4]The concept of an "algorithm" is extended in this paper to reflect a "schematic representation" of procedures that focuses on the processes/skills underlying relationships among the respective concepts. This is in contrast to the typical interpretation of algorithms (e.g., Gibbons, 1977), whereby a given task is decomposed into a set of finite, discrete, step-by-step operations.

based processes, the learner is made to see how different concepts are consistently related to each other through the common features underlying their structures. The "decomposed instructional units" provide the learner with explicit descriptions, then, of how classes of concepts presented in a particular piece of instruction [problems to be solved] are related by the algorithmic (or heuristic) processes underlying acquisition of the concepts [problem solutions].

Landa (1987) illustrates teaching the relational concepts of "convex" and "concave" curved surfaces with the AHT approach. Under some types of conventional instruction, the two lens types would be introduced separately with their own definitions and examples of each, thus creating a separate mental model for each type in the learner's long-term memory. By contrast, the AHT approach focuses on the cognitive operations of "relating" and "classifying." This involves presenting the two lens types simultaneously so that the concepts are learned in terms of their common and dissimilar attributes. For example, both (a) have at least one curved surface, (b) are made of transparent material, and (c) are used to form images. This common set of "critical" attributes qualifies both lens types as members of the same, superordinate concept class of curved planes.

The lenses nonetheless differ on a set of "variable" attributes that discriminate one lens type from the other, such as (a) the relationship between their surfaces (i.e., a convex lens has a pushed-out surface in relation to the opposite surface while the concave lens is pushed in) and (b) the convex lens usually has surfaces that converge to one point while the concave does not. While the variable attributes cause the surfaces to appear quite different in shape, the two lens types continue to share an underlying relationship due to their common set of critical attributes qualifying them as members of the same, larger concept class. Thus, learning how to identify the presence of the critical and variable attributes among a set of concepts should help subjects in the schema-driven processes of "relating" and "classifying" (for a review of the concept-learning literature, see Tennyson & Cocchiarella, 1986). Instruction could be designed to enhance similar skills through a series of examples and questions as shown in Figure 10.5. The examples were selected to illustrate how lenses within a given category might differ in shape (e.g., examine the convex lens figures A, B, and C). Yet, they are members of the same class because each possesses the critical attribute(s) essential for class membership (e.g, the surfaces of figures A, B, and C are curved out and so belong to the convex lens category). Probing questions such as, "What distinguishes figure A from figure B?," "On what trait are figures A and B similar?," "Why do figures A and E belong to different lens categories?," are raised to facilitate generation of useful rules. In addition, an emphasis throughout the instruction on the process of "relating" should facilitate pattern recognition among a wide variety of different examples of convex and concave lenses. As automatic productions of pattern recognition develop (e.g., distinguishing the critical from the variable attributes), the learner should become more skilled in constructing a "bigger" picture or schema for the problem.

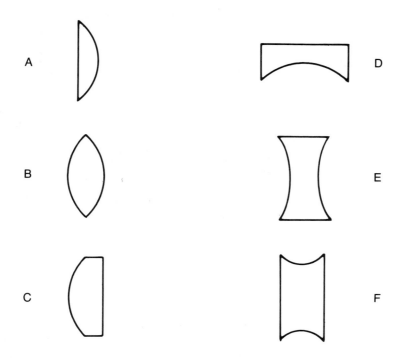

FIGURE 10.5. Convex (left) and concave (right) lenses. The processes of "relating" and "classifying" might be stimulated by asking such questions as, "Which drawings have at least one curved surface?" (critical attribute), "For which drawings do the surfaces converge to one point?" (variable attribute), "Which drawings have a reference surface that is curved away from the opposite surface?" (variable attribute).

The algo-heuristic model describes an approach to instructional design with the goal of enhancing automatic skills development. Its overall prescriptions focus on decomposing the instruction in terms of the network of relationships underlying the concepts to be taught. The next section reports an experimental study involving applications of the algo-heuristic theory in designing instruction in the base-five number system. The overall hypothesis considered the use of schemata as the instructional components for producing both effective and efficient (i.e., in terms of automatic skills development) learning of operating in base 5.

APPLICATIONS OF A SCHEMA-BASED APPROACH TO INSTRUCTION: AN EXPERIMENTAL INVESTIGATION

Landa's theory stimulates the instructional designer to think beyond the paradigm of decomposing instruction into a sequence of low- to high-level skills/procedures. Efforts are extended to designing "automatic processing" components to decrease resource demands in strategy training efforts (Gagné, 1983; Landa, 1983). A few empirical validations of instructional design approaches that focus on automatic skills development in classroom-types of tasks are available (Fisk & Gallini, 1987; Gallini & Fisk, 1987[5]; see also Frederiksen, Warren, & Rosebery, 1985). I focus on one of them here. For instance, Gallini and Fisk (1987) applied the Algo-Heuristic Theory to teach counting, adding, and subtracting in the base-five system.[6] An instructional sequence was designed for each operation (count, add, subtract) according to either (a) a schema/algorithm or (b) a nonschema/algorithm (i.e., traditional task-analytic) approach. The research sample consisted of full-time graduate students enrolled in summer-school courses at the University of South Carolina. None of the subjects were skilled in working in the base-five system. Subjects were randomly assigned to one of the two treatments, with approximately equivalent grade-point averages and GRE scores in the two conditions.

Treatment

Each treatment included approximately six hours of instruction and practice in counting, adding, and multiplying in base 5, with each topic covered on a separate day. In the initial class sessions the experimenter probed subjects' understanding of the material by rasing many questions regarding application of the presented techniques (e.g., when counting numbers, how might you use the digit in "place one" to determine when digit(s) to the left will be changed? Does your obtained sum qualify as a member of the base-5 system?). The experimenter-generated questions served as a model for the participants. Eventually subjects became skilled in self-generating questions during the instructional sessions/practice exercises regarding the appropriateness of different strategies, the tenability of alternative solution paths, the plausibility of their solutions, and so forth.

There were major differences between the treatments in the design and presentation of the instruction and practice exercises. The experimental approach was consistent with the algo-heuristic model of instructional design (Landa, 1983, 1987), based on the cognitive theoretical notions of how expert learners select and integrate information into coherent representations. While the basic context for learning base 5 is procedural in nature, instruc-

---

[5]This research was supported under Rome Air Development Center (RADC, Rome, NY) contract F30602-81-C-0185 with subcontract E-21-669-516 from Georgia Institute of Technology. This subcontract was funded with Air Force Human Resources Laboratory, LDIRP (Labor Directors' Independent Research Program) funds. Larry Reed was the AFHRL, Wright Patterson, OH, technical monitor. A.D. Fisk was the principal investigator.
[6]Most of the automaticity work has been confined to laboratory tasks (e.g., visual search tasks).This study extended the related research to a classroom setting. The base-five tasks were chosen on the premise that most subjects would posses virtually little or no prior experience with the tasks.

1. Start with numbers in foremost right column

2. Add the numbers together

3. Divide the sum by 5

4. Place the remainder in the present column and carry the number of groups of five over to the digits in the column to the immediate left

5. Then ask:

   Is this the last column to the left.

Yes

Record the sum
of that last column

No

Repeat steps
2 through 5

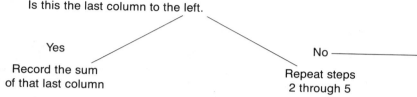

FIGURE 10.6. Algorithm for adding in base 5.

tion was designed to focus on both the concepts and the underlying processes that produce relational links among the concept nodes. The approach is in contrast to the control group instruction involving a separate sequence of steps to follow in solving each problem type (i.e., "addition in base 5"problems, "addition in base 10" problems, and so forth), and is consequently leading to the encoding of a different rule for each type of problem.

Control.

Under the nonschema treatment, subjects were guided by a lecture-example format. A typical task-analytic approach (i.e., "hierarchical analysis"; for discussion see P. Merrill, 1978) was applied to decompose the instruction into components consisting of steps or "simple to complex" skills necessary for solving the arithmetic problems in base 5. For example, the steps for addition were presented in a procedural "how-to" format: (a) Start with numbers in the foremost right column. (b) Add the numbers together. (c) Divide the sum by 5, etc. (see Figure 10.6). Each step in Figure 10.6 represents an instructional component that was presented to the learner either in a verbal or written "list" format. Attention was given to "how to conduct operations in base 5" rather than "how to formulate relationships" among concepts underlying those operations. Such an approach focuses on what one must know in order to add, count, and multiply in addition to the necessary prerequisite skills to accomplish each task (Mayer, 1986). Furthermore, instructional processes to be acquired are typically described in general, indefinite terms such as: The student will be able to analyze the problem" or "establish relationships between the concepts" (Landa, 1983).

Supplementary instructional materials were of the traditional types used in teaching base-10 operations, such as multiplication and counting tables. These materials provided solutions to situation-specific problems in base 5, such as the base-5 equivalents of base-10 numbers 0 to 100; or products of multiplication problems using base-5 numbers 0 through 30 as the multipliers. Many examples covering a variety of each problem type were also provided over the course. In essence, the approach focused on the isolated set of skills or defined steps required to solve a given problem rather than on the general rule(s) underlying problem solutions (e.g., the general rule involved in counting from 30 to 40 in base 5 or from 50 to 80 in base 10).

Experimental.

While the control-group instruction focused on task-analytic procedures, it would be appropriate to describe the experimental treatment approach (i.e., schema/algorithm) as a conceptual elaboration of task analysis (Mayer, 1986; see also Gagné, 1977; Merrill, 1978). Instead of decomposing instruction into specific steps for solving a particular problem, subjects were instructed in the use of schemata or conceptual networks of relationships underlying different types of problems. In essence, the instruction was decomposed into schemata, each of which applied to a range of problems that on the surface appeared to be different. Thus, subjects were explicitly shown, for example, how adding in bases 5 and 10 were very similar since they were both tied to a common schema.

To illustrate further, consider one schema used in the experiment that was based on Greeno's (1980) framework for arithmetic word problems (see Figure 10.7). The schema of Figure 10.7 illustrates how the different operations of adding and multiplying two single-digit numbers (the structure could be expanded to include larger numbers as well) in any base system are conceptually related. That is, shown in the diagram are relationships among major concepts and procedures underlying the different computations. Included are the concepts of quantity change, reference, incremental value, and the conversion procedure.

The use of such schemata in this study was hypothesized to facilitate learning in the base-5 system by relating its conceptual and procedural features to those of base 10 (any other base system could be used as well). Rather than focusing the instruction on a set of specific steps for solving each new problem in base 5 (as was done in the control group), the schema approach demonstrated relationships among concepts and procedures in the base systems that on the surface appeared to be disparate. Thus, subjects were encouraged to search for the common features of solution paths to different problems such as 44 + 32 in base 5 and 56 × 47 in base 10.

Verbal information (e.g., definitions) was highlighted during instruction (Mayer et al., 1984) to develop automatic retrieval of such information. In addition, instruction integrated procedural knowledge with the respective concepts being taught. For example, the process of adding in either base is virtually the same due to the underlying "combination" schema on which the operation is based. Instruction was accompanied by a range of parallel or

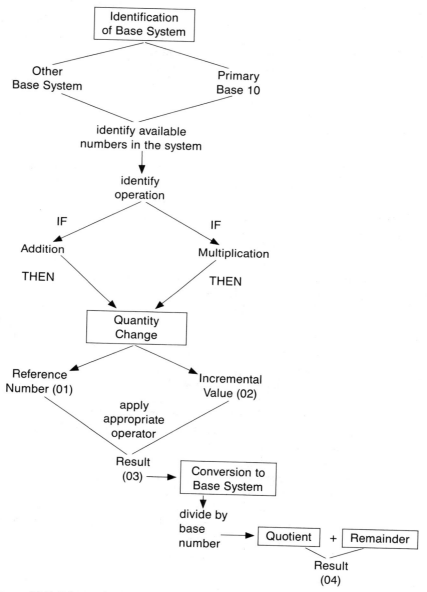

FIGURE 10.7. Schema for addition and multiplication in any base system. Result 03 and 04 yields the same solution in base 10. Thus, the "conversion base system" subschemata does not need to be executed in base 10.

"matched" (see Tennyson & Cocchiarella, 1986; Tennyson & Merrill, 1977) examples/nonexamples in base 5 and base 10 presented concurrently. Thus, subjects could discern the similarities and dissimilarities of the base systems (Tennyson, Chao, & Youngers, 1981). For example, "14 + 3 = 22" in base 5 and "15 + 6 = 21" in base 10 were presented as "matched" examples in that they both illustrated the concept of "carrying" when adding two-digit and one-digit numbers.

Automaticity Assessments

The primary question related to the impact of a schema-based training sequence on the development of automatic skills in base five. To address the question, automaticity measures (e.g., Logan, 1979; Schneider & Fisk, 1982) involving arithmetic verification equations in addition and subtraction were administered on a computer. Both pre- and post-test assessments of subjects' skills in base-10 (pretest) and base-5 (post-test) computations were collected, with daily assessments of skills taught on a given day. Test items were addition or multiplication equations of the form $A [\times$ or $+] B = C$, where A and B were single digits 0 to 4. C could be a one- or two-digit number with these digits ranging between 0 and 9 for base-10 items or 0 to 4 for the base-5 items.[7] Several different types of items were formed (Zbrodoff & Logan, 1986): (a) the sum of A and B correctly equalled C; (b) the product of A and B correctly equalled C; (c) and (d) equations were formed such that C equalled neither the sum nor the product of A and B (e.g., $3 \times 2 = 8$; $3 + 2 = 9$); (e) associative "multiplication" lures were formed such that C equalled the product of A and B (e.g., $3 + 2 = 6$); (f) associative "addition" lures were created such that C equalled the sum of A and B (e.g., $3 \times 2 = 5$). The last two conditions produce a Stroop effect (Dyer, 1973; Stroop, 1935; Zbrodoff & Logan, 1986). The Stroop effect provides for a test of automatic processing of information. For example, when a subject sees $3 + 2 = 6$, associative connections for both addition and multiplication of 3 and 2 are automatically activated (assuming that addition and multiplication have been automatized). In essence, activation of both addition and multiplication tables occurs since the equation indicates 3 and 2 are to be summed; but at the same time, the 6 activates the process of multiplying 3 by 2. In other words, interference results due to the activation of an additional process, regardless of the person's attempt to attend to one process. An increase in

---

[7]The pretest arithmetic verification tasks were administered to obtain a profile of a subject's development, over many practice trials, of automatic skills in the basic operations of addition and multiplication. Since the subjects indicated virtually no prior experience with the base-5 system, pretest assessments were conducted in the familiar system of base 10. The approach provided a more realistic description of the subject's entry status with respect to "automatic skills" in the basic computations of addition and multiplication.

reaction time from pretest to post-test on Stroop items provides an argument for at least partial automaticity[8] in such tasks (Zbrodoff & Logan, 1986).

There was support for the hypothesis that automatic skills development is promoted by a schema-based instructional approach. Difference reaction time (pre–post-test) scores on the arithmetic verification tasks were calculated for conditions 1 and 2 (correct equations), conditions 3 and 4 (incorrect equations), and Stroop conditions 5 and 6. There was a significantly greater improvement for the schema group in their ability to identify incorrect equations quickly, with a marginally greater improvement ($p < 0.08$) for speed of processing in the schema condition compared to the control condition for the correct equations. There was also a Stroop effect for the schema group in base 5, thus suggesting interference from the associative lures (Stroop condition) due to at least some partial development of automaticity in base 5. Subjects in the traditional treatment condition, however, did not exhibit the Stroop effect (i.e., there was no evidence of additional interference at post-test compared to pretest). The effectiveness of the schema-based training was further evidenced by the respective group's higher performance on the most difficult achievement test involving multiplication problems.

The schema-based approach was based on the notion of "consistent component training." That is, subjects were taught how to count and perform multiplication and addition in base 5 by being exposed to sets of rules that consistently applied to particular types of problems. Such consistency promoted automatic skills development in this study.

Concluding Remarks

Instructional theories and models are being expanded to address instructional design issues from the perspective of (a) the mental operations involved in doing a task, (b) strategic processing demonstrated by the expert, and (c) the nature of instructional activities that foster automaticity. This chapter focused on schema-based strategies, including the strategic processes of categorizing problems by problem types and activating existing schema to represent problems. Many learners already use some schema-based strategies. However, qualitative differences at the extreme ends of the expert-novice continuum are quite clear. While the novice's rules for categorizing problems are based on surface features, the expert searches for principles and rules governing the solutions to what appear to be disparate problems. Furthermore, the novice executes a problem solution in a step-by-step format. By contrast, many of these low-level operations have been automatized by the

---

[8]Partial automaticity bears on the issue that automaticity should be construed as a continuous dimension rather than a dichotomy (Zbrodoff & Logan, 1986).

expert. In essence, they are stored as a "chunk" or information and executed by the expert as a single step or production(s).

How can such theoretically-based findings about expert-novice differences be translated into instructional practice? Collaborative efforts by instructional designers, psychologists, and educational researchers are required to design and validate instructional prescriptions that promote automaticity and other expert-like characteristics.

Acknowledgment.. This research was supported in part by the Biomedical Research Support Grant, University of South Carolina.

REFERENCES

Adelson, B. (1984). When novices surpass experts: The difficulty of a task may increase with expertise. *Journal of Experimental Psychology: Learning, Memory, and Cognition, 10*, 483–495.

Anderson, J.R. (1982). Acquisition of cognitive skill. *Psychological Review, 89*, 369–406.

Anderson, J.R., Greeno, J., Kline, P., & Neves, D. (1981). Acquisition of problem-solving skill. In J.R. Anderson (Ed.), *Cognitive skills and their acquisition* (pp. 191–230). Hillsdale, NJ: Erlbaum & Associates.

Anderson, R.C. (1977). The notion of schemata and the educational enterprise. In R.C. Anderson, R.J. Spiro, and W.E. Montague (Eds.), *Schooling and the acquisition of knowledge* (pp. 415–431). Hillsdale, NJ: Erlbaum & Associates.

Bartlett, F.C. (1932). *Remembering.* New York: Cambridge University Press.

Britton, B.K., & Glynn, S.M. (1987). *Executive control processes in reading.* Hillsdale, NJ: Erlbaum & Associates.

Brown, A.L. (1985). Metacognition: The development of selective attention strategies for learning from texts. In H. Singer & R.B. Ruddell (Eds.), *Theoretical models and processes of reading,* 3rd ed. (pp. 501–526). Newark, DE: International Reading Association.

Burton, L. (1984). Mathematical thinking: The struggle for meaning. *Journal for Research in Mathematics Education, 15*, 35–49.

Case, R. (1985). *Intellectual development.* Orlando, FL: Academic Press.

Champagne, A.B.. Gunstone, R.F., & Klopfer, L.E. (1985). Instructional consequences of students' knowledge about physical phenomena. In L.H.T. West and A.L. Pines (Eds.), *Cognitive structure and conceptual change* (pp. 61–90). Orlando, FL: Academic Press.

Charles, R.I., & Lester, F.K. Jr. (1984). An evaluation of a process-oriented instructional program in mathematical problem solving in grades 5 and 7. *Journal for Research in Mathematics Education, 15*, 15–34.

Chase, W.G., & Simon, H.A. (1973). Perception in chess. *Cognitive Psychology, 1*, 55–81.

Chi, M.T., Feltovich, P.J., & Glaser, R. (1981). Categorization and representation of physics problems by experts and novices. *Cognitive Science, 5*, 121–152.

Chiesi, H.L., Spilich, G.J., & Voss, J.F. (1979). Acquisition of domain-related information in relation to high and low domain knowledge. *Journal of Verbal Learning and Verbal Behavior, 18*, 257–274.

de Groot, A.D. (1965). *Thought and choice in chess.* The Hague, Holland: Mouton Press.

Derry, S.J., Hawkes, L.W., & Tsai, C. (1987). A theory of remediating problem-solving skills of older children and adults. *Educational Psychologist, 22*, 55–87.

van Dijk, T.A., & Kintsch, W. (1983). *Strategies of discourse processing.* New York: Academic Press.

diSessa, A.A. (1982). Unlearning Aristotelian, physics: A study of knowledge-based learning. *Cognitive Science, 6*, 37–75.

Dreyfus, S.E., & Dreyfus, H.L. (1986). *Mind over machine.* New York: The Fress Press, pp. 16–51.

Dyer, F.N. (1973). The stroop phenomenon and its use in the study of perceptual, cognitive, and response processes. *Memory and Cognition, 2*, 106–120.

Fisk, A.D., & Gallini, J. (1987). Training consistent components of tasks: Developing an instructional system based on automatic/controlled processing principles. (Technical Report No. 8701). Dayton, OH: Air Force Human Resource Laboratory, Wright Patterson Base.

Frederiksen, J.R., Warren, B.M., & Rosebery, A.S. (1985). A componential approach to training reading skills, Part I. Perceptual units in training. *Cognition and Instruction, 2*, 91–130.

Gagné, R.M. (1977). *The conditions of learning.* New York: Holt, Rinehart & Winston, Inc.

Gagné, R.M. (1982). Developments in learning psychology. *Educational Technology, 22*, 11–15.

Gagné, R.M. (1983). Some issues in the psychology of mathematics instruction. *Journal for Research in Mathematics Education, 14*, 7–18.

Gagné, R.M., & Briggs, L.J. (1979). *Principles of instructional design,* 2nd ed. New York: Holt, Rinehart and Winston.

Gallini, J.K., & Fisk, A.D. (April 1987). *An investigation of an instructional design approach to expert learning: Integration of attention and instructional design theories.* Paper presented at the annual meeting of the American Educational Research Association, Washington DC.

Gick, M.L. (1986). Problem-solving strategies. *Educational Psychologist, 21*, 99–120.

Greeno, J.G. (1976). Cognitive objectives of instruction: Theory of knowledge for solving problems and answering questions. In D. Klahr (Ed.), *Cognition and instruction* pp. 123–159. Hillsdale, NJ: Erlbaum & Associates.

Greeno, J.G. (1978a). A study of problem solving. In R. Glaser (Ed.), *Advances in instructional psychology,* Vol. 1 (pp. 13–75). Hillsdale, NJ: Erlbuam & Associates.

Greeno, J.G. (1978b). Understanding and procedural knowledge in mathematics instruction. *Educational Psychologist, 12*, 262–283.

Greeno, J.G. (1980). Some examples of cognitive task analysis with instructional implications. In R. Glaser (Ed.), *Advances in instructional psychology,* Vol. 3 (pp. 1–21). Hillsdale, NJ: Erlbaum & Associates.

Greeno, J.G. (1983). Understanding in mathematical problem solving. In S.C. Paris, G.M. Olson, & H.W. Stevenson (Eds.), *Learning and motivation in the classroom* (pp. 83–111). Hillsdale, NJ: Erlbaum & Associates.

Hayes, J.R., & Simon, H.A. (1974). Understanding problem instructions. In L.W. Gregg (Ed.), *Knowledge and cognition*. Hillsdale, NJ: Erlbaum & Associates.

Hinsley, D.A., Hayes, J.R., & Simon, H.A. (1977). From words to equations. Meaning and representation in algebra word problems. In P.A. Carpenter & M.A. Just (Eds.), *Cognitive process in comprehension* (pp. 89–106). Hillsdale, NJ: Erlbaum & Associates.

James, W. (1890). *Principles of psychology*, Vol. 1. New York: Holt, Rinehart & Winston, Inc.

Kiewra, K.A., & Benton, S.L. (April 1987). *Cognitive aspects of autonomous learning.* Paper presented at the annual meeting of the American Educational Research Association, Washington, DC.

Kintsch, W., & van Dijk, T.A. (1978). Toward a model of text comprehension and production. *Psychological Review, 85*, 363–394.

Kintsch, W., & Greeno, J.G. (1985). Understanding and solving word arithmetic problems. *Psychological Review, 92*, 109–129.

Krutetskii, V.A. (1976). *The psychology of mathematical abilities in school children.* Chicago: University of Chicago Press.

LaBerge, J.D. (1975). Acquisition of automatic processing in perceptual and associative learning. In P.M.A. Rabbit and S. Dornic (Eds.), *Attention and performance V.* New York: Academic Press.

Landa, L. (1974). *Algorithmization in learning and instruction.* Englewood Cliffs, NJ: Educational Technology Publications. (Russian ed. 1966; German ed. 1969).

Landa, L. (1983). The algo-heuristic theory of instruction. In C.M. Reigeluth (Ed.), *Instructional design theories and models* (pp. 163–211. Hillsdale, NJ: Erlbaum & Associates.

Landa, L. (1987). A fragment of a lesson based on the algo-heuristic theory of instruction. In C.M. Reigeluth (Ed.), *Instructional theories in action.* (pp. 112–159). Hillsdale, NJ: Erlbaum & Associates.

Larkin, J., McDermott, J., Simon, D.P., & Simon, H.A. (1980). Models of competence in solving physics problems. *Cognitive Science, 4*, 317–345.

Lesgold, A.M. (1983). A rationale for computer-based reading instruction. In A.C. Wilkinson (Ed.), *Classroom computers and cognitive science* (pp. 167–181). New York: Academic Press.

Logan, G.D. (1979). On the use of a concurrent memory load to measure attention and automaticity. *Journal of Experimental Psychology: Human Perception and Performance, 5*, 189–207.

Logan, G.D. (1985). Skill and automaticity: Relations, implications, and future directions. *Canadian Journal of Psychology, 39*, 367–386.

Mayer, R.E. (1976). Comprehension as affected by structure of problem representation. *Memory and Cognition, 4*, 249–255.

Mayer, R.E. (1982). Memory for algebra story problems. *Journal of Educational Psychology, 74*, 199–216.

Mayer, R.E. (1986). Mathematics. In R.F. Dillon & R.J. Sternberg (Eds.), *Cognition and instruction* (pp. 127–154). New York: Academic Press.

Mayer, R.E. (1987). Instructional variables that influence cognitive processes during reading. In B.K. Britton & S.M. Glynn (Eds.), *Executive control processes in reading* (pp. 201–216). Hillsdale, NJ: Erlbaum & Associates.

Mayer, R.E., Dyck, J.L., & Cook, L. (1984). Techniques that help readers build mental models from scientific text: Definitions pretraining and signaling. *Journal of Educational Psychology, 76*, 1089–1105.

Merrill, M.D. (1983). Component display theory. In C.M. Reigeluth (Ed.), *Instructional-design theories and models* (pp. 279–333). Hillsdale, NJ: Erlbaum & Associates.

Merrill, P. (1978). Hierarchical and information processing task analysis: A comparison. *Journal of Instructional Development, 1,* 35–40.

Meyer, B.J.F. (1975). *The organization of prose and its effects on memory.* Amsterdam: North Holland Publishing Co.

Meyer, B.J.F., Brandt, D.M., & Bluth, G.J. (1980). Use of top-level structure in text: Key for reading comprehension of ninth-grade students. *Reading Research Quarterly, 1,* 72–103.

Minsky, M.A. (1975). A framework for representing knowledge. In P.H. Winston (Ed.), *The psychology of computer vision* (pp. 211–280). New York: McGraw-Hill.

National Council of Teachers of Mathematics. (1977). Position statement on basic skills. *Arithmetic Teacher, 25,* 18–22.

Nesher, P. (1986). Learning mathematics: A cognitive perspective. *American Psychologist, 41,* 1114–1122.

Pressley, M. (1986). The relevance of the good strategy user model to the teaching of mathematics. *Educational Psychologist, 21,* 139–161.

Pressley, M., Borkowski, J.G., & Schneider, W. (1987). Cognitive strategies: Good strategy users coordinate metacognition and knowledge. In R. Vasta & G. Whitehurst (Eds.), *Annals of child development,* Vol. 5 (pp. 89–129). New York: JAI Press.

Pressley, M., Goodchild, F., Fleet, J., Zajchowski, R., & Evans, E.D. (April 1987). *What is good strategy use and why is it hard to teach? An optimistic appraisal of the challenges associated with strategy instruction.* Paper presented at the annual conference of the American Educational Research Association, Washington, D.C.

Reif, F. (1980). Theoretical and educational concerns with problem solving: Bridging the gaps with human cognitive engineering. In D.T. Tuma & F. Reif (Eds), *Problem solving and education: Issues in teaching and research* (pp. 39–50). Hillsdale, NJ: Erlbaum & Associates.

Resnick, L.B. (Nov., 1979). *Syntax and semantics in learning to subtract.* Paper presented at the Wingspread Conference on Number, Racine, WI.

Resnick, L.B., & Ford, W.W. (1981). *The psychology of mathematics for instruction.* Hillsdale, NJ: Erlbaum & Associates.

Riley, M.S., & Greeno, J.G. (May 1978). *Importance of semantic structure in the difficulty of arithmetic word problems.* Paper presented at the meeting of the Midwestern Psychological Association, Chicago.

Riley, M.S., Greeno, J.G., & Heller, J.I. (1983). Development of children's problem-solving ability in arithmetic. In H.P. Ginsburg (Ed.), *The development of mathematical thinking* (pp. 153–196). New York: Academic Press.

Rumelhart, D.E. (1975). Notes on a schema for stories. In D. Bobrow and A. Collins (Eds.), *Representation and understanding: Studies in cognitive science* (pp. 211–236). New York: Academic Press.

Rumelhart, D.E. (1980). Schemata: The building blocks of cognition. In R.J. Spiro, B.C. Bruce, & W.F. Brewer (Eds.), *Theoretical issues in reading comprehension.* Hillsdale, NJ: Erlbaum & Associates.

Rumelhart, D.E., & Ortony, A. (1977). The representation of knowledge in memory. In R.C. Anderson, R.J. Spiro, & W.E. Montague (Eds.), *Schooling and the acquisition of knowledge* (pp. 99–135.) Hillsdale, NJ: Erlbaum & Associates.

Schank, R., & Abelson, R. (1977) *Scripts, plans, goals, and understanding.* Hillsdale, NJ: Erlbaum & Associates.

Schneider, W., Dumais, S.T., & Shiffrin, R.M. (1984). Automatic and control processing and attention. In R. Parasuraman, R. Davis, & J. Beathy (Eds.), *Varieties of attention*. (pp. -27). New York: Academic Press.

Schneider, W., & Fisk, A.D. (1982). Degree of consistent training: Improvements in search performance and automatic process development. *Perception and Psychophysics, 31*, 160–168.

Schneider, W., & Shiffrin, R.M. (1977) Controlled and automatic human information processes: I. Detection, search, and attention. *Psychological Review, 84*, 1–66.

Shavelson, R.J. (1972). Some aspects of the correspondence between content structure and cognitive structure in physics instruction. *Journal of Educational Psychology, 63*, 225–234.

Shavelson, R.J. (1981). Teaching of mathematics: Contributions of cognitive research. *Educational Psychologist, 16*, 23–44.

Shiffrin, R.M., & Schneider, W. (1977). Controlled and automatic human information processes: II. Perceptual learning, automatic attending, and a general theory. *Psychological Review, 84*, 127–190.

Silver, E.A. (1979). Recall of mathematical problem information: Solving related problems. *Journal for Research in Mathematics Education, 10*, 195–210.

Silver, E.A. (1982). Problem perception, problem schemata, and problem solving. *Journal of Mathematical Behavior, 3*, 169–181.

Soloway, E., Lochhead, J., & Clement, J. (1982). Does computer programming enhance problem-solving ability? In R. Seidel, R. Anderson, & B. Hunter (Eds.), *Computer literacy* (pp. 171–185). New York: Academic Press.

Spilich, G.J., Vesonder, G.T., Chiesi, H.L., & Voss, J.F. (1979). Text processing of domain-related information for individuals with high and low domain knowledge. *Journal of Verbal Learning and Verbal Behavior, 18*, 275–290.

Stroop, J.R. (1935). Studies of interference in serial verbal reactions. *Journal of Experimental Psychology, 18*, 643–662.

Tennyson, R.D., Chao, J.N., & Youngers, J. (1981). Concept learning effectiveness using prototype and skill development presentation forms. *Journal of Educational Psychology, 73*, 326–334.

Tennyson, R.D., & Cocchiarella, M.J. (1986). An empirically based instructional design theory for teaching concepts. *Review of Educational Research, 56*, 40–71.

Tennyson, R.D., & Merrill, M.D. (1977). *Teaching concepts: An instructional design guide.* Englewood Cliffs, NJ: Educational Technology Publications.

Vergnaud, G. (1982). A classification of cognitive tasks and operations of thought involved in addition and subtraction problems. In T.P. Carpenter, J.M. Moser, & T. Romberg (Eds.), *Addition and subtraction: A cognitive perspective* (pp. 36–59). Hillsdale, NJ: Erlbaum & Associates.

Voss, J.F. (1986). Social studies. In R.F. Dillon and R.J. Sternberg (Eds.), *Cognition and instruction* (pp. 205–239). New York: Academic Press.

Voss, J.F., Tyler, S.W. & Yengo, L.A. (1983). Individual differences in the solving of social science problems. In R.F. Dillon & R.R. Schmeck (Eds.), *Individual differences in cognition*, Vol. 1 (pp. 205–232). New York: Academic Press.

Willis, G.B., & Fuson, D.C. (1988). Teaching children to use schematic drawings to solve addition and subtraction word problems. *Journal of Educational Psychology, 80*, 192–201.

Zbrodoff, N.J., & Logan, G.D. (1986). On the autonomy of mental processes: A case study of arithmetic. *Journal of Experimental Psychology: General, 115*, 118–130.

11
Strategy and Expertise in Solving Word Problems

SHARON J. DERRY

This chapter is concerned with how people think when they attempt to solve complex arithmetic problems, like the examples in Table 11.1. Such problems represent realistic daily situations in which adults employ arithmetic, and frequently are encountered on standardized tests that people take for educational and career advancement. Developing solutions to problems like these requires no specialized knowledge — only fifth-grade reading and math are needed. Yet studies recently conducted in my laboratory show that even typical college students can experience great difficulty with arithmetic word problems. This same lack of basic problem-solving capability also is evident within our military services (see, for example, Hechinger, 1983; Derry & Kellis, 1986).

This chapter will describe several attempts to examine those aspects of performance that differentiate (or do not differentiate) unsuccessful from successful problem solving in this domain. The historical development of a domain-specific theory of problem solving will be detailed, the implications of this theory for strategy training will be discussed, and a prototype instructional system for strategy training in the word-problem domain will be described.

The General Strategies View

One influential idea that has been with us for years is that poor problem solvers lack general strategy knowledge — high-level solution approaches that can be used for most subjects and in many different problem situations. Perhaps the best-known example is the general planning model, whereby students control their approach by thinking through such stages as problem analysis, planning, executing a plan, and evaluating results (see Beal, this volume, chap. 8). This type of general planning capability is considered an important aspect of "metacognition" (Flavell, 1979, 1981), which refers not only to a person's knowledge about problem-solving processes, but also the ability to access, orchestrate, and monitor those processes. Because poor

TABLE 11.1. Example Word Problems

Example 1. Semi-Routine Problem

Sam is going out for pizza. Domino's sells large pizzas with three toppings for 12 dollars. Extra cheese is 2 bucks, and additional toppings are one-fifty each. Sam wants two large pizzas, one with four and one with five toppings. Both will have extra cheese. He has a coupon where you get 2 dollars off per pizza for an order of two or more. He now has collected $14.50 and has $4.00 of his own to put in. How much more must he collect from the gang?

Example 2. Nonroutine Problem

Garfield is 6 pounds overweight, so the vet put him on a diet. Garfield is allowed to eat only 800 calories a day. Each 100 grams of cat-food lasagna contains 20 grams of protein, 55 grams of carbohydrates, and 5 grams of fat. Protein and carbohydrates give about 4 calories per gram. Fat gives about 9 calories per gram. So far today Garfield has had 200 grams of cat-food lasagna. But he is still very hungry. About how many more grams of his special cat food can Garfield have today?

problem solvers often seem less controlled and less systematic than good problem solvers, many researchers advocate direct training based on the general planning model (e.g., Baron, 1981; Belmont, Butterfield & Ferretti, 1982; Bransford & Stein, 1984; Polya, 1957; Pressley, 1986; Schoenfeld, 1985).

Other slightly less general strategies are derived from the computational literature on problem solving, and seem especially applicable to domains that involve mathematics. Two popular computational strategies are working backward from a goal and means-end analysis. Working backward involves: (a) analyzing a goal and determining what final operation would be needed to achieve it; (b) if necessary, seeking a subgoal operator that would achieve preconditions for the final operation; and (c) seeking other subgoal operators that would achieve preconditions for the next-to-the-last operation, etc. Means-ends analysis is another goal-driven strategy, whereby operators are sought that will gradually reduce the differences between a desired goal state and current intermediate problem states (E.D. Gagné, 1985; Greeno & Simon, 1984; Sacerdoti, 1979; Schoenfeld, 1985).

An interesting feature of most general strategies is that they can provide the basis for a stage of "front-end" analysis and planning, performed prior to adopting a solution path. For example, the general planning model encourages students to think through plans as fully as possible before attempting to carry them out. Working backward from the goal requires that the problem solver fully trace one or more lines of reasoning before accepting or rejecting a solution path, while means-ends analysis can be used in this manner. When problem-solving training advocates front-end planning, the learner is taught not to jump into a problem and begin to solve, but rather to stand back from the problem and evaluate potential subgoals and courses of action. Often, an aim of this approach is to reduce impulsive tendencies in people who commit to solution strategies before problems are understood.

For this reason, general strategies training frequently is linked to the educational goal of producing more reflective thinkers (e.g., Baron, 1981; Baron, Badgio, & Gaskins, 1986). Currently it is very popular to view the good strategy user as one who approaches problems with a thinking style that is controlled, analytical, and reflective (e.g., Baron, 1981; Baron et al., 1986; Pressley, Borkowski, & Schneider, 1987; Rankin & Hughes, 1987).

The JSEP Study: A Test for the General Planning Model

The general planning perspective influenced my thinking several years ago, when I collaborated with workers from the Center for Educational Technology to design an instructional unit in problem solving for the Army's Job Skills Educational Program (JSEP). JSEP is a remedial program in basic educational skills designed for lower-ability military recruits. The recruits in our population were adept with double-digit arithmetic calculations, yet their capabilities with word problems were very poor; thus, the subject domain chosen as a vehicle for strategies training was prealgebra word problems. These types of problems were found in training materials and on various tests that recruits took for career advancement, and they could be written to represent real-world problem situations that soldiers might encounter.

Since numerous well-known researchers (e.g., Belmont, et al., 1982; Bransford & Stein, 1984; Brown, 1978; Hayes, 1981; Meichenbaum, 1977, 1980; Polya, 1957) had proposed that skilled problem solving proceeds through stages of a general planning model, it seemed feasible to assume that soldiers' problem-solving deficits might stem from lack of this general planning skill. In an effort to assure ourselves of this point, we conducted a think-aloud study comparing eight recruits from our population with eight higher-ability college subjects (Derry & Kellis, 1986). From a general planning model we derived a coding scheme for classifying subject behaviors that occurred during problem-solving sessions. The coding scheme consisted of 27 categories of behavior, each representing an instance of one of the following processing stages: (a) clarifying a problem, (b) developing a strategy, (c) executing a strategy, and (d) monitoring/checking performance. Subjects were first trained to think out loud while solving arithmetic word problems. Then an experiment was run in which each subject individually received six think-out-loud word problems that ranged from easy to complicated. Subjects were allowed six minutes for each problem and as many trials as desired within that time limit. Protocols were recorded, transcribed, and parsed into six-second intervals. Independent raters then coded the intervals.

As expected, college subjects required fewer trials and performed the problem-solving tasks much faster and more accurately than did the soldiers. However, upon analyzing the think-aloud protocols, one of the first things we realized was that for both high- and low-ability subjects, the problem-solving stages almost never occurred in linear order. It was especially common for the

TABLE 11.2. Proportion of Problem-Solving Time, for Six Word Problems, Spent in Major Categories of a General Problem-Solving Model

Group:	Clarify problem	Plan	Carry out plan	Check	Other
Army (n = 8)	44	7	36	3	10
College (n = 8)	41	2	49	3	5

higher-ability college students to begin calculating activity immediately upon scanning the problem statement, seemingly before the problem was fully understood. Furthermore, activity associated with major stages of the general model occurred throughout the solution process. For example, clarification behaviors would frequently occur toward the end of a problem-solving session as well as in the beginning. With this in mind, we proceeded to determine the percentage of total problem-solving time devoted by all subjects to the four general processing categories represented in the coding scheme. These data are summarized in Table 11.2.

As shown in Table 11.2, both soldiers and college students spent the preponderance of their time in verbalizations pertaining to problem clarification and carrying out their calculations, with a little time being devoted to monitoring and almost no time being devoted to overtly planning a strategy. Both groups appeared to carry on the same types of conscious activities. That is, most of their problem-solving time was devoted to alternate bouts with clarifying and calculating, with a small amount of time being devoted to conscious planning and checking. In sum, this analysis suggested that the lower-ability subjects were similar to higher-ability subjects, at least with respect to their general problem-solving schemes. Neither group followed the general problem-solving plan in an invariant, linear sequence.

Beyond this general level, however, there were obvious and critical differences between soldiers and college students, and some of these are illustrated by the two example protocols provided in the Appendix. As illustrated in these protocols, soldiers spent much more of their time in vocalizing or paraphrasing contiguous segments of the problem statement, while college subjects selected, chunked, and sometimes recoded segments of the problem. There was little in the way of verbalization explaining *why* the problems were broken down and viewed in certain ways; such decisions appeared to be spontaneous. Of course the ordering of these spontaneous chunking decisions did influence the choice and ordering of calculations, which were performed immediately as each chunk was created.

A comparison of errors made by soldiers and college subjects also was made. Both soldiers and college subjects sometimes missed or misinterpreted the problem goal, although soldiers committed this error more often. Only soldiers tended to completely ignore some of the important problem information. Given these errors, it was not surprising to discover that soldiers had more difficulty with selecting and sequencing appropriate calculations. Furthermore, despite the fact that all had previously passed a test of calculational competency, soldiers seemed to make many more errors in their calculations. One reason for calculation difficulties appeared to be faulty recording errors. That is, soldiers would sometimes calculate correctly but fail to save intermediate results in a systematic way. In addition, soldiers sometimes attached incorrect "labels" to the facts they did write down. These recording errors encouraged restarts and confusion, such that incorrect numbers were sometimes "plugged into" problem solutions that were otherwise correct. This is shown by the soldier's protocol in the Appendix.

Our essential conclusion was that the process of chunking problems into substructures, and the processes of developing and executing the calculational strategies, were intimately connected during performance. That is, "strategy" in problem solving partly boiled down to making decisions, during the solution process, about what piece of the problem to focus on and process next. Another significant aspect of strategy was deciding which pieces of the problem representation to write down and save in an extended memory. This sort of memory management was necessary because many intermediate processes were performed prior to knowing what information and numbers would be needed at a later point. Yet the limited capacities of subjects' working memories prevented them from holding in mind all potentially relevant details.

There appeared to be very few instances in which decisions about which chunk should be saved or processed next could have been derived from deliberate front-end planning. Both groups demonstrated a lack of willingness (or capability?) to work through an entire plan that would achieve the goal with certainty. Sometimes, in fact, little attention was paid the goal. This may explain why, in both ability groups, there were instances of carrying out entire solution strategies for an incorrect goal.

With respect to providing prescriptions for training, the analysis just outlined raised as many conundrums as it settled. Our first thought was to question the integrity of this nonreflective style as a basis for designing remedial training. Is it reasonable to recommend to poor problem solvers that they proceed without a plan, without analyzing the problem? We hesitated. High-ability problem solvers sometimes do proceed in this manner, presumably because the method saves time. But while this "reflexive" style of thinking was an efficient strategy when it produced a solution, sometimes it was not successful, even for the "experts." Our common sense kept telling us to slow the students down, to make them analyze.

Many such questions were left unanswered by our initial analyses. However, it is often the case with a real-world instructional development contract that research questions must temporarily be set aside so that a product can be developed and delivered on time. Prior to developing the package, we supplemented our own knowledge and findings by seeking advice on instructional content from recognized experts in the field of problem solving. The package we constructed was a fairly standard strategy-training program. And its performance evaluation produced the fairly typical findings, as I will now describe.

The JSEP problem-solving package is a self-paced module requiring less than seven hours' training and a minimum of instructor involvement. Like many extant problem-solving training programs, the JSEP package trains skills associated with stages of the general planning model. It concentrates largely on general strategies for clarifying a problem representation (e.g., breaking problem into subgoals; diagramming and labeling intermediate steps), since this was a deficit clearly spotted within the target population. Use of the program has been shown to enhance performance on the types of skills it actually trains (Derry & Kellis, 1986), and on the types of problems actually practiced. However, a presumed benefit of general strategies training is that it can help people reason about problems that are outside the training domain. We did not obtain this type of transfer in our study, and so conclude that general problem-solving skill per se cannot be improved as a function of using the JSEP package alone. Mayer (1986), as well as Pressley, Goodchild, Fleet, Zajchowski, and Evans (in press), notes that similar results are all too typical of many programs on the market today.

Reflexive, Schema-Based Processing: A Reconceptualization

The JSEP study was unable to demonstrate that training in general planning strategies can improve problem-solving capability. Importantly, the study raised serious doubts about the appropriateness of general planning schemes as process descriptions for either skilled or unskilled problem solving, at least in the arithmetic word-problem domain. In the JSEP study, neither low- nor high-ability subjects engaged in this form of planning. Rather, subjects selected and ordered operators during the so-called problem-clarification stage.

One possible explanation for this finding is that subjects were using means-ends analysis, although not as a planning strategy. When means-ends analysis is employed in the absence of front-end planning, the problem solver merely looks at the goal and the current problem state, and then selects an operator that appears to reduce the difference between them. This process is repeated until a solution is reached. In previous expert-novice studies conducted with adults and physics problems (e.g., Larkin, McDermott, Simon, & Simon, 1980; Simon & Simon, 1978), intelligent novices, who were unfamiliar with the subject domain, appeared to use a form of means-ends analysis. Means-ends analysis, like other general strategies, is a novice problem-solving approach that sometimes works in the absence of domain-specific knowledge.

In the word-problem domain, however, most older children and adults have acquired significant experience. Even poor problem solvers have attained a degree of "expertise" with real-world arithmetic, suggesting greater relevance of an expert performance model. Stemming from the classic chess studies of deGroot (1965), there has been growing awareness that pattern recognition must play an extremely important role in modeling expert problem-solving performance. Researchers working in various domains have observed that one essential, defining feature of expert problem solving is its heavy reliance on domain-specific schemata (e.g., Chase & Simon, 1973; Chi, Feltovich, & Glaser, 1981; Gallini, this volume, Chap. 10). In the context of problem solving, Sweller and Cooper (1985) define schemata as "mental constructs that allow patterns or configurations to be recognized as belonging to a previously learned category and which specify which moves are appropriate for that category." They characterize expert problem solving as a process of recognizing and operating upon schemata.

Unfortunately, there has been too little interest in examining the feasibility or wisdom of training students to employ expert schema-based processing. As Heller and Hungate (1985) have noted, the conventional goal of formal training is to promote competent novice performance, with the hope that some students will continue their development in specific domains to achieve a higher degree of expertise. However, Sweller and Cooper (1985) and Gick (1986) have argued that reliance upon novice strategies, such as means-ends analysis, may actually retard development of expert schema-based processing. General strategies like means-ends analysis do not require domain-specific schemata; thus, practice with these methods does not encourage acquisition of important prerequisites for expert performance.

A potentially fruitful direction for problem-solving research is to identify strategies and training methods that foster learning and expert use of domain-specific schemata. However, there is still much we do not understand regarding the nature of expert performance itself, and so a logical starting point for exploring these issues is to develop better models of expertise. Gick (1986), for one, has argued the need for more basic research on the nature of expert problem solving. To this end, workers in my laboratory currently are conducting a series of model-building studies. These studies have included a reanalysis of the JSEP protocol data, as well as collection and analysis of a new set of think-aloud data obtained from students in grades 5 and 7 (Derry, Hawkes, & Tsai, 1987).

Ericsson and Simon (1984) discuss how theoretical perspectives adopted for protocol analysis influence coding and interpretation of data. It is noted, therefore, that two theoretical perspectives have significantly influenced the coding and analysis schemes employed in these later studies. The first is a theory of set relationships, adapted from Marshall's schema theory (e.g.,

Marshall, Pribe, & Smith, 1987), which provides a system for identifying and defining the domain-specific schemata used during problem solving. Second, a view of how these schemata are employed during processing is derived from Anderson's (1983; Anderson, Boyle, Corbett, & Lewis, 1986) general theory of cognition. Prior to discussing the model-building work, relevant aspects of these theories will be overviewed.

Schema Patterns in Word Problems

To the extent that schema patterns are important in expert problem solving, any domain-specific performance theory must begin by identifying the core set of conceptual patterns that are recognized and employed by domain experts. Following Kintsch and Greeno (1985), Marshall (1985; Marshall et al., 1987), and others (e.g., Briars & Larkin, 1984; Riley, Greeno, & Heller, 1983), recent protocol analyses conducted in my laboratory assume that an important prerequisite skill for expert performance on word problems is the ability to recognize and manipulate certain relational schemata (see also Van Haneghan & Baker, this volume, Chap. 9). Relational schemata are here viewed as simple mental models representing nonarbitrary set relationships that frequently occur in arithmetic problem situations. For example, if John *had* six marbles but *gave away* three of them, this a change schema consisting of a start set, a transfer set, and a result set that is a later version of the start set. The applicability of a particular schema is believed to be indicated by semantic (rather than mathematical) features of the problem.

Solving single-relation word problems involves not only identifying relational schemata represented within the problem, but also attaching correct arithmetic operations to each. The choice among calculational attachments is determined only in part by recognizing the type of schema, as the student also must recognize which version of the relation is indicated, by identifying the position of the unknown. For example, if the unknown in problem 1, Figure 11.1, had been the start set (How much did John have?), then the correct arithmetic procedure would have been addition rather than subtraction.

Marshall has developed a detailed representation system for arithmetic word problems that includes five relational schemata: change, combine, compare, transform, and vary (Marshall, 1985; Marshall et al., 1987). The first four schemata in this list are basic variations on the part-whole relationship, and frequently are associated with the addition and subtraction operations. Multiplication and division are associated with vary, a structure based on the idea of proportion. This system is similar to representational schemes reported by numerous other word-problem researchers (e.g., Briars & Larkin, 1984; Derry, Hawkes, & Tsai, 1987; Kintsch & Greeno, 1985; Vergnaud, 1982, 1983), and has built on work previously conducted by Riley et al. (1983). Schema training based on Marshall's view has been shown to alter students' problem-classification behaviors, such that attention is focused on semantic

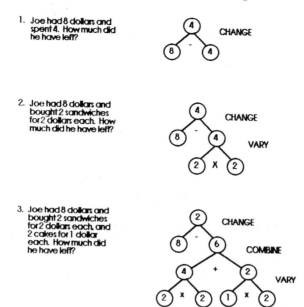

1. Joe had 8 dollars and spent 4. How much did he have left?

2. Joe had 8 dollars and bought 2 sandwiches for 2 dollars each. How much did he have left?

3. Joe had 8 dollars and bought 2 sandwiches for 2 dollars each, and 2 cakes for 1 dollar each. How much did he have left?

FIGURE 11.1. Problem representations illustrating concept of schema chaining.

relations rather than on surface features or operations. Moreover, mathematics textbooks that cover all five schemata appear to produce greater performance gains when compared with texts that concentrate on fewer schemata (Marshall, 1985).

Marshall et al. (1987) have demonstrated that in combination, these five basic concepts characterize a very large percentage of the word problems appearing in widely used prealgebra textbooks and adult-training materials. For example, the first problem in Figure 11.1 can be understood by instantiating a "change" schema. Problem 2 in the same figure is both a "change" and a "vary" problem. Problem 3 represents a more complex situation in which students must instantiate and combine four schemata: a "change," a "combine," and two "varies." This basic idea easily can be extended to encompass additional schemata and very complex problems containing four, five, or more schemata.

For most adults and older children, the solving of nonambiguous one-schema problems is not a difficult test. A learned pattern is encoded in working memory and an appropriate calculational response is activated. However, when a problem is complex, involving two or more schemata as in problems 2 and 3 of Figure 11.1, the solver must also be capable of linking multiple schemata together through common sets, such that a pathway to the goal is created. "Strategies" are required during complex problem solving, partly because the limits of working memory are easily exceeded by the multistep problem. This process is difficult, even for many adults, and is not well understood. A study by Stigler, Fuson, Ham, and Sook Kim (1986) revealed that American textbooks, unlike Soviet texts, currently concentrate on simple, one-step problems.

A General Theory for Strategy Research

ACT* (Anderson, 1983) and PUPS (Anderson et al., 1986) are versions of a general theory of cognition that is capable of modeling various ways in which students might use relational schemata in solving complex arithmetic word problems. Schumacher (1987) has argued that ACT* is a good integrative theory for research on cognitive strategies, since it can provide highly explicit descriptions of processes that simulate human metacognitive and executive functioning, constructs typically described in much more general terms.

A fundamental assumption of Anderson's ACT* and PUPS theories is that much of what is learned, particularly in school, is stored by long-term memory as either declarative or procedural knowledge. Declarative knowledge, which can be called "knowledge that," is exemplified by the networks of facts and ideas that people use to represent the external world. Procedural skills, or "knowledge how," are performance capabilities involving symbol manipulation, such as the ability to write a word or perform a calculation. Although not universally accepted (e.g., Rumelhart, McClellan, & the PDP Research Group, 1986; Rumelhart & Norman, 1981), the declarative versus procedural distinction is fundamental to a number of currently influential theories of learning and instruction (e.g., Anderson, 1983; E.D. Gagné, 1985; R.M. Gagné, 1985). These theories argue that procedural differs from declarative knowledge in a number of important ways. For one, the result of activating procedural knowledge is not simple recall, but operations upon and transformations of information. Whereas declarative knowledge is stored by long-term memory within idea networks believed to contain propositions and images, procedural skills often are viewed as condition-action rules, called productions (e.g., Anderson, 1983; E.D. Gagné, 1985). Importantly, procedural knowledge differs drastically from declarative knowledge in terms of the speed with which it is accessed and used. That is, performance guided by declarative knowledge is relatively slow and conscious, whereas well-learned procedural skills can rapidly be performed with less conscious effort or attention.

These distinctions are important because, in this chapter, "expertise" will be viewed as resulting from domain-specific systems of thought that are largely procedural, rather than declarative, in nature. In Anderson's procedural models, the basic unit of knowledge is represented as a production, which has an IF-clause specifying what conditional patterns must be recognized, and a THEN-clause specifying action sequences that are executed when conditions are met. E.D. Gagné (1985) describes two kinds of productions: pattern-recognition and action-sequence procedures. Pattern recognition underlies the human ability to perceive stereotypical stimulus patterns that are activated in working memory. Realizing, spontaneously, that a particular set of sentences in a word problem represents a vary situation is an example of pattern recognition. Action-sequence procedures, on the other hand, underlie the ability to carry out actions or sequences of operations. Actually carrying out the appropriate arithmetic operation on the vary schema involves action sequences. In order for action sequences to be useful, they should only be executed under certain appropriate conditions.

According to Anderson, the subject interacts with the environment such that features of that environment (e.g., stimulus characteristics of a word problem) are encoded as declarative knowledge into working memory. Through spread of activation, various nodes in declarative memory are activated, creating patterns that set up conditions alerting certain productions. Assuming the subject is sufficiently motivated to perform, a production is executed whenever the declarative knowledge activated in a person's working memory creates the conditional pattern that matches that production. For example, if a learned pattern associated with error conditions is activated, an error-checking routine might be called. Since productions typically operate upon and transform the representation in working memory (or add to it), the result of firing one set of productions may create the conditions for firing of others, and so forth. Many variations in behavior can be simulated in a production system, since productions can be fired in many different sequential orders, depending upon the conditional patterns encoded during problem solving.

Although pattern recognition serves as a mainspring that propels many important problem-solving decisions, some patterns can be imprecise and may simultaneously activate many different productions. Thus, there must be mechanisms for conflict resolution. Anderson has proposed a number of principles for conflict resolution, some of them being data-driven rules. For example, if there is variance in the degree of match to conditions of competing productions, the best match is automatically chosen. Also, the strongest productions are chosen, representing the most practiced, familiar reactions to patterns.

In addition to data-driven processing, Anderson's systems also orchestrate problem-solving performance with the assistance of top-down, goal-directed plans. During processing, there are productions that respond to patterns by setting goals, subgoals, or entire plans that contain multiple goals and subgoals. The goal in effect during any cycle of processing will determine or influence the system's choice of cognitive actions. While executing, Anderson's production systems also can temporarily set aside subgoals for which too little knowledge is currently available, and return to those subgoals after sufficient information has accrued. For example, suppose the first pattern recognized by the problem solver is a combine schema. The system would set a goal to instantiate the schema and carry out the appropriate calculation. If two of the schema's three sets are known, the appropriate operations can be executed to obtain the value for the empty set. However, if three or more set values cannot be obtained from the problem statement, the system must either (a) postpone the combine calculation until a needed set is encountered; or (b) set a subgoal to search for a schema that can calculate the needed set.

In sum, using Anderson's theory, it is possible to develop a problem-solving system comprised of processing agencies that: (a) monitor working memory for the activation of basic conceptual patterns; (b) reflexively select and execute learned responses to the conceptual patterns activated by stimuli encoded in working memory; and (c) set goals and plans to guide the general direction of processing. Although production systems can neither model all aspects of human behavior, such as parallel processing, nor represent the important influence that motivation and effort have upon the human process, the production view of procedural knowledge is adequate for explaining many of the human problem-solving strategies that have been observed in my laboratory.

Toward a Better Model of Problem-Solving Strategy

The modeling study to be overviewed in this section represents a recent attempt to understand how successful and unsuccessful problem solvers construct and operate upon complex problem representations. Conclusions are based in part on a reanalysis of the previously described JSEP data, which were recoded and interpreted in terms of the framework provided by Anderson's theory and by relational schema theory (e.g., Anderson, 1983; Marshall, 1987). Similar analyses were performed on think-aloud data for three complex word problems, which were obtained from 16 fifth and seventh graders enrolled at the Florida State University Research School. These students were selected by testing and teacher nomination to represent a range of ability levels. The data-collection procedures were similar to those used for the college subjects and Army recruits in the JSEP study described previously.

Protocols from both data sets were coded to reveal stages of a comprehension process whereby basic schema patterns are recognized and responses are executed. Specifically, our coding system permitted us to (a) identify sets perceived by the subject; (b) identify the relational schemata constructed with these sets; (c) represent the combining of basic set relations into higher-order schemata; and (d) represent calculational attachments and other operators executed in response to schema recognition. This coding scheme seemed natural, provided good fit to the protocol data, and exhibited fairly high reliability (see Derry et al. (1987) for further details).

The logic of this coding procedure can be understood in terms of Figure 11.2, a tree diagram illustrating the most common representations constructed for "the apartments problem," one of the problems presented to the school pupils. One goal of the study was to develop a process model of how such structures are built. The nature of this construction process is illustrated

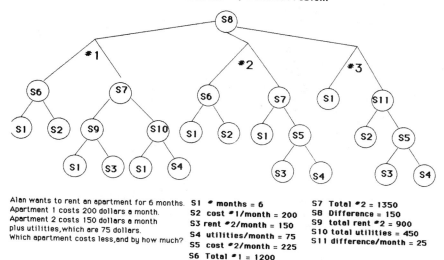

Solution Tree for Apartment Problem

Alan wants to rent an apartment for 6 months.
Apartment 1 costs 200 dollars a month.
Apartment 2 costs 150 dollars a month
plus utilities, which are 75 dollars.
Which apartment costs less, and by how much?

S1 * months = 6
S2 cost *1/month = 200
S3 rent *2/month = 150
S4 utilities/month = 75
S5 cost *2/month = 225
S6 Total *1 = 1200

S7 Total *2 = 1350
S8 Difference = 150
S9 total rent *2 = 900
S10 total utilities = 450
S11 difference/month = 25

FIGURE 11.2. Tree representing all feasible solution strategies.

by the characteristic "expert" protocol (a seventh grader) for the apartments problem, shown in Table 11.3. A comparison of this student's protocol with the problem structure in Figure 11.2 confirms that the subject is gradually building a problem representation, pausing along the way to perform calculations. This protocol illustrates several key features that were observed in many protocols obtained from both children and young adults (see Derry et al. 1987). These are described now.

As hypothesized, subjects do appear to chunk problems during problem solving by connecting problem sets together, giving them roles in basic relational schemata. For example, the seventh-grader working the apartments problem (Table 11.3) conceptualizes the monthly cost of apartment 2 by instantiating a combine relation containing three sets: monthly rent + monthly utilities = monthly cost. Such basic relational schemata can compute an unknown set value whenever a pattern exists such that all of its set values can be determined from existing data (in this example, at least two set values must be known). When a computable relation is in working memory, a calculational attachment is made immediately (unless the calculation is avoided due to its difficulty). The overall modus operandi of problem solving can be described as follows: build relational schema 1: calculate subgoal: build relational schema 2: calculate subgoal 2 . . . build final goal schema, calculate goal.

Because common sets appear in various relations within a problem, individual relational schemata are joined together into an overall problem

TABLE 11.3. "Expert" Seventh Grader Solving Apartments Problem

Subject:	(Reads problem) Alan wants to rent an apartment for 6 months. Apartment 1 costs \$200 a month. Apartment 2 costs 150 a month plus utilities, which are \$75. Which apartment costs less, and by how much? And by how much? OK, apartment number one costs \$200. 150 plus 75, Apartment 2 would be \$225. And the other one, I mean apartment 1 is only \$200, so apartment 1 would be less and by how much? By \$25 a month.
Instructor:	OK, hummm . . .
Subject:	But if it's 6 months, \$200 times 6 is . . . \$1200 for 6 months, \$1200. And, hummm, 225 for 6 months would be 225 times 6 is (works on paper) 1350. OK, 1350 minus 1200 is (works on paper) 150. OK, so it would be 150 more.

structure through a process called "chaining." Subjects appear to use different strategies for choosing the order in which they chunk, calculate, and chain schemata. One strategy involves no planning whatsoever. The subject merely sets a goal to find and operate upon any schema that becomes obvious. This "lazy" form of schema-based processing may continue until the problem solver "happens" upon the goal. This strategy is referred to as "reflexive forward chaining," because the problem solver appears to "react" to patterns, roughly in the order that they are given in the actual problem statement. This strategy can work quite well when there are a limited number of possible pathways to the goal and if there are no irrelevant schemata. When problem conditions are appropriate, this is an intelligent approach in the sense that it requires the least amount of effort. Both experts and novices sometimes use this approach.

Some problem situations do not permit a strategy based entirely on reflexive forward chaining. It is often the case that a spontaneously perceived relational schema is not immediately computable because some prerequisite set values are unknown. For example, the subject in Table 11.3 appears to recognize the following relation before it can be computed: Cost of apartment 2 for 6 months minus cost of apartment 1 for 6 months equals the savings realized by renting apartment 1. Although the monthly costs of both apartments are knowns, the full costs for 6 months must be computed before the relation can yield a set value. When this situation occurs, the problem solver may either (a) set subgoals to find lower-level schemata that will compute the missing set values of the higher-level schema, or (b) attempt to avoid this backward chaining effort by setting the higher-level schema aside until the needed set values are obtained incidentally. The problem solver in Table 11.3 opts for the backward search strategy.

When the problem solver sets a subgoal to obtain needed set values for a higher-level schema, a deliberate search for a lower-level computing schema is inaugurated. Sometimes it is the case that when the lower-level schema is located, it also will not be computable. In this case, a subsubgoal must be set and a search for an even lower-level schema is initiated. When relational schemata are chained together in this manner for the purpose of computing a missing set value, a complex intermediate schema is formed. Such intermediate schemata take the form of "little plans" that involve backward chaining from a subgoal. It is not surprising that many subjects tend to avoid constructing complex subgoal structures, since holding several schemata in mind at once places a significant burden on working memory. However, building such structures may be the major mechanism for acquiring complex domain-specific patterns that combine several relational schemata.

Using a pseudocode notation that omits technical detail, the schematic of a production system that can emulate human word-problem performance is shown in Table 11.4. As in all production systems, the processing in this model proceeds in cycles from top to bottom. Whenever the IF-condition on the left side of a production fails to match the current state of working memory, that production is ignored and scanning proceeds to the next production. However, when the current state of working memory is matched, the action on the right side of the production is executed and processing then returns to the top production as a new cycle begins. One exception to this rule is when the system sets a goal or a subgoal: in these cases processing continues with the next production.

On each cycle, the system in Table 11.4 first ascertains that a problem exists, that the goal has not been satisfied. Problem solving then proceeds by searching for a pattern that matches a schema in long-term memory. Procedures for matching semantic cues in problem statements to set relations in long-term memory have been worked out by Kintsch and Greeno (1985) and by Marshall et al. (1987), and are not detailed here. A schema must be found in order for problem solving to proceed. If a schema match is found, a calculation is performed if the schema is computable. If the schema is not computable, either a subgoal search is initiated for missing set values, or the schema is temporarily set aside, eligible for later recall. Processing returns to the top production (P1) after a schema has temporarily been set aside, or after either a successful or unsuccessful subgoal search. If the goal has been attained, processing stops. If the goal has not been attained and if working memory is filled during any of these processes, the problem solver discards and/or records information from working memory. Processing then proceeds by finding or constructing additional schemata and performing calculations. Cycles continue until the goal is obtained or until the system can no longer locate new schema patterns.

Although some details must still be worked out, the model clearly suggests numerous performance goals for training. It seems clear that performance is facilitated by knowledge of schemata for basic set relations and for higher-

TABLE 11.4.   An ACT Type Production System for Multistep Arithmetic Word Problems

Production #	If clause (condition)	Then clause (response)
P1	If value of goal set computed	Write answer; stop.
P2	If memory overload	Record/discard information. Continue.
P3	If no schema, unsatisfied schema or failed schema	Set goal: find new level 1 schema.
P4	If level 1 schema not found	Give up; stop.
P5	If level 1 schema in WM has 1 unknown	Compute unknown.
P6	If level 1 schema has unknowns > 1	Either: set subgoals for all missing sets 1 . . X, and call subgoal production. Or set schema aside, eligible for later recall.
Subgoal Production		
P7	If memory overload	Record or discard information. Continue.
P8	If all but one level 1 subgoal found	Exit production.
P9	If more than one subgoal not found	Set goal: find level 2 schema for any unknown subgoal set 1 . . X.
P10	If level 2 schema has 1 unknown	Compute subgoal, record, and label.
P11	If level 2 schema has > 2 unknowns	Call subsubgoal production for subsubgoals 1 . . X.
P12	If level 2 schema not found	Make failed schema ineligible, exit.
Subsubgoal Production		
P13	If memory overload	Discard or record information. Continue.
P14	If all but one subsubgoal found	Exit production.
P15	If more than 1 subsubgoal not found	Set goal: find level 3 schema for any unknown subsubgoal. Set 1 . . X.
P16	If level 3 schema has 1 unknown	Compute subsubgoal, record, and label.
P17	If level 3 schema has 2 unknowns	Return to low-eligible schema. Exit to P1.
P18	If level 3 schema not found	Return failed schema.

order combinations. Schema knowledge includes not only the ability to recognize basic relations, but also the ability to attach correct arithmetic operations. It also seems clear that problem solving requires strategies for combining schemata through their common set relations, a capability here labeled "chaining skill." There are metacognitive goals for instruction as well. The system in Table 11.4 includes a number of productions that represent human metacognitive knowledge: memory management, goal checking, a rule for recognizing an overly complex solution path, and at least the need for a rule that chooses between two alternative chaining strategies. The model also possesses a certain degree of error-checking capability. In Figure 11.3, these problem-solving capabilities are organized into an abbreviated hierarchy representing an expert knowledge model.

Instruction for the Acquisition of Expertise

Anderson (1983) believes that the skills associated with a problem-solving domain can be learned initially as declarative knowledge, but must be changed by use into procedural encodings (assuming expert performance is desired). For example, an initial step in learning how to choose and conduct a chaining strategy might be to memorize chaining rules. If these rules were used often in practice, they eventually would become proceduralized. Proceduralization is a form of encoding that reduces the need for conscious interrogation of declarative memory, and increases capability for automatic, reflexive response. The nature of this procedural learning process and instructional implications will briefly be considered for both pattern-recognition and action-sequence procedures.

Pattern recognition

Many pattern-recognition skills are required in the word-problem domain, including the abilities to recognize examples of relational schemata and to perceive problem-solving situations that indicate applicability of metacognitive procedures. Two important processes in learning such patterns are generalization and discrimination (e.g., Anderson, 1983). E.D. Gagné (1985) maintains that there is much a teacher can do to facilitate generalization and discrimination in pattern recognition. One currently accepted procedure is to provide intensive pattern-identification practice with corrective feedback, while carefully controlling the practice examples that are given to students. To promote generalization and transfer of a pattern, example problems should be varied widely on those attributes that are irrelevant to the definition of the pattern, while relevant attributes that define the pattern are held constant across examples. For example, in teaching students to generalize the combine schema, problems could be presented that vary the position of the unknown and the problem context, while holding constant the presence of supersets and subsets, the essential defining characteristics of combine. On the other hand, to promote more accurate pattern discrimination, practice examples should hold constant the irrelevant attributes, while varying those attributes that most clearly define the to-be-learned patterns. For example, to help a child distinguish a problem that will require memory management from one that will not, two example problems might both deal with the same objects and contexts, but be varied in degree of complexity.

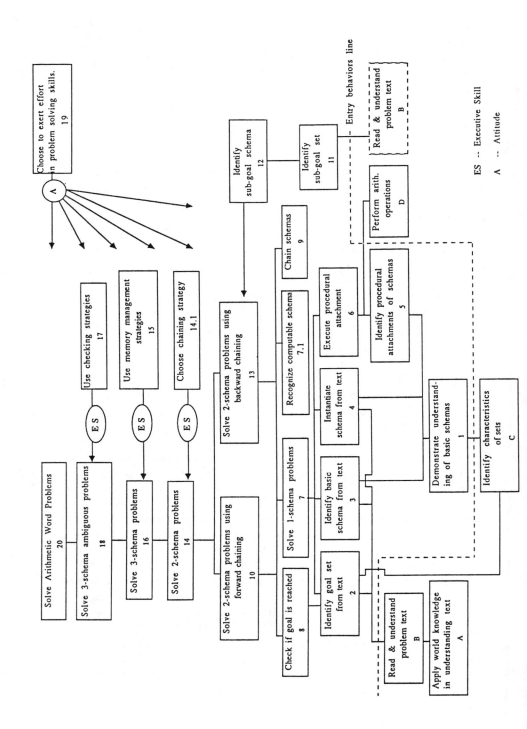

Another procedure for schema training has been investigated by Sweller and Cooper (1985; Cooper & Sweller, 1987), who suggest that having students study worked examples as they practice problem solving improves schema learning and induces automaticity. Presumably, worked examples decrease cognitive load during initial learning, so that more available resources are devoted to learning about problem structures. In studies by these researchers, worked-example groups consistently outperformed conventional practice groups on several performance measures.

COMBINING PATTERN RECOGNITION WITH ACTION SEQUENCES

One important type of action sequence in word-problem solving is ability to carry out arithmetic operations associated with relational schemata. Another example is the ability to link relational schemata through their common sets. According to Anderson's theory (1983; Anderson et al., 1986; E.D. Gagné, 1985), these types of procedural skills are learned in three phases. The initial phase is to create a declarative representation for each step in the procedure. For example, the learner might first learn to perform memory management decisions by memorizing rules, which can then be used as a performance guide. At this novice stage, performance is slow and prone to error.

As the learner attempts to execute and practice the procedure, performance gradually becomes faster and more accurate. This performance change indicates that a new form of memory code is evolving. The process of changing from a declarative to a performance-based representation is called knowledge compilation, and involves two subprocesses: proceduralization and composition. Proceduralization is the creating of mental productions, procedural encodings that no longer rely heavily on step-by-step cues from declarative knowledge. The third learning phase, composition, involves combining elementary productions together, to create larger, more efficient action sequences.

An initial step in this combining process is to bring action sequences together with their appropriate pattern-recognition procedures. That pattern recognition is a prerequisite for cognitive skills use also has been emphasized by metacognitive researchers (e.g., Bransford, Franks, Vye, & Sherwood, 1986; Paris, Cross, & Lipson, 1984; Pressley, Borkowski, & O'Sullivan, 1984). For example, Campione, Brown, and Ferrara (1982) helped popularize "informed training," the practice of enhancing cognitive skills instruction

◄

FIGURE 11.3. Abbreviated hierarchy of component skills required for solving arithmetic word problems.

with explicit information about when and where to employ those skills that are trained. However, informed training of individual problem-solving skills is only a beginning point, since direct, didactic instruction stops short of producing expertise. Problem-solving skills acquired through direct instruction are encoded as declarative knowledge, which must be interrogated consciously during performance. This tends to direct students' attention to processing steps that eventually must be executed without conscious thought. By contrast, expert problem solvers make rapid and flexible problem-solving decisions, indicating a high degree of proceduralization and automaticity at all levels within their domain-specific skill "bureaucracies" (Minsky, 1985).

Schneider (1985) suggests that computer drills be designed to proceduralize specific component subskills associated with a domain, and that these be alternated with "whole" drills requiring students to combine various subskills into higher-order thinking systems. Since intelligent problem-solving strategy emerges from a complex systematic interplay among many cognitive subskills, it seems likely that expertise will develop only if a great variety of problem-solving subskills are sharpened as individual entities and then combined in various practice exercises. This is the kind of practice environment provided by real-world experience. However, Schneider (1985) points out that automaticity of even simple subskills can require thousands of practice trials, while expertise in complex skills often develops slowly through repeated use over an entire lifespan. Lesgold (1988) argues that real-world experience can be a poor teacher, since the right problem situations do not happen frequently enough to promote learning of all needed subskill combinations.

In my opinion, deliberate engineering of problem-solving expertise is a complex educational problem that begs for a technological solution. Only through the application of advanced technology to the design of instruction will it become possible to substantially increase students' opportunities for practice, while also arranging an appropriate sequence of high-quality practice experiences. The following section describes an application of advanced technology for the word-problem domain, which is being developed at Florida State University (see also Lehrer, this volume, Chap. 12).

The TAPS Tutoring System

The TAPS (Training Arithmetic Problem-Solving Skills) Tutor (e.g., Derry, Hawkes, & Ziegler, 1988; Hawkes, Derry, & Ziegler, 1987) is an intelligent computer-based system being designed to help students acquire the skill hierarchy of Figure 11.3 at an expert level of performance. This tutor is best characterized as a plan-based opportunistic system, because it both develops an individualized practice plan for each student, and offers individualized coaching triggered by student performance. Wenger (1987) distinguished plan-based tutoring architectures from opportunistic teaching systems, noting that almost all extant intelligent tutors are based on opportunistic designs. The basic philosophy of opportunistic tutoring is "learn-by-doing" (Sleeman & Brown, 1982; Park, Perez, & Seidel, 1987). Thus, all didactic intervention is triggered by circumstances that occur while a student is engaged in problem solving. Despite the power and appeal of intelligent opportunistic tutoring, the ITS movement can be criticized for its lack of attention to such matters as instructional design theory and knowledge structure. Park et al. (1987) note that developers of intelligent tutors have largely ignored task analysis, which attempts to identify the skills that underlie performance and the pedagogically relevant relations among them. Peachey and McCalla (1986) and Wenger (1987) call for development of systems that constrain the range of student experiences with planning based on task analysis. Our project addresses this issue with the TAPS tutor, which is based on the analysis of problem solving described in this chapter, and which combines the capabilities of global planning with local opportunistic tutoring.

NATURE OF DIDACTIC PLANNING

In plan-based instructional systems (e.g., Peachey & McCalla, 1986; Breuker, Winkels, & Sandberg, 1987), didactic decisions are driven primarily by domain knowledge models rather than by operational models of performance. Thus, an early step in designing our tutor was to construct a model of the expert's knowledge. This model delineates the knowledge components, or capabilities, that presumably are engaged during expert performance. Our model also describes the hierarchical interactions among model components, since some higher-order systems in the model are dependent upon prerequisite learning of other lower-order model components. An abbreviated version of the expert knowledge model resulting from our studies has been provided as Figure 11.3.

Given this expert model, individual student models are expressed in terms of the knowledge components of the expert model. Assessment procedures have been developed to help determine which of the expert components are either missing from a student's model, or should be represented as being weak, or "buggy." Common misconceptions may be associated with the domain, and if these can be identified through further research, misconceptions also may appear in some student models. In the TAPS tutoring system, individual student models will be stored in a temporal relational data base, an innovation that is not described further in this chapter.

The aim of tutoring is conceived as the task of operating on the student knowledge model until it evolves into the expert knowledge model. The TAPS system will accomplish this by building an individualized plan with the instructional goals of adding missing knowledge components to the student model, strengthening existing ones, correcting buggy ones, or eliminating troublesome misconceptions. The structure of the expert knowledge model constrains the order in which these goals must be taught, since it specifies which lower-level components are required as prerequisites for higher-level learning and performance.

PLANNING BY EXPERIENCED MASTER TEACHERS

Observational research by Leinhardt and Greeno (1986) has shown that experienced master teachers employ hierarchical planning in accomplishing their goals. At the most global level, the teacher is guided by a master operational plan called an "agenda." This agenda assembles and organizes goals and operators, and can be tuned and revised during instruction. At a less global level, master teachers also plan lessons. These are characterized in general terms as "action schemata" which use various lower-order "routines." Routines are "small, socially scripted pieces of behavior that are known by both teachers and students," and that are shared by many classroom activities. An important major distinction between expert and novice teachers is that experts possess a much larger array of these "canned" routines. Expert teachers are sometimes observed teaching new routines to their students.

Inspired by the expert teachers observed in studies by Leinhardt and Greeno (1986), we have designed our tutor to carry out three levels of instructional activity: planning an individual's route through the problem-solving curriculum (the agenda); planning practice exercises (using action schemata and routines); and on-line tutorial intervention. At each of these instructional levels, data pertaining to student performance can be collected and made available for use by other levels.

THE CURRICULUM PLANNER

For each student, curriculum planning will begin by establishing that student's current achievement goals. To determine these, the student must be tested on skills in the knowledge model (Figure 11.3), beginning at the lowest prerequisite level. On each assessed skill, the student's level of expertise is classified. In our work we employ the concepts of nonmaster (cannot perform skill), novice master (performs accurately but slowly), and expert (performs rapidly and accurately). If expertise is attained on all skills at one horizontal level in the hierarchy, the testing continues at the next horizontal level and continues until a level is reached where deficiencies are found.

Setting achievement goals is at first conceptually simple. At horizontal level 1 (recall that Figure 11.3 is an abbreviated hierarchy, with skill box 1 actually representing a class of skills), the tutor will set for each skill a performance goal that is an increment above the student's current level. For example, if the student is performing at the level of novice mastery on the skill "understand change schema," the tutor will set a goal for the student to reach an expert level on that skill. This goal-setting heuristic can be stated as follows: Curriculum Planning Rule 1: For any assessed skill, the achievement goal for that skill is set at one level above the currently assessed achievement level.

In addition to setting goals for all eligible skills within a horizontal level, a planner should also set all possible instructional goals for moving vertically from one horizontal level to another. This idea can be stated as follows: Curriculum Planning Rules 2 and 3: A performance goal can be set for any nonassessed higher-level skill that represents a combination of assessed lower-level prerequisite competencies, provided that all involved prerequisite competencies have been mastered at the novice level. The performance goal for the combined skill is set at the maximum possible achievement level that does not exceed the lowest performance goal attained for any single prerequisite competency. For example, if a student has achieved novice competency on skill 4.1 (instantiating change-schema problems) and an expert level of competency on prerequisite skill 6.1 (calculational attachments to change schemata), the achievement goal for the next-higher competency that combines these skills (e.g., instantiating change problems and attaching procedures) cannot exceed novice mastery.

Goal setting becomes conceptually more complicated as the student progresses through the curriculum, since the student will soon be exhibiting multiple levels of performance in different parts of the hierarchy. However, the original goal-setting heuristics can continue to manage movement through the curriculum. These heuristics constrain one another in a convenient manner. The vertical rules cannot set a goal too high because they are constrained by Rule 1. The current achievement goals set by the curriculum planner are recorded in the student's permanent record and remain eligible for that student until they are changed by the planner. Goals are updated after each practice session.

THE LESSON PLANNER AND EXAMPLE INSTRUCTIONAL ROUTINE

The lesson planner selects a lesson goal from the student's currently eligible achievement goals, and then plans a practice drill designed to accomplish a selected goal. As with Leinhardt and Greeno's (1986) expert teachers, the lesson planner eventually will be able to call upon various tutorial routines, which have the capability of teaching these routines to the student.

To illustrate, we are now working on a routine called "Show Me," which has both novice and expert variations. The main purpose of Show Me is to develop schema-chaining strategies, but it also can be used for developing self-monitoring and memory-management skills. In addition, the routine should promote awareness of problem structure—a problem's underlying schemata and how they are joined through common sets. The routine uses a worked-examples approach whereby the student studies and models an expert solution (Cooper & Sweller, 1987; Sweller & Cooper, 1985). Also, in the manner of Collins and Brown (1988), actual tree diagrams are created for each solution, providing explicit representations of problem-solving strategies that can

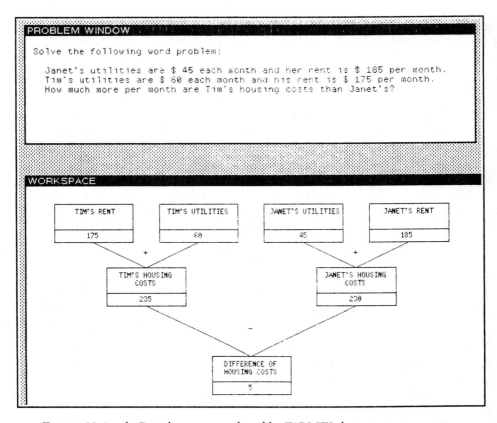

FIGURE 11.4. a–b: Partial screens produced by TAPS ITS during tutoring sessions.

be studied and emulated by students. A system expert illustrates for the student how to solve a word problem by constructing a diagrammatic tree representation. An example of a system expert's tree solution, as presented to the student in the workspace window of a Xerox 1186 screen, is shown in Figure 11.4(a).

Following the expert's demonstration, the student is then presented with a different problem and asked to model the expert's performance by using the system's problem-solving tools. A partial student solution for "the car problem" is shown in Figure 11.4(b), and some of the tools that are used by the student to build the solution are shown in Figure 11.4(c). In Show Me these tools include a set of empty problem schemata that can be dragged by the student to the workspace [Figure 11.4(c)], and a set of labels and operators generated by the system's expert which the student may use if desired. Coaching occurs while the student builds a solution tree [Figure 11.4(d)].

The lesson planner will not only determine when the Show Me routine will be selected for use, but also will develop the particular version of Show Me

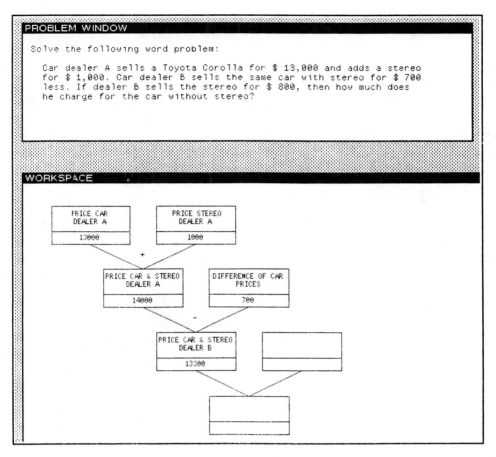

```
PROBLEM WINDOW

Solve the following word problem:

    Car dealer A sells a Toyota Corolla for $ 13,000 and adds a stereo
    for $ 1,000. Car dealer B sells the same car with stereo for $ 700
    less. If dealer B sells the stereo for $ 800, then how much does
    he charge for the car without stereo?



WORKSPACE
```

FIGURE 11.4b.

that will be given in the lesson. One decision that the planner must make is selection of problems that the student will receive. Problems are represented in the system by templates, which are stored in a data base called a problem bank, and which are used to generate the problems requested by the lesson planner. Sets of templates are classified according to the number and type of relational schemata represented. For example, one set of templates is for the one-combine, one-vary problem; another is for the one-vary, one-compare problem, etc. In addition, information regarding other task variables known to influence problem difficulty and interest, such as position of the unknowns and the story context, is also present in the problem bank. Thus the lesson planner will be able to request problems of a specific type and range for the lesson. For example, the planner could request two-schema "difficult" problems that do not employ the vary schema and that are presented in the context of stories pertaining to sports or space fantasy.

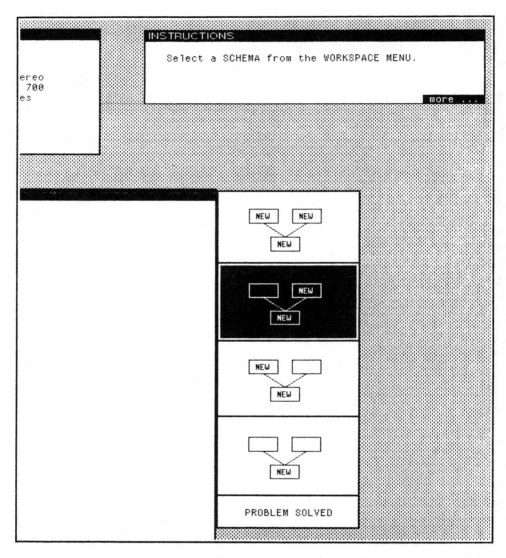

FIGURE 11.4c.

Other decisions to be made by the lesson planner include determination of the particular version of Show Me that will be implemented. Different versions are created, depending upon whether the system is intending to promote novice mastery or expertise. In general, when novice mastery is the goal, students receive easier problems that are isomorphic or very similar to those demonstrated by the expert. Also, the lesson provides a great deal of "scaffolding" (e.g., Palincsar, 1986) in the sense that more tutorial support and

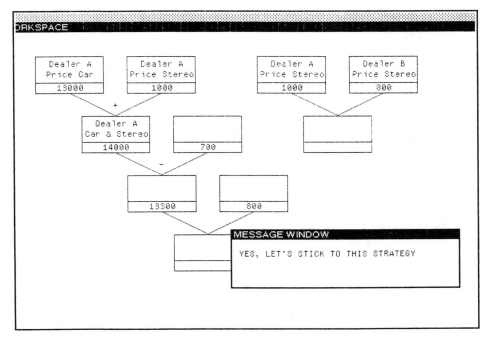

FIGURE 11.4d.

graphic reification are supplied during problem solving. However, when the goal is development of expertise, there is less tutoring and less reliance on graphic scaffolding. Moreover, students are given difficult problems that are structurally different from those demonstrated by the expert, for the purpose of promoting transfer.

INTERVENING MONITOR

Once the lesson is planned and presented on the screen, control is passed to the intervening monitor, designed to observe the student's performance and make specific tutorial interventions. The intervening monitor obtains input from the lesson planner concerning the routine and variations that have been chosen for the lesson plan. Also, the monitor obtains information regarding the student's expected level of achievement for the target skill (either novice mastery or expert), which is used to set an intervention frequency level. If the student is working toward novice mastery, a higher intervention frequency is set than if the student is working toward expertise. At highest intervention levels, students are prompted whenever stimulus conditions indicate applicability of the target action sequences that are being taught. However, as the student gains in expertise, tutorial prompts become less obtrusive and gradually are phased out. By lowering intervention frequencies at later stages of learning, the tutor attempts to encourage self-monitoring, such as error checking and repair.

The monitor observes the user's progress in performing the lesson's problem-solving tasks by comparing student responses to a tree of all acceptable solution paths generated by the expert solutions module (this module has been implemented but will not be discussed here). By comparing the student's solution moves to those recognized by a solutions tree, the monitor is able to obtain on-line observations of such behaviors as how long the student takes to accomplish various parts of the task (a time measure), how frequently the student alters responses (a certainty measure), as well as correctness in schema choices, operators, path, and memory-management decisions. We are attempting to develop the monitor in two parts, one to tutor the lower-level errors (e.g., an incorrect schema is selected) and one for higher-level error patterns. The tutoring of lower-level errors can be implemented in a straightforward manner using production rules that work with the solution tree. The tutoring based on error models is more esoteric. From lower-level measures of time, uncertainty, and correctness, the monitor will calculate how closely the student's performance matches patterns of error exhibited by prototype problem solvers. Four poor problem-solver types and corresponding behavior patterns have thus far been identified: the trial-and-error solver; the wild-goose chaser; the poor memory manager; and the poor calculator (see Derry et al., 1987). Our plan is to associate each prototype with an intervention strategy. However, prototypical error patterns must be investigated further.

Monitoring and intervention continue until the user arrives at a correct answer. A rating is then made of the student's performance, which indicates the current difficulty of the routine. If the rating is within an acceptable range (neither too easy nor too difficult), then the lesson continues according to the current plan. If the difficulty rating is not acceptable, then a lesson repair routine is attempted. When the lesson is completed, performance data are summarized for each problem and the monitor makes a final assessment of the student's performance, which is sent to the student record. If the lesson's achievement goal was clearly attained, the curriculum planner is called to update the list of the student's current available achievement goals. If the goal was not attained, the current eligible achievement goals remain unchanged.

Concluding Comments

Experts solve problems by identifying relational schemata, by attaching correct operations, and by chaining schemata to form complex problem representations that lead to solutions. "Strategies" are employed in constructing complex problem representations, partly because the limits of working memory are often exceeded while the problem is being solved.

Problem solving possibly can be improved to the level of "informed novice" by directly training poor problem solvers to use the skills and strategies employed by high-ability students. However, highly intelligent problem solving is characterized by features that distinguish it from accurate novice performance. Expert problem solving is faster, more intuitive, relatively accurate, and is characterized by a high degree of subskill automaticity and flexible combining of subskills.

It must be recognized that strategic problem-solving ability cannot be developed quickly and easily, or by direct instruction alone. Even in the relatively simple performance domain of arithmetic problem solving, strategic-thinking ability is dependent upon an intricate structure of prerequisite skills, which must operate together with great flexibility in various combinations. The interactional flexibility that characterizes true expert performance may be realizable only through long-term intensive practice with appropriately engineered problem-solving experiences, whereby many different subskills are combined in many different ways. Recent trends toward the integration of cognitive science with instructional technology research should enhance our capabilities for handling such complicated learning problems.

Acknowledgments. This work was partially supported by NSF Grant No. IST851094. The author wishes to acknowledge substantial contributions by Co-PI Lois Hawkes to the ITS project described in this manuscript.

REFERENCES

Anderson, J.R. (1983). *The architecture of cognition.* Cambridge, MA: Harvard University Press.

Anderson, J.R., Boyle, C.F., Corbett, A.T., & Lewis, M.W. (1986). *Cognitive modelling and intelligent tutoring* (Tech. Rep. No. ONR-86-1). Pittsburgh: Carnegie-Mellon University.

Baron, J. (1981). Reflective thinking as a goal of education. *Intelligence, 5,* 291–309.

Baron, J., Badgio, P.C., & Gaskins, I.W. (1986). Cognitive style and its improvement: A normative approach. In R.J. Sternberg (Ed.) *Advances in the Psychology of Human Intelligence, 3.* (pp.172–220). Hillsdale, NJ: Erlbaum & Associates.

Belmont, J.M., Butterfield, E.C., & Ferretti, R.P. (1982). To secure transfer of training instruct self-management skills. In D.K. Detterman & R.J. Sternberg (Eds.), *How and how much can intelligence be increased* (pp. 147–154). Norwood, NJ: Ablex.

Bransford, J.D., Franks, J.J., Vye, N.J., & Sherwood, R.D. (June 1986). *New approaches to instruction: Because wisdom can't be told.* Paper presented at conference on Similarity and Analogy, University of Illinois, Urbana-Champaign, IL.

Bransford, J.D., & Stein, B.S. (1984). *The ideal problem solver: A guide for improving thinking, learning, and creativity.* New York: Freeman.

Briars, D.J., & Larkin, J.H. (1984). An integrated model of skill in solving elementary word problems. *Cognition and Instruction, 1,* 245–296.

Brown, A.L. (1978). Knowing when, where and how to remember: A problem of metacognition. In R. Glaser (Ed.), *Advances in instructional psychology*, Vol. 7 (pp. 55–113). Hillsdale, NJ: Erlbaum & Associates.

Breuker, J., Winkels, R., & Sandberg, J. (1987). Coaching strategies for help systems: EUROHELP. Abstracts of the Third International Conference on Artificial Intelligence and Education (p. 16). Pittsburgh: Learning Research and Development Center, University of Pittsburgh.

Campione, J.C., Brown, A.L., & Ferrara, R.A. (1982). Mental retardation and intelligence. In R.J. Sternberg (Ed.), *Handbook of human intelligence* (pp. 392–490). Cambridge, England: Cambridge University Press.

Chase, W.G., & Simon, H.A. (1973). Perception in chess. *Cognitive Psychology, 4,* 55–81.

Chi, M., Feltovich, P., & Glaser, R. (1981). Categorization and representation of physics problems by experts and novices. *Cognitive Science, 5,* 121–152.

Collins, A. & Brown, J.S. (1988). The computer as a tool for learning through reflection. In H. Mandl and A. Lesgold (Eds.) *Learning issues for intelligent tutoring systems* (pp. 1–18). New York: Springer-Verlag.

Cooper, G., & Sweller, J. (1987). Effects of schema acquisition and rule automation on mathematical problem-solving transfer. *Journal of Educational Psychology, 79,* 347–362.

De Groot, A.D. (1965). *Thought and choice in chess.*. The Hague, The Netherlands: Mouton.

Derry, S.J., Hawkes, L.W., & Tsai, C. (1987). A theory for remediating problem-solving skills of older children and adults. *Educational Psychologist, 22,* 55–87.

Derry, S.J., Hawkes, L.W., & Ziegler, U. (1988). A plan-based opportunistic architecture for intelligent tutoring. *ITS-88 Proceedings*, Montreal, Canada.

Derry, S.J., & Kellis, A. (1986). A prescriptive analysis of low-ability problem-solving behavior. *Instructional Science, 15,* 49–65.

Ericsson, K.A., & Simon, H.A. (1984). *Protocol analysis: Verbal reports as data.* Cambridge, MA: The MIT Press.

Flavell, J.H. (1979). Metacognition and cognitive monitoring: A new area of psychological inquiry. *American Psychologist, 34,* 906–911.

Flavell, J.H. (1981). Cognitive monitoring. In W.P. Dickson (Ed.), *Children's oral communication skills* (pp. 35–60). New York: Academic Press.

Gagné, E.D. (1985). *The cognitive psychology of school learning.* Boston: Little, Brown and Company.

Gagné, R.M. (1985). *The conditions of learning,* 4th ed. New York: Holt, Rinehart and Winston.

Gick, M.L. (1986). Problem-solving strategies. *Educational Psychologist, 21,* 99–120.

Greeno, J.G., & Simon, H.A. (1984). *Problem solving and reasoning* (Tech. Rep. No. UPTT/LRDC/ONR/APS-14). Pittsburgh: Learning Research and Development Center, University of Pittsburgh.

Hawkes, L.W., Derry, S.J., & Zeigler, U. (May, 1987). *A cognitive theory and AI implementation for training problem-solving ability.* Paper presented at the Third International Conference on Artificial Intelligence and Education, Pittsburgh.

Hayes, J.R. (1981). *The complete problem solver.* Philadelphia: The Franklin Institute Press.

Hechinger, F.M. (1983, July 12) Report faults Army's teaching of basic skills. The New York Times. p. C6.

Heller, J.I., & Hungate, H.N. (1985). Implications for mathematics instruction of research on scientific problem solving. In E.A. Silver (Ed.), *Teaching and learning mathematical problem solving: Multiple research perspectives* (pp. 83–112). Hillsdale, NJ: Erlbaum & Associates.

Kintsch, W., & Greeno, J.G. (1985). Understanding and solving word arithmetic problems. *Psychological Review, 92,* 109–129.

Larkin, J.H., McDermott, J., Simon, D.P., & Simon, H.A. (1980). Models of competence in solving physics problems. *Cognitive Science, 4,* 317–345.

Leinhardt, G., & Greeno, J.G. (1986). The cognitive skills of teaching. *Journal of Educational Psychology, 78,* 75–95.

Lesgold, A. (March, 1988). *Intelligent tutoring systems: Practice environments and exploratory models.* Address presented at Florida State University, Department of Psychology, Tallahassee, FL.

Marshall, S. (August, 1985). *An analysis of problem-solving instruction in arithmetic textbooks.* Paper presented at annual meeting of the American Psychological Association, Los Angeles, CA.

Marshall, S.P., Pribe, C.A., & Smith, J.D. (March, 1987). *Schema knowledge structures for representing and understanding arithmetic story problems* (Contract No. N00014-85-K-0661). San Diego, CA: Center for Research in Mathematics and Science Education.

Mayer, R.E. (1986). Teaching students how to think and learn: A look at some instructional programs and the research: A review of J.W. Segal, S.F. Chipman, & R. Glaser's (1985), *Thinking and learning skills, 1, Relating instruction to research* and S.F. Chipman, J.W. Segal, & R. Glaser's (1985), *Thinking and learning skills, 2, Research and open questions. Contemporary Psychology, 31,* 753–756.

Meichenbaum, D.H. (1977). *Cognitive behavior modification: An integrative approach.* New York: Plemum Press.

Meichenbaum, D.H. (1980). A cognitive-behavioral perspective on intelligence. *Intelligence, 4,* 271–283.

Minsky M. (1985). *The society of mind.* New York: Simon and Schuster.

Palincsar, A.S. (1986). The role of dialogue in providing scaffolded instruction. *Educational Psychologist, 21,* 73–98.

Paris, S.G., Cross, D.R., & Lipson, M.Y. (1984). Informed strategies for learning: A program to improve children's reading awareness and comprehension. *Journal of Educational Psychology, 76,*1239–1252.

Park, O., Perez, R.S., & Seidel, R.J. (1987). Intelligent CAI: Old wine in new bottles, or a new vintage? In G. Kearsley (Ed.), *Artificial intelligence and instruction: Applications and methods* (pp. 11–40). Reading, MA: Addison-Wesley Publishing Company.

Peachey, D.R., & McCalla, G.I. (1986). Using planning techniques in intelligent tutoring systems. *International Journal of Man-Machine Studies, 24,* 77–98.

Polya, A. (1957). *How to solve it.* Garden City, NY: Doubleday-Anchor.

Pressley, M. (1986). The relevance of the good strategy user model to the teaching of mathematics. *Educational Psychologist, 21,* 139–161.

Pressley, M., Borkowski, J.G., & O'Sullivan, J.T. (1984). Memory strategy instruction is made of this: Metamemory and durable strategy use. *Educational Psychologist, 19,* 94–107.

Pressley, M., Borkowski, J.G., & Schneider, W. (1987). Cognitive strategies: Good strategy users coordinate metacognition and knowledge. In R. Vasta & G. Whitehurst (Eds.), *Annals of Child Development*, Vol. 4 (pp. 80–129). Greenwich, CT: JAI Press.

Pressley, M., Goodchild, F., Fleet., J., Zajchowski, R., & Evans, E.D. (in press). The challenges of classroom strategy instruction. *The Elementary School Journal*.

Rankin, S., & Hughes, C. (April, 1987). *The Rankin-Hughes list of selected thinking skills and its implications for curriculum and instruction*. Paper presented at the annual meeting of the American Educational Research Association, Washington, DC.

Riley, M.S., Greeno, J.G., & Heller, J.I. (1983). Development of children's problem-solving ability in arithmetic. In H.P. Ginsburg (Ed.), *The development of mathematical thinking* (pp. 153–192). New York: Academic Press.

Rumelhart, D.E., McClelland, J.L., & the PDP Research Group. (1986). *Parallel distributed processing: Explorations in the microstructure of cognition, Vol. 1, Foundations*. Cambridge, MA: The MIT Press.

Rumelhart, D.E., & Norman, D.A. (1981). Analogical processes in learning. In J.R. Anderson (Ed.). *Cognitive skills and their acquisition* (pp. 335–359). Hillsdale, NJ: Erlbaum & Associates.

Sacerdoti, E.D. (1979). Problem solving tactics. *Proceedings of the sixth annual International Conference on Artificial Intelligence, 2*, 1077–1085.

Schneider, W. (1985). Training high-performance skills: Fallacies and guidelines. *Human Factors, 27*, 285–300.

Schoenfeld, A.H. (1985). *Mathematical problem solving*. Orlando, FL: Academic Press.

Schumacher, G.M. (1987). Executive control in studying. In B.K. Britton & S. M. Glynn (Eds.), *Executive control processes in reading* (pp. 107–144). Hillsdale, NJ: Erlbaum & Associates.

Simon, D.P., & Simon H.A. (1978). Individual differences in solving physics problems. In R. Siegler (Ed.), *Children's thinking: What develops?* (pp. 325–347). Hillsdale, NJ: Erlbaum & Associates.

Sleeman, D., & Brown, J.S. (Eds.). (1982). *Intelligent tutoring systems*. London: Academic Press.

Stigler, J.W., Fuson, K.C., Ham, M., & Sook Kim, M. (1986). An analysis of addition and subtraction word problems in American and Soviet elementary mathematics textbooks. *Cognition and Instruction, 3*, 153–171.

Sweller, J., & Cooper, G.A. (1985). The use of worked examples as a substitute for problem solving in learning algebra. *Cognition and Instruction, 2*, 59–89.

Vergnaud, G. (1982). A classification of cognitive tasks and operations of thought involved in addition and subtraction problems. In T.P. Carpenter, J.M. Moser, & T.A. Romberg (Eds.), *Addition and subtraction: A cognitive perspective* (pp. 39–59). Hillsdale, NJ: Erlbaum & Associates.

Vergnaud, G. (1983). Multiplicative structures. In R. Lesh & M. Landau (Eds.), *Acquisition of mathematics concepts and processes* (pp. 127–172). New York: Academic Press.

Wenger, E. (1987). *Artificial intelligence and tutoring systems: Computational and cognitive approaches to the communication of knowledge*. Los Altos, CA: Morgan Kaufmann Publishers.

Appendix 1:   Example Protocols from JSEP Study

Soldier's (Novice) Protocol

Subject and Experimenter read together.

A car rental company rents car A for a $10 fee plus $2 for every hour you have the car. The same company rents car B, a much sportier model, for a $2 fee plus twice that much per hour. Private James has been working very hard. He receives an eight-day leave. He wants to spend half of his leave days (24 hours each) driving around the country. If Private James has $500, how much money will he have left for food if he rents the car with the cheapest total cost for four days of his vacation?

Subject:

Okay, a rental car company rents car A for a $10 fee plus $2 for every hour you have the car.
Per hour, OK, Car B is more expensive.
Private James has been working very hard. He receives an eight-day leave.
OK (pause) OK, $2 times 24 for the hours in the day (works on paper), that's $48 dollars a day, $58.
OK, he wants the car for how long? He spends half of his leave driving around the country.
OK, so we add 48 here three times, multiply it first (multiplies 48 × 3 on paper, obtaining 154), and 154 (adds 58 and 154 on paper) is 12,212.
OK, Private James has $500. How much money will he have left for food if he rents the car for 4 days of his vacation?
OK (subtracts 212 from 500 on paper), $278? (pause)

Experimenter: Work a little longer.

Subject:

Car rental company rents car A for a $10 fee. The fee is not every day is it?

Experimenter:

No.

Subject:

OK. $10 fee plus $2 for every hour you have the car.
OK. 24 hours in a day, 4 days (pause).
48 dollars a day, 4 days is (works 48 × 4 on paper) $192 plus the $10 fee.
OK, be 202 dollars (but writes down 302).
OK, he receives an 8-day leave (subtracts 302 from 500), 302,500 (pause).
What am I doing here?
$198 dollars?

Experimenter:

Not quite.

Subject:

OK, OK
48 dollars a day is 192 and 1, . . . 302 hummmm . . .
Let's see, 8 days. How much money left for food if he rents the car with the cheapest total cost for four days of his vacation?
200
OK, so car B is 4 dollars . . .

(time called)

COLLEGE SUBJECT (EXPERT) PROTOCOL

Subject and Experimenter read problem together.

Subject:

OK, 10, Car A is a $10 fee plus 2 dollars for every hour you have car.
So that'd be $10, 4 days, 24 times 4, 96 hours times 2 would be (works on paper) 192.
So that would bring it to 202 for 4 days for Car A (records and labels as "A")
Car B is 2 cent fee + $4 an hour, so if you got 96 hours, 4 (multiplies on paper), be 382 plus $2 (works on paper) fee brings it to 384 (records and labels as "B."
So he would have cheapest total if he rents car A.
(Subtracts 202 from 500 on paper.) He'd have 298 left for food.

12
Computer-Assisted Strategic Instruction

Richard Lehrer

Children's efforts to learn a programming language provide a looking glass that reflects many of the pitfalls and prospects of computer-assisted strategic instruction. Accordingly, this chapter contains a report of research examining transferable (and nontransferable) aspects of strategies acquired as young children learn Logo. Logo is a programming language suggested as a vehicle for the development of new ways of thinking for children (Nickerson, Perkins, & Smith, 1985; Papert, 1980, 1987).

In the first section, Gentner's (1983, 1988) theory of analogy serves as a platform for the consideration of several forms of transfer from computing environments to other contexts. The second section then presents a study of the strategic teaching of Logo, analyzing transferable components of such instruction. In this section, the influences of instructional method and the type of transfer task are related to the degree and quality of transfer. Here I contend that inquiry-based instruction with Logo helps children decipher problem constraints (and relationships among these constraints) in nonprogramming contexts. The analysis of transfer is extended in the last section by viewing the computer as a tool for helping children create links between what Bruner (1986) describes as two worlds of thought—the narrative world of everyday experience and the paradigmatic world of logic and reason.

Strategies and Transfer

STRATEGIES

Strategies typically refer to an ordered sequence of mental steps enacted to satisfy a goal (e.g., Mayer, 1983). These goal-oriented behaviors may be differentiated according to a variety of criteria, such as the specificity of the goal (Pressley, Forrest-Pressley, Elliott-Faust, & Miller, 1985), the direction of the goal-related processing (e.g., "forward" processes that emanate from given information toward the goal or "backward" processes that emanate from the goal toward given information), and the degree to which goals are integrated with higher-level metacognitive processes (Pressley, Borkowski, & Schneider, 1987).

Although strategies denote goal-driven processes, they also connote wisdom, as described by "the good strategy user" (GSU) model of strategic behavior (Pressley, Goodchild, Fleet, Zajchowski, & Evans, in press; see also Symons, Snyder, Cariglia-Bull, & Pressley, this volume, chap. 1). Briefly stated, good strategy users can behave wisely by selecting strategies after consideration of alternatives, reflecting on their choices, and evaluating the consequences of a particular choice. The GSU model also implies that good strategy users know when and how to apply a strategy learned in one context to another related context. Stated another way, good strategy users can mindfully abstract across contexts.

Transferable Strategies

In defining transferable strategies in educational computing contexts, I draw upon Gentner's (1983, 1988; Gentner & Toupin, 1986) theory of analogy. Briefly stated, she proposes that an analogy succeeds when a system of relations in one domain corresponds validly to a system of relations in a second domain. For example, "an atom is like a solar system" involves mapping relations concerning attractive force from the base domain of the solar system (the familiar objects and their relations) to the target domain of the atom. Literal attributes, however, do not sustain the analogy. For example, the sun does not correspond in any literal way to the nucleus of an atom. Related research indicates that spontaneous application of an analogy is enhanced by easy identification of a common goal structure (Gick & Holyoak, 1980, 1983; Holyoak & Koh, 1987), perhaps because such identification increases the accessibility of important elements of the analogy (Gentner, in press).

In contrast to analogy, Gentner proposes that similarity between objects in different domains involves a mapping process that includes not only relations, as in analogy, but also literal attributes (surface appearances) shared by the objects contrasted. Hence, "she's like Alice" could refer to the brown eyes and gender each possess. As attributes are dropped from a mapping between a base domain and a target domain, the correspondence between domains becomes increasingly analogical in nature. Thus in this view, similarity and analogy define ends of a continuum that differ more in degree than in kind.

TWO TYPES OF TRANSFER

Applying Gentner's theoretical perspective to the transfer of programming skills requires distinguishing two types of transfer. Analogically dominated transfer occurs when relationships (but not literal features) developed in programming contexts are transferred to other contexts. For example, a "break-the-problem-into-components" strategy applied to planning a program could transfer to planning an essay. Here, the notion of breaking a complex program into a set of smaller problems related by a main program shares some relational similarities with the notion of tackling an essay by defining subissues and then connecting these issues with a central, purpose-defining discourse structure.

Analogically dominated transfer is one mechanism by which the "high road" transfer discussed by Salomon and Perkins (1987) can be realized. (High road refers to the transfer of principles across varied contexts.) As Salomon and Perkins contend, such transfer will often require reflective efforts to identify structural similarity between the programming domain and a target domain. For example, the relationship between establishing subgoals when programming and establishing subgoals when writing may be obscure to a novice. Here, pedagogy that helps point out the relationship may be crucial. However, with increasing expertise, such mindful identification may play a less important role. That is, experiences in a domain may automatically "remind" one of analogous experiences in one's domain of expertise (Ross, 1984; Schank, 1980).

Degree of Transfer

The degree of analogical transfer is limited by the "systematicity" (Gentner, 1983) or complexity of the relations to be encoded and mapped from the programming to the target domains. Assuming that more systematic relations place higher demands on working memory, individual differences in working memory constrain what may be transferred. Consider, for example, that higher-order relationships such as "caused by" or "implied by" may entail a chain easily broken by simple forgetting. Such forgetting will adversely influence the prospects for an analogical mapping. However, specific instructional practices may well enhance this type of transfer by buttressing working-memory capacity.

For example, the working-memory demands of a strategy to debug Logo programs appear relatively high. They may be decreased, however, by instruction that decomposes the strategy into component processes, such as those associated with (a) proposing the bug type, (b) specifying the bug location, (c) finding the bug, (d) fixing the bug, and (e) checking the results of the previous step (Carver & Klahr, 1987). Applying such a pedagogy with 8- to 11-year-old children, Carver and Klahr found that debugging Logo programs led to increased ability to identify and repair errors in directions for accomplishing tasks such as setting a table, ordering food, or traveling somewhere. In these transfer tasks, children were presented with a discrepancy between a set of outcomes desired by the direction giver (e.g., a properly set table) and that which resulted when a recipient of the directions attempted to follow them.

Similarity-Based Transfer

At the other end of the spectrum, literal components of programming strategies may map directly to components of a skill in a second domain. For example, a programming template developed to sort numbers may be applied to sort numbers in a nonprogramming context. Here, the literal correspondence between the programming and nonprogramming contexts cues the application of the programming strategy. This similarity-dominated form of transfer will most likely occur spontaneously when programming templates have been repeatedly practiced to the point of automaticity. Salomon and Perkins (1987) characterize this type of transfer as "low road" to emphasize its generally automatic and nonreflective character. However, there seems to be little reason in principle not to expect controlled processes as well in this form of transfer. As in the case of analogy, it is more a matter of degree than of kind. From the vantage of a GSU model, similarity-based transfer is less amenable to strategic instruction because use of the strategy is invoked typically by nondirective spreading activation (e.g., Collins & Loftus, 1975) rather than by deliberate search. In practice, a description of a task as near transfer suggests a similarity-dominated mechanism whereas a far-transfer description indicates an analogy-dominated mechanism.

In summary, analogically based transfer may in principle be differentiated from similarity-based transfer. Consideration of analogical transfer suggests that bridging from a programming context to other contexts most likely requires a pedagogy that promotes reflection (Salomon & Perkins, 1987) and ameliorates working-memory demands. Accordingly, teachers of programming languages need to help children (a) construct and reflect upon different ways of composing programs, (b) evaluate the consequences of their choices, and (c) establish correspondences between programming and nonprogramming contexts (Delclos, Littlefield, & Bransford, 1985; Lehrer, 1986; Lehrer & de Bernard, 1987; Miller & Emihovich, 1986). The next section enlarges upon the importance of instructional method and the type of transfer task in a study of transferable aspects of Logo programming.

A Study of Transfer

With a few notable exceptions (Carver & Klahr, 1987; Lehrer, Guckenberg & Sancilio, 1988; Lehrer & Randle, 1987; Mayer & Fay, 1987), experimental studies of the relationship between experience with Logo programming and subsequent transfer to problem-solving tasks usually fail to substantiate any such association (e.g., Pea & Kurland, 1984). For example, in an oft-cited study, Pea, Kurland, and Hawkins (1985) found no evidence of transfer even when children instructed in Logo planned to perform a series of classroom chores that were presented to them in a programming-like environment. This finding has been likened to an "empirical Waterloo" for advocates of Logo-based instruction in the schools (Broughton, 1985).

In contrast, other studies of Logo-based learning associate such instruction with increases in metacognition and other aspects of successful problem resolution (Clements, 1986; Clements & Gullo, 1984; Degelman, Free, Scarlato, Blackburn, & Golden, 1986). These contrasting findings create a paradox for teachers of Logo. On the one hand, phenomena usually associated with more skilled performance in a domain appear to be promoted by experience with Logo. On the other hand, the integration among these different skills, which might result in more successful planning and problem solving, is less evident.

In the research discussed in detail in this section, Paul Smith and I investigated the influence of (a) instructional method and (b) problem type on the transfer of two kinds of programming strategies. The first strategy entailed problem decomposition; programming problems may be more easily solved by partitioning the problem hierarchically into subproblems. For example, painting a "house" on a screen can be broken down into the subproblems of painting the frame and painting the roof.

The second programming strategy consisted of methods for translating problem constraints into programming goals. For example, to construct a "house" in Logo it is not enough to construct each part (e.g., a square for the frame and a triangle for the roof). Rather, the parts must be related in a particular way—the roof must be on top of the frame and not vice versa. Further, the roof must be aligned so that its peak corresponds to the top of the house. These constraints, known declaratively (e.g., they can be stated by children) in the task environment (Newell & Simon, 1972) must be translated into programming goals in the problem space. This translation promotes reflection about the nature of the problem. In the instance of the house, the child must reflect upon how the constraints of the problem determine the relationship between the two Logo procedures (subprograms) that define each module of the house. This understanding must then be translated into programming statements, usually those that orient the turtle so that consecutive execution of the frame and roof subprograms result in a graphics display that looks like a house. Stated more generally, every programming problem involves deciding on the nature of constraints and then testing these decisions in the crucible of the program.

IMPLEMENTING INQUIRY-BASED LOGO INSTRUCTION

Recalling our desire to promote wise use of strategies learned in a Logo context, we devised an inquiry-based approach to instruction in Logo (Collins & Stevens, 1982; Sigel & Cocking, 1977). Instructional methods included presentation of (a) positive and negative instances of a programming construct, (b) comparison cases, (c) hypothetical cases, and (d) analogical bridges to other contexts. For example, when presenting children with Logo's REPEAT command (a way to specify the number of repetitions of an instruction list) we (a) presented several good and poor examples of its use; (b) asked children to analyze similarities and differences among these examples; (c) elicited predictions, including those for examples that we designed to trap children into making the wrong predictions; and (d) likened the construct to other repetitive activities such as breathing. In the latter instance, we dramatized the advantages of repetition by asking pairs of children to play turtle, treating breathing *in* and *out* as separate commands.

Following a period of several months, during which children acquired the fundamental syntax and semantics of Logo graphics, the instruction was further elaborated in one of two ways. In one group, we taught children to solve graphics problems as follows: (a) identify subproblems (e.g., identify separable components of the problem scene), (b) write procedures to draw each component, (c) check procedures (can the procedure be broken down further?), (d) identify how parts (and their associated procedures) fit together, (e) write procedures to interface the parts, and (f) put all procedures together to form a superprocedure that draws the figure. This partition was undertaken to reduce the working memory requirements of strategy acquisition. Children participating in this problem-decomposition (PD) condition also received assistance in developing strategies to translate problem constraints into programming practices.

At first, instructors guided and modeled the strategies directly. For example, children were directly instructed in how to decompose a drawing of an "alien" (after the science fiction movie) and then were asked to implement the same strategy for "son of alien." During the course of instruction, direct instruction was faded; children used their partners as resources more often. The six-part cycle was applied to problems of increasing complexity during the course of instruction. For example, children constructed a flower that could be decomposed into petals, stems, and leaves. Next, another problem constraint was introduced: "place the flower on top of a table." Introduction of this constraint entailed a redefinition of the problem, ideally by decomposition of the task into subproblems: the new problem (drawing a table), the old problem (the flower), and their relationship (flower on table). Constraints introduced subsequently included "put a chair next to the table," and "put a person in the scene." In this way, old problems formed the basis for the definition of new ones, and children were exposed to a variety of examples that conserved continuity yet introduced moderate degrees of change.

In a second group, children used Logo to learn about geometry (GL = geometry Logo). Programming instruction centered about strategies to satisfy geometric constraints. For example, we challenged children to draw a face with eyes represented by one type of polygon, a mouth represented by a different type of polygon, but all having the same perimeter. This form of instruction did not include any explicit instruction in techniques of problem decomposition. As in the first instructional condition; children were free to pursue personal variations on the themes instructors provided (children also provided a fair number of themes that instructors then implemented for the class as a whole).

DESCRIPTION OF TASKS AND TRANSFER EXPECTATIONS

As noted previously, Pea et al. (1985) assessed children's planning as they solved a scheduling problem involving classroom chores. Although the task

was implemented in a graphics environment similar to that of the Logo programming environment, the task is an exemplar of a problem susceptible to solution by opportunistic planning (Cohen & Feigenbaum, 1982; Hayes-Roth & Hayes-Roth, 1979). This is a type of planning where the satisfaction of one component of the problem may lead to the satisfaction of other, related components, provided, of course, that the solver perceives the relationships. It relies upon the ability of the planner to exploit opportunities as they arise. Yet in Logo environments, children often tend to adopt hierarchical decomposition strategies, either because they receive such instruction (such as that provided in this study), or because the graphics environment provides salient cues for the adoption of this type of strategy. For example, a "house" decomposes obviously into a square and a triangle. Similar features are not present in the chore-scheduling task of Pea et al. (1985), even when such a task is presented in a graphics environment. Thus there seems to be little reason to expect transfer between Logo programming experience and performance on this type of task (except under conditions described later).

I devised two types of tasks to assess the transferability of instruction in Logo—a planning task to assess more analogically based transfer and a hierarchical problem decomposition task to assess predominantly similarity-based transfer. The planning task consisted of household chores performed by a character called the turtle. For example, "the turtle must pick up his toys." The turtle was intended to remind children of the applicability of the Logo context to this planning task. This surface similarity in problem components was expected to make relations between the contexts more accessible (Gentner, in press; Holyoak & Koh, 1987), and hence, more transferable.

The chores were subject to three kinds of constraints. It was this feature of the task that we expected to provide a test of transferability of the Logo experience. One kind consisted of a simple before-after association between two chores. For example, "the turtle must feed the dog before he does his homework. " A second type of constraint entailed a transitive relationship among three chores: A before B and B before C. For example, "the turtle must pick up his toys before he vacuums and vacuum before he dusts." The third constraint specified one chore as the last to be completed. The main assumption was that successful task performance entailed translating and making explicit the problem constraints presented, although the main solution strategy did not involve hierarchical problem decomposition in any obvious or necessary way. As a result, we did not expect any performance differences between the two forms of Logo instruction described previously, but we did expect that children instructed with Logo would manipulate problem constraints more effectively than their counterparts in a control condition (this latter group of children will be described later). Further details about the task and its administration are described in Appendix A.

The hierarchical problem-decomposition task consisted of presentation of a novel graphics design in the Logo environment to children. It involved drawing a windmill consisting of a square base and four triangular blades (see Appendix B). Hence, the figure could in principle be decomposed hierarchically into subproblems and then reassembled for solution. As a result, we expected the form of strategic instruction to make a difference here in favor of the group of children receiving explicit instruction in the use of the problem-decomposition strategy. This problem then assessed similarity-based transfer.

DESCRIPTION OF EXPERIMENTAL PROCEDURES

Our subjects were 45 third-grade children attending an elementary school in southern Wisconsin. Approximately equal numbers of boys and girls were assigned randomly by ability blocks, either to one of the two Logo instructional conditions previously described, or to a third control condition. The control condition also consisted of inquiry-based instruction, but with popular problem-solving software such as Rocky's Boots rather than with Logo (see Lehrer, Guckenberg, & Lee, 1988, for details). In this condition, instructors mediated students' learning by helping them make sense of computer-generated feedback, asking students to predict outcomes, and generally structuring their learning in a manner similar to that employed for the Logo instruction.

Instructional methods then constituted a between-subjects factor. Children in each of the three conditions received 47 half-hour lessons, twice a week. Four instructors rotated among pairs of children who worked on Apple IIe microcomputers in a large room. Children also practiced two or three times each week in their classrooms with one of three computers located in the room for this purpose.

Following the end of the instruction, children in all conditions responded to the planning task, but only children in the Logo conditions responded to the problem-decomposition task (because it required knowledge of Logo for its solution). The problem-decomposition task was administered twice to each child. Hence, the task type was a within-subjects factor with an additional within-subjects factor of trials on the problem-decomposition task. Children thought aloud during each administration of the tasks, and their verbalizations were recorded.

EXPERIMENTAL FINDINGS

Problem Decomposition Task

Table 12.1 contrasts the strategic efficiency of children who participated in the two types of instruction in Logo over the two trials of the problem-decomposition task. Here PD indicates that the children were instructed in the use of the problem-decomposition strategy and GL indicates that they received geometry instruction. Measures of problem-solving efficiency included the number of Logo commands used (steps) and the time to solution, measured to the nearest second (time). Both measures of problem-

TABLE 12.1. Means (and Standard Deviations) for Measures of Decomposition Task Performance

| | Instructional Conditions | | | |
| | PD^a | | GL^b | |
	Trial 1	Trial 2	Trial 1	Trial 2
Moves[c]	7.5 (2.0)	5.4 (1.3)	9.5 (4.3)	7.1 (1.4)
Time (sec)[c]	32.1 (7.7)	23.5 (6.0)	36.3 (11.6)	28.1 (5.2)
Plan statements	7.2 (4.0)	5.9 (2.2)	4.6 (1.7)	4.3 (2.7)

[a] PD = problem decomposition.
[b] GL = geometry logo.
[c] Square root transformations.

solving efficiency displayed in Table 12.1 have been transformed (square root) to stabilize the variance (Box, Hunter, & Hunter, 1978). As expected, children explicitly instructed in the application of the strategy applied it more efficiently. For instance, children so instructed solved the problem in fewer moves and took less time across trials ($p < 0.05$).

Analysis of children's verbalizations during the solution process indicated that children who solved the decomposition problem more efficiently did so because they developed more elaborate plans. *Planning statements* were defined as verbalizations referring to anticipated moves beyond the immediate command being entered, and the total number of such statements clearly favored the group instructed in the use of the decomposition strategy ($p < 0.05$). However, the number of planning statements explicitly referring to the decomposition strategy of partitioning an element into its components did not vary reliably by group. Both groups appeared equally likely to adopt the notion of problem decomposition as a method for solution, but the explicitly instructed group was better able to translate the notion automatically into programming methods designed to accomplish the goal. Stated another way, those explicitly instructed in the use of the strategy constructed a frame for the strategy with slots occupied by the methods taught as components of the decomposition strategy.

Chore-Scheduling Task

Turning to the chore-scheduling task, students receiving instruction in either Logo condition solved the task with an average path length 13 percent longer than the optimal path length. The form of Logo instruction made no difference for this measure. However, children receiving instruction in the control condition solved the task with an average path length 19 percent longer than the optimal path length. Although small, the difference between the Logo and control groups was statistically reliable ($p < 0.05$).

Analysis of children's verbalizations indicated that those in either Logo condition were more likely to coordinate relations among the multiple constraints of the planning task than were their counterparts in the control condition (p < 0.05). For example, a child instructed in Logo was more likely to say, "well, I have to pick up . . . but I also have to feed the dog before I . . .," thereby planning moves in relation to potential links among problem constraints. In contrast, children in the control condition were more likely to search the problem constraints serially, resolving them as they were encountered.

STUDY CONCLUSIONS

The results of this study suggest that transferable aspects of Logo programming are moderated by the relationship between strategies presented in the Logo environment and their applicability in the transfer task, and by the type of strategic instruction provided to students as they learn Logo. Expectations that Logo instruction will serve as a general developer of problem-solving skills appear misguided. Instead, it seems more reasonable to view Logo as an "extensible context" that may be readily exploited for the purposes of instruction in particular strategies or principles (Lehrer & Randle, 1987).

As noted previously, the match between particular strategies taught in the programming context and those assessed by the transfer task must be carefully evaluated before one can reach a conclusion about the success or failure of the transferability of instruction in a programming language (Carver & Klahr, 1987). With regard to planning tasks, I have suggested that the type of planning characteristic of Logo environments is not readily applied to chore-scheduling and other similar tasks. Hence, in this research, children instructed with Logo solved a chore-planning task more efficiently not because they developed more elaborate general plans, but rather because they represented specific problem constraints more abstractly, taking into account relationships among the constraints. This superior handling of problem constraints reflected specific instructional efforts to help children describe constraints procedurally. A study of Logo-based transfer by Littlefield et al. (1988) can also be interpreted in this light. In the research conducted by these investigators, children participating in one experimental condition were instructed in Logo under conditions of mediation similar to those of the current study. Subsequently, in a transfer task involving children's planning in a classroom-cleaning context, those instructed in the mediated environment were more likely to satisfy constraints about the appropriate assignment of students to tasks than were their counterparts in the control condition. Like the students solving the chore-scheduling task, these students also appeared to define the nature of the problem more readily as a result of mediated instruction in Logo.

Although we employed inquiry-based methods to promote reflective use of strategies and to increase the quality of children's understanding, we also permitted children the latitude to pursue their own discoveries and to make their own mistakes. Other research we have conducted suggests that the latter is an important feature of children's experience of Logo; children are apt to cite both the challenge and the feeling of personal control when asked what they prefer about Logo (Lehrer & Guckenberg, 1988). In this regard, children's perceptions accord well with theories of intrinsic motivation that stress the importance of intentional or person-center learning (Lepper, 1985; Malone, 1981; Malone & Lepper, 1987).

In summary, we tested two forms of transfer when children received inquiry-based instruction with Logo. As expected, children instructed in the use of a problem-decomposition heuristic successfully applied this strategy to a novel problem in Logo. This was a form of similarity-dominated transfer, largely regulated by identification of common problem-solving elements in the task and the instructional contexts. More analogically based transfer was evident in a chore-scheduling task; children instructed in Logo detected relationships among different types of problem constraints more readily than did their counterparts participating in an alternative software condition.

Up to this point, we have considered transfer from programming to other contexts from a computational perspective that in many ways amplifies Thorndike's (1903) theory of common elements. However, this mechanistic perspective (Pepper, 1942) fails to capture much about the social aspects of transfer evident when one considers knowledge as communication (Mead, 1932; Vygotsky, 1978; Wenger, 1987). Although communication clearly involves common elements, it also involves more elusive quantities such as context and intention. In this view, transfer denotes successful communication between contexts. The concluding section of this chapter considers the potential of the computer to foster intrapersonal communication between two broad classes of context—the narrative world of everyday experience and the paradigmatic world of formal reasoning and traditional schooling (see Day, Cordon, & Kerwin, this volume, chap. 4, for a related position).

Fostering Contextual Communication

Bruner (1986) suggests that a good story and a well-formed argument constitute different natural kinds of apprehension. On the one hand, stories appeal to what Bruner describes as "epiphanies of the ordinary"; the details and interconnections of everyday events are magnified for readers who then evaluate the author's perceptions by their verisimilitude—their ability to strike a resonant chord in the reader. Narrative worlds then appeal to dramatic origins, fraught with the actions of characters and their intentions, and are perpetuated by the tacit knowledge and presupposition of the reader.

On the other hand, well-formed arguments appeal to the general rather than the specific; they originate in formal procedures for establishing truth. Accordingly, their hallmarks are explicitness and a language of formal description. Above all, well-formed arguments transcend the ordinary, disdaining the particular for the general. One case does not a proof make.

In my view, narrative apprehension is dominant in our everyday thinking and in our construction of ourselves (Cantor & Kihlstrom, 1987; Lehrer, 1988). It also constitutes the epistemological foundations of children's thought, notwithstanding the vast preponderance of research devoted to the development of logical reasoning. Hence, children approach the worlds of mathematics and science with categories of thought anchored in drama, not proof. Accordingly, in these domains and in others that rely upon the development of logic, law, and proof, it would be advisable to provide communicative bridges between the narrative and paradigmatic modes of understanding to facilitate transition between them. To this end, computer-based interaction offers particular promise.

Two types of computer-assisted environments are described briefly to illustrate how these environments can facilitate connections between narrative paradigmatic epistemologies. The first is the Logo-based microworld proposed by Feurzeig and his colleagues to teach children algebra (Feurzeig, 1986). The other is the interactive videodisc environment developed by Bransford and his colleagues to foster scientific and mathematical problem solving (Bransford, Sherwood, & Hasselbring, 1988).

FOSTERING TRANSITIONS: TWO EXAMPLES

Feurzeig (1969, 1986) proposes making Logo's underlying mathematical structure available to sixth-grade children learning algebra for the first time. Accordingly, Logo ideas and programming activities are employed to develop mathematical concepts such as variable, function, and inverse. What seems particularly compelling about the algebra-Logo curriculum is the frequent use of a narrative context to bootstrap the acquisition of the algebraic concepts. In other words, narrative frameworks guide the process by which Logo's internal mathematical structure is made available to children.

To illustrate, children's first activities involve the construction of Logo programs that generate gossip. For example, "Chris likes Alex." As they proceed, students can increase the number of actors and the form of the gossip. They can also represent the gossip ironically in a form that later serves to help define functions. In this instance the conversational form of classroom gossip (and its attendant humor) serves as a framework for creating new definitions of formerly abstruse concepts such as variables and functions. And the narrative framework also provides a common goal with which to link all the various subgoals of the programming activities given to children. In this way, some of the inherent paradigmatic power of the Logo language is amplified by bridging between story and programming structures. By paradigmatic power, I am referring to the opportunities children have to learn about the utility of criteria such as generality and (formal) internal consistency as they define programming procedures and reflect about relations among them.

Bransford and his colleagues, like Feurzeig, employ narrative bridges to help develop mathematical and scientific reasoning. However, rather than employing the narrative context as an external frame, Bransford and his colleagues use an interactive videodisk to embed the narrative directly into the design of instruction. Their efforts are contrived to alleviate the problem of inert knowledge: knowledge tightly bound to its original context of acquisition (Bransford, Sherwood, Vye, & Rieser, 1986).

Consequently, Bransford and his colleagues use clips of popular movies to provide narrative frameworks for the development of mathematical and scientific problem solving. Here, the goals of the main character, such as Indiana Jones, necessarily involve twists in plot that provide a set of subgoals that can be instructionally useful. For example, while viewing a film segment students are asked to consider factors such as the height of various obstacles the hero must negotiate, the probable weight of a golden idol the hero swings so casually, and the like. These factors are all invitations to develop paradigmatic reasoning. Moreover, rather than a disconnected series of rules generated to explain each episode, the interactive computer medium provides the tools and the story framework for integrating information across episodes. For instance, students are provided graphical tools with which to analyze the video experience. Bransford and his colleagues contend that this video medium (videodisk, tools, and carefully selected problems) facilitates the development of integrative knowledge. And in a series of experiments, they demonstrate that such integrated knowledge structures are more transferable than their fragmented counterparts.

Concluding Comments

The computer-based environments described in this chapter all share a commitment to scaffolding the development of learning strategies for children. In this way, children can be the masters of their learning. Computer-assisted instruction of strategies generally presents many of the same opportunities and obstacles than confront more traditional forms of strategy instruction in the classroom (see Duffy & Roehler, this volume, chap. 6; Pressley et al., 1987; Rohwer & Thomas, this volume, chap. 5, for recommendations concerning the latter). However, the increasing application of artificial intelligence techniques to instructional computing design promises to alter this equivalence in fundamental ways, offering tools for reflective thought and planning that should assist wise strategy use (Collins & Brown, 1988, Pea, 1985; Wenger, 1987). Logo merely represents the vanguard of this trend. In this chapter, I have further suggested that some of the more powerful forms of computer-based instruction can serve as tools for bridging the gap between two natural kinds of understanding—the narrative world of intuitive thought and the paradigmatic world of mathematical and scientific reasoning. It seems then that wisdom can be taught, but not directly, only interactively. This was Plato's conclusion as well, albeit argued from vastly different premises.

Acknowledgments. Thanks to the editors of this volume, and to Doug Clements, Joel Levin, and Joan Littlefield for their constructive comments on a previous version of this chapter. Parts of the research reported here were funded by a grant from the Spencer Foundation to the School of Education, University of Wisconsin-Madison.

REFERENCES

Box, G.E.P., Hunter, W.G., & Hunter, J.S. (1978). *Statistics for experimenters: An introduction to design, data analysis and model building.*New York: Wiley.

Bransford, J., Sherwood, R., & Hasselbring, T. (1988). Effects of the video revolution on development: Some initial thoughts. In G. Forman and P. Puffall (Eds.) *Constructivism in the computer age.* (pp 173–201). Hillsdale, NJ: Erlbaum & Associates.

Broughton, J.M. (1985). The surrender of control: Computer literacy as political socialization of the child. In D. Sloan (Ed.), *The computer in education (pp 102–122).* New York: Teachers College Press.

Bruner, J. (1986). *Actual minds, possible worlds.* Cambridge, MA: Harvard University Press.

Cantor, N., & Kihlstrom, J.F. (1987). *Personality and social intelligence.* Englewood Cliffs, NJ: Prentice-Hall.

Carver, C.M., & Klahr, D. (April, 1987). *Analysis, instruction, and transfer of the components of debugging skills.* Paper presented at the society for Research in Child Development, Baltimore, MD.

Clements, D.H. (1986). Effects of LOGO and CAI environments on cognition and creativity. *Journal of Educational Psychology, 78,* 309–318.

Clements, D.H., & Gullo, D.F. (1984). Effects of computer programming on young children's cognition. *Journal of Educational Psychology, 76,* 1051–1058.

Cohen, P.R., & Feigenbaum, E.A. (1982). *The handbook of artificial intelligence,* Vol. 3. Los Altos, CA: Kaufmann, Inc.

Collins, A., & Brown, J.S. (1988). The computer as a tool for learning through reflection. In H. Mandl and A. Lesgold (Eds.), *Learning issues for intelligent tutoring systems* (pp 1–18). New York: Springer-Verlag.

Collins, A., & Stevens, A.L. (1982). Goals and strategies of inquiry teachers. In R. Glaser (Ed.), *Advances in instructional psychology,* Vol. 2 (pp 65–119). Hillsdale, NJ: Erlbaum & Associates.

Collins, A.M., & Loftus, E.F. (1975). A spreading activation theory of semantic processing. *Psychological Review, 82,* 407–428.

Degelman, D., Free, J.V., Scarlato, M., Blackburn, J.M., & Golden, T. (1986). Concept learning in preschool children: Effects of a short-term Logo experience. *Journal of Education Computing research, 2,* 199–206.

Delclos, V.R., Littlefield, J., & Bransford, J.D. (1985). Teaching thinking through Logo: The importance of method. *Roeper Review, 7,* 153–156.

Feurzeig, W. (1969). *Programming languages as a conceptual framework for teaching mathematics* (Rep. No. 188). Bolt, Beranek, & Newman. Cambridge MA.

Feurzeig, W. (1986). Algebra slaves and agents in a Logo-based mathematics curriculum. *Instructional Science, 14,* 229–254.

Gentner, D. (1983). Structure mapping: A theoretical framework for analogy. *Cognitive Science, 7,* 155–170.

Gentner, D. (1988). Metaphor as structure mapping: The relational shift. *Child Development*, 59, 47–59.

Gentner, D. (in press). Mechanisms of analogical learning. In S. Vosniadou & A. Ortony (Eds.), *Similarity and analogical reasoning.* London: Cambridge University Press.

Gentner, D., & Toupin, C. (1986). Systematicity and surface similarity in the development of analogy. *Cognitive Science*, 10, 277–300.

Gick, M.L., & Holyoak, K.J. (1980). Analytical problem solving. *Cognitive Psychology*, 12, 306–355.

Gick, M.L., & Holyoak, K.J. (1983). Schema induction and analogical transfer. *Cognitive Psychology*, 15, 1–38.

Hayes-Roth, B., B., & Hayes-Roth, F. (1979). A cognitive model of planning. *Cognitive Science*, 3, 275–310.

Holyoak, K.J., & Koh, K. (1987). Surface and structural similarity in analogical transfer. *Memory and Cognition*, 15, 332–340.

Lehrer, R. (1986). Logo as a strategy for developing thinking? *Educational Psychologist*, 21, 121–137.

Lehrer, R. (1988). Characters in search of an author: The self as a narrative structure. In J.C. Mancuso & M.L.G. Shaw (Eds.), *Cognition and personal structure: Computer access and analysis* (pp 193–226). New York: Praeger.

Lehrer, R., & deBernard, A. (1987). Language of learning and language of computing: The perceptual-language model. *Journal of Educational Psychology*, 79, 41–48.

Lehrer, R., & Guckenberg, T. (April, 1988). *Children's perceptions of educational software.* Paper presented at the annual meeting of the American Educational Research Association, New Orleans.

Lehrer, R., Guckenberg, T., & Lee, O. (1988). A comparative study of the cognitive consequences of Logo-guided instruction. *Journal of Educational Psychology.*

Lehrer, R., Guckenberg, T., & Sancilio, L. (1988). Influences of Logo on children's intellectual development. In R.E. Mayer (Ed.), *Teaching and learning computer programming: Multiple research perspectives.* Hillsdale, NJ: Erlbaum & Associates.

Lehrer, R., & Randle, L. (1987). Problem solving, metacognition and composition: The effects of interactive software for first-grade children. *Journal of Educational Computing Research*, 3, 407–425.

Lepper, M.R. (1985). Microcomputers in education. *American Psychologist*, 40, 1–18.

Littlefield, J., Delclos, V.R., Lever, S., Bransford, J.D., Clayton, K.N., & Franks, J.J. (1988). Learning Logo: Methods of teaching, transfer of general skills, and attitudes toward computers. In R.E. Mayter (Ed.), *Teaching and learning computer programming: Multiple research perspectives.* Hillsdale, NJ: Erlbaum & Associates.

Malone, T.W. (1981). Toward a theory of intrinsically motivating instruction. *Cognitive Science*, 4, 333–359.

Malone, T.W., & Lepper, M.R. (1987). Making learning fun: A taxonomy of intrinsic motivations for learning. In R.E. Snow & M.J. Farr (Eds.), *Aptitude, learning, and instruction Volume 3: Conative and affective process analyses* (pp 223–253). Hillsdale, NJ: Erlbaum.

Mayer, R.E. (1983). *Thinking, problem solving, cognition.* New York: W.H. Freeman.

Mayer, R.R., & Fay, A.L. (1987). A chain of cognitive consequences with learning to program in Logo. *Journal of Educational Psychology*, 79, 269–279.

Mead, G.H. (1932). *The philosophy of the present.* Chicago: University of Chicago Press.

Miller, G.E., & Emihovich, C. (1986). The effects of mediated programming instruction on preschool children's self-monitoring. *Journal of Educational Computing Research*, 2, 283–297.

Newell, A., & Simon, H.A. (1972). *Human problem solving*. Englewood Cliffs, NJ: Prentice-Hall.

Nickerson, R.S., Perkins, D.N., & Smith, E.E. (1985). *The teaching of thinking*. Hillsdale, NJ: Erlbaum & Associates.

Papert, S. (1980). *Mindstorms: Children, computers, and powerful ideas*. New York: Basic Books.

Papert, S. (1987). Computer criticism vs. technocentric thinking. *Educational Researcher*, 16, 22–30.

Pea, R.D. (1985). Integrating human and computer intelligence. In E.L. Klein (Ed.), *New directions for child development*. No. 8, *Children and computers* (pp. 75–96). San Francisco: Jossey-Bass.

Pea, R.D., & Kurland, D.M. (1984). On the cognitive effects of learning computer programming. *New Ideas in Psychology*, 2, 137–168.

Pea, R.D., Kurland, D.M., & Hawkins, J. (1985). Logo and the development of thinking skills, In M. Chen & W. Paisley (Eds.), *Children and microcomputers: Research on the newest medium* (pp 193–212). Beverly Hills: Sage Publications.

Pepper, S.C. (1942). *World hypotheses*. Berkeley: University of California Press.

Pressley, M., Borkowski, J. G., & Schneider, W. (1987). Cognitive strategies: good strategy users coordinate metacognition and knowledge. In R. Vasta & G. Whitehurst (Eds.), *Annals of child development*, Vol. 5 (pp. 89–129). New York: JAI Press.

Pressley, M., Forrest-Pressley, D., Elliott-Faust, D.L., & Miller, G.E. (1985). Children's use of cognitive strategies, how to teach strategies, and what to do if they can't be taught. In M. Pressley & C.J. Brainerd (Eds.), *Cognitive learning and memory in children* (pp. 1–47). New York: Springer-Verlag.

Pressley, M., Goodchild, F., Fleet, J., Zajchowski, R., & Evans, E.D. (in press). The challenges of classroom strategy instruction. *The Elementary School Journal*.

Ross, B.H. (1984). Remindings and their effects in learning a cognitive skill. *Cognitive Psychology*, 16, 371–416.

Salomon, G., & Perkins, D.N. (1987). Transfer of cognitive skills from programming: When and how: *Journal of Educational Computing Research*, 3, 149–169.

Schank, R.C. (1980). Language and memory. *Cognitive Science*, 4, 243–284.

Sigel, I.E., & Cocking, R.R. (1977). Cognition and communication: A dialectical paradigm for development. In M. Lewis & L.A. Rosenblum (Eds.), *Interaction, conversation, and the development of language* (pp. 207–226). New York: Wiley.

Thorndike, E.L. (1903). *Educational psychology*. New York: Lemke & Buechner.

Vygotsky, L.S. (1978). *Mind in society: The development of higher psychological processes*. Cambridge, MA: Harvard University Press.

Wenger, E. (1987). *Artificial intelligence and tutoring systems*. Los Altos, CA: Morgan Kaufmann Publishers.

Appendix A Administration of the Planning Task

The household chore-planning task was displayed on an IBM personal computer, as depicted in Figure 12.1. Each chore was labeled and dotted lines between chore boxes represented paths or "hallways" between the "rooms" in

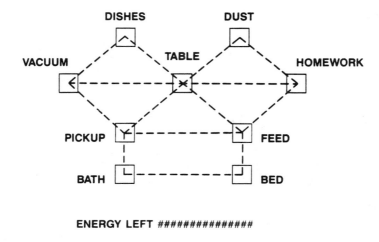

ENERGY LEFT ###############

What chore do you want the turtle to do next?

FIGURE 12.1. Initial display for the errand task.

which each chore would be done. A bulletin board was placed next to the computer; it contained 5- × 11-inch index cards. The title of each chore was displayed in red on a separate card, along with a short sentence printed in black that clarified each chore. Each constraint was listed on a separate index card; students could choose to place these on the bulletin board or could arrange them on the table on which the computer rested. The constraints were printed with the titles of the chores involved appearing in red, and a sentence defining the constraint in black.

Directions to subjects included a description of the overall context of the problem (e.g., "do you have chores to do at home? Well, so does the turtle") as well as a review of each chore, followed by a review of each constraint to ensure that students understood each chore and each constraint. It was emphasized that too much walking would tire the turtle out; children were shown a picture of a "tired turtle" (a cartoon of sweating turtle) that would result from too much exertion. Along these lines, children were also provided graphical feedback of the amount of "energy" the turtle had remaining after each chore was completed.

FIGURE 12.2. Demonstration card for the errand task.

Your job today is to use Logo to draw a windmill.
Here is what that windmill should look like.
Type DONE when you have finished.

PRESS ANY KEY TO CONTINUE

FIGURE 12.3. Initial display for the problem decomposition task.

Before beginning the task, children were required to find the best way to complete the three chores displayed in Figure 12.2 with the constraint that the turtle had to wash his clothes before dusting. In this way, we were assured that children were adopting our minimum-path criterion and that they could resolve a constraint for a small problem (all children could do this).

When the child named a chore, the experimenter entered it into the computer, the turtle went to the corresponding room on the display, and the room was made opaque to indicate that the corresponding chore had been completed. A message appeared at the bottom of the screen stating the turtle had completed that chore. If the constraints were violated by the move (e.g., an illegal move), the turtle remained where it was, and a message explained that another chore had to be done first.

Appendix B Administration of the Problem Decomposition Task

The screen display presented to children in the second task is displayed in Figure 12.3. Children were also presented the same display on an 8- × 11-inch paper for reference as they solved the problem. All children were informed that the orientation of the blades of the windmill need not precisely match that of the standard provided.

Author Index

Numbers in italics refer to pages where references are found.

Subject Index